THOMAS LAWSON
1630 – 1691

CW00517711

The cover design shows *Hieracium Lawsonii* taken from Sowerby's illustration in J. E. Smith's *English Botany* (1809). From a copy in the Minster Library, York, by kind permission.

For Mac
who also loved gardens

THOMAS LAWSON

1630 – 1691

North Country
Botanist, Quaker
and Schoolmaster

by

E. JEAN WHITTAKER, B.A., Ph.D.

Sessions Book Trust
York, England

ISBN 1 85072 003 7

Published 1986

Printed in 10/11 point Plantin Type
by William Sessions Limited
The Ebor Press, York, England

Contents

Illustrations

Abbreviations

Besse	Joseph Besse, *A Collection of the Sufferings of the People called Quakers* (1753).
Braithwaite i	W. C. Braithwaite, *The Beginnings of Quakerism*, 2nd ed., revised by H. J. Cadbury (Cambridge University Press, 1955, Sessions of York, 1961).
Braithwaite ii	W. C. Braithwaite, *The Second Period of Quakerism*, 2nd ed., prepared by H. J. Cadbury (Cambridge University Press, 1961, Sessions of York, 1979).
C.R.O.(C)	Cumbria Record Office, Carlisle.
C.R.O.(K)	Cumbria Record Office, Kendal.
C.T.W.	A. R. Clapham, T. G. Tutin and E. F. Warburg, *Flora of the British Isles* (2nd ed., Cambridge University, 1962).
CWAAS o.s.	*Transactions of the Cumberland and Westmorland Antiquarian and Archaeological Society.* Old series (1874-1900).
CWAAS n.s.	*Transactions of the Cumberland and Westmorland Antiquarian and Archaeological Society.* New series (1901-).
F.H.	Friends House, Euston Road, London.
Fox, *Journal*	John L. Nickalls, *The Journal of George Fox*, revised ed. (1975).
G.B.S.	F.H. MSS, The Great Book of Sufferings.
Henrey	Blanche Henrey, *British Botanical and Horticultural Literature before 1800* (Oxford University, 1975) vol. i.
Hubbard	D. G. B. Hubbard, 'Early Quaker Education.' Unpublished M.A. Thesis, London University, December, 1939 (F.H.).
J.F.H.S.	*The Journal of the Friends Historical Society* (1903-).

Martindale	J. A. Martindale, 'Early Westmorland Plant Records' *The Westmorland Natural History Record* (London and Kendal, 1888-89) vol. i.
NB	Thomas Lawson's MS Botanical notebook, The Linnean Society, London.
N&B	Joseph Nicolson and Richard Burn, *The History and Antiquities of the Counties of Westmorland and Cumberland* (1777).
Nicolson, *Flora*	ed. E. Jean Whittaker, *A Seventeenth Century Flora of Cumbria, William Nicolson's Catalogue of Plants, 1690* (Surtees Society, 1981).
Raven, *Ray*	Charles E. Raven, *John Ray Naturalist, his Life and Works* (Cambridge, 1942).
Ray, *Corr*	ed. E. Lankester, *The Correspondence of John Ray* (Ray Society, 1848).
Ross, *Margaret Fell*	Isabel Ross, *Margaret Fell, Mother of Quakerism* (1949, Sessions of York, 1984).
Swarth	F.H. MSS, Swarthmore.
SYN	ed. William T. Stearn, *John Ray, Synopsis Methodica Stirpium Britannicarum Editio Tertia 1724* (Ray Society, 1973).
T.H.	Tullie House Library, Carlisle.

Preface

Four main things direct and determine a biography such as this: the legacy of what has been written before, the preservation or non-preservation of documents, the influence and help of others and the bias of one's own mind.

The biographical legacy of what has been written before is contained almost entirely in two articles by M. Bennet and S. L. Petty: 'Thomas Lawson, the Westmorland Botanist' and 'Thomas Lawson the Father of Lakeland Botany' and in several passages in Maria Webb's *The Fells of Swarthmoor Hall*. These are all short sketches and, it must be said, are inaccurate in many respects.

To the preservation or non-preservation of documents, the biographer of a man like Thomas Lawson is apt to refer to the nagging question 'what is truth?' In the case of a major figure, an Oliver Cromwell or a King Charles II, the biographer may seek truth in re-interpretation, selecting from the abundant material available, those documents which seem to him to be of special, perhaps neglected, significance. In the case of a man like Thomas Lawson, the documentary material is both scant and patchily preserved and time has imposed its own selective limits to what can be discovered about his life and interests. How much would one not give to find the lost diary that Ellwood speaks of, to see the plan and notes for the 'Floscuculi Britanniae' or to travel back in time and enjoy just one hour of conversation. As it is, we must be thankful for what does remain: for the bureaucracy of Church and State and for the Quakers' own passion for administration that has meant that it has been possible to track Lawson through the episcopal registers, the Quarter Sessions indictment books and the Quakers' own copious records at Friends House, London and in the County Record offices. We may be thankful, too, for the bravery of the early Quaker printers and their zeal for polemics that ensured that nine of Thomas Lawson's works got into print. And lastly, we may be thankful for the care that the Thompson family took of Lawson's botanical notebook which has now found a safe home with the Linnean Society of London.

To that Society my first thanks are due for allowing me to examine the notebook and for permitting a microfilm copy to be made by the University Library, Durham. To the staff of the library and to Miss Elizabeth Rainey, Keeper of the Rare Books, my debts of gratitude extend over many years. My thanks are also due to Edward Milligan, Malcolm Thomas and the staff of Friends House Library, to Mr Bruce Jones, Miss Sheila Macpherson and the staff of the Cumbria County Record Office (Carlisle and Kendal) and to Mr M. V. Mathew and the staff of the Royal Botanic Garden Library,

Edinburgh. Dr Margaret Harvey has given me much help in transcribing and translating the Latin of the episcopal records and I have received guidance on several points from Dr Christopher Brooks, Mr David Crane and Miss Margaret McCollum. Mr Otto Reichwald has given me help with *Eine Antwort* and Miss Joyce Hodgson with criticism of the first and subsequent drafts of the work. My Cousin Sue has put up with me on many visits to the Lake District and my father has given me endless assistance with the research. It remains only to thank those who have capped all this unstinted help by making *Thomas Lawson* financially possible: the Curwen Archives Trust and various Quaker trusts have generously sponsored the text whilst the illustrations have been made possible through a grant from the British Academy.

The reader is now left to pursue the bias of the book. One thing, perhaps, needs to be said: I am not a Quaker and some amongst the Society of Friends may feel that I have used too many military metaphors in describing the early years of the movement. But most Quakers in the 1660s and 1670s saw themselves as engaged upon a crusade – as Christ's apostles in a new age putting on the armour of righteousness. In the words of the title of James Nayler's book they had embarked upon *The Lamb's War*. Against those Friends who would point to the Peace Testimony of 1660 as demonstrating the pacific nature of Quakers from their very early years, I would quote the opening words of that testimony: 'we utterly deny all outward wars and strife and fighting with outward weapons . . .' Outward wars and weapons, maybe: that there was a war of the spirit to be waged and won in a hostile world no Quaker of the early days would have denied. It was precisely because they were such a militant force in the nation that they had to make so official a denial of any military ambition.

Tobermory,   JEAN WHITTAKER
March, 1986

Nineteenth-century view of Vincent's Rocks

THE 1677 TOUR

Itinerary

Lawson's itinerary of his tour is to be found on pp. 326-27 of his notebook. The mileages that he gives measure fairly accurately against the modern mile.

To Kendal 15 miles, To Fell end 7. To Swarthmoor 12. to Marsh Grainge 4, to Fell end 16. To Gunnerthwaite, 10, to Eldroth 13. To Sawley 8. to Manchester 26 calling by the way at Whally Abbey at Sr Raph Ashtons there we saw a Sword Fish From Manchester to Castleton in the Peake Land is 18 miles here is the place called Devil's Arse and the rocks called Mamtor & within a mile or two is Elden hole From Castleton to Leeke 16 to Stafford 16 To Stourbridge 18. to Worcester 15. To Gloucester 18. to Huntley 10 to Nailworth 16. to Bristol 20 To Bathe 10. To Amesbury rather Ambrosbury 26, nigh this is the memorable monument Stonehenge on a river here is plenty of swans, fro Am. to Shifford in Barkshire 19 miles hence to Oxford (leaveing the Vale of white horse on the left hand) 16 miles, To Elnbery in Barkshire 10M. To Oxford again 10 miles thence to Banbury 18 miles; hence by Buckingham to Stony Stratford 19 miles thence by Newport Pannel to Bedford 12: to Riseley 6, from Riseley by Bedford to Barton in Bedfordshire 14 miles, to St Albans 12 to London 20. to Westminster Abby & back 8 to West. Abby againe & back 8 to Deptford in Kent & back 10 to Waltonstow in Essex & back 10 to Westminster & back againe twice 20 miles; to Kingston upon Thames & back againe 20. To Walton Abby in Hartfordshire so on to Ware, Puckridge, so to Cambridge 45 miles, to Wilboram 5 to Gogmagog hills so to Cambridge 8. thence to Over 6 miles, thence to St Ives 6 miles thence to Haddenham in the Isle of Ely 7 miles. thence by Ely to Littleport 9M. thence by Well in Norfolk to Wisbich in the Isle of Ely 15 miles. to Dunnington by which lives Will Dixon 20 miles thence by Deary hill, good for milk Cows & by 40 foot River to Eveden 8 miles, to Lincolne where lives Abraham Morris & Jo Mills 14 miles, To South Leverton in Nottinghamshire by Littlebrook ferry 11 miles; to Balby 14. to Pomfret where is Tho. English 10.M. to Tadcaster where is John Lofte 10.M. to Yorke 8 miles To Tho. Tompsons at Molton 12 To Peter Hodgson at Scarborough 15. by Robbin Hood bay to Whitby 12 to Ellerby where lives Jacob Scarfe 5 miles To Pinchinthorp in Cleiveland 11 To Horton 6. thence by Yarme & Darlington to Ulnaby 13 by Heighington & Bolam to Headlam 6; to Barnard Castle 6 Strickland 30.

LAWSON and THOMPSON FAMILIES

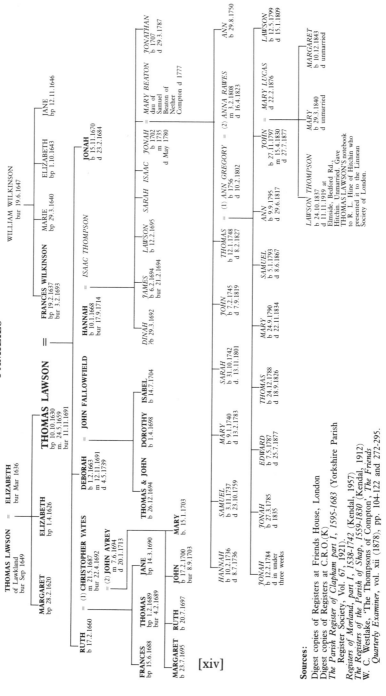

[xiv]

Sources:

Digest copies of Registers at Friends House, London
Digest copies of Registers at C.R.O.(K)
The Parish Register of Clapham part I, 1595-1683 (Yorkshire Parish
  Register Society, Vol. 67, 1921).
Registers of Morland, part I, 1538-1742 (Kendal, 1957)
The Registers of the Parish of Shap, 1559-1830 (Kendal, 1912)
W. C. Westlake, 'The Thompsons of Compton', *The Friends
  Quarterly Examiner*, vol. xii (1878), pp. 104-122 and 272-295.

CHAPTER I

Convinced at Rampside

IN THE EARLY SUMMER OF 1652, a young man who had the care of the souls of the people in the little Lancashire village of Rampside offered his pulpit to a wandering preacher and was himself so convinced by what the preacher had to say that he left his charge and joined the new sect of which the preacher was the founder. The preacher was George Fox, his people the Quakers and the impressionable young man was called Thomas Lawson.

Today Rampside falls within the modern county of Cumbria, reorganised to comprise old Cumberland, Westmorland and that detached portion of Lancashire known as Lonsdale-North-of-the-Sands. In this detached portion lies Rampside. To visit the village, the modern traveller from the South would turn aside at Levens Bridge before Kendal is reached. Kendal is the gateway to the Lakeland hills, but the traveller to Rampside has only distant prospects of the hills – Coniston Old Man and its associates away to the North-west – and soon after entering North Lonsdale he turns his back on the hill country and heads southwards to Ulverston and to Rampside beyond. In this he has described a U-turn that has led him North and West over the head of Morecambe Bay and then southward to the very tip of the Furness peninsula.

For seventeenth-century travellers there was, however, an alternative. Across the sands of Morecambe Bay that lie between the arms of the inverted U was a route passable in favourable states of the tide and with local guidance. It was a route cut by the shifting channels of the Rivers Kent and Leven and subject to the hazards of tide and quicksand. In the Cartmel Register there is, every so often, an entry for the burial of some unfortunate drowned in the crossing.[1] To such travellers, the low hills of Furness must have taken on something of the nature of a promised land seen across the hazardous salt desert of the Sands. Writers of the nineteenth century were apt to draw biblical comparisons with the crossing of the Red Sea and their imaginative eyes saw the caravans of Arabia in the numbers of carts, coaches, oxen, sheep and wayfarers who crossed the Sands on a busy day.[2]

1

For it was undoubtedly a well-used route, shortening the distance from Lancaster to Ulverston by almost half: the modern route cuts across the mosses at the head of Morecambe Bay on a nineteenth-century causeway but the original 'land-way' was obliged to skirt them still further to the North, making the distance from Lancaster to Ulverston 38 miles. The route 'over Sands' was a mere 22 miles – level walking most of the way and at least as good as the atrocious roads of the time. Thomas Lawson certainly knew the route over the Sands, for, amongst the botanical records that he later kept are Sea Lavender, *Limonium vulgare* and Thrift, *Armeria maritima* from Harlsyde (Chapel Island), an island midway in the Leven estuary which sometimes provided a welcome refuge for those who might have got into difficulty in traversing that section of the over Sands route.[3]

Both routes end in the coast road that takes the traveller the last seven miles to his destination, with the Bay on the left hand and the rolling pasturelands of Low Furness on the right, down past Aldingham where the sea licks the churchyard wall and so at last to Rampside at the southernmost tip of the mainland. To the South and West only Walney Island is beyond, lying like a breakwater against the malice of the Irish Sea. To the East, only the oyster-catchers and the waders can go further and sand and sea and sky stretch away to the distant blue outline of the land across the Bay.

To this remote spot between sea and sky came George Fox fresh from his immense preaching successes in Yorkshire and in the Kendal area. He had come over the Pennines from the East; his meetings had attracted many hundreds and he had preached his own special message of hope and religious salvation at Preston Patrick and Kendal. The northern counties of England, poorest in religious and educational facilities were fertile ground and everywhere that Fox went he won followers. From Kendal he came the northern route into Furness. Between the southern end of Windermere and the head of the mosses, the entrance to Furness is narrowed to a five-mile doorway. Through this doorway Fox walked, preaching in the little villages that were strung out along this land route in the strip between the hills and the impassable bog. Beyond Ulverston, he met with a kind reception from Margaret Fell at Swarthmoor Hall,[4] the home of Thomas Fell, a landowner of some substance and a Judge of Assize of the Chester and North Wales Circuit, Vice-Chancellor of the Duchy and Attorney for the County Palatine of Lancaster.[5] Margaret, 16 years her husband's junior, was experiencing some of the spiritual turmoil that was affecting many people in the times that followed the execution of Charles I at Whitehall on a frosty morning in January 1649. The years of war and political controversy that had led up to the execution had given almost everyone a taste for debate and argument and had thrown up a multitude of preachers prepared to travel the country and speak wheresoever they could gain a hearing. Margaret Fell's perplexity of spirit had given her an interest in such travelling preachers and Fox, like others, received hospitality and shelter at the Hall. His reputation had preceded him into the district and when, in that first week in July, he proposed to follow a visit to Aldingham church by preaching at Rampside, Thomas Lawson was full of curiosity. Here was something quite clearly special in the way of prophets and, with a young man's willingness to see justice done, he counselled his congregation at the morning service to give Fox a fair hearing, advising them that he proposed to let him speak in his place at the afternoon service.[6] By this, everyone's appetite was whetted and a good crowd drawn as Fox records in his *Journal*:

> I passed to Rampside and there was a chapel in which one Thomas Lawson used to preach, that was a high priest. He very lovingly spoke in the morning to his people of my coming in the afternoon, and when I was come all the country gathered thereaways.[7]

Thomas, it seems, was not the only one who was full of curiosity and he, wishing perhaps to avert any unpleasant incident that might take place before Fox reached his chapel, went a mile to meet him and conducted him there personally.[8] Probably he met him down on the shore, for the chapel was almost a mile inland from the coast road which Fox would follow from Aldingham. The present chapel is a nineteenth-century building standing on the edge of an eminence commanding views over the land that drops away southwards to Morecambe Bay and westwards to the Walney Channel. The road to it climbs at right-angles to the coast road and it was this way that Thomas and the strange preacher would walk together to confront all the country gathered thereaways to hear what Fox had to say. 'When I was come,' says Fox, 'I saw there was no place more convenient to declare to the people there than in the chapel, and so I went into the chapel and all was quiet,'[9] – though perhaps not as quiet as Fox's writing up of the events would suggest. The Lancaster Monthly Meeting minute book makes it clear that there was some rowdiness amongst those who listened to Fox all that long afternoon and that it was Thomas who kept his people in hand, offering Fox first his pulpit to preach from:

> which the said G. F. refused, but stood up on a form, and livingly declared and held forth the way of salvation to the people for about three hours' space; and when he came forth into the yard, some of the people would have laid violent hands on him, but the said Thos. Lawson forbade them, saying he was greatly satisfied with G. F.'s preaching; and said if our worship and doctrine cannot be maintained without fear and violence, 'tis time to leave it. So the people were quieted and an old woman aged 80 years said she never heard such good doctrine out of the mouth of any black coat all the days of her life.[10]

For her, as for many that day:

> the everlasting Truth was largely declared that day which reached
> and entered into the hearts of people; and the everlasting day of the
> eternal God was proclaimed and all were quiet and received the
> Truth in the love of it.[11]

Like Margaret Fell, Thomas had been perplexed and seeking. Now he had
found what he had sought and the result is recorded by Fox in his *Journal*:

> This priest came to be convinced and stands in Truth, and grew in
> the wisdom of God . . . He threw off his preaching for hire and his
> chapel and came to preach the Lord Jesus and his kingdom freely.[12]

What sort of a young man was this Thomas Lawson and what sort of
position did he hold in his chapel at Rampside? He was certainly not, as has
been said, the vicar of Rampside which was one of three chapels in the
vicarage of Dalton. It is doubtful, indeed, whether Thomas was ever
ordained: it was no uncommon thing for preaching to be undertaken by
persons who were not ordained – the botanist John Ray, for example,
preached both in his college chapel at Cambridge and at St. Mary's for some
time before he took orders.[13] George Fox described Thomas as 'the priest
. . . that was convinced',[14] – a useful and familiar title, for a parson in the
north of England. Nevertheless, one should not disregard the description of
Thomas at the time of his convincement as a 'high' priest. This would imply
a religious bias towards exalted and mystical forms of worship that accords
well with what we know of Thomas' character in early manhood. It required
only the accident of Fox to channel his fervour into Quakerism. In an age of
intense religious feeling Thomas had impressed himself upon the people of
Rampside whose respect he held and who, we must presume, supported
him for 'Ramside hath no maintenance nor Minister' as its inhabitatants had
complained in 1650 when they had appealed to be made parochial.[15] Their
plea had been addressed to a Commission that was set up to survey the
existing parochial system and the maintenance of preaching ministers and it
has been assumed that Lawson was appointed as a direct result of this plea.[16]
But it was 1655 at the earliest before the Registers of the Union and Division
of Parishes (1655-1657) were compiled that related to the returns from this
survey and the action to be taken (for which the approval of the Lord
Protector and Council still needed to be obtained).[17] In them we read:

> the Inhabitants of Ramside pray to be made Parochiall and that
> Rouscoate, Newtowne, Peaseholmes and Salthouse, being 31
> familyes may be added to Ramside and a competent maintenance
> and ministry there setled.[18]

They might have done. The evidence is all against their demands having been met and the records of the Commonwealth are too defective for us to arrive at the real truth of the matter: indisputably, the folk of Rampside, with that desire for independence notorious in the North Country, wanted a minister. Indisputably, too, they got Thomas Lawson. But how the matter was arranged lay, in all probability, between him and them. The most that one can say is that Thomas may have been assisting the vicar of Dalton. As such, he could hardly be said – as has been claimed – to be established in a lucrative living.[19] In 1649, the vicar of Dalton was complaining that whereas in time past he had been wont to receive a stipend of £17 6s 8d, he had not been paid for the past seven years and that he was dependent, besides his tithe, upon the benevolence of his parishioners.[20] There is no reason to suppose that things improved in the lean years of the early 1650s.

●　　　●　　　●

At the time of his convincement, Thomas was 21. He had been born in the North Country in the hilly lands where the eastern boundaries of Westmorland touch the far western reaches of Yorkshire. Though there is some doubt as to his parentage[21] all are agreed that the date of his birth was 1630, the date of his baptism the 10th October and the place was Lawkland in the parish of Clapham,[22] an upland parish of England lying on the North-east edge of the Forest of Bowland with the present M6 less than 20 miles to the West and the valley of the Ribble immediately to the East, where Giggleswick and Settle are planted side by side on either bank of the river. From the Clapham parish register, it is likely that Thomas' parents were Thomas Lawson of Lawkland who was buried in September, 1649 and his wife Elizabeth, buried in March of 1636. Two elder sisters, Margaret and Elizabeth, were baptised on 28th February, 1620 and 1st April, 1626.[22] Such parentage puts Thomas squarely amongst the stock of yeomen and peasant farmers whose isolation and independency of mind made Yorkshire a recruiting ground for Cromwell during the Civil War and a power-house of Quakerism during the inter-regnum. Social life was less varied here than in southern England and its fabric required fewer tugs to loosen the strands. Religious movements caught on quickly in these remote districts and a bare eight miles from Clapham lay the parish of Grindleton where Roger Brereley had raised much controversy in the years before the Civil War and whence his teaching 'that we must not now goe by motives but by motions [i.e. inward guidances]' and that 'when God comes to dwell in a man He so fills the soule that there is no more lusting'[23] gives us some foretaste of Quaker teaching. It was already a sectarian world into which Thomas was born: by 1646, Edwards was to enumerate 199 sects in his *Gangraena*, but even those who did not take upon themselves the label or banner of one particular religious leader were apt to form themselves into small groups, separated from their parish church and humbly calling themselves Seekers. These people pre-dated the Civil War by several years and went on forming little Seeker groups until the early 1650s when many were absorbed into the Quaker movement.[24] In a troubled and discordant world, they were but one protest against the malaise of England, a malaise that was to erupt, when Thomas was nearing his twelfth birthday, in the conflict between King and Parliament. On 22nd August, 1642, in wet and windy weather, the King raised his standard at Nottingham and the Civil War was formally joined. On that fateful day Lawson was still a schoolboy, walking the two and a half miles over the hill to drop down the steep limestone escarpment – running no doubt on the days that he was late – into the village of Giggleswick which had boasted a school since at least 1512 – so says the foundation stone that is now incorporated into the present school – though it is probable that it was in existence a few years earlier, possibly even before the turn of the century. The first school, of which the foundation stone is the only survival, was in the centre of Giggleswick hard by the old church of St. Alkelda and the stone was to be moved four times to be incorporated in four subsequent rebuildings, including that of the present school which has removed 300 yards from the original site and occupies a position above the village, commanding a view that Thomas would have seen many times as he hastened down the hill on his daily journey to his lessons. These began at 6.30 a.m. and lasted until 5 p.m. with a break from 11 a.m. to 1 p.m., though in the darker months boys who lived far off might be let off earlier at the Master's discretion.[25] The accepted curriculum of the seventeenth-century grammar school prescribed a start with easier Latin authors in the lower forms supervised by the Usher. By the time the boys reached the upper school they were working on the whole range of classical authors and Greek and Hebrew had been added to the curriculum.[26] Teaching in the higher forms was largely done by the Master, and Hebrew was very much a thing of the seventeenth century with its deep interest in biblical scholarship and its yearning after the purity of the original word of the scriptures. During Thomas' time at the school, the Westmorland-born Master, Rowland Lucas, was to die and to be succeeded by William Walker, a Giggleswick man who had been a pupil at the school under Lucas. During his nine years as Master, a steady stream of boys went to Cambridge – mainly to Christ's College which took 25 boys during Walker's Mastership. In 1650, the year that Thomas went up to Christ's, two other boys entered St. John's College.[27] In that year his name is entered on the Admission Register of Christ's on July 25th. An entry two years later records the admission of Hugh Lawson who, like Thomas, is described in the register as the son of Thomas, educated at Giggleswick. From this, it has been assumed that Hugh was a brother, but there is no record of Hugh's birth in the registers of Clapham and the connection must remain doubtful. Thomas is registered as a sizar under Mr. Bethell, his sponsor being Mr. Widdrington suggesting that he had benefited, as did the sons of many poor men during the period of Walker's Mastership, from provisions made under the will of Richard Carr which set up eight scholarships worth £5 a year and two Fellowships worth £13. 6s 8d at Christ's.[28] The will makes clear the qualifications that would be required of the holders of the scholarships:

> And my Will is that the Schollars that shall be capable of this Exhibition and partakers of their Schollarshipp afforesaid shall be elected and chosen from amongst the Schollars of the free Schoole of Gigleswick afforesaid . . . My Will is that they make choice onelie of such Schollars as were either borne in the said Parishe of Gigleswick, and whose parents were inhabitants and dwellers in the said parish when the said Schollars were borne or else of the children lawfullie begotten of my brother in lawe Robert Thornton and my sister Jennet his Wife in the parish of Clapham in the Countie of York and of their childrens' posteritie for ever being Schollars brought up in the free Schoole of Gigleswicke, and borne either in the Parish of Gigleswicke or Clapham aforesaid.

And when the founder's kin had been provided for, the choice for the remaining scholarships would fall amongst:

> The poorer sort of Schollars although they be not altogether so well learned as other Schollars which have richer friendes, Yet Provided always that they be fit and meet for the Universitie.[29]

The names of some of the boys who benefited from these scholarships are to be found in the Governors' Minute Book – the 'Shute Book' – of Giggleswick School, but there are no details for boys going up between 1629 and 1680. Thomas, though born in Clapham parish rather than Giggleswick, would appear in every other way to qualify admirably for one of these scholarships.

And so, in the troubled summer of 1650, Thomas Lawson, son of Thomas Lawson of Lawkland, prepared to go up to University. The remote Pennine village of his upbringing may have been a place where the battles for state control between King and Parliament were less real than the necessities of mastering Hebrew and acquiring virtuosity in classical scholarship, but Cambridge was a place where politics were altogether much nearer home. In this summer of 1650, Oliver Cromwell was the unacknowledged king of England. He had removed Charles, had hammered Ireland into submission and, in the early autumn, would move into Scotland to complete his triumphs by the defeat of the strange alliance of Royalists and Covenanters at Dunbar on the wild morning of 3rd September. Victory of a sort there was for the Huntingdon squire, but the health of the country appeared no better than it had been before the war started: many said a good deal worse: and there is no sharper critic than a young man who, having played no part in the battle, has no deep-felt need to find the last state better than the first. Moreover, the universities were themselves under attack from within and without. The year before Thomas went up, William Dell, who objected to much of the traditional university curriculum, had been made Master of Caius. Dell wanted to see a form of university education based less upon the classical texts of the 'wretched heathens'[30] and more upon Christian learning. The political intention of such a course would be to break the gentleman's monopoly of education and consequently of posts in law, medicine and, most especially, in the church.

Outside the university, the cry was taken up by the Levellers and the Diggers and all the radical sects who saw a learned clergy as their chief enemy. In 1653, in the Barebone Parliament, the radicals were to meet defeat at the hands of the conservatives when 80 or so members of Parliament remained in favour of the status quo against 60 who were opposed to a learned ministry.[31] The tide had turned, the dream of the millenium was fading.

Undoubtedly much of this ferment passed over the head of the ordinary undergraduate who was still filling his notebooks with traditional learning and the dicta of Aristotle.[32] But uncertainty was in the air, the universities were demoralised and it was by no means evident that the whole rationale of their existence – the supply of gentlemen to the professions – was not going to be overturned by radical forces. In such an atmosphere, Thomas stayed less than two years – possibly less than one – and took no degree. It has been suggested that during this time he may have met John Ray[33] and laid the foundation of that love of botany which he was later to manifest. John Ray, son of an Essex blacksmith, was to become England's foremost botanist and in 1651 he had been appointed Greek lecturer at Trinity College.[34] It is certainly possible that Thomas met him – Ray, who was born in 1627, was only three years Lawson's senior – but if he did so, it is equally certain that there was no sudden union of minds. It is more than 20 years before we have evidence of Lawson's interest in botany,[35] more than 30 before there is any mention of him in Ray's correspondence.[36] Moreover, Ray himself was only just beginning the study that was to prove his life's work. In 1651, a period of illness forced him to rest and to recruit his strength by riding and walking[37] and it was during this period that his first work – a catalogue of plants growing around Cambridge – was conceived. It took nine years to bring it to publication and the impression to be gained from reading the preface is that they were nine years of rather solitary endeavour. Thomas Lawson, in another college, was not involved in them.

Larger in Thomas' eyes must have bulked the political excitements that were leading up to the final defeat of the Royalist forces. The spring and summer campaigning in Scotland with which the year 1651 opened culminated in a Royalist push southwards to raise England for the new King, crowned Charles II at Scone on 1st January. On 9th August, the Royalists were at Kendal, less than 25 miles from Lawson's home, marching South to their ultimate defeat at Worcester on 3rd September that year. By that time Lawson may have left Cambridge. Possibly he had found himself a poor man in a world that he could not afford. His father had died in the September before he went to university[38] and the sizarship was not really adequate to provide for a student's needs. Fifteen years before, in the mid 1630s, the scholarship of £5 was, even then, proving too small and Giggleswick scholars were finding difficulty in getting Fellows of Christ's to take them on as pupils.[39] It was yet another plank of citicism against the university system that the expense kept poor men out. Thomas, whether he left of his own accord or was forced to turn away through lack of funds, was bound to have sympathy with those who were dissatisfied with the way that post-war England was heading. And, indeed, there was much to criticise and little to praise in the material and spiritual life of the country. The war had left an impoverished land, rife with honest folk forced to turn beggars and the prisons were full of debtors. Those who harked back to the autocratic days of the King's personal rule could remember the success of his administration of the Poor Law.[40] Under the new rulers there was no less autocracy and the Poor Law was in ruins. Everywhere there were signs of misery and confusion. For many it seemed as though the only pre-war ideal to emerge intact from the fighting was the dream of religious freedom, for it was not immediately obvious at the opening of the 1650s that the governance of the country was in the hands of men too fearful of loss of office to remember why they had been entrusted with it, or that Oliver Cromwell himself would be forced to put the security of the state before liberty of conscience.

It was against this background that Thomas Lawson went North again, his experience broadened but his mind not yet cleared by sight of the road ahead. At Rampside, Fox gave him that sight. In a paper written shortly after his convincement, Thomas struggles, in the rather airy language that the Civil War had thrown up, to describe his unregenerate state before he hearkened to Fox:

> there was a time, when I boasted of, and was exalted through the notionary knowledge of god, Christ, the Angells, and high things, . . . and as I grew up . . . so in pride, and selfe conceitedness, . . . in the Pharises steps.[41]

This sketches what his formal education had done for him: what came to him at Rampside was an inner illumination by which, he says, 'I came to see, what I had to stand against, and what to waite in.' He gropes for words to emphasise the change that has come over him in his view of the world: he piles phrase upon phrase to try to make intelligible the unintelligible:

> and here I saw all professions in the will of man to be abomination unto the lord, and that all formes were in the will of man, enimies unto the life of godliness, and so I came to see, and to pitty man run from his maker, seeking a god, but above the way unto him, denying the Crosse of Christ, and going astray from him, so imagining away to life, so I came to pitty man in this bondage, seeing him out of the way unto liberty, not mindeing the light, that shines in a dark place, in the hearte, nor waiteing in it, upon god, to have his Condition opened unto him, and to be brought out of darkness into light.

There were really never enough words for Quakers to express what they truly felt about their religious experience but, a whole 37 years later, Thomas, still walking in the light of that experience, simply and humbly told Fox what his coming had meant to him:

Greatstrickland ye 20 Mo 2 89

Dear George,

> Whom I have, and do love without Eclipse, and I can truly say, the remembrance of thy first comeing, in power and innocency, and thy perseverance therein, hath often sweetly tinctur'd and strengthen'd me in hours of temptations.[42]

AN UNTAUGHT
TEACHER
Witnessed against.

OR,

The old Bottles mouth opened,

It's Wine poured forth, drunk of Drunkards,
denyed of them who have tasted of the new.

That is to say, the unsound, un-

seasoned, unsavory Doctrines, and opinions of *Matthew*
Caffyn, Baptist-Teacher laid open, who in the County
of *Suffex*, is cryed up to be as their Battle Axe, and Weapon of Warre, who as *Jannes* and *Jambres* rides aloft,
and bestirs himself with the Magick Rod of his lies, flan-
ders, asperfions, and unfound Doctrines, labours to
ftrengthen the hands of carnal profeffors, and to keep
the beloved of God in bondage: for whose redemption
the Lord is rifen, and is going forth in majefty, and great
glory, and will triumph over all who have triumphed.

Which Doctrines, and unfa-

vory fpeeches were received from his own mouth, part
of them at a meeting of the people called Quakers, at
Crowley in *Suffex*, others thereof at his own house neere
South-water, before me and *John Slee*, upon the fifth day
of the feventh moneth, 1655.

No Weapon that is formed against thee shall profper, every
tongue that shall rise against thee in judgement, thou shalt
condemn: this is the Heritage of the Servants of the Lord,
and their righteoufnefs is of me, faith the Lord, Isa. 54. 17.

Tho: Lawfon. John Slee.

LONDON, Printed for *Giles Calvert*, at the *Black-fpread-*
Eagle, at the West end of *Pauls*, 1655.

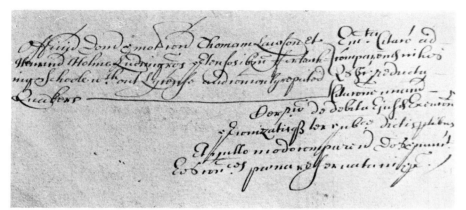

Certification of the serving of a citation on Thomas Lawson and Henry Holmes of Morland 'pretended schoolmasters' to appear to answer charge of 'teaching Schoole without Lycence and commonly reputed Quakers'. C.R.O. (C) MSS, DRC 5/4 f.55v, July 1673

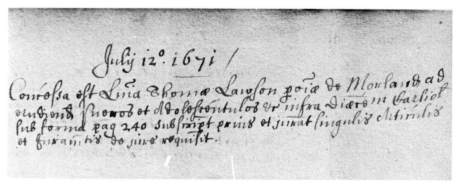

Grant of licence to teach to Thomas Lawson. C.R.O. (C) MSS DRC 1/4 p. 518

Submission of Thomas Lawson to the Church of England. C.R.O. (C) MSS DRC 5/4 f.37

'On Thursday, being the 13th day of the month of July, anno domini 1671. In one of the upper breakfast rooms commonly called the Dining Room, in Rose Castle, there appeared in person before the Rev'd Father and Lord in Christ the Lord Edward by divine permission Bishop of Carlisle a certain Thomas Lawson of Little Strickland in the parish of Morland in the county of Westmorland and the diocese of Carlisle, yeoman, otherwise pretended schoolmaster in that place, placed under sentence of excommunication in due form automatically invoked [lata] against him on account of his obstinacy in not appearing in court to refute certain chief articles of enquiry concerning wholly the salvation of his soul and the reformation of his behaviour. And he humbly begged benefit of absolution from the said sentence of excommunication imposed upon him. At whose humble petition the aforesaid Lord Bishop (because Holy Mother Church never closes her bosom to the penitent and to the soul returning to her) decreed that he thus humbly petitioning (as is said above) should be absolved. And there and then he absolved and restored the same Thomas Lawson to the Church and its sacraments and joined and numbered him with the communion of the faithful'

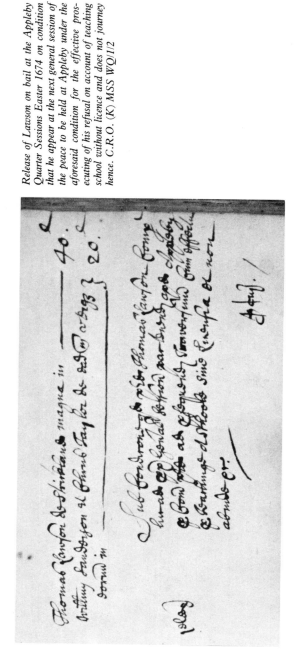

Release of Lawson on bail at the Appleby Quarter Sessions Easter 1674 on condition that he appear at the next general session of the peace to be held at Appleby under the aforesaid condition for the effective prosecuting of his refusal on account of teaching school without licence and does not journey hence. C.R.O. (K) MSS WQ/1/2

John Lawson for his Contemptuous refusall to serve of this Jury is fined —— 00 : 07 : 4
Thomas Lawson for his Contemptuous refusall to serve of this Jury is fined 00 : 07 : 4
Thomas Lawson for keeping Tedders in the feild in the night tyme agt paine — 00 : 03 : 4.
Henry Jameson for this like —————— 00 : 03 : 4

Record of Thomas Lawson in the Court Roll: 'Thomas Lawson for his Contemptuous refusall to serve of the Jury is fyned 00:07:4'
'Thomas Lawson for keeping Tedders in the feild in the night tyme agt paine 00:03:4'

CHAPTER II

Slandered in Clapham

DURING THE REST OF THAT SUMMER and all through the following year, Fox remained in the North-west, preaching his message throughout Furness and up into Cumberland as far North as Carlisle. But it was Swarthmoor that was the beating heart of the movement. His initial kind reception by Margaret Fell had been supported by her husband, Judge Fell, who had been absent in London on the occasion of Fox's first visit to his house.[1] Although the Judge never became a Friend himself he continued, throughout his life, to offer the protection of Swarthmoor to the Quakers. The very fact that he remained within the establishment, continuing to fulfil his function in the judiciary, meant that he was able to protect the Friends to a degree that would otherwise have been impossible.[2] Fox thus had a secure base from which to operate and it was to the hospitality of Swarthmoor that he returned time and again for refuge and refreshment.

In the months following his convincement, Thomas Lawson must have had many opportunities for speech and worship with his leader and with that remarkable woman Margaret Fell and her household. The historian Gerard Croese says that Lawson continued for a while to exercise his function as minister of Rampside,[3] but it was at Swarthmoor that he now had his spiritual home and it was there that he received preparation for the missionary journeys that he was soon to undertake. Whilst Judge Fell lived, there was security to be found at the manor house set in its pleasant surrounds of lawn, garden, orchard and wood. It was a place where domestic business went hand-in-hand with daily experience of God: a place of spiritual uplift but a place, too, of order and comfort under the able management of Margaret Fell. Her practical genius was an essential complement to the flame and fire that Fox's mystic passion gave to his followers. Through her was set up at Swarthmoor an organisation which has best been described as a secretariat:[4] a party headquarters that dealt with planning and finance and kept open the Quakers' lines of communication. Looking at the letters that have survived, it seems as though everybody in

11

the movement wrote to Margaret: Swarthmoor was a clearing house for the information that enabled every member of it, no matter how far from home, to feel that he was an organic part of a larger whole, and that whole embodied in the great-hearted personality of Margaret Fell. There is no finer tribute to her than the hundreds upon hundreds of letters in the Caton MSS and the Swarthmore MSS written by Friends who sought her help, her advice, her support or just the continued assurance of her love towards them. When Thomas was convinced in 1652, it was at a time when the rather random wanderings of Fox had been concentrated on a single point, a place from which a burst of organised energy would carry Quakers throughout England and beyond in a great wave of missionary endeavour. It was a most exciting time to have joined, a most fortunate chance that had brought Thomas to Rampside at just that date.

Surrounded by an atmosphere of apostolic fervour, Thomas would meet and converse not only with Fox, but also with the other leaders in the movement. James Nayler and Richard Farnsworth had followed Fox into Furness[5] and, in these early days, their names were equal with his. This was a time when they were all brothers, all servants of the Lord, seeing themselves as Christ's apostles in a new age. Swarthmoor kept hot the core of the movement whilst Fox travelled in the North, speaking at meetings at Dalton, at Walney, Baycliff, Gleaston and away again to Kendal and Sedbergh to strengthen those whom he had convinced on his way into Furness.

The simple account of the first coming of Fox to Rampside, with its emphasis upon the good – the convincement of Thomas and the quiescence, under his direction, of the congregation – should not blind us to the fact that these were a rural people, as readily turned towards violence by hostile leadership as swayed by the great and simple truths that Fox laid before them. Amongst an easily aroused people, the Quaker was always in danger from sheer mob excitement and, in the autumn of the year, Fox was to receive rough handling from an Ulverston crowd incited by the civil authorities to throw him out of the town after he had come up from Swarthmoor on a lecture day to speak in the church.[6] A regular fray resulted in Friends who had accompanied Fox suffering broken heads and bruises before they were ejected on the North side of the town. The battered little company suggested to Fox that he might return to Swarthmoor, lying South of Ulverston, by a route that skirted the town. This he refused to do. His re-appearance, as he walked back through the centre of Ulverston, delighted the mob who had now tasted blood and were ready for fresh sport. As he came towards the market, a cry went up 'A Fox, a Fox' and the harrying would have begun again had not a soldier, 'one Leonard Pearson, who having seen or heard these former barbarous usages of him, drew his sword and said "let me see whether any dog in the market dare catch this Fox" whereupon G. F. passed quietly through the market, none daring then to lay violent hands on him, and so he went up to Swarthmoor.'

By one man's stand and a simple, authoritative action, Fox was spared further rough handling. The mob was always full of sportsmen who were ready to follow a lead if one were given: a certain callousness was never very far from the surface of seventeenth-century rural life. Many years later, Thomas Lawson was to describe the horse-play that took place around Christmas-time in a way that puts perspective into contemporary accounts of mob action:

> In many places a rude and lewd Rabble meet together in this tyme, with a long piece of wood, and forces such passingers as they meet with, without any regard to their urgent occasions, to sit astride thereon, and force them to Alehouses, and upon resistence they break into houses, force people out of their bedds, and carry them in the aforesaid manner, their priests, or other people, to Alehouses, and thus they use and abuse them till they joyn with them in this folly, or purchase their liberty with money . . . they teare and plough up their heaps of manure, called in the North middens, they teare up Flagstones, and what comes in their way, except prevented by Money, which is their design, and many have received bodily harm in and by the aforesaid vanities, and complaineing to Magistrats, got no other answer, but that these were but Christmas casts, and there was no law to take hold of them.[7]

When we consider that these were the actions of a genial mob, it becomes easier to appreciate the courage of preaching Quakers who faced abuse and violence with extraordinary perseverance and serenity. The soldier, Leonard Pearson, who had protected Fox in Ulverston was later beaten up by a gang of seven men: 'for it was the custom of this country to run 20 or 40 people upon one man,' writes Fox in his *Journal*, adding 'They fell so upon Friends in many places that they could hardly pass the highways, stoning and beating and breaking their heads.'[8] In a little while – a fortnight or so after the incident at Ulverston – he himself was to run into trouble again and the occasion was to offer Lawson a chance to serve him. Fox had gone across to Walney Island with James Nayler and had stayed overnight, holding a meeting at which passions were aroused and a threat made against his life. Later, as he was leaving by boat, he was set upon by a crowd of 'about 40 rude fellows, fishermen and the like' who had got the boatman's wife to let them know of Fox's movements, persuading her that her husband, James Lancaster, had been bewitched by Fox:

So as soon as I came to land they rushed out with staves, clubs and
fishing poles and fell upon me with them, beating and punching and
thrust me backward to the sea. And when they had thrust me almost
into the sea, I saw they would have knocked me down there in the sea
and thought to have sunk me down into the water.

Eventually, after rising and being knocked down again, Fox was beaten
back into the boat and James Lancaster, who had acted throughout with
immense courage, trying his best to shield Fox with his own body from the
worst attentions of the mob, got into the boat with him and rowed him off.
The crowd, diverted from their sadistic notion of either drowning him or
beating him to death, turned on James Nayler, crying 'Kill him, kill him'
and hunted him out of sight. When he had got Fox away, James Lancaster
turned back to look for Nayler, while Fox struggled on, baited by a new
mob wanting only the slightest provocation to use the pitch-forks, staffs,
flails and muck-hooks with which they were equipped. At last, they wearied
of threatening him and dropped away leaving him alone at last. He made a
painful attempt to wash himself in a ditch and then headed for Rampside,
three miles away, where he appealed to a Quaker called Thomas Hutton.
Thomas Lawson, at this time, was still living at Rampside and he lodged
with Hutton. Fox, when the door was opened to him, presented a wild and
bloody sight, despite his attempt to clean up:

> and I could hardly speak to them when I came in I was so bruised,
> and I told them where I left James Nayler[9]

he writes in his *Journal*. Upon this intimation, the two Thomases took each
of them a horse and, riding hard for the shore, they gathered up Nayler and
brought him home that night.

Such experiences served only to bind the Friends together and to
heighten their sense of mission. It was time for Thomas to be up and doing
and, in due course, he, like so many other northern men, was called to the
living witness of his new conviction. In the next few months, the northern
counties were to send out between 60 and 70 missionaries in a great drive to
spread the word to southern England. To these men, history has given the
name of 'the Valiant Sixty'[10] a phrase that has stuck because it so aptly
describes the spirit in which these first missionaries set out. A description of
their going is to be found in Fox's *Journal*:

> And so when the churches were settled in the North, the Lord had
> raised up many and sent forth many into his vineyard to preach his
> everlasting Gospel . . . a matter of 70 ministers did the Lord raise up
> and send abroad out of the North countries.[11]

A list of those 'matter of 70 ministers' – actually between 60 and 70 – may be found in Ernest E. Taylor, *The Valiant Sixty*[12] or, slightly amended, in Elfrida Vipont, *George Fox and the Valiant Sixty*.[13] The list is Quakerism's roll of honour, a perpetual reminder of the lights that shone in the days of the movement's beginning, despite all efforts to extinguish them. Thomas Lawson's name on the roll comes two names down from that of James Lancaster, Husbandman of Walney Isle and two before that of James Nayler, Butcher of Bolton-Forrest.

First, though, Thomas had to win his spurs in the cause. Fox assigns the raising and sending forth of his cohort of missionaries to the Lord, but the guiding and co-ordination of the troop came from Swarthmoor. Shortly after his convincement, Thomas was given his marching orders: 'I was ordered to go to the towne, where I was brought up from a Childe, and declare some thing among them' he writes in a paper[14] that he later put out to tell of his experiences. From other evidence, it is clear that the town was Clapham where Christopher Place was minister: Place being given as Thomas' adversary in the Great Book of Sufferings, that monumental manuscript now in Friends House, London which records the vicissitudes of the early Quakers. From this manuscript, Joseph Besse obtained information for *A Collection of the Sufferings of the People called Quakers*.[15] Thomas' instructions followed a common practice with the Quakers. By this they tested themselves on the depth of their convincement. To stand up in the parish of one's upbringing and preach the message of Fox was to defy the parish authorities under which one had been brought up and to proclaim one's new conviction amongst the people who were least likely to forget – friends, relations, the teachers and workmates who had guided, influenced and known one best. It was a baptism by fire, comparable, perhaps, to Christ's ministry in Nazareth when the people said: 'is not this the carpenter's son? is not his mother called Mary? and his brethren, James and Joseph, and Simon and Judas?'[16] Like Christ, the new apostles were apt to find themselves without honour in their own country. For many, it was the final break with the old life. And so it proved with Thomas.

At first, however, things went quite well. Several people were convinced by what he had to say 'and brought into obedience, and do abide' says Thomas, who was successful enough to anger the vicar and the stalwarts of his congregation who began to be 'in an uprore, and great rage against me'. This was only to be expected: it was the common lot of travelling Quakers who could not hope to find vicars pleased at being called priests of Baal and having their congregations alienated. But things became more serious for Thomas when the enraged vicar and his congregation took to personal abuse. It seems that there was a lot of verbal mud slung and Thomas, in the paper that he wrote afterwards to clear himself, asserts that there was nothing in it. His adversaries were, he says:

> raising filthy lies, slanders, aspersions against me, speaking many filthy things of me, behinde my back without any ground, on my behalfe, as they do on others, in other places, stirring up one another against me, and against any that were brought to owne the Crosse of Christ.

On the precise nature of these slanders, aspersions and filthy lies, Thomas is not specific. The heightened language in which his refutation is couched does not lend itself to the sober recital of particulars and debars us from any autobiographical glimpse of Thomas' life before he left for Cambridge. The aspersions were, no doubt, charges of immorality. There were no holds barred in the polemics of the age: a seventeenth-century churchman in full cry was a man for whom absolutely anything went, and it is as easy to believe Thomas' assertion that the charges were without foundation as it is to believe that there were dark scandals in his past. They were not raked up against him again so far as can be discovered.

Undoubtedly, however, there was a girl involved: 'a young woman, who was and is tender, and faithfull, in what is Committed unto her from the lord, meek, and humble, and truly hungering, and thirsting after righteousness,' according to Thomas' description. She it was who accompanied him when, determined not to be diminished by slander, he went to the church to force a confrontation. Under a statute made in Mary Tudor's time, it was against the law to interrupt a minister in the course of his sermon. It had long been understood, however, that this interdict did not relate to remarks made after the minister had finished and, during the inter-regnum it had become common practice to ask permission to speak at the end of the sermon.[17] Many Quakers attempted to avail themselves of this but many, too, were prosecuted and jailed under the Marian Act.

Thomas' determination to have public and open debate was thwarted – as so many such attempts were, by passion and high feeling, descending at length to blows;

> and the rude multitude were presently beating me, and shamefully intreated me, and the preist his cry unto the people, was severall times kill him, kill him.

In the uproar, Thomas was hustled out of the church – no doubt to give the good people, whipped up into a frenzy by their vicar, a bit more elbow room to give him a drubbing in the churchyard. At this critical moment up on a stall jumps the girl and, with great courage, harangues the vicar:

and was made to fasten her eies on the priest, and speak unto him, the word of the lord in much power, and his mouth was shutt, he could not utter a word, and she said unto him, thou art one of the dumbe doggs, which the prophet Isaiah cryed against, thou cannot speak the pure language, with many other words, to the wondering of many.

But if the uncertain temper of the crowd was diverted for a moment they, and the vicar, soon recovered:

and he sweld with envy, and burst out into waileing speeches, saying away with her, sett her after him, she is his whore, with many other such reprochful words, and hurried her forth.

– and so out of our story, for Thomas mentions her no more and we can only hope that she was allowed to return home unhurt and not ducked in the pond or made to suffer any other of the indignities by which rural folk of the seventeenth century had such a charming way of making their social disapproval known: the Quaker Jane Holmes, for instance, was ducked as a scold for crying her message through the town of Malton in Yorkshire.[18]

After the incident in the church, Thomas made a final attempt to have the matter out with the vicar and his parishioners:

this thing lay much upon me, to declare unto the priest, and the people, that whereas they spoke forth many filthy things as touching us, whom they so slaundered, that if any of them, preist or people, had any thing to lay to our charge, to declare it, and not to fill the minds one of another with lies.

But the vicar was not to be drawn and feelings were running too high for discussion. 'Very little was I suffered to declare,' writes Thomas, 'for the rage of the people was great against me'. In such circumstances, he must be content to have convinced a few, several of whom were 'pretty faithfull, and watchfull, seeing a necessity to waite on the lord, that his owne seed may be raised up to rule, and governe.' Thomas' words reflect the belief of the first Quakers in the possibility of the establishment of God's kingdom here on earth. In Clapham, however, and at this moment, the run of things was against it: Thomas was faced with too much hostility, too many secret enemies whose evil conceivings have been tattled abroad, injuring his character and forcing him to put out this paper in his own defence. 'I speak the truth, and lie not,' he declares, 'and my conscience beares me wittnes herein, that I am not stained with such pollutions, and evills that the wicked one hath raised against me.' Not here or anywhere is he prepared to be specific about the exact nature of the slanders spread about him – he feels that it would be improper to be so – but as he is at pains to deny 'all fleshly unions, relations, and ways' we may be sure that laxness in sexual morality was the substance of his enemies' attack – an easy charge to level at a young man and not one readily capable of proof or disproof. Thomas is firm in declaring his innocence and his 'clearness' and he puts on record his unity with those who dwell in the light:

> and who are in the spirit, and walk in it, in my measure I wittnes them, and am with them.

This foray to Clapham marked a crisis in Thomas' life and the issues were serious enough to have earned an oblique reference in Fox's *Journal*. After describing Lawson's convincement, Fox adds darkly: 'after that some rude people thought to have done him a mischief and cast scandals upon him.'[19] But Thomas has Fox's full support for the *Journal* goes on to record triumphantly that 'he was carried over all.' With regard to the practical results of the mission to Clapham, in terms of the convincement of others it seems unlikely, in the prevailing atmosphere, that much was done. But perhaps there was a seed sown for, years later, in 1669, the episcopal returns to the enquiries instituted by Archbishop Gilbert Sheldon show a 'Meeting of about 60 Quakers' at Clapham.[20]

In his recourse to the written word to appeal for judgment to his fellows, Thomas displays a characteristic that was to become typical of the Quakers. Their desire to record everything exactly as it happened was to become a consuming passion, a testament to their acts, a rebuttal of their adversaries. The paper of justification was the child of the Civil War: the battles of the paper war had been fought as fiercely as those of the real war and had been fostered in it. The Quakers were heirs to an energetic tradition of polemics and many Quaker writings – letters, Monthly Meeting minutes, published and unpublished papers – were accounts of clashes between members of the Society and the hostile world at large. Their enemies might harass them in churches, talk them down in courtrooms, extinguish them in prisons but their words tumbled on, explaining, recording, justifying. In doing battle with his parish priest and putting forth a paper giving an account of it, Thomas is standing up to be counted:

> All freinds, whom this may concerne, this am I moved of the lord to give forth, who is the wittnes of my clearenes, from the aspersions cast upon me, which are under my feet, and here have I declared the truth, my Conscience beareing me wittnes of the same, Tho: Lawson.

Something that Thomas does not relate is that he was actually assaulted by the vicar, Christopher Place. A separate report of the incident appears in the Great Book of Sufferings. In a brief entry under Yorkshire, we read:

Thomas Lawson was throwne over the stalls by Christo: Place priest and the priests hearers beat the said Thomas about the head with their bibles.[21]

The marginal note used in the Great Book of Sufferings as a key to such incidents is 'Fighting Priests'. In many cases it was no more than plain statement. A parish priest carrying a punch hefty enough to knock Thomas over the stalls is a formidable adversary and might leave the victim in poor shape to stand up to a battering of congregational bibles. If there is a touch of humour in the situation, there is also more than a touch of lynch law.

•   •   •

After this exploit, Thomas may have continued eastwards, deeper into Yorkshire. It was fertile ground for the Quakers: a restless county in an England restless and edgy in the last days of the unpopular Rump Parliament. There had been sporadic outbreaks of discontent in 1651[22] and the authorities reacted with repressive measures. York Castle began to see its first Quaker prisoners. Many of these were jailed for the offence that Thomas had perpetrated at Clapham: interrupting a minister in his church[23] and Thomas himself now spent some time in the unwholesome precincts of the castle.[24] Probably it was only a brief imprisonment for it is not mentioned in the Great Book of Sufferings. Our evidence is a book entitled *A Brief Discovery of a threefold estate of Antichrist*, 1653, in which a four-page pamphlet by Lawson 'Of the False Ministry' is included with a tract[25] by three other prisoners who also witnessed Lawson's piece:

Witnessed by the Prisoners of the Lord at York Castle: Thomas Aldam, Benjamin Nicholson, John Harwood.

Of these men, Aldam was the most prominent, a man tireless in undergoing persecution and a conspicuous force in his own county. The entries under his name in the Yorkshire section of the Great Book of Sufferings are legion. In 1653 he was being punished 'for speaking to Thomas Rookby priest of Warmsworth in the steeplehouse'[26] though the Great Book of Sufferings adds that he 'spake not a word till the said priest had donne,' arguing thereby that he was not in violation of the Marian statute. For this, he was imprisoned 44 weeks. Benjamin Nicholson's offence was similar: 'for goeing into the Steeplehouse at Doncaster and speaking in it'[27] he was judged to be a 'disturber of John Jackson Priest of Doncaster' and spent the next five months in prison. Lastly, John Harwood was with a certain Marmaduke Lambert when they were 'taken out of a Friends house where they were mett together in the feare of God.'[28] The authorities, nervous and frightened that such meetings concealed sedition, jailed the two men for 11 months.

'Of the False Ministry' was Lawson's first publication in support of the movement. In it, he attacks the church and the ministers who make their living from service to it. In the polemics of the time, Thomas calls the priests of the world conjurors, thieves, antichrists, witches, lyers, blasphemers and ravening wolves. In the language of the apocalypse they are:

> Scarlet-coloured beasts, trimmed and painted with the Saints words, inwardly full of deceit and self-ends, a wel-favoured harlot, having a golden cup in her hand full of abominations and filthiness of her fornication.
>
> Rev 14. 5,6,7.   Rev 9.2

This is the language that was originally forged in Cromwell's army of Saints. But in a peroration that stands out in simple contrast, Thomas exhorts his readers:

> Wherefore, dear friends, dwell in that which is pure; and come from amongst these Babylonish Merchants, and hear the voice of Christ within; and I will be your God and you shall be my people, saith the Lord.
>
> Thomas Lawson, one which was a Priest in Lancashire.

This pamphlet makes public Thomas' affirmation of his faith and repudiates in print his past life as one who had preached the gospel for hire. He was now ready for whatever service might be required of him.

Missionary in Sussex

WHEN THOMAS WAS RELEASED FROM YORK, he found himself part of an increasingly integrated movement. All our assumptions about Thomas' life during these early years following upon his convincement must needs be conjectural: even his imprisonment at York rests upon the single evidence of 'Of the False Ministry' and may, in truth, have come as easily before the Clapham incident as after. My own feeling, however, is that Clapham was a first test of Thomas' resolution and that the next serious trial of his fortitude was between the stone walls of York Castle. But between June 1652, when he was convinced, and May 1655[1] there is no date that we can assign to any of his movements with certainty. Indeed, we may, if we wish, suppose that he was in prison until the beginning of 1655.[2] Report, however, has it that at some time during his early career, he was wont to engage Dr. Gilpin, the minister at Greystoke in Cumberland in furious debate[3] and I think we shall not go far wrong if we assume that, after his imprisonment in York, he joined up with some such group as were engaged in the guerilla tactics of heckling and harassment in parishes all over the North country. Dr. Gilpin certainly suffered much from the unwelcome attentions of such bands:

> Some time before the restoration, quakerism began to spread, in Cumberland and Westmorland. Among other things, remarkable in their behaviour, the quakers would go into the parish church of Graystock, and disturb Dr. Gilpin, in the pulpit, dureing divine worship. And such were their novel phrases, and crosse questions and answers; that the Doctor seemed, sometimes, at a losse what to say to them.[4]

This was written by Henry Winder, the grandson of one of Dr. Gilpin's flock, also called Henry, who was an eye-witness to Dr. Gilpin's embarrassment. The Quakers 'would come and openly disturb Mr. Gilpin (and hundreds more) in the Church,'[5] he wrote in an attack on the Quakers that he published in 1696: *The Spirit of Quakerism, and the Danger of their Divine Revelation laid open*. Winder had good cause to feel bitter against the

Quakers. His grandson describes how the silencing of Dr. Gilpin by the fierce eloquence of the Quakers had drawn Dr. Gilpin's parishioners away from him:

> Among others, Henry Winder was seduced, to the no small grief of good Dr. Gilpin and his friends.[6]

A duel of words was the way to secure adherents – the Civil War had made preaching the ultimate test. Where the Quakers convinced, they convinced by words, for they spoke to a generation whose ears and minds and judgments were open to persuasion. Winder, however, did not remain a Quaker for long and his later history gives us a strange and somewhat disturbing insight into these early, heady days of Quakerism. When he became disenchanted with the movement and left it, he became the object of a most bizarre accusation by two women Quakers: Margaret Bradley, wife of Thomas Bradley and Mary Langhorne, wife of Thomas Langhorne, both of whom claimed that, by the revelation of Jesus Christ, it had been shown to them that Winder had murdered and secretly hid his own child. The unfortunate Winder was put through a good deal of distress and expense to refute this cruel accusation,[7] and the episode leaves an ugly taste in the mouth, a taint of fanaticism, a reminder that, in all great ventures, there are black patches, sinister areas of unbalance. In later, more pedestrian years, Thomas Langhorne became a most respected member of the Quaker community of Strickland: an executive in the formal structure of Monthly Meetings and Quarterly Meetings that were set up long after to give Quakerism a discipline and an organisation to monitor from within any such wild behaviour as Margaret Bradley and Mary Langhorne had given themselves over to in these early days.

Wherever Thomas was in the period before the spring of 1655, we can be reasonably sure that he was an activist. Probably he was based in the country around Penrith: when next we hear of him, he is accompanied by John Slee, a Greystoke man whom he may have met when heckling Dr. Gilpin if he was, indeed, one of that band. The whole area was one in which Quakerism was strong and growing: its centre might be placed in the village of Great Strickland, five miles to the South of Penrith which was, and remained, Quakerism's most important stronghold in Westmorland. James Nayler had been there in the very first months of the penetration of Westmorland and the people had been much impressed by him and his testimony when he was tried and imprisoned at Appleby in 1653:

> and his Testimony for Truth therein, and upon his Examination at their Sessions was much taken Notice of in that Country; and he was instrumental in Convincing divers Enquirers after the Way of Truth in and about Strickland in the same County.[8]

To have won spectactular success in the North was one thing, but within 18 months of Fox's arrival, ambitious plans were being made to spread the Quaker message wider and, in particular, to try to carry the word to the southern counties of England. Hitherto, Fox had been something of a lone mystic, a wandering prophet who had lit a fire and left it burning behind him. Swarthmoor had given the movement a base and a great executive leader in the person of Margaret Fell. We have seen how, in his *Journal*, Fox records that in late 1653 and all throught 1654 as many as 70 ministers set forth from northern England in a great missionary push to the South.[9] In these early years of the 1650s, the Friends were riding high on the crest of popular acclaim. The earliest successes on a large scale had been in Bristol where John Camm and John Audland, the Preston Patrick men, had been able to report attendances of 3,000-4,000.[10] These figures were soon matched in London where the first northern missionaries to penetrate the city had been the Westmorland men Howgill and Burrough – at 18, Burrough was younger even than Thomas Lawson. They had been instantly and immediately successful: by the autumn of 1654 it had been difficult to find a meeting place large enough for the thousands who wanted to attend and Burrough and Howgill were almost spent with their exertions.[11]

In 1655, they were joined by James Nayler, whom we remember from Walney Island, now the foremost man in the movement after Fox himself. He was at once much in demand in London, repeating the achievements of Burrough and Howgill and adding to them by a charismatic style of preaching all his own.

In the spring of 1655, it was Thomas Lawson's turn to be numbered among the apostles. His assignment was Sussex and his travelling companion was to be John Slee of Greystoke. The dates when the two men were down in the South may be deduced from financial statements sent to Swarthmoor in 1654 and 1655 by George Taylor and Thomas Willan of Kendal.[12] Before the movement was very old, Margaret Fell had seen the need for the establishment of a fund on which the Friends could draw for the inevitable expenses of missionary work. Demand was constant. In 1655, we read that the money was being 'laide foorth of purss the Stock being then emptie since the first of ye 3d month'. Nevertheless, the work went on and Slee and Lawson were able to draw upon the fund for the southern mission. We read:

It. to John Slee for a Bible & other Nessessaries   00 07 06.

For Thomas, there were three entries: five shillings and ten shillings 'to Tho: Lawson' and a further ten shillings 'to Tho: Lawson att his goeinge in to Sury.' If these monies were drawn shortly after the first of the 3d month, we may date the missionaries' departure to the month of May, the year at that time beginning in March. In fact, they must have left very early in the month for a letter of 10th May, written by the Yorkshireman Alexander Parker from London, reports that Slee and Lawson had passed through the city.[13]

Their campaign was to last all that summer and into the autumn. In the financial statements of Taylor and Willan there is a payment of 14 shillings to John Slee noted as 'sent the 1st of the 8 month [October]' We know from other evidence that Slee was still in the South at the beginning of October[14] and the note makes it clear that the money was sent rather than collected. Thomas, however, returned to the North some time towards the end of the year when he appeared in person to make demand upon the fund:

> Since the 1st of the 10th month: 1655 . . .
> To Tho: Lawson wch he sd hee wanted   00 05 00

The 10th month being December, we may accord the missionaries a campaigning season of some six months, spanning the summer. During that time, Thomas made one brief visit back to the North, but he found no rest there, being immediately involved in further controversy. It was to be a very hard year.

In May, however, the companions were keen to begin. Francis Howgill, who was still working in London, corroborates on the 21st May Parker's report that the two missionaries had passed straight through London and 'are gone into Sussex.'[15] There they were joined by another, Thomas Laycock, and the three had the distinction of being the first Friends to 'publish truth' in the county of Sussex. Long afterwards, when Yearly Meeting had been set up in London, it was thought advisable that the records of these 'first publishers' should be gathered together before it was too late and all memory of their coming had passed from mens' minds. When the Quarterly Meeting at Thakeham responded to the directive of Yearly Meeting in a letter of 23rd September, 1706, they were writing of the events of 50 years before: the men they wrote of and the events they described had become an honoured part of Quaker history:

> This blessed Testimoney, & Joyfull Tidings of Saluation, was first preached by friends in the north side of this County of Sussex, about the third month of the year 1655, at the towne of Horsham, vizt. by John Slee, Thomas Lawson, and Thomas Laycock.[16]

The Sussex folk were not immediately receptive. The three Friends were unknown and the reserve of the countryfolk left them isolated and unwelcomed:

> noe man receueing them into his house, some of them Declared the Truth in the open market, in a powerfull manner, directing the

people to yeild obeydience to the heavenly gift of god, the Light of Christ Jesus, as it was made manifest in them.[17]

This teaching met with a very mixed reception:

> This was to the great admiration of some, yet, as in all ages, the most part Reuiled, and some stoned them, others Counted them mad man, yet all did not Dante them, nor stop their Testimoney; but they bore all with such meekness & patience as was wonderfull to behold.[18]

Having finished their testimony for the time being, the missionaries left the village of Horsham and were taken in by a fellow North countryman, Bryan Wilkason or Wilkinson[19] who 'came out of the north of England not Long before' to settle at Sidgwick Lodge in Nuthurst parish, about two miles from Horsham, 'he being Indeed the first man that gaue enterance as well to their persons as to their Testimoney.'[20].

With a base secured, they were able to preach without the threat of stones and rough-handling to which market-place preaching constantly exposed them:

> And the next day, being the first day of the week [Sunday], they had a meeting in his house, which through the power that attended their Testimoney, the Consciences of some were Reached, and soe from that time Truth began to spread it selfe in this County of Sussex.[21]

Once a few convincements had been made, the work proceeded steadily. The next meeting took place at Ifield and an important convert was made in Richard Bax who live at Capel, in Surrey. It was he who, after another Sussex meeting at Twineham – 'a meeting which was very great & seruiceable to the Conuinceing of severall'[22] – extended the hospitality of his house to the missionaries as we read: 'John Slee, & Thomas Lawson, and Thomas Lacock were receivd in Surrey by Rowley Titchbourn, of Rygate, & alsoe by Richd Bax, of Capill.'[23] Perhaps it was Bax who encouraged the companions to spread their endeavours from Sussex into Surrey. He was to prove a notable recruit: a 'Large Convincement' was made at his house and in 1677 Friends were able to record that 'the said Richard Bax hath Continued a Monthly Meeting at his house to this day, being now above 20 yeares.'[24] The Surrey account of the *First Publishers* gives one other meeting for the county, held at the house of John Stedman in Ockley. Laycock, apparently was not present for the names of Slee and Lawson only are mentioned in connection with this meeting.

With the seed sown, Thomas took time to return briefly to the North. Possibly Slee went with him, but it is more than likely he travelled alone, leaving Slee and Laycock to keep the work alive in his absence. Some time before mid July,[25] he passed through London and what he saw there disturbed him mightily. In June, Burrough and Howgill had taken ship for Ireland, intent on spreading the missionary work ever wider and Nayler had been left in sole charge of Quakerism in the restless and teeming capital. A Yorkshireman and a former soldier in the Parliamentary army, he bore a striking resemblance to traditional portraits of Christ and he was soon pulling in the London crowds with a magnetism as powerful as that of Fox. As the year went on, the strain of his frenetic and successful life began to tell on him and to affect the balance of his mind, whilst the fanatical style of his followers was beginning to worry his friends and to cause division between him and the other Quakers working in London at the time. Even before the departure of Francis Howgill and Edward Burrough, it was obvious that a potentially divisive attachment to personalities was beginning to affect the followers. In the Pauline words of the first epistle to the Corinthians, the faithful were splitting into factions: 'One saying, I am of James – another saying I am of Francis and Edward.'[26] Those who were 'of James' unfortunately appear to have been of the wilder sort – mostly women, whose adulation of Nayler brought them to the lengths of suggesting that he make a complete split with Fox.

In London, Lawson met and conversed with Ranters: he may already have been worried for, as we shall see later, Laycock was verging upon Ranterism and it is even possible that Thomas' return to the North after less than three months in Sussex and Surrey may have been prompted by anxiety over the way things were heading. What he saw in London can have done little to reassure him. Nayler himself was now within breathing distance of Ranterism. Certainly we must conclude that some of the people to whom he was giving tacit encouragement were Ranters in the accepted sense of the term, however difficult it may be to define that term in practice. Generally, it was one that was applied by hostile outsiders: a word to be bandied about as 'fascist' might be today. Writers of propaganda in any age are happiest with an unpleasant label at their finger tips and the fringes of most of the sectarian movements of the seventeenth century harboured persons who were described as Ranters. Perhaps the most useful definition to bear in mind when considering Ranters is that they were a people who were characterised as much by their behaviour as by their beliefs. These were often confused and, amongst the wildest of them, amounted to a denial of truly Christian faith even whilst this was being expressed in the traditional language of the scriptures.[27]

In time, the Quakers came to realise that they could not afford to be bracketed with the Ranters. In the popular view, the Ranters excused any excess of behaviour – and there was no vice from drunkeness to buggery that their enemies did not accuse them of – by the claim that they were moved by an inward compulsion. The Quakers countered this with the insistence that the only true voice within was the voice of Christ which could never be the prompter to sinful action but such a claim was dangerous in itself as we shall shortly see, especially as the movement grew in success and came, from sheer size and popularity, to have political weight in the eyes of the authorities. Because of success, because it had the eyes of the authorities upon it, the Quaker movement came to need an internal discipline antipathetical to its original ethos. Association with persons as anarchistic as the Ranters could only be damaging.

When he arrived back in the North, Thomas made for his old haunts in the Penrith area. From Penrith, he writes to Margaret Fell in some perturbation of spirit:

> This is to acquainte the, that while I was in the South partes beyonde London, and on this side I mett with severall of the Ranters, who feed of nothing but the forbidden, abominable, swine flesh, and plead to justify that which they wallow in, even filthynes and ungodlynes it selfe.[28]

The reasons for Thomas' hostility become evident as he goes on to point out the danger that the Ranters constituted to the Quaker movement, the more particularly because some had formerly been good Quakers:

> formerly as thou knows, some and severall of them have tasted of the good word of god, and of the power of that worke, which the liveing god is establishing his people in, which is without end and severall of them, their hearts were truly touched with the love of god, and they led by a principle of righteousnes, tending to life.

Now, however, these people have turned away from the true paths of Quakerism and 'are given up to follow the motions of the wicked one . . . and many simple people were affraid to receive us in whom was secret groneings after righteousness.' The very fact that the Ranters were close enough in spirit to fall in and out of the Quaker movement made a redefining of the Quaker position imperative. Thomas has made notes relating to Ranter arguments which he now sends to Margaret Fell, begging her to initiate some action:

> so ever as I gott their false words from them and the scriptures which they wrest to their owne destruction, and others, I took an account thereof, a Coppy whereof, I have sent the, and if thou bee moved to write any thing, to them, or to send to George, it Could not but bee [?very] serviceable, to scatter an answer to the[se] things up and downe the nation, for with their swelling words they catch severall.

Geoffrey Nuttall implies that these notes may have been the draft of a book that Lawson published against Magnus Byne, vicar of Clayton in

Sussex.[29] This was in reply to Byne's attack on Lawson in *The Scornfull Quakers Answered*. But Byne's book was not published until 1656. Accepting Nuttall's own dating of the letter,[30] July/August 1655, then it is impossible that Lawson's notes should have been the reply to Byne. A more likely candidate as the manuscript of these notes relating to Ranters, is an undated letter or paper addressed to John Webster, rebuking him and warning him to listen to inward wisdom 'soe that thou would come to know the voyce of the true shepphered in thy selfe from the voyce of the stranger.'[31] Webster, a man who passed through many shades of sectarian belief, had attracted attention in a public debate in London on 12th October, 1653 when he and William Erbury had had a 'very famous dispute' (D.N.B.) with two ministers whose names are not known. Erbury was dead now, but he had often been called a Ranter by his enemies,[32] an accusation that it may have suited Lawson to extend to his friend and supporter John Webster. He reproves him in terms similar to those that describe the Ranters in the letter to Margaret Fell:

> soe thou speakes things through the secrett pride of thy heart, both above thy owne condicion and the Conditions of them thou speakes unto, so thou and they are in the generation of busie minds, medlinge with that you have nothinge to doe withall, eatinge the forbidden fruit.

Webster came from Craven and, towards the end of the Civil War, had been given the vicarage of Mitton in Yorkshire only four miles from Grindleton. Lawson may even have heard him preach there in his youth but it is also possible that he was one of the Ranters that Thomas says that he met in London for, at the time of the joint dispute with Erbury, Webster was officiating minster at All Hallows, Lombard Street and he may have been in London in 1655. The fact that Lawson's letter to him is to be found amongst the Swarthmore papers suggests that it was a document for which Thomas sought Margaret Fell's approval – Webster would have been unlikely to return it to the Quakers. This is further evidence that it might have been the 'notes' that Thomas speaks of in his letter to Margaret but it does not exactly fit Thomas' own description of notes summarising Ranter arguments and it may be that there are other papers which we have lost for which the rebuke to Webster was to form a covering letter. Webster's recent book, *The Judgment Set and the Books opened*, 1654, would make him a suitable focus for a Quaker attack.

• • •

If Thomas had hoped to give himself a breathing space for thought by returning to the North, he was to be disappointed. The new movement was being assailed from all sides and the North country was no more peaceful than the South. Thomas had visited the village of Great Strickland in

Morland parish and found the people there in an uproar over tithes. A new minister, Percy Burton had been appointed in November, 1654[33] and Thomas, in a letter dated 17th July, reports to Margaret Fell what had happened:

> the preist of Strickland in Westmorland, lately went through the people, to demande Tyth, and some freinds, denying him the same, hee put forth a challenge that hee and other three of their mynisters with him, would give 4 of the quakers a meeting.[34]

What Percy Burton was suggesting was a good old inter-regnum debate, solemnly recorded to the satisfaction and further dissatisfaction of both parties:

> and hee likewise said, that either party, should have a writer, to write downe the dispute, which among judicious men, should be read over, to bee censured upon.

The Quakers of Strickland stirred into action:

> John Fallofeild and some other said, that to wittnes forth the truth against deceipt, wee should not deny, so the day is appointed, the 26t day of this fift month beeing the next Thursday, but one, so called, from the writeing of this and the thing was published in the streets, at Appleby, the last seaventh day.

The affair was being organised formally, with its own rules of combat:

> 'tis said, that preist Higginson, the dragons mouth is to bee one of the 4, and the preist Burton, and Jackson, and Rowland.[35]

Francis Higginson had been a witness in the trial of James Nayler when he had appeared before the Assizes at Appleby in January, 1653, on a charge of blasphemy. He was active against the Quakers and published two pamphlets against them.[36] Obviously, he was an adversary to be reckoned with and the Quakers of Strickland were apprehensive – 'freinds this away, would see warriers come against the day' writes Thomas though he himself feels that the local Quakers can supply warriors of their own without calling in reinforcements – 'some of them, have strength enuff to encounter with them.' Thomas leaves it to Margaret to decide the course of action 'I thought meet, thee to tell of it, so that thou may do in it, as thou knows to be convenient.' In any case, he prepares to stand by and see the thing out: 'I know not that I shall go from this away, till that day bee over, and gone.'

It is difficult to appreciate how deeply and thoroughly tithe penetrated everyday life:

> two hundred years ago [or, for that matter three hundred] tithes were engraved upon the lives of the entire population: a source of

income, luxury and avarice for the privileged; a tax at 2s in the £, and a source of anger and resentment for everyone else.[37]

Tithes were payable on agricultural produce, were usually payable in kind and, when one looks at the bewildering list of titheable produce, it seems that there was almost nothing that escaped. From the tenth piglet in the sty to the milk from the daily milkings, all was tithed. The parson or his agent was everywhere, assessing crops, cattle and even the very herbs that the country wife grew by her door. Of all these, he had a right to take a literal tenth. When the harvesters cut the corn it was to be left stooked until the parson or parson's agent had come and collected every tenth stook. It all made for great resentment and, in the sort of war of attrition that was being waged between Quakers and the parish authorities, there were times when nobody won. When he had a home of his own, Thomas was to refuse to pay his own tithes and later, when his testimony against tithe is recorded, we find him bitterly reporting that the vicar of Morland's agent simply stole a march on the Strickland Friends by gathering in his tenth before the crop was ripe, just as agents at other times were apt to descend upon Quakers and seize goods or drive off beasts, taking by force what the Friends sought to deny them as of right. His testimony is to be found in the Strickland Monthly Meeting minute book:

> Since it pleased god to open my eyes to see man made Ministers not workers for, or with God, for the good of soules, but for their own ends, I never gave them the least of that they call their dues, nor consented thereto. As for tith settled on Levi, the maintenance of the first preisthood the leave offeringe, Christ put an end to that preisthood, and to tith the leave offeringe, and to the law that appointed these things, beinge the high preist over the Household of God, the one offeringe that perfects such as are sanctified. Therefore my testimony in this thinge, is, that such as pay tyth and such as take tyth beinge truely seen into, are in the denyall of Christ to become in the flesh, soe as touching tyth I never paid it, not consented thereunto, yett true it is, the Farmers thereof for the most part, come to the land, before we Judge it for Inninge, and takes it away.
>
> Tho: Lawson[38]

The outcome of the debate between the Strickland Quakers and the four ministers is shrouded in silence. If papers reporting it were circulated, they are now lost and, in due course, Thomas returned to the southern front.

On his return, he found Sussex fairly humming with activity and at Horsham the lines were being drawn up in what was to prove a long war between the Quakers and the minister at Horsham, Matthew Caffyn. Caffyn had been expelled from Oxford for his Baptist beliefs and he was to attack the Quakers many times in his long life of 86 years.[39] Dying in 1714, he was to outlive most of his adversaries and all of the passions of this summer of 1655. Laycock had not been long in falling foul of him. From Brian Wilkinson's house he had been 'moued to goe into the steplehouse [i.e. church] at Horsham.'[40] To what extent his motion took him may be supplemented from the pages of Besse:

> Thomas Lacock being religiously concerned in one of the publick Assemblies [i.e. church service], after the Priest had closed his customary Performance [i.e. sermon], to give a Christian Exhortation to the People, was for his Love and Goodwill, requited with four Months Imprisonment.[41]

– in other words, he had harangued the minister and the congregation and was summarily silenced – at least for the time being.

Nor was Brian Wilkinson behindhand in activity:

> Also Brian Wilkinson of Nuthurst, for sending some Queries, and writing a Letter to the Priest of Horsham, which the Justices termed scandalous, suffered nine Months Imprisonment, to his great Detriment, being confined during the Time of Harvest.[42]

Late in September, Laycock was brought out of prison to have his case heard at the Quarter Sessions and he made something of a triumphal progress of it. The Sessions were to be held at Chichester and Lawson rejoined Slee to accompany Laycock. They improved the journey by holding a meeting on the way 'att one William Penfolds and Daniell Gittons house, att Binsted, nere Arondell . . . where was Conuinced Nicholas Rickman, Edward Hamper, William Turner, Tristrum Martin, John Ludgater, and seuerall others.'[43] This success was topped by his release at the Sessions but he was a marked man and his triumph was to be short-lived. On the way back, the three Friends, re-united again, held another meeting at the house of Nicholas Rickman in Arundel:

> where, as he was Declareing the truth to the people, there Came in one George Penfold, a Cunstable, Instigated thereto by one John Beaton, a Presbiterian Priest, and assisted by one John Pellatt, and pulled away the said Thomas Laycock, and broke up the meeting, haueing Thomas Laycock before one Thomas Ballard, Mayor, who was allso a Presbeterien, who Imeadiately Committed him againe to Horsham Prison, on the third day of the Eight month, 1655 [3rd October, 1655][44]

Laycock was thus effectively immobilised. The following year saw him in trouble again and sent to the House of Correction:

> where he was whipt, and for some Time kept in Irons, lying several
> Weeks in Winter in a cold low Room without Boards, having neither
> Fire, Candle, nor a Bed to lie on, though no Transgression of any
> Law had been proved against him, nor was there any legal Cause
> assigned for such his barbarous Usage.[45]

These entries present Laycock to us as the most forceful of the trio of
missionaries and this, no doubt, was why he was particularly singled out for
the angry attention of the authorities. It is possible that the outspokeness of
his language was, at times, an embarrassment to his companions. Magnus
Byne of Clayton, Sussex gives a strange picture of a silent Lawson when, at a
meeting, Laycock is said to have claimed to have been Christ – 'this Lawson
yielded unto by his silence.'[46] Already Quakers were running into difficulty
when they tried to define exactly what they meant when they talked of
Christ within a man. Lawson silent may have been Lawson unable to
support the language of extremism. An unpleasant story of Thomas
Laycock is related by Byne:

> Tho Law-cock, who meeting at one Goodman Matthews house near
> me, was called aside by the woman of the house, of good report, but
> almost turned a Quaker; to whom the woman in kindeness said, Sir,
> will you eat something which I have provided? The Quaker replied,
> What shall I eat with Devils and Dogs? and pointing to a Dog,
> There's thy companion, thy fellow-creature, of the same nature with
> thy self (saith the Quaker) and shall I eat with thee a Devil, a Dog?
> And was not this a good argument to perswade the woman to be a
> Quaker? And when the woman began to reply something to excuse
> her great sin of asking this man of God (as he calls himself) to eat, he
> opens his box again, and calls her whore and Harlot; and was not this
> another good argument to perswade her.[47]

Now this is from the pen of a prejudiced witness but the story, if considered
against the contemporary background, cannot entirely be dismissed for it
has about it an authentic whiff of Ranterism. Laycock's abuse of the woman
of the house is in keeping with Ranter foul-mouthedness, his reference to
Devils and Dogs smacks of the desperate Pantheism that marked most
members of this strange group. Ranters were characterised chiefly by a
desire to shock but underlying their wildest utterances was a most persistent
sense of guilt. Calvin had given the world back to men accursed and the
Ranters, seeing God in all things, saw a tortured vision of divinity itself
attainted 'for more than once Thomas Laucock (Quaker-teacher) hath said
that the Lord Jesus Christ is ACCURSED.'[48] This sounds very much like
Ranterism.[49] The great achievement of the Quakers was to draw in many of
the lost and desperate sects who had been thrown up by war and the

inter-regnum and to establish a new hope founded on the belief that a redeeming Christ was to be found in every man. In the early days, therefore, the Quaker movement included many from the dark and confused background of the many sects that had been spawned in the war and its aftermath. If all we know of Thomas Laycock comes from hostile sources it is, nevertheless, difficult to escape the impression that, in these early days in Surrey and Sussex, he was one of the more extreme adherents of the young movement. Francis Bugg gives him a very bad character, putting him into his cage of unclean birds and calls him 'a notorious drunkard.'[50] His reasons may have been better than the prejudices he entertained as an apostate from Quakerism. Quakers, as we shall see, were going to have to beware in the future of the persistent and damaging taint of Ranterism.

Without Laycock, Thomas Lawson and John Slee had been left to carry on the good work together. Whilst Laycock had been undergoing his first imprisonment, it had fallen to them to take up the battle with Matthew Caffyn. At a Quaker meeting near Crawley on 5th September, Caffyn had challenged them and the argument had been followed up and carried into Caffyn's own house not far from Southwater near Horsham.[51] It was the type of full-scale debate so popular at the time, conducted by argument and refutation, point by point, detail by detail, head by head and it looks as though it developed very quickly into a good old slanging-match, seventeenth-century style. On the title-page of the account that Slee and Lawson afterwards published, *An Untaught Teacher Witnessed Against*, 1655, Caffyn's teaching was branded as 'unsound, unseasoned, unsavoury' and he himself depicted as a sort of war-monger 'who as Jannes and Jambres rides aloft, and bestirs himself with the Magick Rod of his lies, slanders, aspersions, and unsound Doctrines, [labouring] to strengthen the hands of carnal professors, and to keep the beloved of God in Bondage.'

This account was divided into 30 heads and Slee and Lawson were not above pulling the usual contemporary tricks of abuse and misrepresentation which make seventeenth-century polemics repetitious reading. There cannot be enough adjectives to describe Caffyn whose perversion of Scripture 'hast got the words of the holy men of God, into [his] vain, wily, shifty, peevish, subtle, crafty and untoward minde.'[52]

Repetitious as it is, though, the account gives us an extraordinarily vivid picture of what was happening. We can see Caffyn growing increasingly angry and harassed, brandishing the scripture: 'And he said he ministered from the Scripture, through the assistance of the Spirit of God.'[53] The missionaries retorted that such a claim is as of the blind leading the blind. But the scripture contains the revelation of God, cries Caffyn, 'as that he walking up to its revelation, to his lives end, with a single heart, shall be eternally saved.'[54] The missionaries retorted that it is God who reveals God, not the Scriptures. Caffyn said that the Scripture *is* the word: they said that God is the word.[55] He said that Scripture is the truth: they said that Christ is the truth.[56] He – doggedly trying to keep the last argument – said that Scripture *leads* to the truth: they said 'another lie.'[57] 'Blasphemy,' he said. 'Slander,' they said, and the wrangle takes another turn and reaches another deadlock. It was not a very edifying debate. Nevertheless, out of mere words and abuse something emerges intact: the central belief of Quakers in the doctrine of Christ within. For Caffyn, the reality is literal. Christ, he declares:

> is now sitting in Heaven, with a body of flesh and blood, with the very same body of flesh and blood, with the which he did eat broyled fish, among his Disciples.[58]

Caffyn expects to see his risen Lord with his own eyes: 'in my flesh shall I see God,' he cries, quoting Job and pointing his fingers at his eyeballs.[59]

Against this literal reality, the two Quaker missionaries posed their own reality of inner light. Fox's doctrine of Christ in every man was, and has remained central to Quaker belief. It was a doctrine that was to lay them open to the charge of blasphemy and Caffyn was not alone in finding the suggestion of Christ in every man infinitely shocking:

> He said no man upon earth sees Christ, he said, he had not seen Christ, and when I asked him, if he had seen God, he cryed out of blasphemy.[60]

Fox's answer was proclaimed once to an angry crowd near Gainsborough, telling them 'that Christ was in them except they were reprobates . . . and I said that if the power of God and the Seed spoke in man or woman it was Christ.'[61]

Lawson and Slee's *An Untaught Teacher Witnessed Against* is typical of most of the early polemical literature of the Quakers which was so often produced to refute the attacks made by Baptists and others, rather than to present and advertise their own beliefs. The charges of blasphemy and sedition continued against the books themselves which were frequently seized and destroyed. In 1656, Brian Wilkinson suffered a 10 month imprisonment 'for buying Friends bookes and bringing them from London into the Country.'[62] *An Untaught Teacher*, fresh off the press, was probably one of them.

The debate was by no means ended by the publication of the missionaries' account of it. Caffyn hit back with his own account: *The Deceived, and deceiving Quakers Discovered. Their damnable Heresies, horrid blasphemies, mockings, railings, unparalel'd Deceit, and Dishonesty laid open,*

1656. This reply does not put over the argumentative immediacy of *An Untaught Teacher*, but it does, in a more collected and ordered manner, set out some of the objections to Quakerism that were most often raised by contemporary opponents. On the title-page Caffyn promises to make known 'the pure use of the holy Scriptures' and to explain the nature of 'the true Christ, and how he justifies, his second coming proved not to be already (as the Quaker affirms)'. It is on these two points that his attack largely rests and he sees them as the two parts of a single issue:

> The Quaker saith, That there is such a light in every man (which they say is a measure of Christ) that leads, and guides into all the ways of God, without the Scripture, or any outward Teachings; and (saith Nayler) is the ONLY revealer of the Gospel; as appears in his Book called, Satans design discovered, page 32.[63]

Caffyn was not alone in finding such a point of view potentially anarchistic. The Civil Authorities, alarmed by this aspect of Quakerism, were asking the same question as Caffyn:

> What then should hinder them (who are so apt to pervert the Scriptures) in time, to bee perswaded in flaming fire, to take vengeance on them that know not God, in their sense, and that offend in their sense; and pretend it to be Christ in them, the flaming fire taking vengeance according to the Scriptures.[64]

It was an alarming thought and the enemies of the Quakers played upon it. To adopt the claim that reliance upon the inner light gave sufficient guidance for a godly life would make every man his own judge. It was undoubtedly this that roused the greatest antagonism from both the civil authorities and those whose profession it was to expound the scripture and explain its law. Christ himself had been a law-giver, Paul the apostle both taught and wrote to give his people guidelines for their lives: he did not tell them that they should rely only upon the light within and when the apostles went to turn the gentiles from darkness into light, it was the enlightenment of knowledge to which their converts were to be brought. When Lawson says that that which may be known of God is manifest within man, he is wrong:

> As Paul informs us that which may be known of God is manifest in (or to) man (saith the Notes) so also he informs us how it comes there, and by that we find him to have a spirit differing from Lawsons: for Paul tells us that God hath shewed it unto man by the things that are made..[65]

In Caffyn's view, the things of the external world – which include the constructions of human learning – show us God, and he quotes scripture to

demonstrate: 'that there is not such a light within us as [Lawson] speaks of.'
The external aids to bring us to a true knowledge of God are the Creation
and the Scripture and to deny the Scripture is to commit heresy. And with
what do the Quakers replace Scripture? Why, with their own voluminous
writings: in their sinful pride they have set up a body of writings that are a
rival to God's word:

> Oh how great are the self-exaltations of these men! how doth their
> arrogancy appear! while they so mightily indeavour to destroy mens
> faith of the Scriptures, as being a discovery of the Lords will, and yet
> in the mean while furnish the Nations almost in every corner with
> THEIR SCRIPTURES (which is writings) calling them a
> DISCOVERY of several particulars.[66]

On these two points: the proper place of the Scriptures and the nature of the
inner light, the Quakers were irreconcilable with most of their generation.
It was the view of Calvin that the inward light comes to the regenerate only
after receiving the spirit. It was not something in the unregenerate waiting
only to be discovered.

From this rock of division, Caffyn passes on to lesser differences,
accusing Lawson of lack of learning as Lawson had accused him, attacking
the Quaker notion of the perfectability of man and defending a literal
interpretation of the second coming and the resurrection of the dead.

The Deceived and Deceiving Quakers is not only a reply to *An Untaught
Teacher*, it is a reply to a whole series of arguments and debates, verbal
battles and papers circulated in manuscript:

> The Quaker saith, that some of them are already come unto the
> END OF FAITH, this Thomas Lawson, John Slee gave me in
> writing . . . and Thomas Lawson, John Slee (Quaker-teachers) gave
> me their understandings thereof in writing (namely) that
> NOTHING that goes into the Grave shall rise again.[67]

Typically, it is Laycock who emerges from the heat of the argument most
strident and shocking:

> As we have heard that Scoffers should come in the last dayes even
> now already are they come, whereby we may know that it is the last,
> of the last dayes; for at a certain time, when I, with other brethren,
> was reasoning with Thomas Laucock concerning the comming of
> Christ, he scoffingly said, WHERE IS THE PROMISE OF HIS
> COMMING, IS HE ASLEEP?[68]

Such reckless fury was something that Quaker opponents could use against
them. Caffyn concludes his counter-blast by referring not only to the pages
of *An Untaught Teacher* but to the wild passion of the Quakers in the

arguments that had preceded it:

> who at several times thus have said to me in great rage, and fury of
> spirit; Thou Beast, bruit beast, thou Witch, thou Devil, thou
> Reprobate, thou Enemy of God, for the Lake, thou Swine feeding
> upon husks, thou Cain killing thy brother Abel, thou Drunkard,
> thou Thief, thou Murtherer, thou Serpent, the Curses, Plagues, and
> Vengeance of God is thy portion, and saith Lawson in his Book
> against me, Thou Image-maker, thou Cockatrice hatching Eggs,
> Vultures eye . . . a Mate for the Night-birds, Cormorants, Bitterns,
> Owls, Ravens, Dragons, wild Beasts, Satyrs, Vultures, Scritch-
> owles.[69]

Did Christ, says Caffyn with assumed blandness, use language like this?
Indeed,

> The Quaker hath pronounced the curses and plagues of God, to be
> my portion, which seemed not a little strange unto mee; that men
> pretending perfection should thus rage.[70]

But the Quakers were not to be demolished by mere urbanity: they were
far too much in earnest for that, and in 1655 satire and sarcasm were
brushed aside by a generation that lived with the millenium too near to their
imaginations for anything but the most literal approach to real life. Thomas
Lawson was soon to go North again and wrote no more against Caffyn, but
the debate that had been initiated was to rumble on through successive
pamphlets and several years, being almost immediately taken up by James
Nayler in *The Light of Christ, and the Word of Life Cleared from the Deceipts of
the Deceiver*, 1656, which lifted the debate out of the mire of unprofitable
wrangling by cutting through to the two central issues at stake:

> There is onely two things which as to the way of God, may prejudice
> some who are simple, which I shall lay open thy deceipts in, and for
> the rest leave it to discover its author, and by what spirit he is guided,
> which the least Child of light may easily Judge.[71]

These two things were 'the light of Christ and the Word.' On these two
topics hung all that was controversial in Quaker teaching. Thomas
Lawson's account of the Caffyn affair, if compared with Nayler, is more
clouded with the immediacies of debate – the point by point scoring of a
furious argument, but all the points enumerated do hinge upon these two
topics of inner light and the true place of Scripture. Thomas had registered
his unity with the children of light in a debate over central issues.

CHAPTER IV

An Abode in the Earth

TOWARDS THE END OF 1655, Thomas Lawson returned North. the winter was a poor time for outdoor preaching and Thomas was probably not sorry to be away from the frenzied atmosphere of southern England. In the super-charged air of London, James Nayler continued to move in a cloud of mass fervour and excitement. Working alone, he was controlled by events more than he was able to control them and until the adulation of his more extreme followers was tempered, there would be no combating Ranterism. Margaret and Fox both wrote to Nayler,[1] much afraid that this most trusted and valued lieutenant would split the young movement apart. It was a crisis to which it was ill-equipped to respond: its very nature had made it vulnerable to just such an emergency. Even if Nayler had not stood so tall in the movement, it would have been difficult to discipline him when the whole basis of Quakerism rested upon individual liberty and freedom of speech and conscience. Margaret and George wrote and admonished: they found it difficult to do more than that. And events were taking over too rapidly and powerfully for a society which had, as yet, little formal organisation and no structure of leadership beyond popular consent. In that, Nayler's title was every bid as good as Fox's. He was now, however, well on course for tragedy and the year 1656 opened with the rift between himself and his old friends growing ever wider.

In the winter of 1655/6, it is very likely that Lawson spent some time at Swarthmoor. He had fresh and first-hand knowledge of what was happening in the South and his concern would make him wish to discuss the problems with Margaret Fell. He was also proposing to publish another book and it is more than likely that he would wish to discuss that too. Even as early as this, a sort of informal censorship was at work[2] whereby the leaders were consulted about proposed tracts and papers. In 1656 was published *The Lip of Truth Opened, Against a Dawber with untempered Morter*. In essence, this was a direct reply to a piece put out that year by Magnus Byne, vicar of Clayton in Sussex, entitled *The Scornfull Quakers answered*, a publication which contained a specific attack on Lawson: *The Scornfull Quakers railing Reply refuted*. This attack and Lawson's reply to it enable us to construct a very real picture of the type of acrimonious controversy in which Lawson was engaged in his Sussex period. The reconstruction is worth doing if only to recapture some of the earnestness with which argument followed argument, point was scored upon point. For us, most of the arguments are dead, the points that divided them so close together as to be inseparable to the twentieth-century eye. If we can hardly understand the points of belief that separated the opponents, we cannot understand at all the heat with which these points were defended unless we work through the print that takes us from point to point and gives us glimpses of the enemy revolving solemnly the points of his own, parallel argument. So it appears that Thomas Lawson presented Magnus Byne with (1) 40 questions in manuscript, to which Byne replied, either in manuscript or verbally. Lawson responded (2) to this reply of Byne and Byne then countered with a series of questions of his own to which Lawson again replied (3).

So far the debate in words and papers. The debate in print opened with *The Scornfull Quakers*. Pages 1-14 are a reply in print to Lawson's original 40 questions (1), pages 14-66 are a reply to Lawson's counter-reply (2), and pages 67 to the end of the book, page 123, are a reply to Lawson's reply to Byne's own questions (3). As to the matter of Lawson's charges against Byne, these follow the well-trodden paths of Quaker anger against the corruptions of the contemporary world. Byne is seen as a lover of darkness, an Antichrist who is a stranger to Christ's cross and an alien to truth. More particularly, Thomas accuses him of social injustices, calling him Tythemonger, enjoying the tithes of two parishes and oppressing the just. His worldliness is to be seen in that he allows men to call him 'Master' and, in his turn, flatters others with titles, conforming to the fashion and practices of the world. From this we may conclude that Thomas had been speaking out for the things in which Quakers believed and for which they were suffering and for which they would continue to suffer for nearly half a century. Both the refusal to pay tithe and the refusal to pay homage to title and authority (even to the extent of refusing to doff the hat to social superiors) were to land Friends in jail. They had launched a social attack on a whole priestly cast and Lawson called on the prisons of England to judge:

> of the Priests Hospitalitie who cast the Saints into prison, some prisons have five, some ten, twenty, twenty four of the Children of God in them.[3]

The words that went down on paper were the token of what Quakers were prepared to suffer in stone and iron. The Quakers' claim to be the children of God and to be the only possessors of truth was understandably infuriating to their opponents. And if some of the theological argument seems to us today to be interminably tedious, we must remember that the Quakers were only one of a number of sects who had gone into battle against a whole cadre in society. It was vitally important to be the only possessors of a single truth 'the truth is pure preciousse and but one'[4] says Thomas in the letter that he wrote to John Webster: 'if we and what we preach, were not foolishness to the covetous and selfish, we could not be of God'[5] he says to Magnus Byne. Other sectaries claimed the same and they fought each other as often as they fought the professional priesthood who, in the face of the common tendancy of them all to make every man his own priest, were out to regain ground and to demonstrate that they alone had the authority to interpret scripture and to provide men with the leadership necessary in spiritual affairs. The wars of society were still being fought on the battlefields of religion. In 1656, the Quaker message of love, light and pacificism was not at all evident in the militancy with which they attacked all who disagreed with them. Whilst there was freedom of speech, the Friends continued to exercise themselves with all the force of their conviction to anyone who would listen.

Early in 1656, Thomas was involved in another debate – a dispute with ministers held in Preston on 4th March. Champions for the Quakers were John Audland, Alexander Parker, Gervase Benson, Anthony Pearson, William Adamson – and Thomas Lawson. There, in a great chamber at the Bull, the Quakers carried the day. In Parker's words: 'we had a gallant charge upon them and got the victory through the love of our God.'[6]

Throughout 1656, the news from southern England grew increasingly ominous. Nayler's preaching successes continued to grow but so, too, did the tales about the type of excitable people by whom he was surrounded. In August, he was travelling towards Launceston to see George Fox who was in prison there, when he was arrested in a move against persons travelling without pass. He was imprisoned at Exeter, but Major-General Desborough of the Western Counties was reasonably sympathetic towards the Quakers and Nayler and other prisoners in Exeter were released at the end of October. In the last wet and wild days of the month, Nayler rode from Exeter northwards with a small band of devotees and entered Bristol. As they came into the city, his adoring companions took off their cloaks and spread handkerchiefs before him, crying 'Holy, Holy, Holy Lord God of Israel.'[7] This parody of Christ's entry into Jerusalem could not be ignored by the authorities: it reinforced their worst prejudices and appeared to confirm the charges against Quakers – that they provoked mob hysteria, that they set themselves up to be Christs on earth and that the doctrine of the inner light was merely a thin covering for blasphemy. A jittery Parliament, fearful of the political potential of any successful movement, was out for blood. On hearing of the incident, they took Nayler's case into their own hands. In November and December of the year, he was tried for blasphemy and found guilty. Lawson, like Quakers up and down the land, would hear with horror the sentence upon the man whom he had once rescued off the shore over from Walney Island:

> That James Nayler be set on the pillory, with his head in the pillory, in the Palace-Yard, Westminster, during the space of two hours, on Thursday next, and be whipped by the hangman through the streets, from Westminster to the Old Exchange, London: and there likewise be set on the pillory, with his head in the pillory, for the space of two hours, between the hours of eleven and one, on Saturday next, in each place wearing a paper containing an inscription of his crimes; and that at the Old Exchange his tongue be bored through with a hot iron and that he be there also stigmatized in the forehead with the letter B; and that he be afterwards sent to Bristol and be conveyed into and through the said city on horseback, with his face backward; and there also publicly whipped the next marketday after he comes thither; and that from thence he be committed to prison in Bridewell, London, and there restrained from the society of all people, and there to labour hard, till he shall be released by Parliament; and during that time be debarred the use of pen, ink, and paper, and shall have no relief but what he earns by his daily labour.[7]

Despite intercession by his friends and by the Protector himself, this savage sentence was carried out to the last detail. Besides the fear that the radicals had raised in the governing powers, the trial of Nayler raised questions of the extent of the judicial power between Parliament and Protector: now the members of Parliament were determined that the sentence should go through.[8] If its barbarity stunned many Quakers, it was also a forcible demonstration of several weaknesses in the new movement.

●   ●   ●

All the while that the Nayler tragedy was drawing to its grim climax, Thomas appears to have remained in the North. At a date between the end of 1655 when he returned to the North and May of 1659, when his marriage certificate describes him as being 'of Newby Stones' Thomas acquired some sort of lodging in the village of Newby near Great Strickland in Westmorland. Perhaps he did so immediately upon his return: his future wife's name was Frances Wilkinson and, as there were Wilkinsons at

Newby at that date, it is pleasant to suppose that there may have been a connection between that Brian Wilkinson in Sussex who 'came out of the North of England not long before' and who gave Thomas hospitality and shelter down there.[9]

Whether or not Thomas had a base at Newby, he continued to travel in the service of truth, glad no doubt to be away from the exaggerated tensions of southern England and to turn his attention to congenial things. In another undated letter to Margaret Fell, he reports that he has been at Newcastle where he has enjoyed 'some conference' with a Hebrew scholar, a distant relation of his,[10] whom he describes significantly as 'a kinde of a moderate man.' No doubt it was restful for Thomas to turn his mind to scholarship and to textual criticism but, as one of a handful of university men amongst the Quakers, it was also his duty to do so. If he was to serve to the top of his bent, then he should not waste his training and Hebrew, in which he had received a grounding at Giggleswick, was important as a key to the original texts of the bible. The bible had become available to men in the seventeenth century as never before: Fox was reputed to know it almost by heart and for most of his followers it was the great textbook for life even when they were most passionate in arguing that it was not the very breath of God. The study of Hebrew could only lead to a more disciplined approach to it as a historical document and Thomas, after conference with his relative of moderate views, is seen hastening down to the stationers in Newcastle to enquire after a Hebrew lexicon. The lexicon was not immediately available, but it seems that Lawson was staying in the town for a few weeks for he thought it worthwhile for the stationer to send off for one from London. Whilst he waited, impatient to see whether the lexicon was procurable from London, he would, no doubt, take the opportunity of further conference and, perhaps, instruction from his relative who, we hear, outstripped any that Thomas had previously spoken to in relation to Hebrew and loved any that sought the language.

Although Thomas has generally been credited with being a Hebrew scholar and botanist as early as his Rampside days,[11] we cannot really know how far his studies had reached at this point or even how far his training at Giggleswick had taken him. Hebrew was a long way from enjoying the accepted status of the classical languages within the school curriculum and, in some schools, its inclusion in the syllabus was mere window dressing. From Giggleswick, Thomas had gone on to Cambridge at a troubled time and left after a year or less without a degree. The following year saw him caught up in the energetic work of spreading the Quaker message. There can have been few quiet times for sustained study. Now there was a further difficulty: the lexicon was not obtainable from London. Thomas therefore approached his relation to ask him whether he was prepared to part with his copy:

> Hee said hee was not willing to parte with it, not knowing how to procure another, yet if I sought after that language he would let mee have it, for hee much loved any that sought it, now I had little mony left mee, so I borrowed 10 shillings of Thomas Turner, and bought my Lexicon.

Probably this was the 'Buxtorfs Heb. Lexicon' which Thomas left in his will to his son-in-law: a much-used work, being the *Lexicon Hebraicum et Chaldaicum* of Johannes Buxtorfius, printed in Basle and immensely successful. First published in 1607, it went into 10 or 12 editions before the close of the seventeenth century, the eighth being in 1655. It is somewhat surprising that Thomas did not already own a copy of this standard work and might be taken as another indication that his determination to immerse himself in the serious study of Hebrew was of fairly recent date. What is certain is that he bore his new acquisition away in triumph to Swarthmoor where he hoped that Margaret Fell would order the re-imbursement of Turner out of the General Fund to which Thomas had had recourse in his Sussex days. Thomas had felt unable to apply in person to Willan or Taylor: he had seen Taylor as he passed through Kendal, but had been reluctant to mention the matter of the lexicon to him 'for hee is against mee in his minde.' Clearly he felt that Taylor would be unsympathetic towards the expenditure. The fund helped to keep missionaries on the road by providing shoes and clothing and though it sometimes included such things as books for Friends in prison, Taylor might have considered that Lawson's lexicon should be a personal expense. Thomas had not yet had the opportunity to show how he might place his learning at the service of Quakerism. His comment on Taylor gives a rather sharp point to that entry in the financial statement of five shillings paid to Thomas Lawson 'which he said hee wanted.'[14] Thomas was obviously not going to have Taylor hold him to account for every penny that he spent on what he considered legitimate Quaker business. One can only hope that his appeal to the higher authority of Margaret Fell was effective in reimbursing the obliging Thomas Turner; especially as he not only loaned Lawson the 10 shillings but also allowed him to take another book that argued for the authenticity of the Greek text of the New Testament upon Thomas' promise that it would be paid for when possible. This book came from a shop that Turner kept in Newcastle:[15] if his was the stationer's at which Thomas had been disappointed in his attempt to purchase a Hebrew lexicon, then he made ample amends.

From Newcastle, Thomas crossed the country back to his old ground in Furness. All these things he had intended to tell Margaret Fell when he saw her again at Swarthmoor, but he was in for a disappointment. When he arrived, Margaret was away from home and his account of his efforts to procure the lexicon had to be related in a letter which he left to await her return. His purchases show Thomas equipping himself for the war of words that was a conspicuous feature of the first decade of the Quaker movement. The work in Sussex had been conducted on the level of pamphleteering – the Quakers, taunted with lack of learning and linked with other sects of the simple and ignorant multitude, were now out to show that they could, if they chose, display an erudition equal to any adversary. Thomas' Hebrew scholarship was a valued contribution to his friends. It has been estimated that, up to the Restoration, the Quakers put out no fewer than 468 separate publications. By the first quarter of the eighteenth century, the total had risen to 2,678 publications.[16] Thomas' contribution to this great burst of writing had so far been three works. During the rest of his life, he was to write 10 more and to publish seven of these. Fox had said 'that being bred at Oxford or Cambridge was not enough to fit and qualify men to be ministers of Christ'[17] and the movement repudiated mere book-learning as the way to true enlightenment. But in order to grapple with their adversaries, the Friends needed to speak their language. Stung by Magnus Byne's jibe that he lacked learning, Thomas turned his attention to scholarship. His conviction that he could make a special contribution thereby made him feel justified in appealing to Margaret Fell for monies out of the General Fund for:

> if it please the lord to give mee an abode in the earth, I know I may do service therewith . . .

and then, rather cryptically, he adds:

> . . . if thou see any thing of this at   [18] Ulverstone, as thou art free speak to thy husband, I have left a few lines for him, that hee may know my purpose from my owne perticuler, I know not but in a few days to come over againe, to morrow I purpose to go toward Kellit, in the measure that lives I salute thee

tho. Lawson[19]

What was this 'purpose' of Lawson's? The tenor of the sentence would suggest that Thomas was referring to his future. Did he hope that Margaret's husband, Judge Fell, would be able to put in a word for him at Ulverston to get him some sort of a job – perhaps a teaching position? At any rate, nothing seems to have come of it but by now it may have been clearer to him how, in the future he should employ his talent and, when the opportunity arose, he would not be slow to take advantage of it.

For the moment, however, nothing was offered at Ulverston and Thomas possibly spent the winter of 1657 in the Great Strickland area, living at Newby. It was a natural place for him to gravitate towards, for to Great Strickland, in this winter, came James Nayler. The savagery of his sentence and his downfall from so eminent a position in the movement might have made him mad or driven him to despair but, in fact, his agony and subsequent close confinement in Bridewell were seen as having brought him sanity and a strange sweetness that drew at the heartstrings of those who were sympathetic to him. He was the martyr of the movement in every sense – as they had been uplifted beyond normality with the exciting vision of a new world, so had he; as he had over-reached himself, so had they; his fall was, to some extent, theirs, and his gentleness in the face of a harsh authority was more and more to be the ideal of future Quaker behaviour. James Nayler was changed but not broken, despite worsening health. In the winter of 1657, the authorities, following a common seventeenth-century practice, allowed him out of prison for a while to recuperate and it was to the Quaker community at Great Strickland that he went and there he had an opportunity to go over those disastrous months of 1655 and 1656 with George Whitehead, later the editor of his life and works.[20] Thomas, somewhere in the North of England, was most likely to have been at Newby and there would have been time for private talk and gatherings of Friends around the still influential figure of James Nayler.

With the spring, however, Thomas resumed his travelling ministry, walking eastwards into Yorkshire whence, in a letter to Margaret Fell dated 11th March, 1658 and written from Bordley Hall not far from Malham,[21] he says that he has been at York and takes the opportunity of forwarding a letter addressed to Margaret which came to his hands there. Sending letters must, at times, have been an erratic and chancy business but, on the whole, one is impressed by the speed and ease with which Friends managed to communicate with each other.

Thomas has been at a Meeting at Scalehouse where an annual series of Meetings was held in the last four years of the Commonwealth. These Meetings were part of the growing organisational structure that the Friends were imposing upon themselves and to the Meetings came representative and leading Friends of the northern counties.[22] In the letter, Thomas passes on to Margaret the good wishes of Gervase Benson, Thomas Goodaire and Thomas Killam. As these Friends came respectively from Sedbergh, Selby and Balby near Doncaster, it looks as though the Meeting that Thomas attended was the annual or general Meeting, rather than a purely local affair and he may have been attending as a representative from the Strickland area of which Newby was part. Each of these Yorkshire Friends 'desires dearly to bee remembered to thee and to Margrett Bridgett and freinds in thy family.' Margaret's brood of daughters always held a fond place in Friends' remembrances and it is remarkable how Swarthmoor was regarded as the home of all Friends however widely scattered.

From Scalehouse, Thomas proposes to attend a Meeting at Skipton on the 13th. He has heard something of a book called 'the testament of the patriarchs': 'it speaks very much of Enochs prophecy, which hints much against the lying priests' and Thomas wonders whether there was anything of Enoch's writings still extant in Jewish literature and whether enquiry might be made by any Friend going to Holland and speaking with Jews there. This, again, shows us Thomas pursuing an interest in Hebrew scholarship although Enoch's prophecy was not destined to become known in Europe for more than a century and a half when it was discovered in an Ethiopic manuscript and published in English, Ethiopic and other languages.[23] Then, with his own love to daughters, Margaret, Bridget and Sarah 'and all in thy family,' the letter ends.

This is the last letter that we date to the wandering years. By the time another spring had come round again, Thomas had found a permanent home. On 24th May, 1659, he married Frances Wilkinson of Great Strickland, the ceremony being performed according to Quaker usage.[24] He had attained his abode in the earth and, for the rest of his life, he was to live and work in the village of Great Strickland, half-way between Penrith and Shap, with the high hills of Lakeland to the West and the long range of the Pennines to the East. If he was not quite done with dispute and contention, he was nearly so. In 1660 appeared what was to be his last work published in England[25] for 18 years: *An Appeal to the Parliament, concerning the Poor, that there may not be a Beggar in England*. This was a short pamphlet, running only to four pages and devoted entirely to practical ends. The sectaries, who drew their support largely from the poor and simple men and women of the country, all had the concerns of the poor at heart. In common with other groups, Quakers found a commitment to social reform and most Quakers of note produced social as well as religious tracts. It is natural to find Thomas turning his pen from the obscurities of doctrine to the detailing of social evils. England at the close of the Protectorate was, it seemed, as full of ills as ever. Military rule had been effective in keeping the peace in the country but the poor and dispossessed were as numerous as they had ever been. Thomas, jailed at York and itinerant missionary in Sussex, had walked and talked with those for whom the promise of a better England free of the crippling effects of monarchial tyranny had faded. The Protectorate, in its last days, had gone sour on the people. It is significant that although Thomas addressed the Parliament as a body still presumed capable of great undertakings, he calls for a revival of the laws of the past in providing for the poor: he opens his appeal:

> In the midst of many and great Undertakings, let not a Settlement for the Poor be forgotten, but revive, ad [act], and execute all wholsome Lawes, and encourage all good Means, to Supply Poor People with Labour and Relief, and so prevent the ill Breeding, wicked Life, and bad End that many Thousands have fallen into through Idleness; To this End, give Order that the ensuing Platform may be fully executed.[26]

It is a call for reform more cogently and clearly expressed than is common with Lawson, and it is in a direct and practical manner that he goes on to outline this platform.

Its chief plank was to be an area office which would function as a sort of employment agency supervised by an organiser or organisers who would collect statistics on the unemployed, find jobs for those who could be fitted immediately to a trade, train those who could not and generally set up a sort of clearing house for those in need and distress. Thomas' spell in jail and his insecure life thereafter had given him a wholesome dislike of arbitrary authority and a sympathy for those who found themselves in prison for little else but the crime of poverty. He desires:

> That no Poor People be denied their former Liberty, nor strict Course taken against them, until some good Means be used to Supply their wants.[27]

And he is emphatic that the poor must have channels through which their grievances may be made known. It should be the desire of the Magistrates and other local authorities to encourage the reporting of injustice and neglect of the poor and it should be the duty of the Judges of Assize and Sessions to see that the poor receive justice and get their dues. None of these suggestions was particularly novel, though earlier Poor Law reformers had, perhaps, emphasised the need for public order where Thomas emphasised the rights of the unfortunate. Like all reformers who had preceded him back to the days of Queen Elizabeth, he saw the problem of poverty as one of waste – of manpower untapped and resources squandered. No one pretended that it was better to have men roaming the roads or begging in the streets than gainfully employed. It was a problem with which successive legislators had grappled and Thomas' suggestion of organisation under local authority with the provision of a Poor Man's Office is very similar to other schemes of social welfare throughout the seventeenth century.[28] The chief interest of the pamphlet is that it is the earliest Quaker publication to treat of the subject. Thomas' appeal is directed towards central government: at the time that he wrote and for long thereafter, the administration of the poor was carried out by parochial authorities, and Friends unwilling to co-operate with a system founded upon the parish unit and its religious authorities, were obliged to institute other programmes for the care of their own poor. The vision of a structure that would enable the poor to be usefully and gainfully employed was one that was shared by the Quakers who followed Lawson. But in later years such schemes relied more upon the administrative network of their own Meetings and looked no more to a hostile government for imaginative programmes of reformation. Thomas' appeal on behalf of the rights of the poor and their humane treatment must be seen against the background of the collapse of the Elizabethan Poor Laws and the present fact of military rule under a Parliament which put peace before liberty in the local administration of England.

Almost as soon as the pamphlet appeared, however, that Parliament had gone the way of the Protectorate and the crowds were cheering Charles II to the throne. The demands of the *Appeal to the Parliament* remained as pressing as ever but the entering of Charles into his kingdom was a distraction and a challenge to the Quakers who, at first, had great hopes of the new regime. They were to prove short-lived. The new king was in no position to make good any promises that he might have given about religious toleration before his accession and new censorship laws and the Acts of 1662 and 1664[29] making all meetings for worship illegal unless they were of the Established Church left the Quakers worse off than they had been in the days of Oliver. The new regime set out immediately to muzzle the press. In 1661 Giles Calvert, who had printed the first three of Thomas' works was arrested and thrown into prison for publishing a pamphlet called *The Phoenix of the Solemn League and Covenant*[30] and although he was released after a few weeks' confinement, neither he nor his widow, who carried on the printing works after his death in 1664, were ever again to enjoy that freedom and government favour that had been theirs during the inter-regnum.

The eclipse of Giles Calvert must have been a blow to the Quakers. Operating from the Black Spread Eagle in St. Paul's churchyard, he published many Quaker works although there is no evidence that he was himself a Friend. His wife Elizabeth continued the business under all the difficulties of Restoration harassment, moving from St. Paul's churchyard to Little Britain in 1666 and to a new Black Spread Eagle in the Barbican in 1667. She was imprisoned at least twice for printing works that annoyed the authorities and although the Calverts were by no means the worst harried of the underground printers of the Restoration, they had enough troubles to make them shy of the Quakers. Elizabeth, indeed, had very little connection with Friends and her will (dated 19th October, 1674) directed that her body be decently buried amongst the Baptists. It may be that when Lawson want the *Appeal to the Parliament* to be published Giles Calvert was already trying to keep himself out of trouble for the *Appeal* was published by Robert Wilson of the Black Spread Eagle and Windmill, St. Martin's le Grand in Aldersgate. Wilson's career was also harassed by officialdom. 'I am exposed in this day,' he writes to a Bristol acquaintance in 1661, 'through many and frequent sufferings to severall difficulties: for very often am I plundered by ye rulers of my goods; burning them at home and abroad.' And that year he was committed to the Gatehouse for selling 'seditious pamphlets against the Goverment of the Church of England.'[31]

We may, if we wish, see the effect of this repression on Lawson over the decades of the 1660s and 1670s: until the end of that period the only work of his to appear was published abroad. Not until 1677 came a work entitled *Baptismalogia* and, with the relaxation of the licensing laws at the end of that decade, three other works in quick succession. This looks as though the authorities were successful in discouraging Quaker publication so far as Thomas was concerned. But other Friends continued to publish and their works appeared unlicensed and without imprint. The underground press poured out a steady stream of Quaker works despite the Government's best efforts to stem the flood. Thomas, however, remained silent during these years. Marriage and a home at Great Strickland were to bring him land, children and responsibilities. Between 1660 and 1670 his four children were born: Ruth in 1660, Deborah in 1663, Hannah in 1668 and Jonah in 1670. With the end of his wandering years, Thomas turned his attention to local affairs and the service of the Strickland community. He was active in the Monthly Meeting and he opened a school in the village. As a Quaker, his teaching was carried on without licence and this, in itself, was enough to bring down the unwelcome attentions of the authorities upon him: during the next many years his battles were all to be fought on a domestic front and the affairs of the metropolis must have seemed ever more remote.

CHAPTER V

Schoolmaster at Great Strickland

IN THE YEAR THAT KING CHARLES II came to the throne, Thomas Lawson was 30. Did he but know it, the most adventurous period of Quakerism was behind him. Upon the King's accession, the hopes of Friends had been raised by the promise of toleration given in the Declaration of Breda in the spring of 1660 even if, as rumour darkly reported, the new King had his own reasons for wishing to see a measure of religious freedom in England.[1] On 25th May of that year, the guns and bells of England clamoured for him and a new age had begun. The Quakers, with almost everyone else in the land, had come to believe that the new regime could only be an improvement upon the old.

That winter, the hope was scattered in the gale of government wrath raised by the Fifth Monarchy rising of January, 1661 when Thomas Venner led his little band through the streets of London with the cry 'King Jesus and their heads upon the gates.' In the resultant government panic, over 4,000 Quakers found themselves in jail.[2] It was a short and furious spasm of persecution but scarcely had the ripples of it died away, than there was a fresh scare, this time in the North and very close to home. At the beginning of 1663, there was a plot hatched to raise the northern counties to force the king to carry out the promises of toleration which he had made when in exile. Westmorland's contribution to the scheme was a small force led by Robert Atkinson of Mallerstang, once a Parliamentary Captain of Horse and former Governor of Appleby Castle. In the autumn of the year, on the night of 12th October, his contingent of about 30 men reached the village of Kaber on the Kirkby-Stephen/Durham road. There he had counted on reinforcements from Kendal who were to join him on a march into Durham to rendezvous with the main body of the uprising. When the Kendal men did not materialise, the sorry little band dispersed and the rising was over. Like Venner's it had involved pathetically few men but its repercussions harmed many. Rebels were hunted down and the unfortunate Robert Atkinson and three others were hanged.[3] Rumour had it that the Quakers were involved and zealous magistrates such as Sir Daniel Fleming of Rydal Hall used the opportunity to take a tough line. In January, 1664, Westmorland Friends, alarmed by the extent to which they were being accused of conspiracy, presented a declaration of their peaceable intent to the King. There were 140 signatures on it[4] but it did prevent Fox, in the month that it was presented, from being taken at Swarthmoor at the instigation of Sir Daniel. Shortly after, Fleming stirred up the magistrates to proceed against Margaret Fell who, for refusing the Oath of Allegiance, was imprisoned at Lancaster and not released until 1668.[5]

By that date, all the legislation aimed specifically against dissenters that is known as the Clarendon Code had been passed.

> The Corporation Act of 1661, which imposed, amongst other things, the sacramental test 'according to the rites of the Church of England' upon officers and members of municipal corporations, had for its object the purging out of disaffected persons . . . The Conventicle Acts of 1664 and '70, to suppress seditious conventicles . . . The Five Mile Act of 1665 was directed at Nonconformist ministers.[6]

In response, the Quakers found a need to define their attitudes. The Friends of Westmorland had, in declaring themselves to be peaceable and innocent of plots, been following the example of London who, after Venner's rising, had made a similar declaration: the Quakers' first offical declaration of pacifism in all circumstances.[7] From henceforth, trouble might come to them but, officially at least, they adopted the attitude that they never sought it.

In the decade following the Restoration, Thomas Lawson was to put his youth behind him and his life came to revolve around the activities of his new life in Great Strickland. His marriage had brought him customary tenancies in the village which was part of the Lowther estates. Manorial court rolls of the 1660s describe Thomas as a customary tenant and also appearing on behalf of his wife (*in jure uxoris*) she holding a tenancy in her own right.

From the rolls, we get glimpses of the Lawsons' life in the agricultural community in which they were placed. The manorial court, held annually, regulated the activities of the estate's tenants and provided for the sharing of communal activities and the conservation of natural assets. It also adjudicated in disputes. The jury of the court that met on 5th April, 1661, for instance, recorded that:

> we find by testimonie by oath that the hedge and gutter at variance between Thomas Lawson and William Fallowfield belongeth to the said Thomas Lawson.[8]

This is interesting in the light of subsequent courts whose rolls show Thomas consistently refusing to serve on the Jury himself or even to appear in court – presumably because an oath was inevitably required for any participation in the court's proceedings. In 1665, for instance, besides a fine of 3/4d 'for keeping Tedders in the feild in the night tyme' he was heavily fined (7/4d reduced from 13/4d) 'for his Contemptuous refusall to serve of the Jury.'[9] In 1666, his fine was a shilling and at the same court Frances Lawson was fined 6/8d for cutting whins of the West side of the common.[10] In 1667 the fine was a shilling (sixpence on his own account and sixpence on his wife's)[11] and there was a further twelvepenny fine again in 1668.[12] These recurrent fines are an indication that Thomas was attempting to be faithful to the Quaker injunction against swearing. Friends were imprisoned for refusing to take the Oath of Allegiance, their refusal based on the literal word of Christ's teaching 'swear not at all' (Matthew 5.34). It was not to be thought that they would unbend to take the lesser oaths of legal proceedings, though in some instances, when authority was sympathetic, ways were found round the difficulty that satisfied officials without compromising Friends. In the case of probate, for example, a Quaker executor was often assumed to have sworn and, if the officer was satisfied, the word 'jurat' went down on paper by tacit understanding.[13] Some such face-saver may have been found when Lawson was in dispute with William Fallowfield over the hedge and gutter. Alternatively, a tacit understanding may have been reached among local Quakers as to the limits of principle. A gesture of contempt for the manorial court was a fine thing but when that court was the final arbiter, Lawson took his case before it. The roll for 1670 records:

> Whereas Thomas Fallowfeild pretends a Title unto one Gabell end nowe in the possession of Thomas Lawson, Wee (the foresaid Jury) doe Fynd the foresaid Gabell end absolutely to belong to Thomas Lawson, and that the said Thomas Fallowfeild tendered Consideration for lyeing his Timber thereupon, as he himself acknowledged before us.[14]

The Fallowfields were as staunch Quakers as could be found in Morland parish. Eight years later, Thomas Fallowfield and Thomas Lawson were both amongst Quakers whose goods were seized by process out of the Exchequer. Neither had any need to prove himself and though, in theory, Quaker discipline urged Friends to come to an accommodation between themselves, there was no absolute forbidding of recourse to worldly courts of justice.

These cases show us Thomas in a new light. The young man adrift from Cambridge, the disciple at Rampside, the firebrand of Sussex has become the small farmer of Great Strickland. The court rolls show the work of the village going on as the court orders improvements to walls and hedges and watercourses and lays down rights of access over fields or to the village water supply. In 1665, the court was concerned to see that every man thatched his part of the town kiln, the following year it ordered 'that none shall cut any Whinnes below the Church gate coming from Woodsyde upp to Robert Stevensons on the East syde of the Common upon paine of xx^d for every default.'[15] And in 1667, a two-year programme was initiated to replace the pasture hedge between Newby Pasture and the White Lees with a stone wall, every man to do his share upon pain of a 6/8d fine.[16]

In such communal activities and in the improvement of his own holding passed Thomas' life at Great Strickland. In 1667, he increased his acreage when a Thomas Robinson surrendered to him parcels of ground of an annual rent of 2/6d[17] and, by 1686, he is being described as Thomas Lawson 'Gent' (with the abbreviation 'Exc[used]' after his name) in the court roll of that year.[18] Later rolls, up to the year of his death, continue to style him 'Gent' and he is again excused from attending the court in 1690. Neither the tradition of his descent from the elusive Sir Thomas Lawson (see p. 209) nor his illegal schoolmastering can plausibly explain this sudden acknowledgement of status. The interest of the manorial court was in land, and it is much more likely that we should look to Thomas' position as a holder of land for an explanation of his gentry status. One quite common practice in Cumberland and North Westmorland was for a manorial tenant to increase his status by becoming a sub-lessee in the same manor or even in other manors. This does not, however, show up in the court rolls. Eventually, he might increase his holdings to such an extent that he was able to live off his rentals and assume a more leisured and gentlemanly way of life. Local folk generally knew exactly who was and who was not a gentleman and although the old definitions were crumbling by the end of the seventeenth century, the tenure of land was still the surest way of being a gentleman. At the end of his life, Thomas is being described as a tenant of both John Dalston and James Grahme.[19] Late in his life, also, Thomas is using a seal on his letters with the device of a bird cut upon it.[20] If any credance at all is to be placed upon the idea that he was related to some branch of the northern Lawsons, one might be inclined to suppose that the bird is the martlet which appears in the various Lawson coats of arms.[21] My own opinion, however, is that Lawson, casting about for a seal device, was not unwilling to appropriate the martlet of his notable namesakes.

Thomas' growing prosperity was not achieved without difficulty and in the face of the harassment of the Church. We have seen how he recorded his tithe testimony in the Strickland Monthly Meeting minute book but tithes, if the most bitterly resented, were but one part of clerical exactions. The Established Church also operated a system of church rates, intended mainly for the repair and maintenance of church fabric. To these, of course, the Quakers refused to contribute. The pages of the Bishop's Correction Court Act Book for Carlisle diocese are full of the names of Quakers who were cited 'for refuseing to pay their several proporcions of the Church assesse.' Ever amongst them, is Thomas Lawson. The same names appear time and again: Rowland Wilson of Newby, representatives of the Fallowfield family, maintaining a clannish obstinacy: 'Richardus Holme, Henricus Lycock de Morland, Johannes Robinson, Nicholanus Denkin . . . Johannes Robinson de Newby, Thomas Willan, Henricus Baxter de Thrimby, Williamus Morland, Thomas Smith, Christoferus Robinson, Mabella Smith, Johannes Smith, Agneta Teasdale et Williamus Hobson de Slegill'[22] – the names come again and again in repeated citations. Sometimes there is a little variation: a name drops out or one is added, William Hobson falls foul of the law and the clerk records (no doubt with immense satisfaction) 'in gaola.'[23] Two years later he is dead and a relentless church pursues his executors for the money owed to the assess.[24] The Church's ultimate sanction was excommunication but, unless this could be followed by action in the civil courts, it was a fairly toothless threat. Church rates had, in fact, no statutory basis[25] and it is not surprising to find one of the post-Restoration bishops lamenting that 'fanatics fear as little our excommunication as the Papists and indeed I find no sect much dreading it.'[26] Things were altogether more serious if an action was brought in the civil courts and we shall see later how Thomas was to suffer for continuing a school without licence. In the meantime, he continued to stand out against tithe and church rates with the quiet obstinacy that was Quaker policy and to try to pursue the ordinary life of a small farmer.

Besides his farm, however, Thomas had a small school and the running of this was to expose him to far more harassment than the refusal of tithes and church rates ever had. When he had written to Margaret Fell to justify the purchase of his Hebrew lexicon, one of his hopes had been that if God granted him a settled home, that he might find the lexicon useful in employing his training to good purpose. Hardly was he married and settled at Strickland than he began to bring home that promise by opening his school. Indeed, one of the first pupils arrived a bare two months after the marriage and the project of starting up a school must have been discussed by the young couple prior to their union. It has been suggested that this school was the building listed as no. 5 on page 220 of the report of the Royal Commission on Historical Monuments, Westmorland, 1936: 'House formerly school . . . built c. 1700'[27] but it is unlikely that Thomas ever taught anywhere but from his own home: certainly some pupils in the 1680s are known to have come for tuition to his house which was big enough to have had an upper storey.[28] On his marriage, Thomas held no property in Great Strickland: he is described as being 'of Newby Stones' in the marriage register and it would seem that his house must have come to him through his wife or his wife's family. The court rolls support this. William Wilkinson, Frances' father married a Margaret Stephenson in October, 1634.[29] She was a customary tenant on the Lowther estate when she got married, her name appearing in the court roll, 1632. Even in 1639 she is recorded as Margaret Stephenson but in 1647 the correction is made, Stephenson is crossed out and is followed by 'modo Margaret Wilkinson.'[30] In that year, her husband died and she inherited the tenancies. On William's death there were four girls of the marriage: Frances, baptised on 19th February, 1637 and Marie, Elizabeth and Jane, baptised in 1640, 1643 and 1646 respectively.[31] Margaret Wilkinson continues to appear in court rolls of 1657, 1661 and 1662.[32] In the roll of 1662, her name is crossed out and that of Thomas Lawson is inserted above. This kind of entry often occurs when a tenant dies: the clerk has made out the roll beforehand and corrections and amendments are made when the court is assembled.[33] If Margaret had been living when Thomas first settled in Great Strickland and died in 1661 or 1662 it seems likely that he started his married life with Frances in the house of his widowed mother-in-law and it was in this house that he opened his school and continued when, on the old lady's death, the property passed to her eldest daughter Frances.

The first pupil of whom we have any information was the son of Francis Howgill. The father writes from Kendal on 22nd August, 1659 to Edward Burrough in London:

> This we[e]ke I intend to cary my boy to Thomas Lawson to schole, into the Further parte of the County and may stay a few dayes.[34]

It is possible that this early pupil lodged with the Lawsons and his father wished to see him well settled before he returned to the work of his calling. In the early days of Quakerism, when Friends' schools were thinly scattered, it was quite acceptable for children to travel very long distances[35] to their schooling, so that it is not too surprising that Howgill, a Kendal man, should take his boy to Great Strickland for his education. But it does say something for his confidence in Lawson. Howgill was a well-educated man, his prolific writings well thought of, and he might be supposed to have wanted a good education for his son. The choice of Lawson as his son's schoolmaster suggests that Thomas' writings and other activities had brought him some reputation for learning.

This early pupil was the son of a father famous amongst the first martyrs of the movement. If one had to choose a Quaker whose life was both typical and exemplary in those first vital years, one would not go far wrong in choosing Howgill. Born in 1620 and brought up in Westmorland, he had been committed to Appleby jail with James Nayler in 1652.[36] He accompanied Edward Burrough on missionary work in Bristol in 1654 and in Ireland in 1655. At Bristol, the two missionaries attracted large crowds and at the instigation of local clergy were ordered by the magistrates to leave the city. Francis Howgill replied that they had served the commonwealth faithfully, abided by its laws and that the magistrates had no power to order them to leave. They continued to preach. In the summer of 1655, after preaching for three months in Dublin, they continued to preach in other places in Ireland until arrested in Munster. On an order from the Lord Deputy, Henry Cromwell, they were deported back to England.

In July 1663, whilst going about his own affairs, Howgill was taken up at Kendal market and was tendered the Oath of Allegiance. When he refused to take it, he was committed to Appleby prison, refusing the Oath again at the Assizes in the following month. An indictment against him was drawn up and he was set free until the next Assizes in Lent.

Judge Twisden at the Lent Assizes in Appleby, 1664, cautioned Howgill:

> The Time being dangerous, and Things having now a worse Appearance than at the last Assizes, and People, under Pretence of Conscience, violating the Laws, and hatching Treasons and Rebellion, although I have nothing of that Kind to charge against you, yet seeing you did refuse to take the Oath of Allegiance at the last Assizes, the Law doth presume such Persons to be Enemies to the King and Government, however I shall give you Time to prepare for your Trial till the next Assizes, only you must enter into Recognizance for your Appearance then, and for your good Behaviour in the mean Time.[37]

In the uneasy years after the Restoration, the Judge thus expressed the fear of the times that there might be further rebellion. Pacifism was by no means so clearly formulated a part of Quaker belief in 1664 as it was to become later and the peaceful nature of Friends was not at all evident at a time when their public utterances often led to violent disturbances. There had not been a rebellion yet in England whose leaders did not protest that they came in peace. Judge Twisden's requirements of good behaviour included attendance at church and no further meetings. Howgill refused to enter into such a bond and was returned to prison.

Judge Turner at the Assizes in August, 1664 was less sympathetic. After Howgill continued to refuse to swear, he pronounced the dread sentence of *praemunire:* 'You are put out of the King's Protection, and the Benefit of the Law. Your Lands are confiscate to the King during your Life, and your Goods and Chattels for ever, and you are to be Prisoner during your life.'

For Francis Howgill's sake, Thomas Lawson broke the long silence between 1660 and 1678 when nothing of his work was published in England. In 1668, he published abroad a book entitled *Eine Antwort auf ein Buch* – 'An answer to a Book given forth in the Latine Tongue, called the Scum (or Dross) of the Quakers' as Smith renders it in his *Catalogue of Friends' Books*, delicately translating *Colluvies Quackerorum*, the book which is being answered and which was by John Joachim Zentgraff and published in 1666. Zentgraff had attacked Howgill and sought to demonstrate that the Quakers had taken their origin from the Seekers. With Howgill in jail, Thomas took up his pen to defend the cause against Zentgraff's accusations. The charges and Lawson's responses are very much what we have come to expect. Thomas defends the practice of quaking with Job 4.14 'Fear came upon me, and trembling, which made all my bones to shake'; he defends liberty of prophesying with 2 Peter 1.21 'holy men of God spake as they were moved by the Holy Ghost'; he defends the doctrine of Christ within with Luke 17.21 'behold, the kingdom of God is within you'; and he defends the perfectability of men on earth with 2 Cor 5.17 'therefore if any man be in Christ, he is a new creature: old things are passed away.' On these and like texts he holds an amalgam of views that we have come to recognise as distinctively Quaker. Again, he has to repudiate the suggestion that the prompting of the inner spirit may be a licence to sin, again he conveys the sense that the Friends had of being reborn into a brotherhood of new believers. Zentgraff has scorned Howgill's expectations of grief and misery as a prerequisite of rebirth. Lawson quotes David, swamping his tent with tears, Job with boils that ran like water and Jeremiah cursing the day that he was born. For the Quakers, as for Bunyan, the road to heaven lay through the Slough of Despond.

The trend of *Eine Antwort* is to disassociate the Quakers from the other sects. Zentgraff had tried to link them with the Seekers: by 1668 Lawson – in line with the Quaker movement as a whole – would wish to deny the connection. And there were others whose names they would not wish to have linked with theirs: Millenarians, Menandrians, Basilidianians, Socinians, Ranters, Brownists, Anabaptists and Antiscripturists[38] – not to mention Thomas Venner and his Monarchy Men. From all of these, the Quakers early withdrew the hem of their garments. How much Howgill, a humble seeker from 12 years old, would have cared for this pharisaical withdrawal, we cannot know. On 20th January, 1669 he died, still in Appleby jail 'a faithful Martyr, who laid down his Life in Testimony of his Obedience to the Precept of Christ, *Swear not at all*'.[39]

This was the man whose son was entrusted to Thomas Lawson's care. During his life, he had been an active missionary and a prolific writer and in death he became a perfect martyr. The lines of Thomas' life were to be laid down differently, but much of his early experience was similar and he too looked upon the inside of Appleby jail.

As time went by, Thomas acquired a reputation and his school began to attract others, not all of them Quakers. It was not unknown, even in the early days, for non-Friends to send their children to a Friends' school if it had a good reputation: then, as now, much might be done for the sake of a good education. Certainly by the end of the century, there were many children of non-Friends attending the famous Quaker school at Sidcot in Somerset[40] and, of the 28 children at the Friends' school in Lancaster in the early eighteenth century, only four came from Quaker families.[41] What little information we have about Thomas Lawson's school suggests that there too the intake was mixed. It has been said that amongst his pupils were some of the sons of local gentry and of one such boy there is a record. John Smith was the son of William Smith, rector of Lowther. Clergymen were always rated as gentry: whatever their origin and income, their education and authority in the community automatically made gentlemen of them. William Smith's provisions for the education of his son had mixed results which are best described in John Nichols' *Literary Anecdotes of the Eighteenth Century*, a work which comprised the biographical memoirs of William Bowyer, which Nichols edited:

> the Rev. William Smith . . . after being himself for some years the superintendant of his son's studies, was unfortunately advised to send him to Bradford, under the care of Mr. Christopher Nesse, a leading man among the Dissenters; with whom he continued two years, and lost almost all that he had learned from his father; but recovered it again under Mr. Thomas Lawson, a Quaker, who was a favourer of learning, an excellent school-master, and grounded Smith well in the learned languages.[42]

Thomas, indeed, tutored the young man to such good effect that he was able to complete his education by going to University in 1674. Nichols relates an extraordinary chapter of accidents whereby young Smith, originally intending to go to Glasgow, was eventually enrolled upon the register of St. John's College, Cambridge.

> An early foundation in classical learning being thus raised, his father conceived thoughts of sending him to an University. The nearness of

the place, and the company of a young student who was going thither, recommended Glasgow; and the day was fixed for the journey; but it proved so rainy and tempestuous a season, that his father would not venture him from home: and the family, it is said, always looked upon this as a providential escape from the Scottish religion, to which his intended companion was made a proselyte. Oxford was now thought of, two sons of a neighbour going at that time to St. John's College in Cambridge, Smith's father yielded to the great desire of his son to go with them.

Whether Thomas would have preferred his old university to that of Presbyterian Glasgow, is a nice point. Rescued from the Scottish religion by the providential opening of the heavens, his ex-pupil progressed in an entirely conformist way from B.A. into holy orders, a progress which can hardly have met with unqualified enthusiasm from his former school-master. Thomas, had he lived to see it, however, would have had good reason to be proud of his pupil's subsequent career: John Smith built upon the sound classical foundation given him and became a 'learned and eminent Antiquary,' the editor of Bede's *Ecclesiastical History* in Latin and Saxon.

Other pupils of Thomas are more shadowy. His son Jonah composed 'several Affectionate Epistles written in Verse to one John Hall, School-Master in Cleeve-Land, his Quondam School-fellow'[43] but though several John Halls are recorded as passing through university at this time, none looks likely to have been a school-fellow of Jonah Lawson. On Thomas Lawson's death, it is said that it was a former pupil who erected the tombstone over him but the name of the perpetrator of this act of piety (against all Quaker rulings) is now lost to us.

Five more pupils who were definitely not Quakers – since they went to University – may be turned up from Foster's *Alumni Oxonienses* and Venn and Venn, *Alumni Cantabrigienses*.[44] Interestingly, two of them are from County Durham: John Johnson of Whorlton and Humphrey Hagget of Barnard Castle, both of whom went up to St. John's College, Cambridge. Johnson, who is described as son of Ambrose, yeoman, went as a pensioner in 1672, aged 18 and Hagget, described as son of William, husbandman, as a sizar in 1675, aged 19. Both men give as their school 'Great Strickland' and we may safely conclude that this was Lawson's. And so with three other boys who went up to Oxford without giving the name of their school in the register but giving the place of their birth or origin as Strickland. All three went as commoners. Bernard Gilpin, son of Alan, went to Queen's College, matriculating 13th February 1674, aged 18 and proceeded to his B.A. in 1678. Richard Hebson, son of Richard of Little Strickland, also entered

Queen's – a college with strong Cumbrian connections. He matriculated the same day as Hebson, took his degree the same year and in 1691 is found as vicar of Middleton or Longparish in Hampshire. Lastly, Allan Towson, son of Allan, entered Brasenose in 1678. The date of his B.A. is not given but was presumably conferred in that he later proceeded to M.A. at Sidney Sussex, Cambridge in 1697.

The curriculum of Thomas' school was probably very similar to that of William Jenkins of Hertford who, a generation later, was the first schoolmaster of the Friends' school at Sidcot. Jenkins' pupils, in 1699, paid 20s a year to learn reading, writing and arithmetic and 30s to learn Latin, Greek, writing and arithmetic.[45] To these subjects, Lawson, with his personal interest in the language, probably added Hebrew. It gave, as we have seen, a certain cachet to a school and we know for certain that Thomas gave adult instruction in Hebrew. In 1679, the Quaker, Christopher Taylor, was to publish his *Compendium Trium Linguarum*, a dictionary of Latin, Greek and Hebrew. The inclusion of all three in one compendium suggests that all were commonly taught in Friends' schools at that time.[46]

From the evidence we have, it is clear that Thomas' establishment was more than just another village school. Those boys who came from a distance would lodge in the village – one or two may even have boarded with him. If we take Sidcot again as an example, the fee for a border in 1699 (and prices were fairly static between the end of the Civil War and the end of the century) was £9 per annum.[47] By far the most part of the boys, however, would be local lads, earnest to equip themselves in a world that was rapidly becoming more commercial. The fact that a school was needed in the area is demonstrated by the attempt many years later, in 1685, to start a school at Thrimby, two miles from Great Strickland. A Thomas Fletcher 'for and in consideration of the great love and respect which he beareth towards the Inhabitants of Little Strickland and Thrimby' made funds available for the provision of a schoolmaster/curate to teach 'an English and Grammar Schoole' in the chapel at Thrimby not only 'for the better educateinge and instructeinge of the Children within the said Two Townshipps' but also for the benefit of 'other adjacent Places.'[48] The first curate in post under these provisions was to play an explosive part in the life of the Lawson family as we shall see later.

A small school at Lowther had been endowed in 1638 but it was not until towards the end of the century that John Viscount Lowther's more ambitious school was established, described by Nicolson and Burn as an 'ample foundation . . . for the benefit of all the northern counties.'[49]

These schemes take us well beyond the date of the foundation of Lawson's school, but they do serve to illustrate that there was a need in the area that he strove to meet despite difficulties and harassment. For all his commitment to it, however, teaching was not the only way that Thomas sought to 'publish truth.' Neither his activities as a schoolmaster nor the upkeep of his land prevented him from continuing to travel from time to time, still spreading the message that Fox had brought to him at Rampside. About these journeys we can know very little. Thomas kept a record of only one and, from the scant documentation of others we might, perhaps suppose that were still more completely undocumented. We tend to know about Quaker journeys only when they lead to trouble with the authorities. From the scraps of evidence that we do have, we know that Thomas was away from Great Strickland, preaching, teaching or in jail in 1666, 1673, 1674, 1677 and 1687. In 1666, Thomas was amongst a dozen Quakers rounded up by the Trained Bands under an order issued by Bishop Cosins and John Tempest, Justice of the Peace in Durham. Most of the captured were described as yeomen and came from various places in an area South of Durham city. In the Great Book of Sufferings at Friends House, which records the taking of these men, Thomas is described as 'Tho: Lawson of Great Strickland in Westmoreland Schoolmaster.'[50] The Great Book does not make it clear whether these prisoners were taken individually and at intervals or whether they were all gathered up at a Meeting. When Fox had visited Durham three years before, a General Meeting had been held at Heighington in the home of Christopher Richmond, one of the present prisoners.[51] However taken, they were all conveyed to Durham city where, says the Great Book of Sufferings 'most of them continued in the Custody of Wm Wilkinson called Marshall one month and the rest put into the Common Goale.'[52]

What Thomas was doing in South Durham is not apparent, but it is most likely that he was on a mission, strengthening the faith of the convinced. In the same year, his wife was also in trouble. An entry in the Great Book under the heading 'Sufferers For Meeting Together to worshipe God' records 'Frances Lawson Elizabeth Gibson for the first ofence for meeting with Gods people was sent to the house of Corection for a month'[53] and, under the heading 'For not Going to the publicke worshipe' 'Frances Lawson being fined 3s had two Quishons taken from her worth 5s 6d.'[54] We know so little of Frances: one suspects that much of the organisation necessary for a reasonable existence under the uncertainties of persecution must have fallen to her charge and much, too, of the work necessary to sustain life on the land and to allow Thomas to pursue his calling. But we have only one picture of her outside of the dry documents of officialdom – when she supported her daughter Ruth in marrying against her father's wishes. It is somehow typical of Frances that it was her household cushions that the authorities chose to distrain when she refused to pay the fine of 3s imposed on her.

It was, however, in the running of his school that Thomas stood most into danger. No government can feel happy at the sight of the nation's children being taught by a man who belongs to what it considers a subversive group. The machinery for repression had always been there. In 1581, *An Acte to reteine the Queenes Majesties Subjects to their due Obedience* (23 Elizabeth cap 1) made the authorities liable to a fine of £10 per month for allowing a non Church-going schoolmaster to teach and the schoolmaster himself liable to proscription from teaching and a year's imprisonment. By the first year of King James' reign, the fine had gone up to 40s per day, half of which was offered as an incentive to the person or persons who brought the action. This act (1 James I cap 4)[55] which was aimed chiefly against Roman Catholic recusants was used, in the latter half of the seventeenth century against other groups who refused to take part in the services of the Established Church and, in 1662, with Charles II on the throne, the Act of Uniformity[56] gave the authorities the further power of requiring a schoolmaster who applied for a licence to subscribe to a declaration of conformity to the liturgy of the Church of England. The hopes of a kindlier regime that Charles had raised amongst Quakers were disappointed. When Thomas opened his school in June or early July of 1659, Cromwell was dead and the Protectorate dead in all but name. In months, the king's restoration was to bring back the old forms and customs of the Anglican settlement and to empower the restored bishops to exact conformity thereto from tutors and schoolmasters. These measures were soon applied and in 1664 Thurston Read, a Friend teaching in Essex, was imprisoned in the Moot Hall in Colchester by the Mayor, William Moore, for teaching without a licence. In the insanitary conditions of the prison he 'continued there till he died.'[57]

Initially, Thomas' position as a schoolteacher appears to have been somewhat ambiguous. He is present, for instance, at a General Chapter held at Appleby on 27th April, 1664,[58] along with parish priests and officially recognised schoolmasters although he was already under threat of excommunication[59] and later in the year his old enemy, Percy Burton, was to declare him excommunicate following upon letters issued by the ecclesiastical office on 1st May.[60] With Thomas was excommunicated Henry Holmes, who may have been employed by Thomas as an assistant. By December of the year, Lawson and Holmes are cited 'for teaching School without licence and for not coming to Church.'[61] A day and place had been appointed where they and several other offenders (mostly cited for refusal to go to church) might appear to give reason why their names should not be signified to the kind and a writ taken out for the capture of their persons.

This is interesting as part of a process which is thought to have fallen into disuse almost a century earlier although it remained a part of canon law and Richard Burn describes it in his *Ecclesiastical Law*, 1763 under the heading 'Excommunication'. It was a procedure of gradual stages: the offender, having first been presented at a visitation of the archdeacon (or, more rarely, the bishop) was usually admonished and dismissed with an exhortation to mend his ways. If he persisted in error, then he was cited to appear before the ecclesiastical court and might continue to be cited thereafter. Excommunication was the ultimate weapon in the bishop's armoury. Beyond that, he was dependent upon the assistance of the secular arm, the machinery for it being the bishop's signification of an offender to the king. A writ, *de excommunicato capiendo* would then be issued out of Chancery and it would be the duty of the sheriff to whom it was issued to capture the excommunicate.[62]

How this machinery worked in practice is difficult to discover. People were certainly allowed to remain excommunicate for many years[63] and there is, as we have seen, already much evidence that excommunication was regarded as a fairly toothless threat in a way that it would not have been had church and state truly been working in concert. It was expensive to procure a Chancery writ and, so far as Carlisle diocese was concerned, Bishop Rainbow was a moderate man and he may well have taken the view that the backward North-west was not so well provided with schools that the authorities could afford to extinguish a useful schoolmaster. The Archbishop of Canterbury, Gilbert Sheldon, might, in 1665, demand that bishops enquire into the religious conformity of schoolmasters within their diocese and find out whether those 'yt keep schollars in their Houses to board or sojourn, and privately teach them or others within their Houses . . . do themselves frequent the publick Prayers of ye Church and cause their Schollars to do ye same,'[64] but Bishop Rainbow of Carlisle does not seem to have exerted himself unduly in this matter. His return to Sheldon's enquiries of 1669, for instance, makes no mention of Quakers at Great Strickland and names only a handful of teachers in his diocese.[65] In 1664, Lawson and Holmes showed their contempt for the church court by not appearing before it to say why they should not be signified and the signification appears never to have been proceeded with.

So things went on in the 1660s. Each year after his excommunication Thomas is to be found faithful amid those Friends cited for refusal to pay church rates. As the 1670s opened, however, life became harder – the clergy began to make concerted effort to resist nonconformist encroachment on their teaching monopoly. The old days of the blind eye were over and Thomas found himself unable to operate without a licence to teach. The difference was that the civil authorities now had their eye upon him and in 1671 he had to appear at the Midsummer Sessions at Appleby where he was released on bail of £40 (his sureties being Bernard Bainbridge and Christopher ?Couplin):

> Condicione that he shall appear att the next Sessions and that he shall keep nor teach schoole till he have A Licence thereunto by the D[ean] and C[hapter] of the Diocesse.[66]

If this was a crisis in Thomas' life then he appears to have faced it in the immediate knowledge of what he would do. He had taught through long years of quiet obstinacy without a licence now, if the only means of continuance was to go through the motions of conformity, conform he would. He lost no time. On 12th July, he went before the bishop and adopted the posture of a penitent. After humble submission and a promise of future obedience, he was accepted back into the fold of the Anglican church.[67] He had subscribed to the articles required by law, taken the necessary oaths and was promptly – the same day – granted a licence.[68] His submission was not without its humiliation. The Bishop's Correction Book, under the date of 13th July records that in a room 'vulgare vocato ye Dining Room' in Rose Castle, the Episcopal Palace, Thomas Lawson, yeoman, alias pretended schoolmaster of Little [sic] Strickland, making petition, begged for forgiveness and was granted absolution and restored to the sacraments of holy mother church.[69]

Less than a year later, Thomas may have been regretting his humiliation as Charles II issued his Declaration of Indulgence, sweeping away the need for a schoolmaster to conform to the Established Church. The resultant flood of applications for licences to teach bore witness to the numbers of schoolmasters who had been teaching illegally and frightened Parliament into forcing the king to cancel the Declaration only a year after its proclamation. Subsequent pressure from Archbishop Sheldon led, in 1675, to a public withdrawal of all licences granted under the Act. Long before that, the authorities had swooped upon Thomas Lawson. Despite the fact that licences issued before the Declaration were supposed to be valid, Thomas was in serious trouble. No doubt he had seen the Declaration as freeing him from the need to keep up even a pretence of continued conformity. It must have seemed a chance to wipe out the smart of having to bow down to the despised church. If he blatantly ignored his recent recantation, then he reaped the rewards of cynicism. In July of 1673, he and Henry Holmes, 'Ludimagistros pretensos' were again cited 'for teaching Schoole without Lycence and commonly reputed Quakers.'[70] The Book of

Sufferings of Friends within Westmorland Quarterly Meeting tells what happened:

> First of all Robert Wilkinson Constable of Clifton, and Thomas Wiber called Church Wardens of the same gave in a Testimony which they were enjoyned to do by a Warrant Issued out by the Justices upon the Kings declaration above mentioned ['the Kings declaration against Recusants'], that they had no popish Recusants within their parish, But John Thwaits Clerk of the Sessions bid them go again and bring in a List of the Quakers within their parish which they did accordingly and was presented that day before two Justices, Thomas Fletcher and Robert Hilton as in this Following schedule vizt . . .

> presented by Tho: Docker) Lancelott Fallowfield and his wife
> Warden of Morland parish) James Fallowfield and his wife
> and Tho: Ayrey Constable) Thomas Fallowfield and his wife
> of Great Strickland   ) Thomas Lawson and his wife

> Also the said Tho: Lawson was Indicted and Imprisoned at Appleby upon the said Statute 23d Eliz: for teaching school without a Licence . . .

> All these above named were presented as abovesd and convicted and returned into the Exchequer as Popish Recusants.[71]

Once again, Thomas was obliged to find sureties. This time William Sanderson and Christopher Taylor pledged £20 each and Thomas was released on condition that he appeared to answer two separate indictments at the next Sessions.[72] The two indictments were for not repairing to church for a month and for teaching a school without licence. If he was imprisoned for any length of time, I can find no record of it. Perhaps the imprisonment referred to in the Westmorland Book of Sufferings was a temporary one, pending bail. Certainly by the time of the next Sessions, he looks to have made his peace with authority. If he was jailed at all, it can only have been for the briefest of periods, for by July of the year he had departed the Great Strickland area to find refuge in Lancashire. For the present the Establishment had won.

CHAPTER VI

Swarthmoor Interlude

IN THE SUMMER OF 1674, Thomas Lawson might reasonably consider himself lucky to be still at liberty. There was no question of his being able to re-open his school and it probably appeared to him that withdrawal from the Great Strickland area was politic. As in the old days, it was Swarthmoor that offered him sanctuary: an entry in the *Household Account Book* kept by Sarah Fell, fourth daughter of Margaret Fell and the family accountant reads:

> 1674 July 5th By m⁰ to Bro: Loweʳ yᵗ hee gave Thomas Lawson foʳ comeinge over hitheʳ to Instruct him and his sistʳˢ in the knowledge of herbs   000 10 00¹

Shut out of his old employment by the officers of the state, Thomas had been taken in by the family at Swarthmoor. Thomas Lower was Margaret's son-in-law, the husband of her daughter Mary and a man of strength within the movement. Like Margaret herself, he was a great executive rather than a great mystic. The 'sisters' referred to in the account book would, according to the common usage of the seventeenth-century, be his sisters-in-law. Besides Mary and Sarah, the other Fell girls who were at home at that time were Susannah and Rachel, aged 14 and 11.²

The real significance of this entry in the account book is that it is the first piece of hard evidence that Thomas was known as a botanist. We have seen how Isabel Ross, like others who have provided biographical notices of Lawson, accorded him an interest in botany from his very early, Rampside days.³ But there is not a scrap of evidence that he was interested in plants much before the 1670s. Amongst his surviving plant records, there is no find that we cannot more plausibly ascribe to journeys and expeditions made in the period after 1670 than in the period before. And there is one piece of evidence that points fairly positively against Lawson's having been interested in botany at an early date. When, in 1661, John Ray made his botanising tour that brought him into the northern counties, he makes no mention of having met Thomas, despite the fact that he botanised in the

66

Shap area only five miles from Great Strickland. Indeed, approaching Shap from the North, he would pass within a mile of Great Strickland and it is certainly tempting, as Ray's biographer, Charles Raven says, to suppose that Lawson and Ray met on this or on two other occasions when Ray was in the Shap area.[4] The 1661 tour is well documented in the 'Itinerary' that Ray compiled to describe his expedition.[5] A previous tour, in 1660, is not documented, but it seems unlikely that if Ray had met Lawson then, he would have passed by his door a year later without visiting. Fellow botanists were not so thick on the ground that Ray could afford to neglect a valuable contact in the remote North-west. His tour of 1668 is only briefly documented in a letter to Martin Lister[6] but Thomas Lawson is not mentioned in it and Ray, who was generous in acknowledging his friends and botanical helpers, attributes no plant to Lawson in the *Catalogus Angliae* published two years later. In other works, published very much later, Lawson's name was to be of frequent occurence but always in respect of records that can be traced to later communications. Tempting as it may be to suppose that the two men met, the evidence is all against it. On the contrary, it would suggest that Lawson was not at all known as a botanist in the 1660s since Ray did not detour a mere mile to see him. To say, therefore, as M. Bennet does in *The Westmorland Note Book*, that the friendship between the two men was 'intimate' and to go on to say that Ray 'is said to have performed a journey on foot from his residence in the south of England in order to visit him'[7] is pure invention.

But if Ray never came to sit at Lawson's feet and if his passing just a mile from Great Strickland must be reckoned one of history's near misses, there is one other, even more interesting moment when the two men's paths might have crossed. In 1661, Ray was offered and refused the living of Kirkby Lonsdale. His reasons for refusal were various – one was financial. But he had been sorely tempted:

> One great motive to have induced me to take it was, because of its vicinity to the Yorkshire Alpes, and especially Ingleborough Hill, which is not above six or seven miles thence distant. Indeed the whole countrey of Westmoreland, for variety of rare plants, exceeds any that I have travailled in England; perhaps Carnarvonshire in Wales, may vie with it.[8]

At Kirkby Lonsdale, he would have been only a day's ride from Lawson. Barely a year later, however, Ray found himself unable to accept the Act of Uniformity and was thereby debarred from the clerical profession. If the same scruples had operated at Kirkby Lonsdale, he would have come and gone again in a few months at a time when Lawson's interests in natural history were undeveloped. If Ray had been an admirer of Lawson, then

Thomas' name would certainly have appeared in the *Catalogus Angliae* and we might have expected some correspondence between the two men – especially in view of the desire expressed by Ray above to know more of Westmorland. On the contrary, it was Lawson who was stimulated by the *Catalogus Angliae* and only when Ray was collecting for the projected third edition did Lawson submit any records and plant material to him. Thomas, like other naturalists up and down the country, was greatly stirred by its production. The *Catalogus Angliae* was the first pocket flora of England. Unlike the massive herbals of the past, it was affordable and it was the product of extensive local research by Ray – research of a sort that could be carried on and extended by anyone with a working knowledge of plants and the energy and opportunity to get out into the field. It was a tool for the working botanist and, in the last three decades of the seventeenth century, all the botanists of note were mentioned in it or in the various works of Ray that succeeded it and enlarged upon its findings. For anyone with any leaning towards botanical studies, the publication of the *Catalogus Angliae* would have been example and spur. If we were to look for a point in Thomas' career when he first started to become seriously interested in plants, then I think we would not go far wrong in choosing 1670 and the publication of the *Catalogus Angliae*. In all his travels around England before that date, he shows no sign of having taken the opportunity to observe plants or record them: the records that have come down to us can all be dated more probably to a date after 1670 than before. In 1674, on the other hand, he was known to the Swarthmoor household as a man qualified to instruct them in the knowledge of herbs. His interest, therefore must have been awakened at least a year or two prior to that date.

Another assumption which needs, in my opinion, to be corrected, is that Thomas gave his pupils instruction in the medicinal properties of herbs. It seems to me somewhat unlikely that Thomas Lower, who had qualified as a physician, would need any such instruction. The suggestion that Lawson himself undertook an occasional bit of medical practice in Great Strickland appears likewise to be grounded on little more than the fact that he was interested in botany.[9] It is too easy to assume that every plant hunter in the seventeenth century was a herbalist. No doubt Thomas knew as much as any educated man in the age about the virtues of herbs, but there is no evidence that he was especially interested in that aspect of plant lore. He was a follower of Ray and his interests lay with the identification and establishment of the British flora. It was the distinguishing of species that he taught to Thomas, Mary and Sarah and perhaps also to Susannah and Rachel.

Those summer days teaching Lower and the Fell sisters must have afforded a measure of peace to Lawson. For the moment, he was resigned to the cessation of his normal teaching activities: he had lost the weary battle to keep his school open and now he was prepared to turn his mind to other things. A month later he is the subject of another entry in the *Household Account Book*:

> 1674 Aug 4th by m^o p^d Tho: Lawson fo^r a booke called ye yonge Clarkes Tutor fo^r mee   000 01 06[10]

The Young Clerks Tutor was the most popular home lawyer of the day. Written by Edward Cocker who also wrote several works on arithmetic and accounting, it went into many editions of which the sixth of 1670 would have been the latest available in 1674. The preface to the work bills its contents:

> Here is presented to thy Hand a faithful Collection of Presidents of all sorts, which for the variety will fit every Mans Occasions: and for the clearness will be useful to any Understanding.[11]

Cocker had already pointed out how, in this captious age, every man needs a defence against those who so busily examine and eagerly pursue 'all advantages and shifts whatsoever.' He concludes with his own encomium of his work:

> Hereby it will not be easie to mistake, and cheaper than this no man can purchase greater quiet and security
>
> Farewell.[12]

Cocker's work so satisfied a need that his name has come down to us in the popular phrase 'according to Cocker'. Sarah probably wanted the book to help her with the management of Force Forge, the iron smelting furnace in the Rusland valley which the Fells had owned since 1658. In 1666, George Fell had sold the forge to his four younger sisters who, for some time employed a manager, Thomas Rawlinson. In 1668, a dispute had arisen over his stewardship that had resulted in Sarah's taking over the forge and managing it herself. As the only woman to manage a Furness iron forge, she was not going to rely entirely upon the Quaker way of settling disputes by bringing the parties together at the local business Meeting of the Society: it had not been very successful in reaching agreement with Rawlinson.[13] So Thomas had recommended *The Young Clerks Tutor* to her as a guide to legal practice and perhaps it was his own copy for which the Fells paid 1/6d. It is pleasant to think of Thomas helping Sarah, the most business-like of the remarkable Fells, in her business affairs.

This summer period passed at Swarthmoor must have been a time of refreshment and renewal for Thomas in the midst of any troubles. Although he had escaped the worst of the authorities' wrath and was a free man, it was a taste of what they could do if they were so minded. Moreover, he still had the prospect of a hefty fine hanging over him. We remember from the Book of Sufferings that, apart from his indictment for teaching school without licence, Thomas had been presented along with Frances and three Fallowfield men and their wives 'and convicted and returned into the Exchequer as Popish Recusants.' The financial penalties for this were extremely stiff: heavy fines were imposed or the recusant might be liable to forfeiture of two-thirds of his land. Thomas had been returned into the Exchequer; now he could only wait while the legal wheels ground on, using his time to recuperate and to gather strength for what might lie ahead.

In the process of re-structuring his life around new interests, Lawson was to discover a deep and abiding love for botany. We live in a country which prides itself on the tradition of the clergyman-naturalist and both John Ray and Thomas Lawson have been described as though they fitted into that mould. Indeed, popularised in a television programme, John Ray has been described as 'a 17th-century parson'.[14] He was nothing of the sort and neither, of course, was Thomas Lawson: even in his Rampside days it is stretching a point to apply the term clergyman to him. Ironically enough, it was precisely the intolerance of the church that diverted both men into the paths of natural history. When, on refusing the Act of Uniformity Ray had found himself 'free and unemployed, a teacher without pupils, a cleric without a charge, debarred by his profession from secular employment, debarred by the law from his profession,'[15] he had thrown himself wholeheartedly into the study of natural history to which he had been attracted whilst still a Fellow of Trinity. From then on it became his life's work. Thomas Lawson, also debarred from *his* profession – teaching – by the law, likewise sought to occupy his mind with the study of natural history. Before the July of 1674, when he retreated into Furness we have nothing to indicate that he was interested in botany. After that date, evidence of his botanical studies comes thick and fast. Like Ray, he had found a new vocation and, in the last half of his adult life, we shall see him more and more as a botanist. In later years, Low Furness was one of the areas which his extant records show him to have known best and the basis of that knowledge was surely built in the summer of 1674 when he had the demands of the Swarthmoor botanical pupils to satisfy. For himself, it probably reinforced a philosophy of education that matured with him all his life.

The belief that the observation and detailing of the natural world had educative value was not special to the Quakers. It had its origin at least half a century earlier and its chief spokesman was Bacon. The Baconian ideal of learning from practical observation found expression in many of the educational treatises of the century. John Dury's *The Reformed School*,

1651, for instance, includes instruction 'in the observation of Husbandry and Gardening; of Fishing and Fouling; and the generall Rules thereof'[16] and prescribes Pliny's *Natural History*[17] and the Latin authors on agriculture. This type of emphasis in education came, however, to be particularly associated with the Quakers as, excluded from positions of state by their religious beliefs, they turned their attention to the mastery of the practical sciences. It was one of George Fox's strengths that, although not well-educated himself, he had a vision of Friends' education that enabled him to make constructive and practical suggestions to others. Towards the end of this year of 1674, it seems that he got word of Thomas Lawson's difficulties for, on 10th October, we find him writing to William Penn from Worcester Prison. He asks Penn in London to remember his love to various people 'and Th: Lawson if that waye'. Then Fox put down some thoughts on the establishment of a school:

> & it might doe well if Tho: L. & R[ichard] R[ichardson][18] did sett vpp a schoole in ye country neere London: ffor if thou didst discourse with Tho: L. thee wouldst vnderstande farther: ffor I doe not vnderstande yt ffreinds at London can aunswer R. R.'s way of teachinge, whoe is a man fitt to perfect scollars, rather then to pupill them: butt these thinges I shall leaue to themselues.[19]

Left to themselves, these things did not, apparently, move forward, though Fox continued to be interested in a type of education that would include the study of botany. Early in 1675, we find him in London, recovering from his imprisonment at Worcester and, at his suggestion 'Six Weeks' Meeting considered setting up a school to teach, in addition to languages, the nature of herbs, roots, plants, and trees.'[20] Years later, Lawson describes the scheme to set up what he calls 'a Garden School-house' in a letter that he wrote towards the end of his life to a prospective pupil, John Rodes of Barlborough Hall:

> Now some years ago, George ffox, William Pen, and others were concerned to purchase a piece of land near London for the use of a Garden School-house and a dwelling-house for the Master, in which garden, one or two more of each sorte of our English plants were to be planted, as also many outlandish plants. My purpose was to write a book on these in Latin, so as a boy had the description of these in book-lessons, and their vertues, he might see these growing in the garden, or plantation, to gaine the knowledge of them; but persecutions and troubles obstructed the prosecution thereof, which the Master of Christ's Colledge in Cambridge hearing of, told me was a noble and honourable undertaking, and would fill the Nation with philosophers.[21]

The Master of Christ's College was Ralph Cudworth, the noted Hebrew scholar and author of the neoplatonic work, *The True Intellectual System of the Universe*. As a neoplatonist, Cudworth was sympathetic to the study of the natural world as a means of approach to God. In all nature he saw God's hand operating by means of a vitality which he calls the 'plastic principle' and, like John Ray, he would have agreed that 'a spoyle or smile of grass showed a Deity as much as anything.'[22] At what stage Thomas spoke to Ralph Cudworth we do not know. We do know that he was in Cambridge in 1677,[23] but it is also possible that he visited London in the winter of 1674 and continued on from there to Cambridge. If the Garden School-house had been any sort of a serious proposition, Thomas would have needed to visit London to size up the situation and to meet Richard Richardson and prominent London Quakers who might have been expected to support the venture. There might, too, have been legal business to organise in connection with the impending Exchequer Process whereby Thomas was to be fined for recusancy.

In many ways, it was a pity that the scheme had to be abandoned. Thomas was now approaching 44 years of age: for all of his adult life he had been engaged in the struggle to be a Quaker and to perform what he believed was his best service: teaching the young. Fox's comment on Richard Richardson that he was 'a man fitt to perfect scollars, rather then to pupill them' is, by implication, a great tribute to Thomas. If Thomas' written work appears sometimes to get bogged down in matter, if his expressions sometimes want clarity and his presentation lacks force, no such caveats attended his teaching. The respect in which he was held was derived from his person as much as from his works. In approaching Lawson, one is always left with the feeling that the man was greater than his remains.

In the meantime, Thomas diverted his energies into building up a proficiency in botany. No doubt his friends in Furness who had already helped him by financing him to instruct them in botany, continued to encourage him at what must have been a rather depressing period in his life. Sharing an interest, however, is always rewarding and the Furness area, with its shoreline of sand and marsh, gave him the opportunity to look at plants which were not to be found at Great Strickland. Our evidence for his botanical activities derives from a notebook in which he recorded plants seen on a tour that he was to make in 1677. My own feeling is that this notebook was not started much before that date: it was organised on a county by county basis and was intended, I think, to act as a search list specifically for the tour. When compiling this search list, he worked from the records available to him in contemporary herbals and floras and, in the case of Lancashire and Westmorland, from records of his own. When we look at the lists for these two counties, we find first an alphabetical list of plants with locations followed by a further list that is randomly put down. I argue that the alphabetical list represents those records available to Thomas at the moment of sitting down to compile his notebook (which could be sorted and organised) and the randomly noted plants are those that he found during and post 1677 (which were put down as and when he found them).[24] The question that then remains is what form his records took before he set them out in the notebook of 1677? It is possible that he had an earlier notebook whose records he transferred and which he abandoned.

The first impulse of most people when starting to botanise, however, is to start a collection – something tangible to which to refer. When the botanist is secure in the recognition of species, he becomes content to write them down in a notebook – location then becomes more important than recognition. Today this attitude has been qualified by repeated injunctions to take the book to the flower and not to pick flowers indiscriminately. Lawson would have felt no such restraint and the books that he would have had to take to the flowers might measure 13″ by 8½″ and weigh 11 lbs.[25]

Let us then suppose him collecting for his herbarium. We may imagine him beginning to botanise around his home at Great Strickland at some time prior to 1674, building up that knowledge of plants that was going to lead, in the July of that year, to the invitation to Swarthmoor to instruct Lower and the Fell daughters. There, in the fields about his home he saw Black Bindweed, *Polygonum convolvulus* 'in Great Strickland field', Bird-Cherry, *Prunus padus* in 'Croft Short Close', Winter Cress, *Barbarea vulgaris* and the Small Bistort, *Polygonum viviparum*, which Thomas also knew of from Crosby Ravensworth, a famous locality for this plant.[26] Then there are a few records that come from land that may be identified as Thomas' own: Grass of Parnassus, *Parnassia palustris* grew 'in my Holme' and at Limethwaite bank. Thomas obviously had land down by the River Leith in his holding – 'holms' were the marshy lands close to the river which might, in times of flood, become little islands. They were to be popular plant-hunting grounds, rich in wet-loving plants. On higher ground grew Buckthorn, *Rhamnus catharticus* 'by Sheriff Park' and again, to the North, 'by Waterfall Bridge.' Two other plants found in Thomas' holdings were 'Campanula lactescens', 'in my open Garth' and, an interesting record, the Melancholy Thistle, *Cirsium heterophyllum*, which grew 'at my field house by Backstanbar.' This field and the field house were to feature in Thomas' will, being his own property held in fee simple at the time of his death.[27]

Other locations are within easy walking distance of home. In the neighbouring village of Morland, Pellitory-of-the-wall, *Parietaria diffusa* had gained a footing amongst stonework and at Newby 'on the bank of

Rowland Wilsons' there was a Mallow, which Thomas calls 'Alcea vulgaris', adding doubtfully 'ut suspicor'.[28] In the open country round the villages, Pepperwort, *Lepidium campestre* grew on Lance Moor where there were cornfields and Cat's-foot, *Antennaria dioica* grew at two local stations: 'Newby pasture', and 'nigh Common holm bridge.' On Newby pasture too, grew Bog Asphodel, *Narthecium ossifragum*, whilst Commonholme Bridge was to become a favourite botanising ground for Thomas, producing Shepherd's Cress, *Teesdalia nudicaulis* and Marsh Pennywort, *Hydrocotyle vulgaris* 'a little above Common Holme bridge in the ditch divideing the Common and Medowe.'

Other finds reflect wanderings only a little further afield – an afternoon's outing rather than a walk around the village. A stroll over Commonholme Bridge might take Thomas to Cliburn via the forest of Whinfell, a good gathering ground for Whortleberries and Bilberries, *Vaccinium uliginosum*, *V. myrtillus* and *V. vitis-idaea* and a place for Crowberries, *Empetrum nigrum* and the delicate Maiden Pink, *Dianthus deltoides*. Hedge Mustard, *Sisymbrium officinale* was found behind Cliburn Parsonage and at Lowther and Knotted Pearlwort, *Sagina nodosa* was a plant that Thomas noticed everywhere: round his home at Great Strickland, South on Little Strickland pasture and North on Clifton Moor. Clifton was on the road to Penrith, of course, but Thomas, a Westmerian, was more often in Kendal and his collecting reflects this. The route South took the traveller over Shap, a ground famous amongst seventeenth-century botanists in the days when the exploration of mountain vegetation had scarce begun. Shap was a good deal more accessible than central Lakeland. On a 'scar betwixt Little Strickland and Shap' grew Mossy Saxifrage, *Saxifraga hypnoides* and up on the bleak moorland, Thomas recorded Stag's-horn Clubmoss, *Lycopodium clavatum*. Not far from the road to Kendal – at a place where the present A6 is re-aligned a little to the East of the road that Thomas knew – the bright spikes of Bog Asphodel, *Narthecium ossifragum* gladdened the eye 'on both sides Hause house, very nigh the same'. Ogilby's map of the London to Carlisle road calls this Horse House.[29] The Mountain Sorrel, *Oxyria digyna* was probably found hereabouts, too: Thomas gives no location for it, but inserts it in the Westmorland list and he was later to find it in Longsleddale. A fellow-Quaker, Reginald Harrison lived there and he showed Thomas a plant to which he gives the name 'Gratiola angustifolia.' This is the polynomial for *Lythrum hyssopifolia*. Other claims for the occurence of this plant in Cumbria have been made. In this case, the plant may well have been *Scutellaria minor* as suggested by J. A. Martindale. Martindale points out that Lawson was to use the polynomial again for a plant that he saw on

Clapham Heath, but subsequently crossed out 'Gratiola angustifolia' and replaced it with the polynomial 'Lysimachia galericulata minor', the binomial of which is, indeed, *Scutellaria minor*.[30]

A handful of other plants are listed under Westmorland with no particular location: Procumbent Pearlwort, *Sagina procumbens* must have been a very common sight on the edges of the tracks of that pedestrian age – as common as the Ivy Duckweed, *Lemna trisulca* that greened the trackside ditches. Brookweed, *Samolus valerandi* and Marsh Speedwell, *Veronica scutellata* were plants to which Thomas never gave specific Westmorland locations although he found both in several places elsewhere in England and there is a moss or fern 'adiantum aureum fol. bifidis etc.' which is not identifiable with certainty. To three others recorded in this way: Mountain St. John's Wort, *Hypericum montanum* and Rusty-back Fern *Ceterach officinarum*, and Tower Mustard, *Turritis glabra*, Thomas later added specific locations.

On a trip or trips to Kendal Thomas saw Wood Cranesbill, *Geranium sylvaticum* and Hemlock Water Dropwort, *Oenanthe crocata* and he climbed up on Cunswick Scar to find Ploughman's Spikenard, *Inula conyza*. In the town, he took the opportunity of visiting a couple of keen gardeners: in Thomas Sands' garden he notes white lilac – he himself had a purple – at Dr. Whitaker's he saw Starry Saxifrage, *Saxifraga stellaris* and admired some interesting or striking species brought in from the countryside. There was, for instance, the Royal Fern, *Osmunda regalis* which Thomas had also seen growing by Reginald Harrison's home in Longsleddale and he examined the stem of a Purple Loosestrife, *Lythrum salicaria* and observed that it was six-sided. On Dr. Whitaker's authority, Thomas also accepted Heath Bedstraw, *Galium saxatile* from Kendal Fell and a stachys that should, from the polynomials be *Stachys germanica*.

South of Kendal were other things of interest. Marsh Fleawort, *Senecio palustris* grew 'in Hilderston Mosse by Burton' and at Levens there was James Bellingham's White Cedar, *Thuja occidentalis* to admire and Thomas spent some time distinguishing *Sorbus torminalis* which had been planted in Levens Park near the bridge from the White Beam, *S. aria*, growing conveniently next to it 'called . . . Cumberland Hawthorne.' He noted the distinctive grey pubescence of the undersides of the leaves of the latter and the long leaf petioles on the former. Then swiftly on to Lancaster where he saw Sea Bindweed, *Calystegia soldanella* and southwards still for *Senecio palustris* again in Pilling Moss. Perhaps on the way back his horse cast a shoe and he stopped at the smithy at Carnforth and recorded Soapwort, *Saponaria officinalis* while he waited. A few plants defy attempts to fit them into imagined journeys. The locations are so scattered that the prime object of his going cannot have been botany. He has Black Bryony, *Tamus communis* recorded between Kendal and Levens, and he also has it recorded from Fell End almost 10 miles away. Business took Thomas diverse ways and perhaps sometimes the botanising habit led to his bringing home single plants from locations where he records no others: on Arnside sands he found Glasswort, *Salicornia europaea*, Touch-me-not, *Impatiens noli-tangere* from near Ambleside and at Kirkby Lonsdale, Windermere and Orton, Northern Bedstraw, *Galium boreale*. Not far from Orton too 'between Greenholme and Roundthwaite on the Common' he saw Cat's-foot, *Antennaria dioica*, marking the eastern extent of his botanising as Lancaster had marked the southern. One record that is almost certainly an error is Cornish Moneywort, *Sibthorpia europaea* 'in Brakinthwait well nigh Brokill houses in Orton parish and in springs upon the fair mile in the way to Sedberge.' It was suggested by Martindale that this was 'a lax form of *Chrysosplenium oppositifolium*'[31]

With his herbarium building, Thomas became known as an interested botanist and, in 1674, as we have seen, came by invitation to Swarthmoor. Three records mark the route into Furness: Solomon's Seal, *Polygonatum multiflorum* at Underbarrow, White Beam, *Sorbus aria* at Witherslack and Bog Asphodel, *Narthecium ossifragum*, 'beside Winandmer water' – probably at the southern end of the lake.

In Furness, his records show him making a trip or a series of trips that must have brought back many memories. Perhaps it was deliberate; perhaps at this critical juncture in his life he needed to make something of a pilgrimage, to refresh himself with the memory of those days of Fox's first coming – that remembrance of power and innocency that so sweetly tinctured and strengthened him in hours of temptation. To Rampside, then, he went and botanised along the shore to Walney, the records afterwards tracking North in a circular route past Furness Abbey and up to Dunnerholme Rock on the Duddon estuary.

On the way down the coast to Rampside, he found Fleabane, *Pulicaria dysenterica* at Aldingham and, between Aldingham and Roosebeck, Seakale, *Crambe maritima* which had been reported to him by Joseph Sharp, bailiff of Marsh Grange, one of several friends who were to report unusual plants to Thomas when it became generally known that he was interested in collecting such records. Another, Dan Abraham, who was to become the husband of Rachel Fell, described the Elder, *Sambucus nigra* growing in the hedgerows about Manchester. The record is of interest as suggesting that Daniel Abraham may have been a visitor at Swarthmoor as early as 1677 – Ross rather tentatively dates the first meeting of Daniel and Rachel to 1681.

At Roosebeck, there are several records: Yellow Horned-poppy, *Glaucium flavum*, Sea Milkwort, *Glaux maritima*, and Sea Rocket,

Cakile maritima (which is ticked in the search list) present no problems, but 'Atriplex maritima nostras' is the subject of a short note by Thomas on the variability of the genus – clearly he is having difficulty with it. Martindale suggested that his find was *Atriplex glabriuscula*.[32] 'Crithmum spinosum, pastinaca marina,' on the other hand, is clearly enough *Echinophora spinosa* according to the synonyms, but did Thomas really see this Mediterranean umbellifer which is not recognised as a member of the British flora? There have been other, later, notices of the plant from a handful of stations in Dorset and Kent, but all of these records have had doubt cast upon them and it has been suggested that an error for *Crithmum maritimum* could have been made. E. J. Salisbury, in *Watsonia* finds such a suggestion implausible: 'No one who knew *Crithmum maritimum* could mistake it for the other plant.'[33] Well, Lawson did know *Crithmum maritimum*, whose English name is Samphire: it was quite a table delicacy in his day.[34] Under the polynomial 'Crithmum marinum vulgaris' he enters it directly above his disputed record of *Echinophora spinosa* with the locations Dunnerholme and Harleside Rock. We must, of course, still allow for the fact that he was not yet a completely experienced botanist but, on the other hand, one must at least consider that the Furness shore, with its maritime links, is not an improbable place to find a plant which was probably introduced in ballast and which may have flourished on the Lancashire shore for only a brief period.

From Roosebeck, Thomas trod the road that Fox had walked upon almost a generation ago when he came to Rampside and Thomas was convinced. Lawson marked this later occasion by noting Hedge Mustard, *Sisymbrium officinale*. Walney Island also had associations with Thomas' early life, but at this stage he had not appreciated its richness as a collecting ground and two plants only he records: Sea Aster, *Aster tripolium* and Sea Sandwort, *Honkenya peploides*. Inland from Walney, Furness Abbey receives a mention for a plant notorious on its own account: Deadly Nightshade, *Atropa Bella-donna*, had long been a famed plant of the old Cistercian Abbey and it was incorporated into the Abbey seal:

> It consists of a circle, within the circumference of which is a figure of the Virgin Mary beneath a canopy of three compartments, the centre one filled in with stars, and the other two with sprigs of nightshade . . . Below and supporting the shields are two monks in full dress, with cowls, before each as well as overhead are three sprigs of nightshade.

J. M. Mawson who quoted that explanation of the device on the Abbey seal to the Barrow Naturalists Field Club, pointed out that the members might easily observe the seal 'as the Furness Railway Company have appropriated it, and it is conspicuously painted on all their railway carriages.'[35] The

Furness Railway Company has long gone, but the Nightshade remains, still a feature of Furness Abbey.

Also at the Abbey, grew Pellitory-of-the-Wall, *Parietaria diffusa*, growing on the ancient stone 'on the mannour house and Abbey in Furneis', a monks' remedy for troubles of the bladder and of the stone.

Northwards again went Thomas to Dunnerholme, a locality which he was to explore in more detail when his botanical pupils, Thomas and Mary Lower moved to Marsh Grange in 1676. Now he records only Thrift, *Armeria maritima* (also at Chapel Island) and the record of Samphire, *Crithmum maritimum* which we have already discussed.

As in Westmorland, there are a few plants for which he gives no specific location, merely listing them in the Lancashire search list. Greater Bladderwort, *Utricularia vulgaris* is listed in this way and against Jew's Ear, *Hirneola auricula-judae*, he writes 'At –' and gets no further. Five others have 'Ray' after them, although a Lancashire location is not to be found in Ray's *Catalogus Angliae*: Tutsan, *Hypericum androsaemum*; Common Meadow-rue, *Thalictrum flavum:* Lesser Marshwort, *Apium inundatum;* Smallage, *Apium graveolens* and Water Dropwort, *Oenanthe fistulosa..* Specific locations in the North were later given by Lawson for all these five.

Lastly, there are three records from Durham which complete his own collections as he wrote them down initially in his notebook – one wonders whether these three were remembered from times past. There may have been some special reason to remember Pepperwort, *Lepidium campestre* from near Headlam, Glasswort, *Salicornia europaea* from the seashore at Hartlepool and White Bryony, *Bryonia dioica* along the roadside between Ulnaby and Darlington. All might have been recalled from the days in the 1660s when he travelled in Durham as a missionary.

When Thomas came to write out his records in initiating his botanical notebook, he inserted, in the appropriate alphabetical order, the records of other botanists who had made finds in the various counties. This was to be the body of data on which he hoped to build when on tour. So far as Westmorland and Lancashire were concerned, he had come to know plants in his own neighbourhood around Great Strickland and when the opportunity had arisen, he had looked at a very different flora along the coastline of Furness. In a year or two's time, he was ready for a much more ambitious venture: a tour of England that would combine botany with Quaker business. In ways that were not of his own choosing, the Established Church, in the last 15 years of his life, was going to make a botanist of him.

CHAPTER VII

On Tour: walking to London

THE YEAR 1675 OPENED WITH THOMAS' FUTURE UNCERTAIN and the opposition of state and clergy as fierce as it had ever been. However, early in the year there was good news for northern Quakers. Fox had been freed from his 14 month imprisonment in Worcester and, after a short period in London, was now coming North. In June he came up to Swarthmoor amid scenes of Quaker rejoicing which culminated in the reception of Fox and Margaret Fell at Lancaster. Judge Fell had died in 1658 and Margaret had married Fox 11 years later, in 1669, so this was truly a homecoming for Fox; one of the few occasions when he and Margaret were able to spend any length of time together. At Lancaster, the couple were met by their family and many Friends who formed a large party to cross the Sands with them and see them home to Swarthmoor[1] where Fox was to spend nearly two years writing up his *Journal* for publication and heartening, by his presence, all the Quakers of the North.

During this time, Thomas would, no doubt, return to Swarthmoor to visit him. His school was closed and it would look as though there was a lengthy break in his life at this time. Fox's letter of 1674 suggesting that Thomas and Richard Richardson set up a school together in the London area shows that he was taking an interest in Lawson's future and what could be more natural than that Thomas should spend time with George at Swarthmoor: they had both gone through recent tribulation: both needed to recoup and recover and plan for the future.

All during his sojourn at Swarthmoor from June 1675 until March 1677, Fox laboured to set the records straight for Quakerism, working away at his *Journal*, looking over Friends' letters which were stored at Swarthmoor, making records of Quaker missionaries who had gone out of the North and all the time writing and writing. When Thomas visited him during these months as he was almost bound to do, Fox probably suggested to him that it was time that he too published something for the edification of the movement. It is likely that Thomas already had a body of notes requiring only to be worked up for publication. As a young missionary in Sussex, his first controversy had been with the Baptist, Matthew Caffyn, and, over the years his interest had not diminished and it is very likely that he collected material for the tract that he now proposed to publish: *Baptismalogia, or a Treatise concerning Baptisms: whereto is added a Discourse concerning the Supper, Bread and Wine, Called also Communion.* It is Thomas' longest treatise and differs from his earlier works in that it is not the product of immediate controversy. Gone were the heady days of ding-dong debate, gone the stridency that made every word of the printed page jump off the paper as though it had been shouted from a public platform. *Baptismalogia* was constructed in the study, not forged in the white heat of argument. It was to set the pattern for works to come and it may be that it was Fox's presence in the North that gave Thomas the encouragement to set his notes in order and also, pehaps, to take the manuscript across to Swarthmoor and discuss it with Fox and maybe the rest of the Swarthmoor household as well. It is a heavily historical work, braced and counter-braced by quotation and reference to authority. No-one should accuse him of lack of learning in the preparation of this work. Thomas' faith – the faith shared by all early Quakers – lay in the possibility of return to an ideal primitive state: a time when Christian thought was clear, Christian customs unsullied by the overlay of later usages. From this purity, man had declined:

> Herein also thou mayst see, that after the Primitive Times, The Fall of the Star from Heaven was manifested, Sun and Air (thorow the Smoke of the Bottomless Pit, Maman Wisdom, Heathenish Learning, Spoiling Phylosophy, School Divinity) was darkned, thorow the steaming in of which Christ's Baptism in and with the Spirit came to be lost, then Water-Baptism and Rantism came to be reassumed.[2]

And so Thomas prepared to hit back at old enemies: Baptists, Ranters – anyone who, in his view, had allowed abuses to obscure the real meaning of Christian baptism. These abuses he details: the baptising of people earlier and earlier, as soon as they are capable of it or, most shockingly, even 'Children in the Womb, before they were born.' At the other extreme is the baptism of persons already dead or the baptism of the living for the dead. And if this were not strange enough, people have, in the name of religion, turned to self-abuse: 'some have had the Character of a Cross made in their Fore-heads with a Burning Iron, which was called Christ's Baptism with the Holy Ghost and with Fire'. All these, along with naked Baptism and Baptism every year, Thomas uses as bizarre and outré examples through which to mount an attack on the whole sacrament of baptism. His discourse is divided under four heads, ending with some supplementary observations.

To the whole is added a separate treatise, having its own title-page (though no date, printer or any other indication that it was separately distributed). This was entitled 'A Testimony for the Evangelical Communion, in the Bread of Life, in the Cup of Blessing'. The four heads under which Thomas argues his main thesis are first that the baptism of John the Baptist with water and the baptism of Christ with the spirit were baptisms of two entirely separate and distinct kinds: John's baptism being a prefiguration of Christ's.[3] Second, that Christ's baptism was a once-and-for-all event. When Christ was baptised with the spirit, He was baptised for us all.[4] For ever. Third, that this baptism of Christ in the spirit is the only baptism that should continue in the church until the end of the world.[5] And the fourth and last:

> Rantism, that is Sprinkling of Infants, is a Case unpresidented in the Primitive times, an Irrepetitious Custom, sprung up in the Night of Apostacy, the Falling Away from the Primitive Order.[6]

All these things Thomas would want, if possible, to discuss with Fox for they pertained to matters central to Quaker belief: baptism could do nothing for a man who had not been convinced by the inner truth of Christ but for such a man baptism was simply an irrelevancy, a superstitious custom as vain as whistling in the dark. These tenets Thomas had shaped into a book and, with it, renewed his commitment to Quakerism whilst Fox was yet in the North to give advice and encouragement.

•   •   •

Early in 1677 Fox got ready to resume his travels. His strength was recruited and there was to be no resting in these stern days. It is, perhaps, no coincidence that Thomas Lawson, at about this time, made his own plans for a journey. With his teaching employment gone and life being made increasingly difficult for him, it is possible that Fox had suggested that he might be more usefully employed away from home than he was at Great Strickland. A journey would, moreover, give great scope for Thomas to enlarge his botanical experience: Fox would encourage such a project most wholeheartedly for he was interested in botany and was at one with Thomas in believing in the application of talent to good ends. Ideas took shape: Thomas would take the completed manuscript of *Baptismalogia* down to London, he would do some botanising on the way there and back and he would, as always, travel in the service of truth.

Such were his plans and he set about preparing for the botanical side of his projected tour by starting the notebook. Some records he already had from the Furness area and from around his home. We have seen how he collected these and I have supposed that they were most likely to have existed in the form of herbarium specimens. Now, settling down to compile his notebook for the tour, he arranged them in alphabetical order under the county headings of Lancashire and Westmorland. For the rest of England, he had to rely upon others to provide him with data about what he might hope to see. County by county, he lists plants from all the sources available to him. Such a county-by-county flora may seem ambitious in the extreme but the compilation of county lists had scarcely begun in Thomas' day and it was possible to extract all the available data from a comparatively few sources and to list it in relatively small space. On tour Thomas could look forward to adding to these lists and so extending his knowledge of the distribution of species without necessarily envisaging anything so exhaustive or so impossible of achievement as separate county floras.

The importance of distribution was coming to be recognised and whilst the emphasis tended to be on 'specialities' of each county this, in itself, fostered a county pride that led to an enormous increase in local research. Much of this was, of course, genealogical or antiquarian but natural history was finding its place in county description and many county histories and topographies were to include plant lists. And they were coming into vogue. In this year of 1677, Robert Plot was to publish his *Natural History of Oxfordshire* with the ambitious subtitle *an Essay towards the Natural History of England*. Although much of it related to family history and antiquities, there were observations on the natural world and Plot included plant lists in the manner adopted later in the magnificent 1695 edition of Camden's *Britannia*. The success of the *Oxfordshire* encouraged Plot to produce *The Natural History of Staffordshire* in 1686 and he proposed a 'Natural History of London and Middlesex' which was never published. Other papers, complete and incomplete might be found up and down the country[7] and, when Gibson's edition of Camden was published in 1695, much of this scholarship found a home in it. Thomas' project is put in perspective if we consider that he pre-dates this edition of Camden by almost 20 years and that in it, under the heading 'An Additional account of some more rare plants observ'd to grow in Westmoreland and Cumberland' there are several plants of Lawson's collection and others are to be found under the like heading for Lancashire, Yorkshire and Wiltshire.

Thomas, then, was something of a pioneer as he sat down to extract the necessary data from his sources. John Ray, it is true, had once suggested that such an exercise would be worthwhile, but Thomas was the first to try it. The sources that he used were Thomas Johnson's edition of Gerard's *Herball* (1633 or 1636), John Parkinson's *Theatrum Botanicum* (1640), William How's *Phytologia* (1650), William Coles' *The Art of Simpling* (1656) and *Adam in Eden* (1657), John Ray's *Cambridge Catalogue* (1660), Christopher Merret's *Pinax* (1666 or 1667) and Ray's *Catalogus Angliae* (1670).

The use of the *Catalogus Angliae* fixes the date of of the compilation as no earlier than that year. As it does not seem likely that Thomas would have gone to the considerable trouble of writing out the county lists unless he had his proposed tour in mind, I think we may date it quite close to 1677[8] though some records – those of Chaper VI that I have suggested came from a herbarium – are earlier. If we look at the notebook (see Appendix 2) we find that it is a medley of different things – neat county lists, jumbled plant records, extracts from religious writings, a few notes on curiosities, a few notes of people to visit or addresses to remember. And all in Lawson's space-saving handwriting. It is, though, principally a botanical notebook – the other matter occupying only a few pages. When we come to look at the botanical records – apart from the difficulties in looking over someone else's field notebook – there are also problems of order and arrangement: the first tour notes, for instance, relate to plants around Cambridge, directly under the heading 'In my journey -77' as though Thomas has inserted the heading at a later date to section off that part of the notebook used on tour. Such gross displacements can usually be dealt with by reference to an Itinerary at the very back of the notebook.[9] This is a brief, but extremely useful list of the places that he visited and the distances between them, but only to a certain extent can it be said that it 'clears up the medley and uncertainties of his collecting.'[10] It is difficult, for instance, to explain why, in the midst of plants gathered in London, he has the droseras, *D. intermedia* and *D. rotundifolia* 'in Mosey Mire in Witherslack copiose' and, in the same place, other plants of the North: Marsh Arrow-grass, *Triglochin palustris* 'frequenter by ?Blea Crag bridge which divides Lancashire and Westmorland the Lancashire side of the bridge' adding 'there also is gramen parnassi [*Parnassia palustris*]': Alpine Lady's Mantle, *Alchemilla alpina* 'plentiful in the scar 2 bowshots south of Black Crag belonging to Bannisdale Head in Westmorland': Flea-sedge, *Carex pulicaris* in the same vicinity: All-seed, *Radiola linoides* 'on Clifton moor in Westmorland' and Cloudberry, *Rubus chamaemorus* 'between Bannisdale head and Water Sleadale.' Concluding the list is *Ornithopus perpusillus* from an unidentified location 'on Sandforth Moor, nigh the Thorn.'

Apart from the gross displacements, there are a few other minor anomalies that interrupt the consistency of what, otherwise, seems to be day-to-day recording. The most plausible reconstruction would seem that Thomas collected his specimens in the field and wrote them up each evening: a pen with an ink horn would be an awkward thing to manage out-of-doors and the handwriting shows a uniformity rarely achieved when note-taking in the field. If we assume that he gathered specimens from which to write up his notes, then minor displacements of records become explicable by supposing that he was not immediately able to identify everything that he gathered: it might be a day or two before he was able to consult someone who was capable of identifying them for him or to look them up in an illustrated work of reference. The *Catalogus Angliae* had no cuts and the illustrated works of the day were all large folios, impossibly heavy to carry around the country, even supposing that Thomas possessed a Gerard or a Parkinson. It is, indeed, difficult to imagine of what Thomas' library consisted. A letter to Ray, written 11 years later, would seem to suggest that he had both Gerard and Parkinson, but it may only mean that he had access to these fine volumes in the library of some nearby gentleman. He is referring to the difficulty of identifying two species of orchid separated by Parkinson:

> I have consulted Park. and Ger. Emac., and see no reason to distinguish them. Pray consult Park. and Lobel. Lobel I have not.[11]

Even in 1677, it was a long time since he had been too poor to buy himself a Hebrew lexicon, but his way of life since then and his growing family responsibilities make it unlikely that he was a man of great resources. The only three books that we know for certain that he owned were the Hebrew lexicon (mentioned in his will), a copy of Camden's *Britannia* (also in the will) and his *Catalogus Angliae* which later became the property of his daughter.

In the spring of that year, 1677, he was on his way, his notebook, perhaps, in one pocket and his copy of the *Catalogus Angliae* in another. Down through Longsleddale he went, noting Bog Pimpernel, *Anagallis tenella* 'at the foot of Sledale some 4 miles from Kendal' and Alpine Lady's Mantle, *Alchemilla alpina* 'on a rock towards the foot of Sledal, copiose.' A mile or two further on and he saw Greater Broomrape, *Orobanche rapum-genistae* 'in Broom Closes by Skelsmoor hall, or Dodding green, copoise.' Then he was in Kendal and in holiday mood, keen to go visiting gardens. He called again on Dr. Whitaker, noting the Starry Saxifrage, *Saxifragra stellaris* once more and adding Alexanders, *Smyrnium olusatrum* and 'Anthora, The wholesome helmet flower or Counterpoison Monkshood.' Some of these entries are duplicated, appearing out of alphabetical order at the end of the search list for Westmorland and the same has happened with Lancashire plants as though, in these first two counties to be visited at the beginning of his tour, Thomas had tried to keep his county lists and his tour notes running in parallel. Later he seems to have found this system of double entry too laborious and though he continued to use his prepared lists to tick off plants seen and occasionally made a jotting at the end of the county list, most of his finds are listed only in the long running notes of his tour. The Monkshood in Dr. Whitaker's garden reminded Thomas of his own and when he transferred it into the Westmorland list, he wrote down above it 'Napellus verus *flore* caeruleo, Blew Helmet flowre, or Monkshood, in horto meo.'

The contents of Dr. Whitaker's garden suggest that he treated his patients from herbs within it, not relying entirely upon the apothecary's shop. That Thomas noticed these may be another small indication that he took an interest in the virtues of herbs but he had an eye, too, for the purely ornamental and his fancy was much taken by the 'Campanula persicifolia, peachleafed Bell flower' that grew 'In George Walkers and Thomas Warriners garden in Kendale copiose.' When he came to transcribe the plant at the bottom of the Westmorland list, he added 'There roots may be had. See Parkinson paradisi' a reminder to look up the horticultural notes that Parkinson gives in his gardening book, *Paradisi in sole, paradisus terrestris* (1620). His advice is that it 'requireth . . . to be planted in some shadowie place' being susceptible to drought. With regard to another plant 'Pyrancantha, The ever green hawthorne, or prickly Corall Tree' which grew in Thomas Sands' garden in Kendal, Lawson's curiosity impelled the note 'See if it be not the same that grows in Mount Sorrill.'

These gardens were chiefly the object of Thomas' attention in Kendal – Herb Robert, *Geranium robertianum*, growing abundantly on a wall caught his eye but he was not very serious about botanising around old familiar Kendal. When the time came to leave the town, he made a short day of it, walking down to Fell End, right underneath the southern neb of Whitbarrow Scar where Ivy, *Hedera helix*, covered the rocks. A few records from Witherslack mark this stop: English Stonecrop, *Sedum anglicum*, Royal Fern, *Osmunda regalis* and Water Betony, *Scrophularia aquatica*.

The following day he saw a plant that puzzled him:

All along the way between Newton and Penny bridge grows a small plant From a small woody fibrous root arises a very small stalk or stalks about halfe a span high full of joynts at each joynt [very narrow, deleted] leaves after the manner of St. John wort but very narrow and every way lesse than those of St. John wort at the top stand flores lutie pentapetali mucronati   hypercei.

Thomas wondered whether the plant was *Hypericum pulchrum*, but he was not happy about the idea and his alternative, *Hypericum humifusum* was the correct identification.

Beyond Penny Bridge, the white stars of the English Stonecrop, *Sedum anglicum* kept him company all the way to Ulverston. Journey's end for this day lay at Swarthmoor, just beyond, and there is only one more record: White Climbing Furmitory, *Corydalis claviculata* at Dragley Beck.

At Swarthmoor he would have had business to transact. He was, after all, about to embark on a major tour and, prior to his departure, there is likely to have been much consultation. A fern which may have been *Thuidium tamariscinum* engaged his attention but, with this exception, botany was laid aside for a while and only resumed when he moved on to Marsh Grange, a house on the Duddon estuary which had been part of Margaret Fell's marriage portion when she married the Judge. For some time, it had been the home of George Fell, Margaret's only son, who had died in the house in 1670. The property had then been acquired by Sarah Fell, from whom Thomas Lower had bought it in 1676.[12] It is thus very probable that this was Lawson's first visit to his former botany pupils in their new home. No doubt they were keen to show him how much they had profitted from his instruction of three summers back and several forays were made into the marshy and maritime habitats of the immediate neighbourhood. Marsh Grange was a happy place for wet-loving plants and Thomas was able to record Pennywort, *Hydrocotyle vulgaris*, Bogbean, *Menyanthes trifoliata*, Apple-scented Mint, *Mentha rotundifolia*, Bog Myrtle, *Myrica gale* and the Great Water Dock, *Rumex hydrolapathum*. Seeing Purple Loosestrife, *Lythrum salicaria*, he was reminded that he had seen it in Dr. Whitaker's garden in Kendal and he observes the two stages, one with hexagonal and the other with quadrangular stems. A plant that he had recorded from Witherslack, the Royal Fern, *Osmunda regalis*, grew within the grounds of Marsh Grange itself – common enough in Lawson's day, its majestic fronds had begun to attract gardeners.

Within a short walk was Dunnerholme, a rocky knob of raised ground, a thumb of land poking out into the Duddon estuary from the largely flat and marshy coastal strip. Walking out there, Thomas noticed the English Stonecrop, *Sedum anglicum* which he remembered both from Witherslack and the road between Ulverston and Penny Bridge. On the promontary itself were Kidney-vetch, *Anthyllis vulneraria* and Bladder Campion, *Silene vulgaris*. Common Rockrose, *Helianthemum chamaecistus* grew there 'copiose' and, most glorious of all, Bloody Cranesbill, *Geranium sanguineum* flourished in absolute profusion ('copiosissime'). To round off his examination of Dunnerholme, Thomas turned his back on all this colour and poked about amongst the seaweed, noting two that are not now possible to identify: 'Muscus marinus albidus' and 'Muscus marinus rubius pennatus.' To this visit to Furness, too, we must date the record of Sea

Lavender, *Limonium vulgare*, found at Chapel Island.

These brief excursions were all that there was time for and, once he had left behind the hospitality of his Furness friends, Thomas was truly on his travels. He missed out Kendal on the return out of Furness, cutting South of the town and finding Fly Orchid, *Ophrys insectifera* 'on the right hand under the wall in the lane as one goes from home park house up to the yeat [gate] that opens to Home Crag [near Burton], about a stone cast short of the yeat,' a good find with its location carefully noted. From there, he continued eastwards, walking through Gunnerthwaite where he found a white-flowered Lousewort, *Pedicularis sylvatica* as well as white forms of Marsh Thistle, *Cirsium palustre* and Self Heal, *Prunella vulgaris*. These last two, together with Royal Fern, *Osmunda regalis* and All-seed, *Radiola linoides* are also among those entered in his notebook at a much later date, being found among his London plants.

From Gunnerthwaite, Thomas made towards his old home at Lawkland. He stayed at Eldroth, a bare mile away, pleased no doubt, at having found Lady's Slipper, *Cypripedium calceolus* as he passed through Ingleton, a famous location for this very rare plant and one known to Parkinson. In the late eighteenth century the orchid disappeared, from this locality, dug up for sale by an Ingleton gardener.

From Eldroth, it was a long haul to Manchester: 'To Sawley 8' writes Thomas – a slip, I suppose, for 18. Then 26 miles to Manchester. At Sawley Abbey, the finding of Water Betony, *Scrophularia aquatica* reminded Thomas that he has seen it before – at Witherslack – and he noted too Wild Carrot, *Daucus carota*.

There was to be no time to botanise on the long trek to Manchester, but it was broken by a call at Whalley Abbey, the home of Sir Ralph Ashton. The Ashtons had always been zealous Puritans and Sir Ralph was implacable in proceedings against Quakers who refused to pay their tithes. Several entries in the Lancaster Quarterly Meeting Sufferings show Sir Ralph sending in his bailiffs to take by force what his Quaker tenants denied him as of right. It is possible that Thomas' visit was a diplomatic mission: since he was an outsider, local Quakers may have hoped that he would receive a less prejudiced hearing from Sir Ralph. Perhaps, too, they felt that his stature was such as to carry weight with the proud Ashtons. If so, Thomas' style of persuasion must have changed since the hectic days of Sussex and his youth – 'Sir' Ralph gets his proper title in the notebook from a man who, long ago, had attacked Magnus Byne for allowing men to call him 'Master.' It seems to have been a gentlemanly meeting altogether for Sir Ralph appears to have entertained Thomas – in the garden Thomas saw Lamb's Lettuce, *Valerianella locusta*, perhaps even ate it at lunch since it is the only herb that he bothers to record. One other curiosity alone attracted him: the notebook records 'there we saw a Sword Fish.'[13] More than half a century ago the Ashtons and Whalley Abbey had been involved in the dramatic and tragic fate of the Lancashire witches: in the first magical days of the movement, the Quakers themselves had sometimes been accused of witchcraft. Now, in 1677, they might hope for a fair hearing though political circumstance might have changed the accusation of witchcraft to one of sedition. Thomas says 'we' saw a sword fish – were 'we' a deputation waiting upon Sir Ralph? There is no other indication that Thomas was travelling in company nor any suggestion as to who his travelling companion might have been. We do not even know whether he was horsed or on foot, although the distances covered are strongly suggestive of the latter. The longest distance that he logs is the 26 miles to Manchester which, though a goodly step, was well within the capacity of an active pedestrian of the time: we remember that, a century or so later, Sir Walter Scott had Jeanie Deans walk from Edinburgh to London at the good round pace of 'five-and-twenty miles and a bittock' per day. And perhaps, like Jeanie, Thomas would have been able to say:

> And I didna just a' thegither walk the haill way neither, for I had whiles the cast of a cart; and I had the cast of a horse from Ferrybridge, and divers other easements.[14]

In general, moreover, Thomas' daily distances were under 20 miles and sometimes under 10 with, we must assume, days of botanising, missionary work or just plain resting in between.

As he went into and out of Manchester, Thomas recorded a couple of plants. North, there was White Climbing Fumitory, *Corydalis claviculata* 'at Berry [Bury] nigh Manchester' and when he passed out to the South of the town he took the road to Stockport or, as he calls it Stopford, and notices the Sour Cherry, *Prunus cerasus* 'Plentiful in the way between Manchester and Stopford.' Then he adds: 'Plentiful in Worcestershire and Gloucestershire. Merry tree at Berry or Bury in Lancashire.' The plant also earns an entry in the Cheshire search list where it is preceded by a record of *Gentiana pneumonanthe* on Rud Heath in Cheshire a little South of Knutsford and, on the face of it, several miles off Thomas' direct route. In the tour notes, apparently written up much later and included amongst London records, there is an expanded note:

> On Rudheath in Cheshire grows a Gentianella with very small leaves 2 set directly opposite tis undoubtedly pneumonanthe (1) Calathian violet.

From Manchester, he moved on into the Peak District, making for Castleton where, like any other tourist, he found time to view the sights:

'From Manchester to Castleton in the Peake land is 18 miles, here is the place called Devils Arse and the rocks called Mamtor and within a mile or two is Eldon hole.'[15] These were well-known tourist attractions, featuring in Camden who reckoned the great cavern of Devil's Arse 'among the Prodigies of England.'[16] and Thomas may, like Ralph Thoresby, the Leeds antiquarian who visited Castleton four years later, have taken a guided tour of the cavern:

> Of a marvellous capacity is the mouth of this Cave, wherein are five cottages, whence, furnished with candles, we descended lower and lower, till we were forced to creep upon our hands and feet till we came at another large place, called the Belfrey; then lower again to a water, which was then so high that it almost touched the lowering rock, that we could not possibly get farther, else, beyond this, they say is a narrower and then more spacious place, to a second water; and after a third interval a third river, which, *ut vulgo traditur*, never any passed and returned again.[17]

An eerie place indeed, lit only by the lights of flickering candles, and no less marvellous was Mam Torr, a hill from which as Thoresby describes it 'incredible heaps of sandy earth'[18] were perpetually falling without the hill being in any way diminished.

These natural curiosities probably occupied a good deal of Thomas' attention but he found time to view the pretty Mountain Pansy, *Viola lutea*, in flower near Eldon Hole, for the appropriate entry taken from Merret: 'Jacea, sive herba Trinitatis elegantissima flore lutea amplissimo, pansie with a most ample yellow flower, near Elden hole, and Buxton, Mer' is marked with a cross in his search list and his running notes of the tour mark it down as found 'copiose' near Eldon Hole where he also observed 'hoary wild time' *Thymus drucei*. And Buxton held other attractions. At the end of his search list for Derbyshire, Thomas jots down: 'Here is Buxton well, wholesome for stomach, sinews, and the whole body, frequented by the Nobility, Camb.'[19] There was a brisk seventeenth-century tourist trade there too where visitors were crowded into low wooden sheds, and regaled with oatcake and with a viand which the hosts called mutton, but which the guests strongly suspected to be dog.

Leaving these dubious pleasures behind him, Thomas travelled on southward in a direct line, covering the ground in even stages from Castleton to Leek (20 miles), to Stafford (16 miles), to Stourbridge (18 miles) and to Worcester (15 miles). Either he was keen to put the miles behind him on this stage of his journey, or his visits to Leek, Stafford and Stourbridge were in connection with missionary work of which we know nothing, for he records little of botanical interest over these 69 miles of his journey, though he did notice Milk-vetch, *Astragalus glycyphyllos* 'nigh Stafford at the town end' and a plant which he calls 'trifolium echinatum' having 'little long small narrow leaves at Stourbridge in Worcester by an iron forge.' Two other plants from Staffordshire do exercise a good deal of his attention. In a sandy lane between Leek and Leekbrook he sees a plant growing in profusion which he is unable to identify but which Charles Raven identified from the description as Birdsfoot *Ornithopus perpusillus*:

> From a white small fibrous root arises several stalks about halfe a foot high, with little hoary winged Leaves on diverse foot stalks grow tripetalous very small flowers, 2 whereof standing opposite are white or whitish, the single one, is purplish mixt white and red after which succeeds small crooked Cods resembling a birds claw [deletion   ] Ornithopodium.

A second paragraph of description relates to another plant at Saltheath, shown on Ogilby's map of the London to Holyhead road as about three miles North-easterly from Stafford:

> To a small fibrous root springs up a stalk or stalks which seldome stands erect, but creeps on the ground with little roundish winged leaves from the bosome of the leaves grow on small foot stalks pentapetalous flowers of colour mixt betwixt white and red, this short plant so trails in the grasse, that seldome any thing appears but the flowers sometyme one for the most part severall or many.

After this, Thomas writes 'See if it be not nummularia minor' – i.e. *Anagallis tenella*: from the description the most likely candidate. Then he adds another location: 'this plant is also plentifull at Stonyford or Stainby brook in the way as one goes from Sommerford to Wolverhampton, Staffordshire.'

Puzzling over this plant seems to have absorbed most of his botanical attention between Buxton and Worcester but at Worcester there was fresh interest in the gardens there and in the immediate surroundings of the town. The Yellow-wort, *Blackstonia perfoliata* attracted his attention and as he approached the town, the fields were blue with Cornflowers, *Centaurea cyanus* while on its outskirts he saw and recorded Moth Mullein, *Verbascum blattaria*. Worcester may have been a place where he stayed a day or two: he had time to stroll around the town and look into a few gardens, seeing red and purple cultivated varieties of *Centaurea* and two plants which he calls Shrub Mallow and Vipers grass. There was also a garden having in it Spanish Broom. In another, that of a man called Edward Burns, the Great Plantain, *Plantago major* had been brought into cultivation. Perhaps Burns tolerated it – may even have encouraged it – for its long-standing reputation as a medicinal herb. Or perhaps what he had in his garden were abnormal forms: Plantain has a tendancy to run to these abnormalities which were held in high regard by herbalists and garden-lovers of the time. The garden catalogue of the herbalist, John Gerard, tells us that he cherished two: 'Plantago rosea' and 'Plantago rosea incana'.[20] These were forms which resembled double green roses and were highly prized.

When the time came to leave town, Thomas was in a mood to observe and record and he botanised his way down to Tewkesbury and on to Gloucester. Traveller's Joy, *Clematis vitalba* gladdened his eye as he passed by the hedgerows of the Severn Valley and he distinguished the two bindweeds, *Calystegia sepium* and *Convolvulus arvensis* climbing vigorously over the hedges on the road between Worcester and Tewkesbury. At Ripple, just North of Tewkesbury, he records Chicory, *Cichorium intybus* and beyond, the Flowering Rush, *Butomus umbellatus* gave him a display from the ditches – perhaps in the same place as he found Arrow-head, *Sagittaria sagittifolia* which he added to his Gloucestershire search list. The last plant that he records on this section of road before entering Gloucester, was the wayside weed, Swine-cress, *Coronopus squamatus*.

Quakers in the town of Gloucester were, in 1677, suffering from the excessive zeal of Justice John Meredith who signalised himself in this year by beating two Quakers unmercifully 'with his own Hands'[21] and in one incident seizing another Quaker, John Selcock, by the hair and dragging him from French-hay meeting house into the yard, where he drew his knife 'and said he would mark him'. On this occasion, he was restrained by one of his own servants, although it was a brave man who interfered with Meredith's notions of justice – John Fryer and Joseph Glover, two of his officers, received a beating from the fiery magistrate 'because they would not abuse people so much as he would have them.' Nor was Meredith responsible for all the brutality in Gloucester – Besse has a long, sad list of Quakers who were punched, thrown against walls and over gates, dragged through the dirt of the streets: one trundled round in a wheelbarrow whilst being drenched with water, others having their flesh bruised, their ears nipped, their heads beaten against posts and their persons generally abused in what amounted to a year of legalised terrorism. One informer was heard to say that it was no more sin to kill one of the Quakers than to kill a dog, and certainly the justices do not seem to have discouraged the view that anyone who killed a Quaker would not be hanged for it.[22] So there were plenty of horror stories for Thomas to listen to. But there were plants and flowers too: the pea flowers of the Restharrow, *Ononis spinosa* were blooming to vex the hearts of Gloucestershire farmers and there was Yellow-wort, *Blackstonia perfoliata* to be seen again 'in many places' and Creeping Jenny, *Lysimachia nummularia*, whose cheerful face met Thomas' many a time.

Beyond Gloucester, the road to Nailsworth yielded more plants that were novel to Thomas' northern eyes: *Trifolium scabrum* is a possibility for a plant he saw, 'by a dry ditch in a Corn-field by Eastington' the same that he had seen by the iron forge at Stourbridge and called 'trifolium echinatum.' At Buckall Hill there was Viper's Bugloss, *Echium vulgare* and some fine Beeches, *Fagus sylvatica*: the very name of the hill is suggestive of Beeches for 'bucks' was a name used for Beeches and it was said that the county of Buckinghamshire owed its name to its reputation for growing quantities of Beeches; indeed, they were tithe-free, other timber being scarce in the county.[23] In Cumbria, though, they were less common and Thomas was later to have a Beech tree in his garden that he was proud to point out to visitors.

Beyond Nailsworth, where Thomas stayed – perhaps just overnight – the botanical riches of the Avon Gorge called to him and he covered the 20 miles between Nailsworth and Bristol in one day.

The floristic treasures of the gorge had long been known to botanists: its crowded ledges had drawn William Turner and Matthew de L'Obel, John Goodyer and Thomas Johnson and its fame had been perpetuated in their writings.[24] Thomas' footsteps must have quickened and his heart been light with an anticipation of good things that no remembrance of Nayler's folly of 20 years ago could dispel. Bristol had been a peaceful place for the Quakers in the past five years[25] and today Thomas' mind was running on botany: he could see Pennywort, *Umbilicus rupestris* established on the old walls of the villages that he passed on his route: Thornbury, Olveston, Tockington, and again on the walls of Bristol. As he proceeded, he could see in the hedges the Hedge-parsleys, *Torilis japonica* and *T. nodosa* and we must imagine that he paused and spent a little while getting the differences between these two similar umbellifers clear in his mind before he pressed on down the lanes where the heady scent of Honeysuckle, *Lonicera periclymenum* was the smell of the ripening summer.

Such sights sweetened the last miles between Olverton and Bristol. Ringing in his head were the names of the rarities that he must look for at Bristol: 'Peucedanum minus' (*Trinia glauca*), found as early as 1562 by William Turner, 'Veronica spicata recta minor' (*Veronica spicata* ssp *hybrida*) which had been the discovery of Thomas Johnson and all the other exciting plants that the writings of Ray had made known to him[26] and which he must have longed to see with his own eyes.

The first place to visit was obviously the gorge and the most famed spot for botanists was St. Vincent's Rocks, just a little downstream from the present Clifton Suspension Bridge on the North bank of the river. Thither Thomas hurried, pausing only to note Bristly Ox-Tongue, *Picris echioides*,

on the way. At the Rocks, he saw the Honewort, *Trinia glauca* for himself
'one of the choicest indigenous plants in the country; and of great local
interest on account of its historical associations'[27] says J. W. White in his
Bristol flora with justifiable pride. William Turner had discovered it,
Gerard mentioned that the Bristol people found the root good to eat,
Thomas Johnson's steps were drawn to Bristol by it and the other Vincent's
Rocks attractions when he made his tour around Britain that provided the
material for his *Mercurius Botanicus*, 1634 and, 90 years after Lawson, Sir
Joseph Banks was to take an evening stroll to see it 'in full bloom plentifull,
just above the Rock house.'[28]

The rest of Thomas' finds at the rock are, generally speaking,
unremarkable: the Wayfaring Tree, *Viburnum lantana* was in flower, its
creamy-white sprays 'About Vincent's Rocks and all over in the hedges' and
other Rocks plants were Dogwood, *Thelycrania sanguinea*, Wild Basil,
Clinopodium vulgare, Wood Spurge, *Euphorbia amygdaloides*, Hedge
Bedstraw, *Galium mullugo*, Mountain St. John's Wort, *Hypericum
montanum* and Black Spleenwort, *Asplenium adiantum-nigrum*. Hunting
around a bit, Thomas then found Field Madder, *Sherardia arvensis* 'on the
rock foot opposite to Vincent's Rock' and, in the same place, Blue
Fleabane, *Erigeron acer* and Hemp Agrimony, *Eupatorium cannabinum*,
whilst two casuals found lodgement in the broken ground: Weasel's Snout,
Antirrhinum orontium and the Hemp-nettle, *Galeopsis angustifolia*. Lastly,
there must have been a foray over the other side of the river for Thyme-
leaved Sandwort, *Arenaria serpyllifolia* is recorded 'over the water against
Vincent's hill' and Rusty-back Fern, *Ceterach officinarum* – a plant
remarked upon for its abundance by many of the botanists who visited
Bristol, is noticed by Thomas 'from Vincent's rock and on the rock over the
water.' One other most interesting record of a previous botanist – Thomas
Johnson's of Spiked Speedwell, *Veronica spicata* (ssp. *hybrida*) is not given
specifically from St. Vincent's Rocks but Lawson appears to have no
difficulty in finding it, for he notes it down as occuring 'at or about Bristol.'

One of Bristol's charms for a man who was always drawn to marshy and
maritime habitats was the tidal Avon. Thomas spent at least as much time
'by the water side at Bristol' as he had at the famed St. Vincent's Rocks.
Bristol was the second largest seaport in the kingdom and Thomas, hunting
along the waterline and in the ditches might raise his eyes from time to time
to one of the ships that, perhaps even then, was carrying away some of the
10,000 emigrants who passed through Bristol between 1654 and 1685,
sailing for a new life in America.[29] Thomas might well have wondered if he
should join them and take his family away from England but there was as yet
no freedom for Quakers on either side of the Atlantic and Thomas turned

his attention back to the plants that grew along the water's edge of this western shore of the old world. Sea Aster, *Aster tripolium*, he knew already from Furness but now he records for the first time Sea Beet, *Beta vulgaris*, the Sea Plantain, *Plantago maritima* with its narrow unbranched leaves and the smaller, Buckshorn Plantain, *Plantago coronopus*, whose branched leaves might just remind the fanciful observer of the antlers of a red stag. There were also two Goosefoots to tell apart: Red Goosefoot, *Chenopodium rubrum* and another which Thomas called 'Atriplex sylvestris latifolia seu Pes Anserinus' which grew at Bristol in quantity. Other maritime plants that grew in plenty were Wild Celery, *Apium graveolens*, Sea Purslane, *Halimione portulacoides*, Sea Wormwood, *Artemisia maritima*, Lesser Sea-spurrey, *Spergularia media* and a plant that Thomas calls 'Gramen palustre spicatum, Salt Marsh Spiked grasse,' *Triglochin maritima* 'in a meadow betwixt Bristol and Vincents Rock' where, too, he saw Strawberry Clover, *Trifolium fragiferum*.

Five last records complete his list of Bristol plants: Crow Garlic, *Allium vineale* and Swine-cress, *Coronopus squamatus* were both found 'copiose' and, 'at Red Cliff by Bristol', Thomas records Sea Buckthorn, *Hippophaë rhamnoides*, Elder, *Sambucus nigra* and Spotted Medick, *Medicago arabica*, a plant that he had first noticed growing in a garden on the way into Bristol. It was a plant that he was to record again and again: perhaps the story of the dark spots on the leaves which were said to be drops of Christ's blood fallen from the cross, gave it a special place in Thomas' heart, perhaps the blood spots seemed to him peculiarly appropriate to a plant growing on Red Cliff Hill, Bristol's place of execution: in just eight years, Judge Jefferies was to visit Bristol on the notorious assizes that followed Monmouth's 1685 rebellion and six people were hanged on Red Cliff Hill.

From Bristol, Thomas travelled on up the Avon to Bath and jottings at the end of his search list for Somerset give a clue to his interests: 'In this County is Glastonbury' – though he did not visit it, for it was a long way out of his way. But 'Cainsham' or Keynsham was on his route and he may have searched there for 'ophiomer phitis, Snakestones'[30] which he had jotted down from Merret. Keynsham's ammonites feature in Camden, too, though later editions adopt a superior tone to those who, through 'overcredulous temper' believed serpents to have been changed into stones 'because they found in the quarries thereabouts, some such little sporting miracles of Nature.' Alas, the notion that Nature herself had, in playful mood, sculpted these fossils in the bowels of the earth proved a scientific theory as unacceptable as the snakestone theory and still later editions come nearest the truth in having the fossils formed in the shells of nautili.[31]

Lastly there was Bath, with its chief attraction the hot baths, enjoying the seventeenth century boom in the popularity of medicinal waters.

After Bath, Thomas records little until he reaches Oxford. Before he got there, his itinerary notes record that he made a long deviation southwards to reach, at Amesbury, not far from Salisbury plain, the southernmost point of his tour. In his search list for Wiltshire, he makes a note taken out of Camden of its most conspicuous monument:

> In this County is the Stonehenge reared up by Ambrosius Aurelius in memoriall of the Brittains slaine by the Saxons at a parley. Camb.[32]

Undoubtedly he visited it, for he records from 'in or nigh Salisbury plain copiose' Hare's-ear, *Bupleurum rotundifolium* and a plant note below the Camden note gives us 'Eruca Nasturtio cognata tenuifolia' – ?*Eruca sativa* – 'on Salisbury plaine' a location which was expanded to 'on Salisbury-plain not far from Stonehenge' when John Ray accepted it for inclusion in *Synopsis*,[33] ascribing it to Lawson as a unique find.

From Stonehenge, Thomas turned North again and two days travel via Shefford brought him to Oxford and its gardens under the superintendance of Jacob Bobart the elder. Like Bristol, it was a place that no serious botanist would want to miss. Designed as a demonstration garden, it was the first of its kind in England, having been founded in 1621 on a site down by the Cherwell raised with '4000 load of mucke and dunge laid by H. Windiat ye Universitie scavenger.'[34] On this good foundation, the garden prospered and now, in 1677, it was in an extremely flourishing state having been under the care of Jacob Bobart the elder for over 30 years:

> ye man yt first gave life & beauty to this famous place, who by his care & industry replenish'd the walls, wth all manner of good fruits our clime would ripen, & bedeck the earth wth great variety of trees plants & exotick flowers, dayly augmented by the Botanists, who bring them hither from ye remote Quarters of ye world.[35]

Bobart was now an old man, nearing or into his 80s and it was something of a historic event for Thomas to see the gardens while they were yet under his superintendance. In a little over two years he would be dead and his stewardship would have passed to his son, Jacob the younger, of whom Baskerville says disparagingly that he was but a shrimp compared with his father.[36] Certainly, though the gardens continued to flourish, the younger man lacked the weight and presence that had made his father's name a legend amongst gardeners. The portrait of the elder Bobart shows a man with long luxuriant hair, a great beard falling over his chest and squared at the bottom, bushy eyebrows and the fierce look of an old testament prophet. The beard, it seems, had its uses: Bobart, born in Brunswick, was not without a certain Germanic freakishness and Baskerville tells the story of how, one Whitsuntide, he had a fancy to tag the beard with silver 'which drew much Company in the Phisick-Garden.'[37] Thomas may have turned to lesser men to have his detailed queries about the plants of the botanic garden answered for there is an entry in his notebook 'Rob. Wells servant or undergardiner to Jacob Bobart.'[38]

Queries there would certainly have been, for the garden was a rich storehouse of plants that Thomas had never seen before. Loggan's plan of the Oxford Garden, dated 1675, shows us the formal layout – the straight paths and geometrical beds of a garden of the time. Thomas gives us some account of what was in those beds – a couple of hundred plants, listed in nine pages: mostly exotics but with a few interesting natives scattered amongst them. Often the writing is larger than Thomas' normal hand as if the entries were put down in haste, frequently the names are abbreviated to one or two elements as though Thomas was feasting his eyes and trying to write at the same time. And when Bobart or one of his minions had showed Thomas round the gardens, there would be opportunity to make the acquaintance of Oxford's Professor of Botany, Robert Morison. There is a note that Morison showed Thomas a species of spurge from Crete which was, apparently, flourishing spontaneously in the gardens.[39] Morison had been working for some years on a History of Plants and Lawson also makes a note of 'Morrison's Herball in Folio'[40] as though he had seen sheets of this work, the *Plantarum historiae universalis oxoniensis pars secunda* (the first part, which was to have dealt with trees and shrubs, was never printed). The work was published by the Oxford Press in 1680 and this contact with Morison was to lead to correspondence – when the *Historia* was published a few records of Lawson's were to appear in it and more appeared in the pars tertia of 1699 for which Bobart the younger was largely responsible.[41] A third note: 'Morisons hortus regius blesensis or his Praeludia. At the Rose and Crown in Duck lane'[42] refers to Morison's first published work, the *Praeludia botanica*, 1669, the first part of which bore the title 'Hortus regius blesensis auctus' and consisted of an alphabetical list of the plants in the Royal garden at Blois.[43] Thomas Lawson, excited by all the exotics that he had seen in the Oxford garden was after a reference work to guide him through the new species that were being introduced into England.

Viewing the gardens at Oxford and conversing with their keepers seems to have taken up most of Thomas' time in the city for his recording of plants that occur naturally in Oxford and environs is scant. The Pondweeds, *Potamogeton perfoliatus* and *Groenlandia densa* caught his eye 'in the ditch of Christ Church Meadow,' along with Skull-cap, *Scutellaria galericulata* and Flowering Rush, *Butomus umbellatus*, Frog-bit, *Hydrocharis morsus-ranae* and a plant Thomas identified as *Ranunculus circinatus* but later determined was the Horn-wort, *Ceratophyllum demersum*. A few other plants: Milk-vetch, *Astragalus glycyphyllos*, Birdsfoot, *Ornithopus perpusillus*, Hard-fern, *Blechnum spicant* and Bastard Toadflax, *Thesium humifusum* are recorded 'nigh Oxford.' The search list also received some attention in this county. Coles' record of Greater Bladderwort, *Utricularia vulgaris*, Lesser Butterfly Orchid, *Platanthera bifolia* and a specis of *Chara* 'in Stow wood by the Road that leads to Islip' have crosses against them as have several of Merret's: Water Violet, *Hottonia palustris*, Bladder Campion, *Silene vulgaris*, Wild Thyme, *Thymus drucei*, Frog Orchid, *Coeloglossum viride*, Bee Orchid, *Ophrys apifera* (originally a Coles record), the two sedges, *Carex pulicaris* and *C. dioica* and at Battle (?Botley) *Anagallis arvensis* ssp. *foemina*. Merret had also recorded Ivy Campanula, *Wahlenbergia hederacea* from Bagley Wood just a little to the South-west of Oxford and Thomas made a short excursion into the wood, possibly on a trip that he made down through Abingdon to Elnbery in Berkshire. Leaving Oxford, he recorded the White Poplar, *Populus alba* about two miles out of town, remembering that he had seen it also in the gardens and, a little further on, Squinancy Wort, *Asperula cynanchica*. A look into Bagley Wood revealed, besides the Campanula, Bog Pimpernel, *Anagallis tenella* again and Barren Strawberry, *Potentilla sterilis* both 'nigh the rows of planted willows copiose.' He did not linger long in the wood, however, these being the only three plants recorded there: the interest of Bagley Wood's peat would not seem very novel to Thomas' northern eyes and it may be that he was keen to press on to business in Abingdon and Elnbery. Between Oxford and Abingdon, he records Woolly Thistle, *Cirsium eriophorum*. At Abingdon 'in the river side' there was Yellow Loosestrife, *Lysimachia vulgaris* and Arrow-head, *Sagittaria sagittifolia* and, beyond the village, Thomas notices Water Parsnip, *Sium latifolium*. Whorled Water-milfoil, *Myriophyllum verticillatum* may belong here or in Gloucestershire – the notebook is not clear.

Whatever his business in Elnbery, it seems to have taken Thomas' mind off botanising. Instead of following the Thames on down to London, he turned back to Oxford and set off in the opposite direction, making for Banbury in the northern corner of the county and then turning East into Buckinghamshire: 19 miles to Buckingham and so on to Stoney Stratford, on again to Bedford via Newport Pagnell (12 miles) to Riseley (6 miles); from Riseley by Bedford to Barton in Bedfordshire (14 miles); to St. Albans (12); to London 20. All this while, he never recorded a plant.

CHAPTER VIII

On Tour – Return Journey

IN LONDON, THOMAS WOULD HAVE had plenty of places to stay. Quaker houses abounded in the City and, from distances of excursions from his London lodgings which he gives in his itinerary, we may deduce that he stayed North of the river, perhaps not in the City itself but in that part of London which was spreading northwards from the old City walls towards the country village of Islington. Post-plague and post-fire, it was a very different London from the one that he had known 22 years ago. The fire of 1666 had swept away five-sixths of the city that had been familiar to him then: the notebook records only the botany of expeditions into places that Thomas must have had to re-discover. Elizabethan and Stuart London were burned away and Thomas, no doubt, would walk to Fish Street to see the Monument, completed in the year of his visit near the spot where the fire had first started. Built of Portland stone, designed by Sir Christopher Wren and 202 feet high, its flaming vase of gilt bronze at the top was an emblem of London arising from the ashes – not, unfortunately, to the town plan suggested by Sir Christopher, but in a jumble of brick buildings, shops, eating houses and the new coffee houses which were to take the place of the old taverns. At the time that Thomas visited, the re-building of London was only part complete and there were still waste places created by the fire: an analogy with post-war London is not unapt. But by 1677, much re-building had taken place and there was already a denser texture to the town – former gardens were being built upon and the houses of the nobility were disappearing and being replaced by squares and terraces, often bearing the names of their former owners.

There were also several gardens, designed and maintained for the cultivation of physick plants and of the introduced species that had been coming into Britain steadily over the past century of commercial expansion. When speaking with Morison in Oxford, Thomas would, no doubt, have been recommended to see the Westminster garden under the superintendance of Edward Morgan. Morison thought highly of Morgan, praising him for the best collection of plants in England.[1] On arrival in London, Thomas lost no time in making an excursion out to Westminster to see this famous garden which was situated near the West Cloister of the Abbey and had been established as early as the beginning of the 1650s or perhaps even earlier. The diarist Evelyn had visited it in 1658 and John Ray made at least two trips there in the 1660s and referred to it in the *Catalogus Angliae* in 1670. In an age of intense interest in gardens, its reputation stood very high, and for Thomas, it was an opportunity to see all sorts of exciting plants from Europe, Asia, North Africa and North America – the rewards of a hundred years of colonial enterprise. The scope of the garden was such, and many of the plants in it so new to Thomas' eyes that he kept returning to it to find fresh things on every trip. In four separate visits, he wrote down the names of nearly 500 different plants. Through this list, the most comprehensive we have of the Westminster garden and estimated by R. H. Jeffers as about a third of the total plants growing there, it has been possible to make a theoretical reconstruction of the garden.[2] Its fame was later rivalled by the garden at Chelsea founded by the Society of Apothecaries but in 1677 this was having teething troubles and all interest centred upon Westminster where, besides the Westminster garden, there were at least two other gardens in existence. Thomas Lawson in his Middlesex search list puts a cross against Parkinson's record of the Mediterranean Holm Oak, *Quercus ilex* 'in the Kings privy Garden at Whitehall.'

All this was very stimulating and Thomas was botanising avidly now, learning new things every day. Westminster was a village, separated from London by fields and open ground. Where government offices now stand was once the bare ground of 'Tuthill' or 'Tuttle' fields, a large area in the bend of the Thames and entirely open apart from two or three isolated buildings and the cemetery where a special part had been reserved for victims of the plague in 1666. It was a place with a varied flora and one where the characteristic plants of waste ground flourished. There Thomas noticed Chamomile, *Chamaemelum nobile*, Stinking Goosefoot, *Chenopodium vulvaria*, Sand-spurrey, *Spergularia rubra*, Creeping Jenny, *Lysimachia nummularia*, Subterranean Trefoil, *Trifolium subterraneum*, Buckshorn Plantain, *Plantago coronopus*, Swine-cress, *Coronopus squamatus* and, in a damp place, Marsh Speedwell, *Veronica scutellata*. With his head reeling with the names of the foreigners that he had seen in the Westminster garden, it must have been a relief to record these natives. One that he would be particularly pleased to identify was the Sun Spurge, *Euphorbia helioscopia* on which he had made a careful note in the Oxford garden. There was also Merret's record of Tobacco, *Nicotiana tabacum*, springing up 'betwixt St. James's and Hide Park' which Thomas ticked in his search list.

Twentieth century records of tobacco are referred by D. H. Kent, *The Historical Flora of Middlesex* to *N. alata*.[3] Another of Merret's Westminster plants received the same treatment in the search list: 'near the gate as ye go into Kingstreet' is a location for a fern which Merret calls 'Filix saxatilis crispa.' King Street, leading from Charing Cross to the Abbey, was Westminster's high street. It had two great gateways across it: Holbein's gateway and King's Gate, both of which feature on many a contemporary view of Westminster.

London gave Thomas the opportunity that he needed to get acquainted with many plants that he was unlikely to see in the North of England. Another of its advantages was that there were books and people to whom he could turn for help whenever he was puzzled about an identification. This, perhaps, accounts for some apparent confusion in his record keeping: sometimes a plant is displaced from the locality in which it was found and appears amongst a group of other plants from a very different locality as though Thomas had carried a specimen around with him for some time before positive identification could be made.

If much of what Thomas saw is now obliterated by bricks and concrete, his records are still interesting as his own contribution to an area of Britain for which the historical record in botany is richest and most complete. Particularly is this true of his excursions to the villages of Deptford, Greenwich, Charlton, Woolwich and Lewisham where nothing now remains of the rural countryside into which he made his first field trip out of London. Deptford and Greenwich were attractions in their own right: the Dutch wars had turned the eyes of Englishmen towards the sea and the king's personal passion for yachting ensured patronage for the dockyards. He had several royal yachts built for himself, including the famous *Fubbs* which was to be built at Greenwich in 1682 by Sir Phineas Pett. Thomas, like any other visitor, would enjoy the sights of the busy maritime village of Deptford, but he was there to botanise too. Hoary Cinquefoil, *Potentilla argentea*, *Lemna trisulca* and another weed of the ditches 'Conferva Plinii,' together with Deptford Pink, *Dianthus armeria*, Upright Chickweed, *Moenchia erecta* and the two Mulleins, *Verbascum lychnitis* and *V. nigrum* were all recorded at Deptford before he moved a little further down river to Greenwich. There he explored along the shore, finding the Sea Club-rush, *Scirpus maritimus*, Marsh Sow-Thistle, *Sonchus palustris*, a plant which he calls 'alsine hirsuta altera viscosa' which was probably Common Mouse-ear Chickweed, *Cerastium holosteoides* and the Sandworts, *Minuartia hybrida* and *Arenaria serpyllifolia*. The latter is also given with Woolwich as a location where he also saw the cornfield weeds Buckwheat, *Fagopyrum esculentum*, Field Madder, *Sheradia arvensis* and Venus's Looking-glass,

Legousia hybrida. Apparently, he had now moved a little way from the river. Inland from Greenwich, Knotted Hedge-parsley, *Torilis nodosa* was a plant that he had already taken some care to identify near Bristol but there were others that he had not noted before: Small Toadflax, *Chaenorhinum minus*, Slender St. John's Wort, *Hypericum pulchrum* and Ramping Fumitory, *Fumaria capreolata*. Musk Mallow, *Malva moschata*, he is now confident of having seen. A few more plants were recorded still further away from the river at Blackheath: Subterranean Trefoil, *Trifolium subterraneum*, Creeping Jenny, *Lysimachia nummularia*, White Climbing Fumitory, *Corydalis claviculata* and Sun Spurge, *Euphorbia helioscopia* were added to the bag before Thomas pressed on to Charlton where he was to find a whole host of plants that were new to him. As he went, he noted Tower Mustard, *Turritis glabra* growing in a lane between Greenwich and Charlton Wood and Butcher's Broom, *Ruscus aculeatus* near to the wood. John Ogilby and William Morgan's map of 'The Country about 15 miles any Way from London' shows the wood as occupying an area South-eastwards of Charlton and North of Shooters Hill. Nearly all Thomas' Charlton plants were to be found in or around it. The damp woodland under the underscrub of Alder Buckthorn, *Frangula alnus* and Goat Willow, *Salix caprea* harboured Wood Spurge, *Euphorbia amygdaloides*, Slender St. John's Wort, *Hypericum pulchrum* and two Speedwells, *Veronica serpyllifolia* and *V. montana* whilst Bird's-nest Orchid, *Neottia nidus-avis* was one of several orchid finds in Kent. Hoary Cinquefoil, *Potentilla argentea* and the Three-nerved Sandwort, *Moehringia trinervia* were a reminder of how close was the tidal Thames. Four other plants complete the list for the wood: Bog Stitchwort, *Stellaria alsine* which he observed had a quadrangular stem, a species of trifolium which Thomas called 'Lotus quadrifolia phaeum fuscus' and two mosses which he sought to distinguish – species of Polytrichum of which one was probably *P. formosum* and the other *P. commune*.

Charlton proved an attractive place to botanise, providing Thomas with several plants that were new to his northern eyes: some reflect the pattern of agriculture in this prosperous coastal strip: the Long-stalked Cranesbill, *Geranium columbinum* was as much at home in the cornfields as it would have been on the fringes of the wood, its cousin, Musk Storksbill, *Erodium moschatum* had spread inland to flourish in the fields where the Cudweed, *Filago germanica* grew in drier places and Marsh Cudweed, *Gnaphalium uliginosum* in damper. A quick glance into the ditches and wet places yielded little out of the way: Duckweed, *Lemna trisulca*, a Potamogeton, *P. crispus* and the Pondweed, *Groenlandia densa* summed up his researches there. But he was botanising carefully all this while. Prickly Lettuce, *Lactuca serriola* and Great Lettuce, *Lactuca virosa* probably caused him some head-ache and there were also a few peaflowers that need to be sorted out: Spotted Medick, *Medicago arabica*, Black Medick, *M. lupulina* and the Lesser Yellow Trefoil, *Trifolium dubium* all grew in the Charlton area. So did Greater Knapweed, *Centaurea scabiosa*. One last plant, the Toad Rush, *Juncus bufonius*, is jotted down without location but amongst others from Charlton.

In the notebook, there is now something of a break between these plants collected in North Kent and another series recorded mainly about Lewisham and Brockley. Plants from Westminster and the Westminster garden form the break and this suggests that Thomas returned to London from Charlton and that he made a second expedition down the river at an interval of a day or two. During this interval, while he was revisiting the garden, he walked down by the river and recorded Skull-cap, *Scutellaria galericulata* 'by Thames side near Westminster' along with Great Yellow-cress, *Rorippa amphibia* and Marsh Speedwell, *Veronica scutellata* with a white flower which is given without location but entered in this place. Turnip, *Brassica rapa* might also have been seen by the river or elsewhere in waste ground 'nigh Westminster.'

Amongst a separate list of Westminster garden plants is another record of Skull-cap 'plentifull by the way side in the ditches between Horsadown and Deptford in Kent.' Horsadown is upriver from Deptford and it is possible that Lawson crossed London Bridge and walked down on his second trip, but more than likely he went by boat and disembarked at Deptford again, for he records Wild Basil, *Clinopodium vulgare* and Basil-thyme, *Acinos arvensis* between Deptford and Lewisham. Then at Lewisham itself, his list consists of Scarlet Pimpernel, *Anagallis arvensis*, also seen elsewhere in Kent with a white flower, Common Hemp-nettle, *Galeopsis tetrahit*, Small Fleabane, *Pulicaria vulgaris* which were seen growing between the furrows in the cornfields and Dark Mullein, *Verbascum nigrum* in Lewisham churchyard.

The list for this excursion is not a long one – perhaps Thomas had other business to transact that day, but it contains some interesting plants and Thomas, again, was on the look-out for things that he had not seen before. Another cornfield weed of the South-east: Sharp-leaved Fluellen, *Kickxia elatine* attracted his attention 'in the corn about Brockley' as did Weasel's Snout, *Antirrhinum orontium* which was already known to him from a less typical location at Vincent's Rocks near Bristol. Water Purslane, *Peplis portula* and Ivy-leaved Water Crowfoot, *Ranunculus hederaceus* are two more plants given with Great Brockley as their location and there is a handful of other records that are listed in this group of Lewisham/Brockley specimens and may be supposed to have been collected on this expedition:

Marsh Ragwort, *Senecio aquaticus* find a place amongst the list of other plants all with Kent locations and Marsh Thistle, *Cirsium palustre*, Yellow Vetchling, *Lathyrus aphaca*, Glasswort, *Salicornia perennis*, Sea Lavender, *Limonium vulgare*, Wild Oat, *Avena fatua* and the Soft Shield-fern, *Polystichum setiferum* are all recorded simply as growing 'in Kent'. So too are some orchids – Thomas did not overlook this most interesting feature of the Kent flora. His 'Orchis abortiva violacea' defies identification and may not be an orchid but his 'Orchis Arachnitis', a Merret polynomial for a plant found at Walcot near Rugby, is Early Spider Orchid, *Ophrys sphegodes* and his 'Orchis sphegodes sive fucum ferens' found 'in a close adjoyning to Charleton Church' is Bee Orchid, *Ophrys apifera*. And last among these plants listed as growing simply 'in Kent' we may regret that there is no specific location for Golden Samphire *Inula crithmoides*.

Another expedition took Thomas into Essex on a day when the Petty Whin, *Genista anglica* was to be seen, although the summer must have now been getting on: perhaps Thomas saw the bushes without flower. On his way, Thomas passed through Hackney, recording Stone Parsley, *Sison amomum*, Sharp Dock, *Rumex conglomeratus*, Water Dropwort, *Oenanthe fistulosa* and Fine-leaved Water Dropwort, *O. aquatica*. It was to be an excursion to record the flora of heath and marsh: Cross-leaved Heath, *Erica tetralix*, the Great and Lesser Reedmace, *Typha latifolia* and *T. angustifolia*, Rampion, *Campanula rapunculus* and the Lesser Water-Plantain, *Baldellia ranunculoides*. A few more plants are given without location but immediately follow upon the Essex records so that we may assume that Thomas simply continued jotting: Lesser Sea-spurrey, *Spergularia media*, Sea Heath, *Frankenia laevis*, Sea Bindweed, *Calystegia soldanella*, the Glassworts, *Salicornia europaea* and *S. perennis*, Saltwort, *Salsola kali* and Annual Beardgrass, *Polypogon monspeliensis*. Essex was a good place to improve Thomas' knowledge of sedges and rushes: Bulbous Rush, *Juncus bulbosus* is recorded and the two carices, *Carex pendula* and *C. divisa* – the latter, recorded from near Hackney, is noted to have concave stalks. To these plants there was, as yet, little guidance in the literature, still less was there any for mosses and liverworts. Thomas struggles with *Marchantia polymorpha*, recording it twice under different polynomials for the two different fruiting bodies.

These expeditions – two into Kent and one into Essex – were Thomas' major botanising forays from London. He had other matters to attend to amongst the Quakers of the city and there would be social calls to pay. His itinerary for instance, records a visit to Kingston-upon-Thames and in his scribbled notes of persons to see we find 'Marg. Rouse'.[4] Margaret, eldest daughter of Margaret Fell, had married John Rous, son of a Barbados sugar planter. The Rouses, father and son, had been the first people in Barbados to be convinced when the thrust of missionary endeavour had propelled the Friends across the Atlantic in 1655. John Rous, the son, later undertook a missionary journey on his own account to New England whose Puritan people, having come to America to win the right to worship in their own way, were not disposed to allow that worship to be undermined by anyone else seeking freedom of conscience. Rous and those with him were treated to a truly ferocious reception and suffered a series of imprisonments and floggings, culminating in the punishment of having an ear cropped – a piece of judicial mutilation enacted under Massachusetts law.[5] These events were long past by 1677, however, and the day at Kingston would pass pleasantly as Thomas renewed his ties of affection with the Fell family, met the younger Margaret's husband for the first time and passed on the news from Swarthmoor. Margaret would want to know how her mother was keeping and how her younger sisters looked and Thomas, so many miles from home, would be glad to exchange North Country gossip and to tell of his journeying down the western side of England. In his itinerary, he writes 'to Kingston upon Thames 20 miles' which suggests that the trip was a day's outing from his London lodgings – perhaps on this occasion he hired a horse for we find only two botanical records that might be ascribed to this trip. With a cross in the search list is Merret's 'Muscus denticulatus major et minor. Toothed or Dented mosse: at the Neat houses, and Kingstone bridge is the greater.' It is difficult, however, to know how much weight we should give to records that are marked in this way. 'Sinapi Genevense syl. J.B.' for instance, a Merret record 'beyond Southwarke in the way to Lambeth' has a cross against it and could have been seen on the way to Kingston. A plant under this polynomial appears in the Morisonian herbarium identified as the rare casual *Erucastrum nasturtifolium*[6] and it is odd, if Lawson really saw this or some other strange casual crucifer, that he did not make a detailed record of it in his own notes. Meadow Cranesbill, *Geranium pratense* that he gives from Kingston 'flore albo' is a much surer record.

This was one trip westwards from London. Another took Thomas as far as Henley – trip that we must deduce from the plant records for there is no note of it in the itinerary. This is something of a puzzle: Thomas compiled his itinerary meticulously, noting the distances between each stop with the care of a man who has watched the miles stretch out in front of him and fall away behind him all the way around England. But a round trip of 40 miles which appears to have taken him South of the river to Clapham and then westwards through Staines and Maidenhead to Henley and Caversham and back again goes inexplicably unrecorded and can only be reconstructed from the plants that he listed.

On this journey, Thomas may have crossed the Thames by the Westminster horse ferry: he records several plants in his notebook down by the waterside and it is impossible to be definite as to when he actually collected then. Alternatively, he may simply have crossed London Bridge from his lodgings. Either way could have taken him across the open spaces of St. George's Fields that lay behind the marshes of Lambeth. There he hunted the ditches to find Frog-bit, *Hydrocharis morsus-ranae*, the Skull-cap, *S. galericulata* a species of *Chara* which he calls 'equisetum foetidum sub aqua repens' and the two docks, Curled Dock, *Rumex crispus* and Fiddle Dock, *Rumex pulcher*: the last an interesting find as Thomas later reckoned to have seen it in Westmorland. On Clapham Heath another reminder of how close the cornfields grew to London – Field Woundwort, *Stachys arvensis* as well as some wet-loving plants that are unfamiliar in these days of lowered water tables: a moss, probably *Thuidium tamariscinum*, the Marsh Speedwell, *Veronica scutellata* and Water Purslane, *Peplis portula* which he had recently seen near Great Brockley. Here he gives it a slightly different polynomial though obviously recognising it as the same plant. Thrumwort, *Damasonium alisma* is recorded by him for the first time and there is Lesser Skull-cap, *Scutellaria minor* and All-seed, *Radiola linoides* which he recorded again as he continued up the Thames valley 'on the Common between Hersham and Walton in Surrey and on Ditton Heath eodem comitate.' At Hersham, too, there was Rampion, *Campanula rapunculus*.

On up the river then, recrossing it to Staines where another cornfield weed, *Xanthium strumarium* was one of the two of Lawson's southern records that was published. Beyond Staines 'in the corn between Staines and Colnbrook in Buckinghamshire' he saw *Galeopsis ?angustifolia*. Between Maidenhead and Henley the day was, perhaps, running out on him – he appears to have concentrated on trees and shrubs: Spurge Laurel, *Daphne laureola*, Juniper, *Juniperus communis*, Beech, *Fagus sylvatica*, Wayfaring Tree, *Viburnum lantana* marked this section of the route.

At Henley he probably stayed. He was 50 miles out of London now and there are a few records that point to more leisurely collecting: Field Madder, *Sheradia arvensis*, the Hemp-nettle, *Galeopsis angustifolia* again, Musk thistle, *Carduus nutans* and the two Fluellens, *Kickxia elatine* and *K. spuria*, all 'on Stanhill West of Henley Wood.'

At Henley, he would not have been far from Caversham where Man Orchid, *Aceras anthropophorum* had been reported and included in Merret's *Pinax*. Thomas writes down very careful directions for finding the plant:

Orchis Anthropophora, Man Orchis, at Cawsham nigh Reading.

From the bridge pass to Cawsham Church, crosse the Church yard to the West then turn short down towards the River Thames, by the Garden wall, when within 100 yards of the Thames, at the place where one leaps down the bank, turn short on the right hand, passing along on the ledge of the brow of Cawsham hill Westward, this ledge is nearer the bottom by 2 parts then the top, and is a Level green walk, both on the right hand and on the left of this walk this plant grows, being about halfe a quarter of a mile from the said garden wall sub finem maij floret.

This, entered at the end of the Berkshire list rather than in the running notes of the tour, has the look of directions written in advance. Following it, is a note written at a later date 'Orchis Galea et alis fere Cinereis Jo. Ray Jo. Watts, who also found the female of this.' If Thomas went to see the plant and wrote that note when he had looked at it, then his later polynomials identify it not as *Aceras anthropophorum* but as *Orchis militaris*, to which Druce, in the *Flora of Oxfordshire* referred the record that appeared in Merret's *Pinax*.

The mention of John Watts in connection with this record suggests that Thomas met Watts in London. Watts was very highly thought of as a botanist by contemporaries and, in 1680, he was to be appointed to superintend the Apothecaries' garden at Chelsea at a salary of £50 per year, stocking the garden with native and foreign plants at his own expense. Watts, however, was a better botanist than he was a business man and arguments over the financing of the garden characterised his tenure of office.

If Thomas went as far as Caversham, we may log it as the most westward point of this trip out of London, the last he was to make from the capital. It would soon be time to think of turning his face to the North again. As he walked back to London, however, he found time to visit Nonsuch Park, the Elizabethan palace that had been granted to Barbara Villiers, Charles II's mistress in 1670 – a parting present when her charms ceased to interest the king and she was forced to give way to Nell Gwynn. The park had once been famous for its trees but had suffered from the attentions of the Parliamentarians in the Civil War and, by the Restoration, all that remained were the elms and walnuts that Samuel Pepys described in his diary (21st September, 1665). The palace, which Barbara Villiers pulled down shortly after she acquired it, consisted of two courts, the outer of stone and the inner of timber.[7] Probably it was the outer which was Thomas' 'Nonsuch Over Court' where he found Blue Fleabane, *Erigeron acer*, Rampion, *Campanula rapunculus* and Vervain, *Verbena officinalis*. Some trees and shrubs there must have been, for he notes that in the park the Mistletoe, *Viscum album* was abundant and so too was the Stemless Thistle, *Cirsium acaulon* whilst near to Nonsuch he saw again Stone Parsley, *Sison amomum*. Perhaps like Pepys too, he walked in the ruined garden for there is a short list of 10 plants given without location but following upon the Nonsuch plants, including Broad-leaved Spurge, *Euphorbia platyphyllos* and the Welsh Poppy, *Meconopsis cambrica*. This list is followed by another of plants from wildly different localities. The last eight are from Lancashire and Westmorland locations and have been entered in their place although it is difficult to imagine how they should have got so separated from the rest of the northern records. Before these stand two other plants: 'Hieracium fruticosum latifolium hirsutum et glabrum, by Henly in Warwickshire.' and *Calluna vulgaris* with a white flower 'by Sherly [Shirley] street in Warwickshire.' Neither of these places was on Thomas' route when he walked South: at the nearest, passing West of Birmingham, he was 12 miles from Shirley; when he came up again to Oxford and Banbury he was 25 miles from Henley-in-Arden. It would be nice to think that he was on his way up to Middleton to see Ray, but there again there is too much against such a supposition and these two plants must remain a puzzle.

These lists are at the end of the London notes, marking the last planned trip that Thomas took out of the city. We might, perhaps, venture upon Star Thistle, *Centaurea calcitrapa* ticked in his search list 'between London and Mile end copiose' as the last plant recorded when he tramped out of town heading for Cambridge and the long road home.

Before we accompany him on that journey, we might look at what remains of his botanising in London itself – the evidence of continual collecting on days when he was not embarked upon a planned expedition but simply observing in the streets or foraging in the waste places and watery ditches with which untidy, semi-rural, semi-urbanised London abounded. It was a city of contrasts where narrow streets as pestiferous and as colourful as an eastern bazaar gave way to gracious gardens and the prostitutes and the beggars rubbed shoulders with the dandy, the nobleman and the self-important man of affairs. For Thomas, it was a city where he was out to make the most of an opportunity to see plants and to talk to people who were unlikely to come his way once he had returned to the remoteness of Westmorland. His eyes were everywhere on his walks about the town and Fool's Parsley, *Aethusa cynapium*, Yarrow, *Achillea millefolium*, Hairy Brome, *Zerna ramosa*, Lamb's Succory, *Arnoseris minima* and another composite which he describes as 'Hieracium montanum non ramosum caule aphyllo' are all given with London locations. Once he stopped to remark how the end of the leaf of the Wall Lettuce, *Mycelis muralis* 'resembles an ivy leafe, frequens.'

The waterside, as always, drew him. He records Marsh Ragwort, *Senecio aquaticus* 'nigh London', open ditches yielded *Glyceria maxima* and *Phalaris arundinacea* and on one or more of the occasions when he was in Westminster he walked down by the river – no embankment in those days – and recorded Arrow-head, *Sagittaria sagittifolia* and an *Oenanthe*, probably *crocata* 'nigh Westminster horse Ferry'. So too, Great Burdock, *Arctium lappa* had been recorded by Coles 'on the bank side between the horse Ferry and the Neat houses' and Thomas puts a cross against this record in his search list and independently noted it 'on the mill bank.' Perhaps these plants were found whilst Thomas waited for the ferry, for Marsh Arrow-grass, *Triglochin palustris* is recorded 'by Thames side nigh Westminster' and 'on the other side of the bank' – i.e. the shore opposite Millbank.

One plant that was then not uncommon along the muddy banks of the Thames was the Triangular Scirpus or Bulrush, *Schoenoplectus triquetrus*. Many of Thomas' contemporaries recorded it – Thomas, besides entering it himself 'at Thames side nigh Westminster' ticks Merret's record in the same place. It became immediately scarcer upon the building of the embankment in the mid-nineteenth century and has since disappeared altogether in Middlesex[8] as has the Long-leaved Scurvy-grass *Cochlearia anglica* for which Thomas put a cross against the Merret record across the river from Blackwall. These records, like those on the Essex marshland, show Thomas specialising to a certain extent and trying to get difficult plants clear in his mind. St. Pancras Church was probably no more than a few minutes walk from his lodgings and, in a potter round the precincts, Thomas was able to add another carex to his list of identified species: the False Fox-sedge, *Carex otrobae* and to distinguish besides other sedges, rushes and grasses: *Eleocharis palustris, Juncus inflexus, J. conglomeratus* and *J. effusus; Alopecurus geniculatus* (noted twice in London) and *Glyceria fluitans* as well as Stone Parsley, *Sison amomum* which he had already seen in Hackney. He also verified a record of Grass Vetchling, *Lathyrus nissolia* which he had taken from Ray and now notes 'this grows nigh Pancras Church and nigh Highgate.'

Another group that Thomas was trying to get clear in his mind at this time was that of the Goosefoots and Oraches. He had found Red Goosefoot when he was in Bristol: now, quite close to where he was staying 'on our dunghill' he found a profusion of plants of this group. It is a sudden reminder of the filth of seventeenth-century London, but it was a perfect place, if scarcely salubrious, to work at the discrimination of the various species. Red Goosefoot, *Chenopodium rubrum* was to found again there and he could distinguish it from the common Fat Hen, *Chenopodium album*, while Stinking Goosefoot, *Chenopodium vulvaria* he knew from Tothill fields. The chenopodium 'Atriplex sylvestris latifolia seu Pes Anserinus' at Bristol was found here too and there is another puzzler 'Atriplex halimi folio' which Thomas was quite certain was distinct from the other Goosefoots on the dunghill, for he wrote 'ni fallor' by it. The binomial equivalent is *Halimione portulacoides* but a specimen under the polynomial in the Dillenian herbaria is *Atriplex pedunculata*[9] and there is no way of being certain as to what Thomas actually saw.

Continuing with chenopods, Thomas was able to compare Common Orache, *Atriplex patula* with Hastate Orache, *Atriplex hastata* and to note of the latter its diagnostic feature: the delta-shaped leaf. A last member of this group, Herbaceous Seablite, *Suaeda maritima* completes this enterprising list of plants 'on our dunghill.'

Other plants from the eastern end of the city were entered up or ticked on the search list. White Clover, *Trifolium repens* 'betwixt Virginia House and Naghead's Inn in the way to Hackney' is Thomas' own: others are marked down with crosses: Milk Thistle, *Silybum marianum* 'by Lord Southamptons house and about Islington', Bishop's Weed, *Aegopodium podagraria*, a Merret record from Moorfields and Creeping Thistle, *Cirsium arvense*, a Parkinson record 'on Kentish Town green copiose.' London Rocket, *Sisymbrium irio*, which Thomas also saw at Kensington grew as a defiant reminder of the Great Fire 'within the walls of Pauls.' The old St. Paul's where John Donne had preached his powerful sermons in the early days of the Stuart monarchy had been left a pile of ashes, the new cathedral, designed by Sir Christopher Wren, was still under construction. Where the fire had burned, the London Rocket flourished, vigorous as the Rose Bay Willow Herb on the bomb sites of the Blitz. A century later and it was fighting for its foothold in London – by the early nineteenth century it was apparently extinct. Now, however, it is back again, its revival dating from the last war.[10]

One Middlesex habitat that has almost totally disappeared is the vast heathland that once made up a good proportion of the vegetational cover of the county. At the beginning of the sixteenth century it has been estimated that there were about 45,000 acres of common and waste land. A century after Thomas there were still about 30,000. The nineteenth century dramatically altered this: 200 years after Lawson's visit there were less than 2,500 acres remaining and our own century has completed the vegetational transformation by drainage schemes that have lowered the water tables until the heaths of Middlesex are largely a thing of the past.[11] The most famous of them, however, still remains though its vegetation is much modified.

Hampstead Heath was a classic locality that was in easy reach of Thomas' lodgings: a collecting ground for London apothecaries that was already well documented in his day by Gerard, Johnson and Merret.[12] Thomas amused himself checking off his search list the plants recorded by his predecessors: the Hampstead plants in the Middlesex list have been combed through and crosses have been placed against several of them: 'Aster Atticus' and the 'Aurea virga of Arnold of villa nova' which was the Golden-rod, *Solidago virgaurea* as well as the more readily identifiable Common Cow-wheat, *Melampyrum pratense*, Birdsfoot, *Ornithopus perpusillus* (for which Blackheath is also given as a location); Hornbeam, *Carpinus betulus*, Lesser Skull-cap, *Scutellaria minor*, Butcher's Broom, *Ruscus aculeatus*, Hard-fern, *Blechnum spicant*, Bulbous Rush, *Juncus bulbosus* and the Service Tree with its wild cousin, *Sorbus domestica* and *S. torminalis* which Merret had recorded as growing 'in ye [?privie] walks by Hampstead Heath.'

In Thomas' day, the Heath was a large wild tract with woods and villages all around[13] – his recording reflects this picture. The Wild Service Tree is noticed again forming part of the woodland mix that chequered the fringes of the Heath. In the lanes through the woodland grew Rosebay Willow-herb, *Chamaenerion angustifolium*, rather an uncommon plant in Thomas' day. There, too, grew Lily-of-the-Valley, *Convallaria majalis* and Bitter Vetch, *Lathyrus montanus* which reminded Thomas of home where it grew 'in Strickland Woods.' Where patches of woodland gave way to enclosure there was Wood Horsetail, *Equisetum sylvaticum*, Saw-wort, *Serratula tinctoria*, Smooth Tare, *Vicia tetrasperma* and Hairy Tare, *V. hirsuta* and a composite which Thomas calls 'Hieracium fruticosum latifolium hirsutum.' Beyond the enclosures again was the open expanse of the Heath, clothed with Bell Heather, *Erica cinerea*, Ling, *Calluna vulgaris*, and in the damper spots, Cross-leaved Heath, *Erica tetralix* where Marsh Speedwell, *Veronica scutellata* also flourished. On the Heath, Thomas found the parasitic Dodder, *Cuscuta epithymum* which Parkinson had reported as growing on bracken. Thomas made a note of the species that he found it growing on:

> found on several plants in Hampstead Heath as on heath (1) Ling on Furze (1) Whins, on Bilberry bushes, so Epierica, so Epigenista, Epivaccinium.

These are apothecaries' distinctions. John Gerard recommends the virtue of Dodder parasitic upon Thyme – epithymum – and nettles – epiurtica – for a variety of ailments. 'Epiurtica', indeed, 'is prouved oftentimes in the West parts with good success against many maladies' he says embracingly but Culpeper voiced a more common opinion when he said that 'he is a Physitian indeed that hath wit enough to chuse his Dodder according to the

Nature of the disease and Humours peccant.'[14]

Hampstead Heath, the apothecaries' gathering ground, was an appropriate place to bend one's mind to the medicinal virtues of herbs. Again, though, one cannot read into this anything more than a normal interest in their properties. There is no evidence, for instance, that Thomas sought to become acquainted with any of the physicians in the city or that he took an interest in the medical experiments conducted by the Royal Society. He had jotted down the name of Walter Charlton, the Royal Physician, but only in connection with his garden in Kent.[15] If Thomas was not botanising he was more than likely interesting himself in Quaker affairs. His expeditions alone are indicative of some lengthy stay in London: four times to Westminster garden, once at least into Kent, once into Essex, the trip to Hampstead Heath and some more local forays around his North London lodgings must all have taken time. In between, he transacted other business in London. I have suggested that he very likely took the manuscript of *Baptismalogia* with him and at a Second Day Morning Meeting of Ministering Friends of 6th August, we read in the minutes: 'A treatise concerning Baptisme etc. Also a discourse Concerning the Supper etc by Tho. Lawson being formerly read ordered to be printed.'[16] The Second Day Morning Meeting had been established as an editorial board to read and, in effect, censor all Quaker manuscripts intended for publication. The need for group solidarity had always been felt in a world of hostility: we have seen how Thomas, in his early years, had submitted manuscript material to Margaret Fell for her approval and during the Commonwealth many Friends had submitted manuscripts both to her and to George Fox.[17]

In the early days of enthusiastic visionaries and prophets, Quaker writings had been full of the language of the apocalypse and the fantastic imagery of a people passionate to express themselves. But sometimes such passion had drawn its writers into language and sentiments which the Friends, as a whole, felt uneasy about endorsing. The Second Day Morning Meeting was set up with two aims: to curb excesses of language and to prevent anything being published that might bring ridicule or outright discredit upon the Society. It became, therefore, one of the moderating forces that, in the last three decades of the century, set the Society in a more conservative mould. The minutes of its proceedings, volume after volume in folio, are a continuing record of many patient hours and the burning of much midnight oil as individual members of the committee sat up late reading yet another Friend's tract; evaluating, commenting upon it, censoring it ready for the final yea or nay at the next Meeting. Thomas' treatise concerning baptism, the *Baptismalogia*, passed through this process of censorship apparently without comment: the editorial committee of

6th August merely recording that they had now passed the manuscript for printing. Possibly, as I have suggested, it already bore George Fox's seal of approval.

When it came out, there was no printer's name on the title-page. A copy in Friends House in London has on page 105 verso a list of 'Books Printed and Sold by Andrew Sowle at the Crooked Billet in Hollaway-Lane in Shoreditch' and we may take it that he was the printer. Soule's imprints did not appear on his books until 1680 when he opened a shop in Devonshire buildings, but he was certainly printing for the Quakers as early as 1672 and two years later the Second Day Morning Meeting minutes reveal him as established as a printer for Friends. He was to become one of the best known of all Quaker printers: Thomas Lawson's *A Mite into the Treasury* was printed by him in 1680 and, after his death, Tace or Tacy Sowle, probably his daughter, carried on the business. Like anyone else engaged in the risky business of printing Friends' books, Sowle suffered his own vicissitudes. His premises were repeatedly turned over by the authorities, his presses damaged and, on one occasion a thousand reams of printed books were confiscated. Throughout all this harassment and bullying, Sowle serenely went on printing. Sir Richard Browne, before whom he was once brought, might threaten to send him after his brother Twyn who had been executed in 1664 for printing a seditious book but Andrew is reputed to have responded to his enemies by setting out food and drink before a party of officials who were searching his premises in accordance with the command of *Romans* xii 19,20 to feed even your enemies. Of such is hagiography made and the purveyor of this particular story says, in unconcealed satisfaction, that one of the chiefs of this search party 'survived not long after, but died in a miserable condition.'[18] The Sowles, on the other hand, father, daughter and another member of the family, J. Sowle, continued printing well into the eighteenth century.

Thomas may have stayed in London to see his work run off and, perhaps, to carry a few copies into the North with him. If the 6th August, the date on which it was passed by the Second Day Morning Meeting, represents a date shortly after his arrival in London, one might, perhaps, allow at least a fortnight after that for his botanising trips and arrive at a date late in August for his departure from London. He could not delay much longer if he wished to travel home whilst there was yet a bit of the summer left and plants to see on route.

In fact, as we shall see, the return home through the eastern counties was to be, floristically, the poorest part of his tour. But Thomas did have one more place of botanical pilgrimage to see: Cambridge. Ray's *Catalogus Angliae* had been his constant companion on his tour and he had used it extensively in the field and as a source of reference. Many of the Cambridgeshire records in that work derived from Ray's own first work in botany, the *Catalogus Plantarum circa Cantabrigiam nascentium*, published in 1660 – the first flora of a British county. In the preface, Ray explains how enforced leisure following an illness had turned his attention towards botanical studies. He had ridden and walked the Cambridgeshire countryside during convalescence from this illness. He has been fascinated and absorbed by the rich spectacle of the meadows in spring-time and filled with wonder and delight by the intricate structures of individual plants.[19] From that time on, John Ray had never looked back; the study of the natural world became his vocation and he travelled all over England extending and completing the work begun when he was a young Cambridge don.

In its early stages, though, it had not been an easy task. The science of botany was not one that had any place within the scholastic studies of Cambridge. Like the herbalist, William Turner, more than a hundred years earlier, Ray had discovered:

> to my astonishment, among so many masters of learning and luminaries of letters I found not a single person who was deeply versed in Botany, and only one or two who had even a slight acquaintance with the subject.[20]

Thomas Lawson was to make his own comment on the neglect of the study of the natural world by the universities in two works published shortly after his return from this tour. Now he was to follow Ray's footsteps in a literal as well as metaphorical sense and to visit many of the places where, for John Ray, it had all begun. Thomas would view for himself a lot of the plants through which Ray, as he tells us, 'became inspired with a passion for Botany.'

One of the first places that Thomas visited was the Gogmagog hills, one of about a dozen locations that were repeatedly botanised over by Ray during the period that he was collecting for the *Cambridge Catalogue*. Of the 14 plants that Thomas records from the Gogmagogs, 10 were Raian finds from that location, the remaining four being found by Ray elsewhere in Cambridgeshire. Purple Milk Vetch, *Astragalus danicus*, Field Fleawort, *Senecio integrifolius*, Perennial Flax, *Linum anglicum*, Sainfoin, *Onobrychis viciifolia*, Dark-winged Orchid, *Orchis ustulata*, Pasque Flower, *Anemone pulsatilla*, Wild Mignonette, *Reseda lutea*, Wild Thyme, *Thymus drucei*, Horse-shoe Vetch, *Hippocrepis comosa* and the Common Rockrose, *Helianthemum chamaecistus* had all been first recorded by Ray from the Gogmagogs and it must have been a great source of pleasure to Thomas to walk the same ground and to find the same plants flourishing in the place where Ray had botanised more than 17 years before. His own additions were generally unremarkable: Common Milkwort, *Polygala vulgaris*, a Harebell, *Campanula rotundifolia*, the Bulbous Buttercup, *Ranunculus bulbosus*. But there is always a chance of finding something new, even in a well-worked area, and Thomas' seeing eye noticed a white-flowered Rockrose amongst the yellow and he was later to send this record to Ray and to receive acknowledgement in the *Fasciculus* of 1688 and in Ray's great work the *Synopsis Stirpium Britannicarum*:

> Mr Lawson gathered it on Gogmagog Hills with a white Flower; which Variety is very rare in this Plant, and never observed by me.[21]

Another locality which had been much visited by Ray during the first years of his collecting was Madingly and Lawson made a short excursion out there and recorded Black Bryony, *Tamus communis*, Marsh Pea and Narrow-leaved Everlasting Pea, *Lathyrus pratensis* and *L. sylvestris*, Woolly Thistle, *Cirsium eriophorum* and Crested Cow-wheat, *Melampyrum cristatum*. And there were others from the Cambridgeshire fields and hedgerows: the Corn Crowfoot, *Ranunculus arvensis* was a common weed in the Cambridge meadows and there was the Corn Caraway, *Petroselinum segetum*, Milk Vetch, *Astragalus glycyphyllos*, Alexanders, *Smyrnium olusatrum* 'in a close at Cambridge' and the Wild Radish *Raphanus raphanistrum* growing 'in Foulmire cornfields.' Ivy Duckweed, *Lemna trisulca* spread its green mat over stagnant waters where the Brookweed, *Samolus valerandi* also grew and the Field Mouse-ear Chickweed, *Cerastium arvense* flourished 'on the hill of health[22] and by Cambridge Castle.' Less specifically, there is Squinancy Wort, *Asperula cynanchica*, another mention of *Linum anglicum* 'about Cambridge', and a plant which Thomas calls 'Eruca Italica' which may possibly be identified as Tall Rocket, *Sisymbrium altissimum*. Harder to identify is his 'Trifolium virginiarum' with 'leaves as large as those of hedera virginiana quinquefolia' – an exotic, perhaps, seen as Thomas strolled around the town, noting the white umbels of the Bur Chervil, *Anthriscus caucalis* abundant 'on the mud walls in and about Cambridge.' A walk out towards Barnwell produced the Great Hairy Willow-herb, *Epilobium hirsutum* and Spotted Medick, *Medicago arabica* which Thomas had last seen at Charlton on the day that he had enjoyed botanising in Kent.

Apart from the white-flowered variety of the Rockrose, though, none of Thomas' Cambridgeshire observations were new. He visited many of Ray's locations to see what he had seen, making a deliberate expedition, for instance, to 'an old Gravel pitt near Shelford by the footway from Trumpington to Shelford Church' where Ray had seen the Early Spider Orchid, *Ophrys sphegodes* – by the hundred as he recorded in the appendix to his Cambridge Catalogue which was published in 1663. Thomas' wording is exactly Ray's taken from the *Catalogus Angliae* in which the record was later incorporated. The total impression is one of the natural impulse of a keen botanist gravitating towards known botanical high spots. A lucky white-flowered Rockrose was as much as might be expected from a few days' stay in an area where John Ray had spent nine years collecting records and Thomas must have left Cambridge content with the time spent there. He was, perhaps, rather over-occupied with white forms, but the Rockrose earned its place in Ray's *Synopsis* and Ray, ever generous, acknowledged the plant.

At the end of the Cambridgeshire search list, there are a few additional notes:

Otis, The Bustard, New market-heath.

In the Isle of Ely is an Artificial River called Hundred foot river, from its bredth, when made, tis 20 miles or more in length.

There is another called 40 foot River a latitudine

Below these is one more plant, Brookweed, *Samolus valerandi* found with a white flower 'plentifull on a rotten moor between Cambridge, and Wilborham.'

When Thomas left Cambridge, he was in no hurry to press on home even though his botanical recording is tailing off as the year grows late and he has, perhaps, other business to attend to: the distances between the next stages of his journey are short: 'to Over 6 miles; thence to St. Ives 6 miles; thence to Haddenham in the Isle of Ely 7 miles; thence by Ely to Littleport 9.' Such distances allowed for some plant collecting by the way: Venus' Looking-glass, *Legousia hybrida*, Corn Gromwell, *Lithospermum arvense*, Water Parsnip, *Sium latifolium* and Great Yellow-cress, *Rorippa amphibia* are all noticed at St. Ives, the last two, perhaps, from down by the River Ouse where Oliver Cromwell had once pastured cattle in the marshy fields that bordered the river.

Back eastwards again for the last records from Cambridgeshire, – Thomas' zig-zag departure from Cambridge is strongly indicative of Quaker business about which we know nothing and he was now headed for Lincolnshire where the movement had gained greatly in the early days – in the late 1650s Lincolnshire had been among the top contributors to Quaker funds and by the end of the century its Meetings were still growing. Thomas, walking 'betwixt Haddenham and the windmill in the Isle of Ely' no doubt thought about these things even as he recorded Small Fleabane, *Pulicaria vulgaris* and stood to contemplate the water flowing under the 'great wood bridge on Audrey Causey in the Isle of Ely' where he recorded Water Soldier, *Stratiotes aloides* – 'standing on the bridge looking into the water, it appears very plentifully.' In the Isle of Ely, too, he noticed the White Poplar, *Populus alba* giving, at the same time, Lincolnshire as another location but there was little time to stand and stare now for he was truly on the move again: the plants in this sequence are all seen as his tramping feet took him ever deeper into the Fen country: Sea Aster, *Aster tripolium* 'very plentifully at Long Sutton in the ditches by the High-rode' receives mention in the tour notes but Brookweed, *Samolus valerandi*, Creeping Jenny, *Lysimachia nummularia* and Marsh Mallow, *Althaea officinalis* all, seemingly, 'in a ditch on the left hand of the highway leading from Hallbich to Gedney in Lincs' are added to the search list. They are records of a man who has become a botanist by habit, compulsively noting but unable to spare time for extensive search. For a while we must rely upon his itinerary: no plants mark his track 'to Dunnington [Donington] by which lives Will Dixon 20 [miles]; thence by Deary hill good for milk cows and by 40 foot River to Evedon [by Sleaford] 8 miles; to Lincolne where lives Abraham Morris and Jo Mills 14 miles.' The names of Quakers are punctuating the brief narrative. Abraham Morrice, prominent in Lincoln was in 1690 to marry Isabel Fell, Margaret's third daughter. He may have been the Abraham Morrice for whom Thomas Lawson had left a parcel of books when he was in London. A cryptic memo in his notebook reads 'John Dew a joyner on the north side of pauls, my books to be left with him for Abr. Morrice.'[23] It sounds like an arrangement to have Lawson's works distributed in Lincolnshire – perhaps he was now in the county on a follow-up mission. There is much we can only speculate upon.

The impression that there was activity of another sort on Lawson's mind at this time is confirmed by the negative evidence of the botanical records. Only Crow Garlic, *Allium vineale* 'nigh Monks Mill by Lincoln' and an abundance of the Horse-shoe Vetch, *Hippocrepis comosa* by St. Giles at Lincoln were sufficient to divert him but then it may be that time and his home were calling him and once he left behind him the flat lands of Lincolnshire and the hospitality of Abraham Morrice he was truly returning to the North Country: 11 miles brought him to South Leverton in Nottinghamshire and a longer stage of 14 to Barnsley in Yorkshire, collecting by the way Venus' Looking Glass, *Legousia hybrida* again and Water Violet, *Hottonia palustris* both from Retford and Barnby Moor just five miles short of the Yorkshire border. In Yorkshire, the records thin still further. He went to have a look at Robin Hood well near Wentbridge and noticed Water Betony, *Scrophularia aquatica* and Celery-leaved Crowfoot, *Ranunculus sceleratus* by the waterside and North of Pontefract had another tourist's record: Meadow Saffron, *Colchicum autumnale* 'in the closes adjoining to Sherburn' but the work of Quakerism was more on his mind as he jotted down the names of Friends with whom he stayed in the county. In Pontefract, he stayed with Thomas English who was later to be imprisoned for non-attendance at church and features in Besse, for that reason.[24] And there are others who can be tracked down in Besse: John Loft at Tadcaster, Thomas Thompson at Malton, Peter Hodgson at Scarborough and Jacob Scarfe at Ellergy, all good Quakers who had suffered fines and imprisonments and have earned their places in the *Sufferings of the People called Quakers*. John Loft was a Quaker of long standing, imprisoned in 1655 for getting up in the parish church of Newton to declare that the Prayers of the Wicked [i.e. the assembled congregation] were an Abomination to the Lord.[25] In 1684, he was to be imprisoned again for a similar offence when, having been invited to hear the vicar of Wetherby preach, he was moved to say 'somewhat' to him that interrupted the sermon, earned him a fine of £40 and landed him in jail when he refused to pay it.[26] Thomas Thompson and Peter Hodgson were likewise prominent in their own areas: Meetings were held in their houses and in 1666 Fox had had a Meeting in Hodgson's house after a terrible imprisonment in Scarborough Castle when he had been kept in a cell open to the driving sea winds so that his bed and his clothes were constantly being wetted and the water 'ran about the room, that I was fain to skim it up with a platter.'[27] By such events and such examples were Friends kept true to their original ideal and Thomas, travelling in the service of truth, would have much to listen to and discuss in the strongly Quaker lands of Yorkshire. Beyond Scarborough, though, he paused again to botanise, recording not far from Scarborough, Bog Pimpernel, *Anagallis tenella*. Between Whitby and Lythe, the shore drew him and he records Sea Buckthorn, *Hippophaë rhamnoides* 'on the sea bank between Whitby and Lyth plentifully.'

Now the route home lay directly due West of him, and he began to pace off the miles, turning inland to Pinchinthorpe, near Guisborough, 11 miles away and then 'to Horton 6; to Barnard Castle 6.' Only a record of Corn Gromwell, *Lithospermum arvense*, jotted down at the end of the Durham county list, gives any indication that Thomas was still collecting and we cannot be certain that it was gathered on this occasion. Now only the long haul over Stainmoor confronted him, a well-trodden road between East and West and one on which, surely, he got a lift, for it is more than 30 miles from Barnard Castle to Great Strickland and he records no stopping place between. In his tour notes he mentions no more plants and though his search lists for Yorkshire and Durham record a few plants that might have been picked up in these last 80 miles or so homeward, it is more than probable that they were collected in later excursions. By now it really must have been late in the year for a botanist and even a traveller in the service of truth had a home to go to.

CHAPTER IX

Educational Theorist

ON HIS RETURN FROM LONDON, Thomas found that little at home had changed. Under the Elizabethan statutes against recusants, Thomas faced the authorities yet again. The Quakers might protest that they were no Papists but they continued to be prosecuted. In the Great Book of Sufferings there is a list of 76 persons who:

> have been Prosecuted upon the 23th and 28th of Elizabeth made against Popish Recusants, and two thirds of their Estates thereupon seized and sequestered into the King's hands by the Statute of the 3d of King James provided Against Popish Recusants, and Leavyes for the Yearly profitts of their said Lands; thereupon made by the Sheriffs Bayliffs of the said County, by process out of the Excheqr for the year 1677 as followeth vizt as they were collected and brought up out of the said County presented and Witnessed unto by Wittnesses to the Members of the Aforesd Parliament in the month called Aprill 1678[1]

Thomas Lawson's name is amongst those familiar to us: Rowland Wilson, value of lands seized, 10s; Nicholas Denkin, 6/8d; James Fallowfield 18s; Lancelot Fallowfield, £1; Thomas Lawson, £1.

In various ways, though, the zeal of the authorities was beginning to over-reach itself. There were many in the country who did not wish to see the harrying of a people now generally regarded as inoffensive. Another entry in the Great Book reads:

> A true Account of the Sufferings of the People called Quakers belonging to Strickland Meeting in the Bottome of Westmerland in the Year 1678. Upon the Statute made against Popish Recusants etc.

> All these as followeth were paid to the Bayliff Jo[h]n Wilkinson without Friends Consent by one or other – vizt

> [List of Names][2]

118

Amongst these names is Thomas' together with three Fallowfields. It was
not very satisfactory. By refusal to pay the state, the Quakers challenged its
right to fine them. To have others pay their fines was to weaken their case
when what they really needed was recognition of a right to worship as
Protestant dissenters. A letter from Robert Barrow in Kendal, dated
8th October, 1680, tells of Friends' attempts to obtain recognition of a
status separate from the Papists.[3] They appeared before the zealous Sir
Daniel Fleming at the Quarter Sessions 'and had Certificates under the
hands of the Priest, Constables and Church Wardens that they were noe
Papists Recusants, but Prodistant Disenters Known by the Name of
Quakers.' It made little difference. Sir Daniel was determined upon
enforcing the letter of the law and, in the matter of the law there were, as
always, pickings to be had:

> Likewise Robert Nicolson Deputy Sheriff for the Barony of
> Kendall doth much abuse us, many of our Friends Lands being
> Customary Tenant right and himself gote about forty Friends off
> from the Sequestration and an Order out of the Court not to proceed
> against them . . . Yet nevertheless made Distress: and Afterward
> said he could get soe many off if wee would give him twenty pounds a
> month and hath made Distress in severall places.

In this time of trouble, with his school closed and his lands under threat,
Thomas busied himself with writing. Towards the end of 1679, there was
suddenly new opportunity for having works published that might, in
normal times, have been suppressed.[4] Under an Act of 1662 (14 Charles 2
c. 23) 'An Act for preventing the frequent Abuses in printing seditious
treasonable and unlicensed Bookes and Pamphlets and for regulating of
Printing and Printing Presses,' books were required to be licensed by the
authorities and Quaker printers were, as we have seen in the case of
Thomas' first printer, Giles Calvert, frequently in trouble for flouting this
law which, renewed by successive legislation, continued in force until the
Parliament of 1679. The last time that the law had been renewed in the
previous Parliament, it had been laid down that it should stand 'until the
[end of the] First Session of the next Parlyament' at which time it would
expire unless steps were taken to renew it. Now the Parliament of 1679 was
very short-lived: the king found it intractable and dissolved it before it had
got round to renewing the Act of 1662 which was not to be renewed until the
first year of James II's reign, 1685. From late in 1679 until the new king's
accession, therefore, there was freedom of the press. Of the four works of
Lawson published during these years: *Dagon's Fall before the Ark*, 1679; *A
Mite into the Treasury*, 1680; *A Treatise Relating to the Call Work and Wages
of the Ministers of Christ*, 1680 and *A Serious Remembrancer to Live Well*, 1684

only the first appears without any printer's name, indicating that it was published before the lapse of the licensing Act.

This sudden burst of writing after long silence suggests that Thomas was working rapidly from accumulated notes. He had put his time in London to effect by making copious extracts from theological writers such as John Trapp, Puritan author of several commentaries. His botanical notebook is interspersed with pages of notes incorporated into *Dagon's Fall* and *A Treatise Relating.*[5] No doubt he had also talked with fellow Quakers in London who had stimulated him into organising other notes which he had accumulated over the years and making them fit for publication and it is probable that, besides these works that were published around 1680, Thomas had three other treatises in draft. These were later found amongst his papers at his death.

Both *Dagon's Fall* and *A Mite into the Treasury* deal with the subject of education: if Thomas was banned from teaching, he would at least make his own contribution to educational theory. The two works stand full in the mainstream of radical anti-scholasticism. Protest against the intellectual content of the university curriculum had long been an expression of sectarian discontent and criticism against the established order. The Puritans of Queen Elizabeth's day had attacked university preoccupation with Aristotelian learning and, as the seventeenth century progressed, it became increasingly difficult for those who attacked the professional priesthood to defend learning when the universities, the highest seats of learning, were primarily concerned with the training of that priesthood.[6] A strong current of anti-scholasticism runs through all the reformers of the century.

Excluded from the universities and from official posts, the Quakers were to become prominent in the emergent industries of England: they were to be the ironmasters and industrial businessmen of the future.[7] This development, involving knowledge of the applied sciences, was one consequence of their exclusion from politics and the universities. But even before the legislative moves, whereby the establishment closed its ranks against dissent, there were those who pressed for a different sort of training. The emphasis whereby many Quakers were led into the mastery of business and industry had its roots in the very early days of the movement and in the intellectual underground of the seventeenth century. The old radicals of mid-century who had rejected the *status quo* of their time had sought to establish a culture to run counter to that of the ruling elite who had made a university training the mark of a gentleman. Whatever might have been the reasons for Thomas Lawson's abandonment of his own university career after a year or less, his subsequent activities amongst the poor and the dispossessed had left him with strong feelings against the establishment and a conviction that the traditional learning of schools and universities was a formula and a ritual rather than a real education. Such objections were by no means new: there was a good deal of truth in the long-running criticism that a university education was a formality that put more emphasis upon polish than upon learning. Like the Puritans, Thomas complains of the trivial nature of the classical works studied in schools and university: plays and poems are light stuff, it is absurd that they should be hallowed merely because they are written in the classical tongues. The whole philosophy of the pagan world has been exalted to an eminence that it does not deserve.

Central to all Puritans and sectaries was the belief that the bible contained more truth than all the works of classicism put together. Could we but return to the innocent state of Adam before the Fall, we would know all things. It was common belief that Adam in Paradise had an intuitive knowledge of all things: that he had no need to toil after learning or to use a microscope or a telescope to see the imperceptible details of the universe:[8] he saw and knew it all by instinct just as he knew the language of the beasts and comprehended the voice of God. As Joseph Glanvill had said 'Causes are hid in night and obscurity from us, which were all Sun to him.'[9] After the Fall, of course, things were very different. Glanvill again:

> For whereas our ennobled understandings could once take the wings of the morning, to visit the World above us, and had a glorious display of the highest form of created excellencies, they now lye groveling in this lower region, muffled up in mists, and darkness: the curse of the Serpent is fallen upon degenerated Man, To go on his belly and lick the dust.[10]

Thus, with Adam's loss of innocence went the loss of true knowledge and, as Thomas Lawson sees it, its replacement by a depraved and degenerate interest in the trivial and inconsequential:

> Yea I say, if Adam and his posterity had kept their standing in Heavenly wisdoms dominion, we had had no lascivious Poems, no wanton Comedies, no vain Tragedies, no foolish Fables, no bewitching Orations, no spoiling Philosophy, no Pagan Ethicks, Physicks, or Metaphysicks, which are the infatuating dregs of the Hellish dead Sea, the smoak of the bottomless Pit.[11]

But Adam did not keep his standing in Heavenly wisdom's dominion. He fell. The Adam of Milton's *Paradise Lost* was brought the herb Eyebright, *euphrasy*, by the angel Gabriel to help clear his sight,[12] dimmed by his sin, but no such artificial means ever could restore to him the vision of what he had lost and his posterity became increasingly corrupt in post-lapsarian times, declining both physically and intellectually. Thomas

Lawson paints a picture of increased lethargy and depravity of appetite. The power of men to see and understand the truth has declined and they have opened their ears to diviners, wizards and sorcerers. They have turned away from God and paid heed to Pagan philosophy. And now this was what was taught in our schools in place of bible learning and the honest truths of the world about us. Against the classical curriculum of the schools, Thomas marshals a formidable array of testimonies, quoting Bishop Wilkins, Tertullian, Martin Luther, St. Augustine, Calamy, Gregory the Great, Queen Elizabeth and many others.[13]

Thomas would have the traditional learning of the schools replaced by a learning that looked towards the bible and the world of nature. This apparently contradictory programme – there is little encouragement to nature study given in the bible – can be supported by one key text of the old testament. Thomas calls upon King Solomon as a witness:

> That he had a clear understanding of the Lords Creation, is demonstrable from Scripture records, for he spake of Trees, from the Cedar Tree that is in Lebanon, even unto the Hysop that springeth out of the Wall; he spake also of Beasts, and of Fowl, and of creeping things, and of Fishes, 1 Kings 1.[14]

This was a crucial text for the apologists of the study of nature. The botanist, William Turner had used it in 1551 in the prologue to his herbal, arguing that in the bible:

> I do not remembre, that I have red anye expressed commendation of Grammer, Logick, Philosophie, naturall or morall, Astronomie, Arithmetyke, Geometry, Cosmographie, Musycke, Perspective, or any other such lyke science. But I rede amonge the commendatyons and prayses of kyng Salomon, that he was sene in herbes shrubbes and trees, and so perfectly that he disputed wysely of them from the hyghest to the lowest, that is from the Cedre tre in mount Liban unto the Hysop that groweth furth of the wall.[15]

More than a hundred years later, Lawson is finding it necessary to use the same text in argument against an educational establishment that had virtually stood still since Turner's day. He pleads with the instructors of youth:

> You Teachers of Schools and Colledges . . . were it not more God-like, more Christian-like, to instruct Youth in the knowledge of God, whom to know is life Eternal, and in the knowledge of his works, being very good, and useful and necessary things, then in the knowledge of Heathen Arts and Sciences, brought in by the Serpent.[16]

The educational establishment, however, had ignored more influential critics than Thomas Lawson and the universities continued to provide a curriculum that was unsuitable preparation for nearly all of the new professions that were coming into being, as Britain, in the late seventeenth and eighteenth centuries turned itself into a commercial and then an industrial society.[17] Numbers in the universities dropped dramatically and others besides Quakers found that they could get along very well without a university training. There was a popular feeling that learning should be more useful and tell us more about the world we live in. The view that amateurs were carrying forward the torch of learning in the period after 1660 had enough foundation in fact to make it a commonplace of history.[18] Thomas claims to have abandoned the usual school authors in favour of writers whose bias was utilitarian. He does not quite demote the classical languages from their position of pre-eminence but he does suggest that they might be a vehicle whereby other things may be learnt:

> Now if Languages must be Learned, were it not more Christian like, that out of Latin, &c. Books for that purpose provided, Children and Youth read the Natures of Trees, Birds, Beasts, Fish, Serpents, Insects, Earths, Metals, Salts, Stones, Vulgar and Precious, as also rules for Gardening, Agriculture, Grazing of Cattel, Buildings, Navigation, Arithmatick, Geography, Chronology, sound History, Medicine, knowledge in Law, Improvement of Lands, Chirugery, Traffick Government, ordering of Bees, Propagation of Plants, by Roots, Seeds, Slips, Layers, Suckers, by Grafting, Inoculating, Imping, and of Geometry.[19]

No doubt he put such utilitarian ideals to work when he saw opportunity in his own teaching but the early years of his schoolmastering probably saw little scope for advanced methods. Then, as now, the requirements of the universities tended to influence all education down to the lowest levels and until they changed their requirements he would be unable to depart from the accepted curriculum: the parents of children entrusted to his care would expect them to be trained in the conventional disciplines. He himself says that he taught the usual school authors in the early part of his career[20] – we remember that he grounded John Smith sufficiently well in the learned languages for him to become a noted antiquary.

His trip to London, discussion there and the interest of Fox and Penn had, however, stimulated Lawson into setting down his educational ideas. When he had first begun to teach, the need for a separate Quaker education had not seemed so urgent, for Friends had hardly come to appreciate that their belief was going to lead them into social isolation. On the contrary, in the very early years, they saw a movement that was capable of leading the rest of the country: the country would change, not they. As time went on, the movement grew old and the university men in it grew old with it and were not replaced by men who had had the same training. The Quakers came to see the need to establish an educational system of their own and Thomas, in the last third of his life, came to be involved in a variety of schemes that show him, a man in his forties and fifties, still evolving with the movement. His grandson, Jonah Thompson, was to claim that there was an 'intimate acquaintance'[21] between Thomas Lawson and William Penn and though Jonah had special reasons for trying to establish intimacy, Lawson certainly was well enough acquainted with Penn to include him in a list of Friends to whom he wishes Fox to remember him in a letter written 20th April, 1689: 'Remember me to William Mead, William Pen, John Rous and their wives, George Whitehead, Alexander Parker, James Parke etc.'[22]

The most obvious time for Lawson to have met Penn was in 1677, at some time before Penn's departure for Holland in late July of that year. The plan of the Garden-schoolhouse of which Fox had written to Penn in 1674 seems to have fallen into abeyance but Penn had a multitude of schemes in his head and when he began to form a project to acquire a large area of the new world, Thomas became interested. There is evidence that he went so far as to attempt to purchase land in the new colony, which was to be named Pennsylvania, and perhaps he even did so, though his claim was never established despite the efforts of Jonah Thompson. In 1750, Jonah left Sherborne in Dorset where he had settled as a schoolmaster and took ship across the Atlantic. A letter written to Thomas Penn, 30th March 1751, by Richard Peters the Penn family secretary and agent, reads:

> I write this at the Instance of Jonah Thompson, a Publick Friend, who is, I suppose, well known to you, either in Person or by Character. He and his Brother in England are Grandsons and Heirs-at-Law of the late Thomas Lawson, deceased, whose name you will see the last in the City List as an original Purchaser of 250 acres, for which quantity and Lot appurtenant thereto, and Liberty Land, Mr. Thompson applied to the office, and desired a Warrant to take them up, as it was found none had hereto fore issued, on a careful search of the Books.[23]

This is a remarkable piece of evidence. William Penn did not become owner and Governor of Pennsylvania until 1681, when he acquired it from the crown, partly by exerting his considerable influence and partly through the relinquishment of a claim of £16,000 which was due from the crown to his father's estate for a loan and interest on it.[24] As Governor, Penn had the power to form the constitution and laws of the new colony subject to the consent of the settlers. As owner, he would sell land to whomsoever he wished and, as there was plenty of land and he needed settlers, he sold it cheap.[25] He also wished to encourage rapid settlement so we may assume that Lawson became involved in the venture early in the 1680s when he had just entered his fifties. It was a goodly age to contemplate beginning life anew across the Atlantic. When Penn sailed in the autumn of 1682, nearly a third of the hundred who set out in the *Welcome* died of small-pox on the way.[26] Thomas' desire to uproot himself and his family probably sprang from a weariness of the difficulties of pursuing his calling under constant persecution in England. Perhaps, to the Quaker dream of peace and freedom of worship, he added his own private dream: a full, unharassed life as a schoolmaster with ample facilities and a plot of ground to act as a demonstration garden for his own joy and his pupils' edification.

When Jonah attempted to establish his grandfather's claim in 1751, he told Peters that the deeds had been entrusted to William Penn who was to establish the claim on Thomas' behalf:

> He said the Deeds, by a Family Tradition were said to be given to your Father, & that he engaged to take the Land up for Mr. Lawson who was of his intimate acquaintance, and as may you receive Satisfaction of this upon the spot, he desired my Letter to you, setting forth his application and Disappointment, for he expected to have found the Deeds here, and the Land well located.[27]

writes Peters, who had already declined to give Jonah a warrant to take up the land 'since he had not the Original Deeds, which I told him must be produced, the Descent proved before a Warrant could issue.'

Thomas Penn was in no doubt that his agent had acted correctly:

> With respect to Jonah Thompson, you are not to grant him or any other Person a foot of Land, without their producing my Father's Deed & the regular conveyance from the Person to whom it was granted; for if the Person has not the Deeds the Land may be sold. I never heard of these Deeds.[28]

So Jonah returned home disappointed but certainly not disenchanted with the American colony, for he returned in 1753 to spend two years in Philadelphia, part of which time he was Latin master at the Friends' School there and he seriously considered moving with his family to Pennsylvania. Like his grandfather, however, he never made the break with England and it was left to his son, John Thompson, Thomas Lawson's great-grandson, finally to cross the water and settle in America where he was at first schoolmaster at the Friends' School at Philadelphia and then, in the late 1770s or 1780s, he turned to business. Thus a teaching tradition that had come down in the family for a hundred years was broken.[29]

By that time, the Quakers had made their own dispositions with regard to education and had ceased to attack the establishment with the kind of heat that Lawson raised in *Dagon's Fall*. But for Thomas, the fight was still on and the arguments of *Dagon's Fall* were continued in a work that he published a year later in 1680. This, *A Mite into the Treasury*, his second work on education, is a subject by subject attack on the seven liberal arts which still formed the basis of the scholastic curriculum: Grammar, Logic and Rhetoric, the subjects of the trivium whilst Music, Arithmetic, Geometry, Logic and Astronomy formed the quadrivium. In turn Thomas attacks them: Grammar and the knowledge of tongues are nothing to be proud of when we consider that diversity of tongues was the direct result of man's temerity in daring to build the tower of Babel: 'not learning will open the Book of seven seals, the book of knowledge, but only the Lion of Judah'[30] and Logic and Rhetoric are likewise unnecessary prerequisites of faith. Stephen did not bandy logic with his adversaries but donned the armour of faith:

> Thus Stephen obtained Victory over the Champions of the Dragon: and how? Not by Heathen Wisdom, Pagan Logick, Spoiling Philosophy, but by the Sword of the Spirit, Shield of Faith, Wisdom from above; in this Armour he prevailed.[31]

Nor did Christ promise his disciples that they should be conquerors through such sophistical devices as Pagan Logic and the Rhetoric of the schoolmen and lawyers. Rhetoric is mere Phrase-making and, in the words of Bishop Wilkins 'The grand imposture of Phrasing hath eaten out all sollid Learning.'[32]

The quadrivium, teaching the mathematical arts, might be expected to fare a little better in Thomas' hands as being of more practical application and, indeed, Arithmetic and Geometry do receive a grudging allowance as arts useful to government. On the whole, however, he neither attacks nor defends them. This has rather the air of special pleading: the fashion of the times was growing towards the mechanical arts and Thomas' avoidance of the subject of mathematics has rather the air of a deliberate blind eye. Cambridge had taught him pure mathematics as an intellectual discipline as acceptable as Greek and his knowledge of applied maths was probably as shaky as most of his contemporaries.[33] In any case, he is quick to point out how mathematics may be turned to perverted reckonings and how it is worth nothing unless allied to spiritual understanding. A similar criticism attends music: music and singing are nothing if not performed from the spirit:

> Now who are of God, they are distinguishing Persons, and with us they contend for singing in the Spirit, and with Understanding; this

Song none but the Redeemed can learn; this Song of the Lord cannot be sung in a strange Land, Captivity, Spiritual Babylon; and such as are of God, they deny all dead formal Singing and Singers, who formally sing other Mens Conditions, out of the Spirit, without Understanding.[34]

The implications are obvious: the Quakers were a people in captivity, their spirits blanketed by the formalism and insincerity of the established church which had allowed all sorts of artifice to come between the people and the natural expression of rejoicing in the Lord. A whole chapter follows entitled *Of the Rise of Musical Instruments in the Churches Professing Christianity*.

Now only Astronomy remains to be considered and again Thomas is careful to select the aspects of the subject that suit his case, concentrating his attack upon astrology and upon those who claim to predict the future from the stars. Against these, he sets the true prophets of the old testament:

> The Prophets of the Lord, his holy Seers, (as holy Records tell us) fore-saw things, and what should befall in the World, to Men, States, Persons, People; but this they did by the Indwellings of the Anointing, the Word of Prophecy; not by the observation of Celestial Bodies: And how fallible Astrologers in this thing are, we have annual evident and pregnant Demonstration.[35]

It was an old-fashioned view of Astronomy and if Thomas had heard of the speculations of the Lucasian professor at Cambridge, a man called Isaac Newton, he gives no sign of it. On the other hand, there were still many respected practitioners of astrology around in 1680 and Newton himself made serious excursions into astrology.

If one is left with the impression that Thomas has set up paper tigers with which to fight and if one has the feeling that his thoughts on education do not go as far in imagination as they might, one must remember that his tigers were real enough to ensure that a curriculum little changed since the middle ages still dominated the universities. If Thomas is only groping towards a vision of how things might be changed, he is at least at one with John Locke in seeing that things must change and that children must be taught:

> Useful and Necessary things, whereby they might be Qualified for Concerns of this Life, for the Help, Benefit and Advantage of others in their respective Generations, then to be trained up in Lascivious Poems, Comedies, Tragedies, Frivolous Fables, Heathen Orations, Pagan Philosophy, Ethicks, Physicks, Metaphisick, which after the Apostles Days darkned Sun and Air, disfigured the Face, spoiled the Glory of the Primitive Church.[36]

The book concludes with an argument that is again the product of many bitter years of debate. Quakers had consistently preferred to go to prison rather than doff the cap to authority. Thomas embarks on a lengthy and serious attack on reverential titles and the whole complicated ritual of attire pertaining to authority and to the clergy with its 'Gowns, Hoods, Tippets, round Caps, square caps, Gowns with standing Collars, the Pall, Rochet, Surplice, Copes, Bonnets, Cowls, Black Coats, Miters, Girdles, Sursingles etc.'[37] No such forms and distinctions were known in the first days of the church when a man was known simply by his calling as an Apostle or an Evangelist. Only when the simple light of vocation was lost was it necessary to institute titles and all the evils that they brought with them – the itch after titles for their own sake and the ostentatious display of the robes of office – 'and if any conformed not thereto, What followed? A Thunderbolt of Excommunication, Suspension etc.'[38] Thomas uses the last five chapters of *A Mite into the Treasury* to attack cap and gown, pall and surplice and the whole hierarchy of reverential titles in church and university.

All these works published around 1680 have an out-dated feel to them; as though Thomas was working from old notes that still contained the hope that things might change from within. The Quakers, with other dissenters, were to be in the forefront of a new age that brought in commercial and industrial skills but they did it because they were outside the system, not because they changed it. In his life, Thomas was to keep pace with the trend, making new friends among virtuosi and Fellows of the Royal Society and coming to be styled as a gentleman. But in his writings he remains at heart a millenarian of the 1650s. Gentleman or not, he was to publish one more attack on the respectable clergy. His other work of 1680 had the title *A Treatise Relating to the Call, Work and Wages of the Ministers of Christ; as also to the Call, Work and Wages of the Ministers of Antichrist.* The material for this book had been gathering some time. Twenty-five years ago, a young and fiery Thomas had followed where the calling had led him even into exile and opposition to the paid and professional ministers in the church. Now he calls upon his fellow Quakers to hold firm to that calling for they have good examples to follow:

> Most of the Ministers among the Waldenses were Trades-men, as Merchants, Fisher-men, Taylors, Shoe-makers, Husband-men; and these Waldenses, antient Protestants, Witnesses against the apostatised Roman Church, bare Testimony, That it were lawful for any to Preach, who were called of God: Though Strangers to Natural Tongues, Arts, Sciences, Philosophy, such the living God is raising up to stand on their Feet, and they must bear their Testimony in order to Season, and rectifie the Nations; though by the Sons of

Belial, under the Delusion of Anti-christ, they be branded as Anti-magistratical and Anti-ministerial, and Persecuted.[39]

This is an attack on the hierarchy of society indeed: shoemakers and husbandmen are to put the world to rights and those who are to be ministers of Christ must put the call of Christ above eduction and training. No man can be made Christ's minister by the university: he cannot be 'bred and qualified in the Smoke of earthly Wisdom',[40] which is all that a university training can do. Nor do laws enacted to keep the ministry professional – and Thomas gives a history of these[41] – have any justification.

These are old arguments for Thomas: arguments originally rehearsed in his first publication, *Of the False Ministry*, exactly 25 years before. In Chapter IV of *Of the Work of the Ministry of christ and of Antichrist*, Thomas compares and contrasts the beliefs and procedures of Quakers with the beliefs and procedures of the paid clergy and, point by point, we see repeated the central arguments of the light within, of baptism of the spirit, of liberty of prophesying, of God the only word and of the possibility of freedom from sin in this world.

The rest, and by far the greater part of the book, is devoted to the subject of tithe. Thomas presents a detailed and documented account of the church's coercive and, to Quaker eyes, unscriptural demand for tithe as well as demand for other monies for all sorts of services performed by the church. All, in the Quaker view, should be performed of free will. Christ did away with tithe and though he commanded the scribes and pharisees to pay tithes they were Jews and under Levitical ministration: 'Neither Christ nor the Apostles ever ordained any other Maintenance for the Gospel Ministers, then what was Free and Voluntary, and that from such as received them and their Message.'[42] Mathew 10, Mark 6 and Luke 9 all say that if a disciple should not be received by a particular people in an area, he should shake the dust off his feet and go on his way.[43] But the clergy of the Established Church exact their dues whether the people receive their teaching or not, and the Quaker is punished if he does not render his goods to them. Not by history or mosaic law or apostolic practice or even simple social necessity can the church's claim to the exaction of tithe be justified. Chapter after chapter the arguments go on, full of historical and biblical reference, full too, of the seventeenth-century's particularised examination of the words and deeds of the past in order that they might be related in all small details to the practices of the present. It is Thomas' longest work apart from *Baptismalogia* and it was printed by Benjamin Clarke who, for his printing of Quaker works, was dubbed 'Thee and Thou Clarke.'[44] It was also Thomas' last work relating to controversy and this, perhaps, is the moment to consider his controversial writings and to arrive at some assessment of them.

The first thing that must be said about them is that they are not great literature: it was a literary principle with the Friends that their writings should not embody any ornateness of style or fanciful diction – only plainness could convey the plain truth of Christ. But Thomas' plainness is not the homely plainness of Fox in his *Journal*, nor is it the plain struggle to express, through the imperfect medium of language, the soul's approach to God. It is a plainness that is somehow caught between two modes of expression. As the century wore on, ornateness generally went out of fashion and the plain style in diction was being put across by such pulpit exponents as Isaac Barrow and the silver-tongued John Tillotson who was to become Archbishop of Canterbury in 1691. Balance and decorum were the measures of literary criticism and urbanity the most admired quality of the day. But Thomas never seems to have made the transition from the mid-century plainness of the sectaries, rushing to put their words on paper with an urgency that disregarded style and shape, and the elegant plainness that had begun to prevail after the Restoration. The natural way of writing had come to life and flourished with all the sappy vigour of a neglected rose during the argumentative years of the Civil War. By 1700, style had been pruned and shaped and its natural effect was very much a product of study. In such a context, Thomas' language seems old-fashioned, somehow fossilised at a period when the simpler prose had not yet shaken itself free from the clutter of controversy in which it had been born and from adherence to every word and phrase of the King James bible which had been its godfather. The figure of Antichrist is as sinister to Thomas as it ever was to a King James Puritan and he attacks his adversaries out of the armoury of scripture and Hebrew scholarship and Church history. The closer he is tuned to the authorised version, the clearer his language. At the opening of *Dagon's Fall* he borrows the words of Proverbs (3. 14-17) and Job (28. 16-19) to describe the nature of true wisdom:

> There is a wisdom, whose Merchandize transcends the Merchandize of Silver, whose gain surmounts the gain of the purest Gold, more precious than Rubies, than the Onyx, Saphire, Chrystal, Coral or Topaz of Ethiopia; her ways are ways of pleasantness, all her paths are peace.[45]

Occasionally, too, a phrase comes at us in a way that is pure seventeenth century:

> Through this, Adam was all fair, through a Garment conferred upon him; out of the Wardrobe of Eternity[46]

Such images, however, are rare with Thomas. The tricks of imagery and style were generally eschewed by Quaker polemicists as the dangerous shifts of rhetoric. One could read the whole of Thomas' polemical works and have no inkling that he was a naturalist. No image from botany shall lead the fancy astray or dupe the intellect into acquiescence: the study of plants was a plain matter of science and utility. It should not be allowed to intrude into another sphere. If Thomas does use an image taken from the natural world, it is purely conventional. In *Dagon's Fall*, for instance, he sees youth as being overwhelmed by a great flood of erroneous and corrupt teaching as mariners are endangered by sea monsters:

> as the Sea Monster called Physeter, as naturalists write, mounts above the tops of Ships, standing upright in the Sea, like a Pillar, and spouts out great flouds of water, whereby it overwhelms or indangers them.[47]

This was traditional stuff – straight off the pages of Pliny's *Natural History*.[48] But Thomas had made his attitude to imaginative writing quite clear when he decried the reading of the plays and poetry of the classical world in schools. Such an attitude was common to most Quakers: they distrusted the exercise of imagination and fancy even when much of what they wanted to say fell more naturally into the passionate expression of the seventeenth century than the urbanity of the eighteenth. This tends to make Quaker works heavy-going: the issues over which such passions were roused 300 years ago are strange to us now, the relation of minutiae is tedious, and bad printing and a liberality of italicisation often make the books physically hard on the eyes. Thomas' printed works are fairly typical of his age and the movement which he served.

The books that Thomas published on his return from his tour around England are the contribution of his learning to his Friends in both senses of the word. In part they represent the payment of a debt and it was the contacts made on the tour that stimulated him to pay it. Once the debt was discharged, he was the more free to concentrate on the other product of that crucial year. Through the 1677 tour notebook we have been enabled to see the development of a new and abiding interest in his life which belongs, essentially, to that year. We know that he continued to collect – for there are many records sent to other botanists after 1677, but the data from this later collecting was not entered in the old notebook and it looks very much as though Thomas abandoned it (probably in favour of another notebook) almost as soon as he got home. Before we do the same, and before we go on to look at the nature of Thomas' later botanising, we should, for the sake of completeness, look at a few records not previously considered which were collected in the counties of Yorkshire, Durham and Northumberland. These counties present special problems: the records are sketchy, they are all in the form of additions to the county search lists and only for a few plants are specific locations given. The most interesting are the notes following upon the Yorkshire search list which are as follows:[49]

Trifolium ornithopodii siliquis Ray.

Gramen nemorum hirsutum majus, The greater hairy wood grasse, in the beck between Jo. Blaiklings and Francis Blaiklings Sedberge, see park and Ray. Cat. pl. *Luzula pilosa*. [This record is repeated in the tour notes with the addition 'also about Kendal'.]

Regia hasta, the kings speare, at Brignell nigh Bernard Castle. ['Hastula regia' (King's Spear) is a name applied by Turner, *Names*, [Aiij] to Asphodel or 'Whyte Affodil.'[50]]

Scilla between Scarbrough and Burlington, enquire of Tho. Shipton. [Probably son of Richard Shipton who built Lythe Hall, near Whitby, as Raven suggests.[50] See Fox, *Journal*. pp. 506, 533.]

Caryophyllus montanus C.B. where thlaspi fol. glob. grows Hinckel Haugh. *Armeria maritima* and *Thlaspi alpestre*. [Hinckel Haugh is Rye Loaf Hill. See Raven, *Ray*, pp. 160-61.]

Juncus Capitulis equifoli minus et fluitans. ?B. nigh York found by a freind of J. Newton. *Eleogiton fluitans*.

Lysimachia lutea fl. globoso park. nigh Yorke by a freind of J. Newton. enquire of J. Newton for these 2. *Naumburgia thyrsiflora*.

From York to Hull one may go by Boat, at Hull is the Apparel of a wild man in his strange boat, called Bony boat man.

Nigh Sel[?b]y by water is a winding place, called Nulli Amicus. No mans freind.

Christophoriana. Among the Shrubs by Mallam Cove, on the lower side. *Actaea spicata*. about the midle thereof bursa pastoris etc. Thlaspi veronicae folio, affinis pulchra planta.

This is an interesting list. The record of *Naumburgia thyrsiflora*, if correct, is as Raven points out, much earlier than Dodsworth's which appeared in Ray's *Synopsis* in 1690. Of *Actaea spicata* Ray observes 'Mr. Newton and Mr. Lawson found it among the shrubs at Malham Cove.' James Newton did not begin to botanise until about 1680. Two years later, he would appear to have joined Lawson in a botanical trip in the Lake Counties. As the results of that expedition were not entered in the 1677 notebook, we may date these additions to the Yorkshire search list as between 1680 and 1682 – perhaps the last entries that Thomas made. In many ways they have the appearance of memos – things to look for rather than things seen, and

perhaps the same may be said for a number of additions that Thomas made
to the Durham search list. In each case the attribution 'Ray' is to be found
after the plant but Ray does not give a Durham location and we can only
assume that Lawson knew of or had seen the following within the county:

Astragalus glycyphyllos
Centaurea calcitrapa   These all given also with
Eryngium campestre   Northumberland locations
Lathyrus nissolia
Reseda lutea

Picris echioides   Also given with a specific location in
                             Durham

Carduus nutans   Also given with a specific location in
                             Westmorland

Onopordum acanthium   Not recorded again by Lawson
Sagina procumbens

The difficulties of interpreting Thomas' record-keeping multiply when
we regard the Northumberland list and its additions. As with Durham,
there is a list of plants which are attributed to Ray though Ray did not find
them within the county. All the plants are uncommon and none was found
elsewhere by Lawson. Overlapping this list, one might make a list of plants
that Thomas has ticked. This brings in two further plants for which Ray
does give a Northumberland location – faithfully reproduced by Lawson.
Does the tick mean that he had also seen it? In other counties, such ticks
have been accepted as proof of sighting but the probability of Lawson's
having seen the plants was also high. In Northumberland, with a large
proportion of uncommon plants and no corroborative evidence of an
expedition having taken place, we must regard the whole list as suspect: our
disappointment lessened by the fact that there are no original locations and
by the knowledge that Thomas, having served his apprenticeship in the
1677 notebook and observed all manner of good things in his walk around
England is now to turn his attention to the charting of his home county.
Thomas Lawson is the first botanist to give us detailed information on the
flora of Cumbria.

CHAPTER X

Contact with Ray

THESE HIGHLY PRODUCTIVE YEARS AROUND 1680 saw Thomas settled back into the community life of Great Strickland once again. There was much to do. The year 1681 saw the building of a Meeting House in the village:[1] hitherto the Quakers had met in each others' houses or on the open hillside. The venue in the open was a small hill sloping East and West near the present farm called Gunnerwell. There is a tradition that Meetings were held 'on the side favoured by the weather on the occasion.'[2] Foul or fine, the open-air Meeting did at least ensure that enemies could be seen from afar: the Meeting House provided a focus for Friend and foe alike. In 1685, the Quaker Samuel Bownas describes how he went to a Meeting at Strickland with his mother when about eight or nine and 'persecution being still very hot, and Friends lock'd out of our Meeting-house at *Strickland*, we met at the Door.'[3]

The 1680s were to see no diminution in the extent to which Quakers were harassed. In 1682, a directive from Yearly Meeting in London was circulated to suggest:

> That in such counties where there are any severe and immediate sufferings, they, out of their respective Monthly Meetings, appoint some honest and knowing Friends, to be as a Meeting for Sufferings for that county, who may take care, with all possible exactness, to state and draw up the cases for sufferings.[4]

The directive goes on to remind Friends of the proper action to be taken: formal complaint should be lodged with the proper authority, be it the magistrates, the Judges of the Assize or the Bishop if the case was being dealt with by the ecclesiastical courts. Only when these had been applied to and found unrelenting was it time to bring in Yearly Meeting. Moreover, in sending accounts of sufferings to Yearly Meeting, it was important that these should be scrutinised: the Friends of Yearly Meeting wanted to be properly informed of all particulars of sufferings 'to prevent mistakes, and loose unrestrained Accompts of things complained of.'

These instructions show the Quakers exercising their passion for exact documentation. Over the years, they had come to cherish a reputation for truth in all things and, becoming increasingly emphatic about pursuing their aims by peaceful means, they took, ever more, to fighting the authorities with paper: the long-compiled records of patient sufferings under injustice and abuse. And so the directive warns county Friends:

> that the friends coming up from the severall Counties to the yearly Meeting bring up an Accompt of their sufferings – from their respective Quarterly Meetings not in loose papers, but fairly Entered in a Book, under distinct Heads and causes.

The Booke of Minutes of General Meeting of Northern Counties 1658-1700 gives details of how this directive from Yearly Meeting was received and acted upon. Thomas Lawson is nominated as Strickland's executive in establishing a Six Weeks Meeting:

> for Friends that are sufferers to repair unto on the occasion of such sufferings as may require more speedye consideration and care then to staye untill a quarterly meeting can be dispened with.[5]

The other concern of Yearly Meeting: that all cases should be most carefully checked and faithfully recorded before being passed on to headquarters also fell to Thomas' charge:

> to give account thereof to London in Relation to advice and assistance touching the same . . . such sufferers may have Recourse for advice and assistance in sending up an account thereof as there may be occasion and necessitye seene for it.

In other words, Thomas, as Strickland's representative, was to act as a sort of monitor for sufferings endured by Friends within his Meeting, making sure that no cases were overlooked and also making sure that the accounts sent up to London to be entered in that monumental record of Quaker persistence, the Great Book of Sufferings, were accurate. There is some hint, perhaps, that he was to act in an advisory capacity, perhaps helping the less articulate to frame their complaint in suitable form. Such activity would have suited him well whilst he was unable to re-open his school. For a few years he would wish to avoid drawing attention to himself and he settled down to manage his land and to play his part in local Quaker affairs. On 31st August, 1683, his name appears on the marriage certificate of Robert Winter of Morland and Janet Sutton of Moorhouse who did 'in the publick Meeting place at Greatstrickland of the Parish of Morland afforesaid . . . take each other in the relation of marriage.'[6] The phrasing reflects a slight awkwardness as Friends used the conventional term grudgingly. Marriage was a sacrament of the Anglican church – the Quakers, retaining a strong belief in its religious and civil importance, had to find a way to give it due and proper weight in their own practice. Quaker marriages were hedged with preliminary safeguards and abundant witnesses. Certificates were always clearly set out, noting that the couple had announced their intentions beforehand and each had been 'cleared' of relations with anyone else by persons nominated so to do by the Monthly Meeting. Inevitably, this was not unlike the ritual of the Anglican Church with its formula of banns and its regulations about performing the marriage in public and between stated times. So too, Quaker marriages were always well witnessed and in this case Thomas Lawson's name appears amid a host of Winter and Sutton relatives and two dozen others assembled to put their names or marks to the paper that declared the couple well and truly wed.

These routine activities and the writing of three books must have absorbed quite a lot of Thomas' time. It is unlikely that he re-opened his school immediately upon his return – there is no steady trickle of boys of his entering Oxford and Cambridge in the 1680s as there had been in the 1670s and, as Samuel Bownas puts it, persecution was still 'very hot'. We have only to turn again to the pages of the Bishop's Correction Court Act Book to find Thomas, once more, being cited amongst many other Friends 'for being Quaker and not repairing to the Church to heare divine service and to receive the sacrament'.[7] Thomas may have steered clear of trouble where his school was concerned but the recusancy laws, when the authorities chose to apply them, swept Quakers up by the drove. Besse has compiled a long list of over 150 names 'of the People called Quakers, in this county . . . prosecuted by statutes made against Popish Recusants.'[8] Frances and Thomas are amongst them.

This, though, was no more than the usual price of being a Quaker and at some time during the decade Thomas found the courage and resource to re-open his school. But it may not have been until quite late in the 1680s – the first we hear of his following his 'ancient employ of schooling' is in a letter written to Fox on 20th April, 1689. He had reason enough to abandon his teaching for a while and he had, on his return, much else to occupy and to interest him: the visit to the South had been stimulating, he had energy to spare and he was become a capable and confident botanist. On his return, he started to enlarge his knowledge of the flora of the North and to become known as an authority on it. Before the 1680s, we hear nothing from other people of Mr. Lawson as a botanist: after that date there are continual references. Contact with Morison and Bobart brought him compliments in the second part of Morison's herbal, the *Plantarum historiae universalis oxoniensis*: Thomas had become known as a diligent explorer, a most

knowledgeable investigator of the plants of northern parts, through whose
energy and industry Morison had received records of Shrubby Cinquefoil,
3 records sent Morison, *Potentilla fruticosa* and Bird's-eye Primrose,
Historia, Pars 2 *Primula farinosa.* There is also a third record of
Mountain Sorrell, *Oxyria digyna*[9] which,
although it is ascribed to John Watts is, from its location (Buckbarrow Well
in Longsleddale) most surely of Lawson's origination. Possibly he sent it to
Watts whom we think he might have met in 1677.

Nine more Lawson records appeared in the Pars Tertia of Morison's
Historia which was compiled by Bobart the younger after Morison's death
and came out in 1699. Of these, five had been sent by Lawson to John Ray
9 records sent Morison, and appeared in his works in the interval between
Historia, Pars 3: the publication of the second and third parts of
5 previously sent Ray the *Historia.* Only one record, however looks as
1 in known Lawson Mss though it has simply been extracted from Ray. In
Morison only source for 3 the case of Cotton-grass, *Eriophorum vaginatum*,
the remarks in the *Historia* are almost identical
with those in Ray's *Synopsis* (1690 or 1696). These remarks show that
Thomas' opinion was coming to be respected: he had pointed out that
Parkinson had entered this plant under two different names, making two
species of it. This error, Thomas, from his own observation, takes leave to
correct and Ray and Bobart accepted the correction.[10]

The remaining four plants were almost certainly sent to both men. Two
– a hieracium which Lawson calls 'hieracium leptocaulon hirsutum folio
rotundiore'[11] and a narrow-leaved form of Lily-of-the-Valley, *Convallaria
majalis* – are represented by specimens in the Morisonian herbarium.[12] This
herbarium, though it bears Morison's name, was organised by Bobart to
illustrate the Pars Tertia of the *Historia*: all the names on the sheets are in his
handwriting and there is no date prior to 1680 when the Pars Secunda of the
Historia had been published.[13] Against the hieracium we have 'D[octor]
Lawson', against *Convallaria majalis* we have 'from Westmoreland' and it is
the form with narrow leaves which we are told in the *Historia* that Thomas
had sent Morison when it was found by him at Waterfalls bridge and
elsewhere in the county. The other two plants which he contributed to the
Historia do not appear in the herbarium with his name against them as
donor. Oyster Plant, *Mertensia maritima* he reported to Bobart 'in insula
quadam Lancastriae vicina' – almost certainly Walney – as well as other
places on the northern coasts and if he did not send Bobart a specimen of the
Beech Fern, *Thelypteris phegopteris*,[14] he certainly did to Ray, who mentions
receiving the fern some time before June of 1689.[15]

Four plants, then, remain for three of which Morison is our only source of Lawson recordings. The fourth, English Stonecrop, *Sedum anglicum* occurs in Lawson's notebook with locations in Low Furness and about Witherslack, but Bobart chose to adopt the Raian station near Windermere as confirmed on Lawson's authority. So too, the Alpine Bartsia, *Bartsia alpina* found by Ray near Orton as early as 1668 was communicated by Thomas from the same station and Yellow Mountain Saxifrage, *Saxifraga aizoides*, a Raian find in wet places on the high slopes of Ingleborough had been found in Westmorland.[16] Bobart was happy to cite Thomas: he had become the man to quote on northern and mountain plants. The other botanist in Britain particularly interested in mountain vegetation was Edward Lhwyd, Keeper of the Ashmolean Museum, a Welshman who had botanised in his native hills. Both he and Thomas sent Bobart our third plant, a fescue which should, from the polynomials, have been Viviparous Fescue, *Festuca vivipara*. In the Morisonian herbarium, however, one of the specimens under this name is *Deschampsia cespitosa* Beauv. f. *vivipara*, the other *Festuca ovina* L. f. *vivipara*.[17]

Lawson's contribution to Morison's *Historia* brought him wider notice as a botanist. Ray was not notably fond of Morison who had attacked him over the system of classification that Ray had supplied to John Wilkins' *Essay towards a Real Character* in 1668 but he was bound to peruse his *Historia* and, in an abstract of Ray's correspondence with Lister and Tancred Robinson made by Dr. William Derham at the time when he was editing Ray's letters, we see under 'Books recd' on 29th November, 1681, the tart comment 'Dr. Morison no grammarian and full of errours.'[18] The two plants contributed by Thomas would not have escaped Ray's attentive eye.

By the mid 1680s, Lawson's name was well known to Ray. In the Derham abstract we see that at some time prior to the autumn of 1685, Thomas sent Ray some plants: 'Mr. Law[son]s n[on] descr[ipt] plants' apparently featured in a letter to Tancred Robinson in September.[19] One could wish that Derham had abstracted more fully – the letter together with 349 others to Robinson are now lost.

In February, 1685, Ray is writing to Hans Sloane with whom he had been exchanging records. He writes:

> I am not sure that Mr. Newton was the first inventor of that plant I put under his name. I rather suspect Mr. Lawson might be. I mean no more by putting his name to it than that it is published in his work under that name, as I do by the names of other authors, v.g. Abies *Ger. Park*. However, he was the first showed it to me, and gave me as much as I have set down of the history of it. Dr. Plucknet's

observation of the vesicles on the back side of the leaves deserves to be added to its description.[20]

The last sentence gives us the clue to what the plant was: it was *Hymenophyllum wilsonii* to which Ray gave the name 'Adiantum petraeum perpusillum Anglicum foliis bifidis vel trifids *Newtoni*' in his *Historia Plantarum* published the following year, being as good as his word in adding Pluckenet's comments to the description. In 1689, the plant was still engaging his attention. In a letter to Lhwyd in August that year, he writes:

> I conclude your *Adianthum trichoides* to be ye same wth Mr. Newtons, but whether it be mosse or fern I cannot easily determine; only I incline to ye latter because Dr. Plukenet hath with his microscope discovered certain bladders on back side of the leafe, probably ye seed-vessels.[21]

This Filmy Fern was the second plant listed in a letter that Lawson wrote to Ray on 9th April, 1688. This letter was published in Derham's edition of the correspondence of John Ray.[22] Derham appears to have taken a certain amount of editorial liberty with it. It is difficult to believe that the letter could have started 'Mr. Ray – *Acetosa scutata repens* C.B.' – plunging straight into a plant list with no preliminary niceties. It looks like a case of Derham having left out 'all that might be of little use, such as private business, compliments, &c.'[23] as he himself describes his editorial policy. Whilst he was working on it, some of Ray's correspondence disappeared, this letter amongst others. Such letters as are extant, give evidence of his 'reprehensible practice of . . . [marking] the original letters with red pencil to show the printer what he wished to reproduce and what he desired to be left out.'[24] If Lawson opened with any private business compliments they have, it seems, been red pencilled out. It would have been useful to have known how the letter originally began.Charles Raven supposes that this letter was the one from which a list of plants was drawn that Ray published in the Preface of the second volume of his *Historia Plantarum*.[25] Even allowing for the fact that Ray tells us that this list was a last-minute addition run off when the bulk of the *Historia* was already in the press,[26] there are problems with the dating. By December of 1687, Tancred Robinson is reporting that 'Mr. Ray's second volume [of the *Historia*] is now finished'[27] and, on 8th April, 1688, the day before Lawson wrote his letter, Robinson is found sending a copy to Hans Sloane in Jamaica saying that the volume had been published three months previously.[28] It is difficult to see how the list of plants in the *Historia* which Ray acknowledges to Lawson could have been extracted from the long list sent to him by Lawson on 9th April. The strange thing is, however, that out of the 22 plants in the *Historia*, 16 are to be found in the letter. It is equally difficult to imagine why Lawson should send two letters containing very nearly the same information, though if we suppose that there was only one letter we have now, in addition to the dating difficulty, six extra plants to account for.

The dating difficulty might possibly be got over by supposing either that Derham mistook the date on Lawson's letter – both he and Edwin Lankester, who re-edited his collection of Ray's correspondence, sometimes make mistakes in dating – or that Sloane's copy went off without the Lawson list which was only bound in at the last minute to copies that were circulated some time after 9th April, 1688. It is not very easy to imagine how a mistake in dating could have arisen when the supposed 'real' date of the letter would have had to fall some time in the autumn of 1687 and although it is inherently more likely that Thomas wrote only one letter it begins to look as though too much special pleading has to be made to establish it. If there were two letters, the difficulties over the dating and the extra plants disappear and we are only left wondering why Lawson repeated the *Historia* plants in the April letter. If Derham had not pruned so ruthlessly, the opening sentences of the letter might have told us. Possibly, since there is considerably less detail regarding locations given in the *Historia* list, Ray replied to a first letter with a request that Lawson give more information (perhaps asking for specimens) and extend the list if he had other records that would be of interest.

Whichever theory we prefer, the fact remains that at some time in the autumn of 1687 or the spring of 1688 Thomas Lawson sent John Ray a series of records of, mainly, northern plants. In the *Historia*, Ray divides these records into two sections: a short one of plants that were unknown to him until Lawson brought them to his attention and a longer one of plants already known, though not necessarily with northern locations. These two groupings have been denoted H.P.a and H.P.b in the tables at the end of this chapter. The six plants which do not receive notice in the April letter all fall within the latter grouping. Hairy Violet, *Viola hirta*, Marsh Violet, *Viola palustris* and Cut-leaved Cranesbill, *Geranium dissectum* are all reproduced by Ray without location. From near Manchester, Thomas had given the Elder, *Sambucus nigra*. A white-flowered gentian which was probably *Gentiana pneumonanthe* had caught his eye: Ray gives this with the location of Westmorland. Lastly, there is a plant which Ray had forgotton to include in his *Catalogus Angliae* although he knew it: a fescue which was probably Sheep's Fescue, *Festuca ovina*.

The remaining plants of the *Historia Plantarum* are better studied from Derham's printing of the letter to Ray, as edited by Edwin Lankester which, imperfect as it may be through Derham's omissions, is a much longer list than that selected by Ray. Because it is upon this letter that

Lawson's reputation largely rests, since it was used by most of the later compilers of Lake District records, it deserves a very special kind of attention.

In the first place, we may divide the records listed in the letter into plants already known to us in 1677 by virtue of having been listed in the tour notebook and a much larger group of plants which have either been found in localities other than those given in 1677 or are completely new finds. In the first group, nearly half the records are plants that Thomas saw in the South of England: *Ophyrs apifera*, *Ruscus aculeatus*, *Wahlenbergia hederacea*, *Blackstonia perfoliata*, *Kickxia elatine*, *K. spuria*, *Butomus umbellatus*, *Damasonium alisma*, *Trifolium repens*, *Umbilicus rupestris* (white and yellow flowered), *Helianthemum chamaecistus* and the plant found on Salisbury Plain which was probably *Eruca sativa*. We may also conveniently here include the Mountain Pansy, *Viola lutea* seen on tour 'by Eldon Hole in Derbyshire' – not, perhaps, quite in southern England, but a long way South to a man who lived at Great Strickland.

These are the only southern records that Lawson sent Ray: he had, therefore, nothing to send that we do not know about from 1677 so we may conclude that he never went South again between 1677 and the writing of the letter.

The remaining records in the first group include some plants from localities in the North that are rather distant from Great Strickland: *Ophrys insectifera* (Holme, North of Carnforth), *Saponaria officinalis* (Carnforth), *Pedicularis sylvatica* (seen with a white flower at Gunnerthwaite in Lancashire), *Actaea spicata* (Malham), *Erigeron acer* (Sawley Abbey), *Hippophaë rhamnoides* (between Whitby and Lyth) and *Bryonia dioica* (West of Darlington). These are all interesting plants; rarities such that Thomas considered the old record worth sending to Ray even when he did not find closer locations. Ten plants from stations nearer home complete this first group: *Sorbus torminalis* (Levens Bridge), *Vaccinium vitis-idaea*, *V. myrtillus*, *V. uliginosum* (all from Whinfield), *Drosera rotundifolia* and *D. intermedia* (both from Witherslack), *Mentha rotundifolia* (Marsh Grange) and *Aster tripolium* (Walney). There is also the debateable record of *Echinophora spinosa* which Thomas, although he had been back to botanise along the Furness shore, never saw there again. He was, apparently, confident enough of having made no mistake on the first occasion to send the record to Ray 11 years later.

These repeated records are a small proportion of the list that Lawson sent to Ray – little more than a couple of dozen out of a total list of 161. The records that comprise the bulk of the letter – 133 of them – are the witness of Thomas' activity in the field in the years between 1677 and 1688. We may make of them two further groupings: one will comprise those plants which Thomas has recorded before in his notebook but for which he now gives new locations; the other will comprise totally new finds, not recorded at all in the notebook.

With regard to the plants which have been supplied with additional localities we can see that precise locations have been found for plants that were previously listed simply under 'Westmorland', 'Lancashire', 'Durham'; northern locations have been discovered for plants that were seen in the South and additional locations have been found for northern plants. It all adds up to a fair amount of activity, much of which was conducted round and about Thomas' home as he discovered that many plants with which he had become acquainted on his travels were also to be observed nearby when they were but looked for. Ramping Fumitory, *Fumaria capreolata*, seen in Greenwich and another Kent plant, *Senecio aquaticus* can both be seen about Great Strickland, the last 'in the watery places by Cliburn Bridge.' 'Betwixt the inn and smithy at Sir John Lowther's new town' Thomas found a plant which the polynomials identify as Fiddle Dock, *Rumex pulcher*, but which was probably something else, although Thomas did know the Fiddle Dock, having seen it in St. George's Fields when he was in London. On Lansmoor grew *Galeopsis angustifolia*, last seen near Henley and another cornfield weed, Corn Gromwell, *Lithospermum arvense* which had been plentiful at St. Ives but also grew on Lansmoor, both rare plants, Thomas remarking of the latter 'it is not so plentiful with us.'

It was pleasant for Thomas to discover friends made in southern England in the fields and woods of home. Alder Buckthorn, *Frangula alnus* had been part of the composition of Charlton Wood. Now he knew it grew 'in Thorny Holme, in Whinfield Forest' and two other Charlton finds: Tower Mustard, *Turritis glabra* and Slender St. John's Wort, *Hypericum pulchrum* grew at nearby Cliburn, the latter in 'Trowgill' or Trough Gill, a new botanising spot that Thomas had discovered. There, also, he saw quantities of the Black Spleenwort, *Asplenium adiantum-nigrum* as much at home on the rocks of the ghyll as it had been in the Avon Gorge, and two other ferns that were new to him: Oak Fern, *Thelypteris dryopteris* and Brittle Bladder-fern, *Cysopteris fragilis*. Trough Gill and the ancient remains at Mayburgh where Thomas now found Lamb's Lettuce, *Valerianella locusta* were to produce a long list of plants for Thomas at a later date.

Hampstead Heath friends were also to be seen near at home: Saw-wort, *Serratula tinctoria* grew about Great Strickland and Lily-of-the-Valley, *Convallaria majalis* 'on the Scar near Waterfall Bridge by Great Strickland and in other places West[morland].' This was the narrow-leaved form of which Lawson sent specimens to Ray and Bobart. The usual form he had found in Witherslack Park.

Another bridge that became a favourite spot for Thomas to botanise was Commonholme Bridge, spanning the River Leith two miles from home. There he found Shepherd's Cress, *Teesdalia nudicaulis*, previously just listed under Westmorland and, in a sandy place, Maiden Pink, *Dianthus deltoides*, a nearer location than Whinfield, given in the notebook. Other finds show Thomas supplying Ray with evidence of a more general distribution than had been given in his notebook. Buckthorn, *Rhamnus catharticus*, for example, was abundant around Great Strickland 'in the rocks and hedges' and if he supplied Ray with the old location at the foot of Longsleddale for Bog Pimpernel, *Anagallis tenella*, he also adds that it was to be found in abundance 'near the Cloven Stone on Great Strickland Moor', a place which, with Mayburgh, was also a station for Lesser Marshwort, *Apium inundatum*. Abundant, too, in the days before chemical control was White Climbing Fumitory, *Corydalis claviculata* – the notebook locations are remote from home whereas in the letter he offers 'at Thornthwaite, foot of Longsledale, on the thatched houses in Kentmeer, Isan Parles Cave mouth copiose'. In other ways, his interest was deepening as well as broadening: Subterranean Trefoil, *Trifolium subterraneum* was amongst plants that he had established in his garden in order to study them. Lastly, Knotted Pearlwort, *Sagina nodosa*, a common plant with a Great Strickland location in the notebook is sent to Ray from another of his favourite spots 'in Troutbeck Holm.'

These are plants that Thomas already knew long before he wrote to Ray. A fresh look around the pastures of home showed up some unusual or inconspicuous plants: an odd form of Scentless Mayweed, *Tripleurospermum maritimum*, the Lesser Water-Plantain, *Baldellia ranunculoides* 'near the Cloven-Stone on Great Strickland Moor'; Clustered Bellflower, *Campanula glomerata* and Fragrant Orchid, *Gymnadenia conopsea* 'in Troutbeck Home', another orchid, Dark-red Helleborine, *Epipactis atrorubens* 'in the lane by Abbot Wood Close, near Great Strickland; Stinkhorn, *Phallus impudicus* and Moonwort, *Botrychium lunaria* 'in Croft Short Close' another field close to home. He observed that the leaves of Moonwort were sometimes entire, sometimes crenate and was inclined to make two different species of these but Ray, while noting Thomas' observation, later put them together.[29] These were interesting plants to have found – a constellation of good things to set beside Devil's Bit Scabious, *Succisa pratensis*, a double-flowered Water Avens, *Geum rivale* – Thomas later sent Ray a specimen of this[30] – and the large flowered sort of Lady's Smock, *Cardamine pratensis* for which Thomas' other location is Pen-y-Ghent.

Besides these rarities, Thomas was also on the look-out for something different or unusual and, in a limestone quarry in Great Strickland he saw a monstrous thistle which he calls 'Carduus monstrosus Imperati', probably *Carlina vulgaris*, though the Emperor's thistle was actually *Cirsium acaulon* which had, according to legend, been pointed out to the Emperor Charlemagne by an angel to cure his army of the plague.

As before, we can see Thomas making short excursions to places that are within an afternoon's walk: taking a stroll out to Waterfalls Bridge where the Rowan trees, *Sorbus aucuparia* found footing in the rocky clefts. There, too, grew the shade-loving Figwort, *Scrophularia nodosa*. In the fields between Melkinthorpe and Waterfalls Bridge, grew Small Scabious, *Scabiosa columbaria*; abundantly at Cliburn Field grew Golden-rod, *Solidago virgaurea*, and the small inconspicuous All-seed, *Radiola linoides* known from Clifton Moor, found lodging on Cliburn Moor. A dip into the recesses of Whinfield Forest completed Thomas' tally of vaccinia species with Cranberry, *Vaccinium oxycoccos*. This was getting quite far away. Tall Melilot, *Melilotus altissima* at Langwathby was definitely farther than an afternoon's stroll and we might imagine that the village of Temple Sowerby where Thomas saw the Common Tormentil, *Potentilla erecta*, marked the limit of his strictly local foraging.

Parklands offered an alternative to distance – another habitat different from the patchwork of common land and enclosure that characterised the lands of the tenantry. In the old deer park of Thornthwaite, former hunting seat of the Curwens, Thomas found a geranium 'flore eleganter variegato' which could have been either *Geranium pratense* or *G. sylvaticum*. Later he was to send Ray a specimen of this.[31] The biggest landowner in the area was Sir John Lowther; his woods 'directly against Askham Hall' provided cover for White Helleborine, *Cephalanthera damasonium*. Sheriff Park Woods on the other side of the Leith were especially good for Goldilocks, *Ranunculus auricomus* and in the same area 'among the rocks south of Sir John Lowther's' Thomas had Mossy Saxifrage, *Saxifraga hypnoides* which he also saw at Malham Cove. South again, between Hackthorpe and Lowther grew Cat's-foot, *Antennaria dioica* (also between Shap and Anna Well) and a grass that I have not been able to give a binomial to which Lawson calls 'Gramen sparteum capite bifido vel gemino.'

Other locations show Thomas ranging far afield in the Lake District or, at the very least, acquiring contacts in remote Cumberland and eastwards into the Pennine country and southwards into Lancashire. The only reason to suppose that he did not collect every one of these plants himself, is that many of the records are rather isolated – here a one and there a one, often rather uncommon plants. This phenomenon could, however, just as easily be explained by the fact that Thomas may, at the same time, have been paying social calls or travelling as a Quaker and recorded only what immediately drew his eye. The pretty Mountain Pansy, *Viola lutea*, which he had seen near Elden Hole in Derbyshire, he now knows from Stainmoor; Vervain, *Verbena officinalis*, seen growing in Nonsuch over Court, he has seen growing in abundance at Cockermouth.

As for complete novelties, he has noted the Aspens, *Populus tremula* on St. Herbert's Isle in Derwentwater and maybe we can also assign a white flowered Foxglove, *Digitalis purpurea* 'in a close called Millbank at Lorton Town End' to this time. To the Vervain in Cockermouth, he could add Water Lobelia, *Lobelia dortmanna* 'in Grayson Tarne near Cockermouth.' Thomas' other location for the Water Lobelia – Windermere – still provides it with a home but you would search in vain for Grayson tarn by Graysouthen village: drainage has turned it to pastureland.

Another expedition – perhaps more than one – took Thomas southwards. It is possible that this was a trip arranged with James Newton, a keen botanist who collected plants throughout the British Isles but about whom little is known. He may have been a Leeds man – the diarist Ralph Thoresby says that he was apprenticed to a whitesmith in the city – and it may be that Lawson arranged to meet him in the Malham Cove area. Although, as we have seen, Thomas knew Baneberry, *Actaea spicata* from Malham as early as 1677 it was almost certainly at a later date that he found it in company with Newton and the Mountain Pansy, *Viola lutea* 'Malhame Cove in Yorkshire' is a new location in the letter. If we look up the entry for Wilson's Filmy Fern, *Hymenophyllum wilsonii* in Ray's *Historia Plantarum* we find that Newton observed it on Wrynose in July of 1682. In 1685, Ray is writing to say that Lawson was actually the 'first inventor' of that plant and in the 1688 letter Thomas says 'I was with Ja[mes] Newton when it was found.' The location where the two men found it in company was 'on Buzzard rough Crag, close by Wrenose, in Westmoreland'. This is across country from Malham and there is some slight evidence pointing towards a trip that took the two men to Kendal, Ambleside, over Hardknott and Wrynose and back by a similar route to Kendal and home through Tebay, Orton and Crosby Ravensworth to Great Strickland. Such evidence as there is rests upon plant records. Newton has Hoary Rockrose, *Helianthemum canum* at Kendal, Lawson has Sneezewort, *Achillea ptarmica* 'in the small holm in Winander Mear' – a little boating expedition for a guest, which included another island, Lady Holme, site of an ancient chantry and home of Tustan, *Hypericum androsaemum*. At Troutbeck he noted the fern *Ceterach officinarum* which he already knew from the Avon Gorge. Newton had Soft Rush, *Juncus effusus* at Ambleside, Lawson had a handful of plants out of the country West of Windermere: Great Spearwort, *Ranunculus lingua* and Gipsy-wort, *Lycopus europaeus* from the marshy land near Hawkshead, Touch-me-not, *Impatiens noli-tangere* 'by the cloth-mill in Saterthwait parish' – a nice location to add to his previous one near Ambleside. This, so far as we know, was new territory for Thomas – his Quaker journeyings had not taken him into High Furness and the trip up over Hardknott and Wrynose, culminating in the joint Newton/Lawson discovery of the Filmy Fern must have been quite an adventure. Few people ventured upon the fells in those days. A century later, Richard West writes: 'The shepherds only are conversant in the traditional annals of the mountains, and with all the secrets of the mysterious reign of chaos and old night.'[34] The summit of Hardknott, 1291 feet above sea level on the wild, if fairly well-used route to the port of Ravenglass was almost as high in the mountains as Thomas Lawson ever went.

Ravenglass, the point of departure for the Isle of Man, produced Birdsfoot, *Ornithopus perpusillus*, which had given Thomas such trouble in Staffordshire. No doubt he looked longingly over the sea to Man, visible on a good day from the top of the pass that they had just surmounted. When he wrote to Ray, he was still hoping to visit the island – he writes that he means to observe the Isle of Man cabbage, *Rhynchosinapis monensis* there at Pentecost [Whitsun], giving, in the meantime, locations at Marsh Grange, Walney and along this present coast: 'in Sella Fields, Sea Bank, Cumberland.' There were miles of interesting new coastline to explore – westward-facing and more exposed than the familiar shores of Furness. Thomas found Narrow-leaved Everlasting Pea, *Lathyrus sylvestris* 'on the rocks by the Red Neese, by Whitehaven, cop[iose]' and by Whitehaven, too, he saw Oyster Plant, *Mertensia maritima* with another station 'over against Biggar in the Isle of Walney' given in the letter, whilst Newton found Darnel Poa, *Catapodium marinum* 'near the salt pans' a mile out of the village. These were all excellent finds and the most northerly discovery was the plant that commemorates the man to whom Newton and Lawson owed so much of their botanical enthusiasm: Ray's Knotgrass, *Polygonum raii* was seen 'between Workington and Whitehaven.'

These finds conclude this part of our conjectural tour: perhaps it happened like that, equally it is possible that Newton found his plants independently and Lawson travelled the coast road in quite the opposite direction as part of the trip that took him to Derwentwater and Cockermouth. We have only two certainties: Baneberry at Malham and the Filmy Fern on Wrynose were joint finds – the plants from each man's collecting activities strung out in a chain linking the two points form a circumstantial but plausible story.

Thomas Lawson's botanical notebook, p. 147

The modern names for the plants listed are Thuja occidentalis, *Levens;* Barbarea
vulgaris, *Great Strickland;* Polygonum viviparum, *Crosby Ravensworth and
Great Strickland;* Tamus communis, *between Kendal and Levens, about Fell
End;* Geum rivale, *recorded from Westmorland by Ray in the* Catalogus
Angliae; Prunus padus, *various places in the county and at 'Croft short Close';*
Cirsium heterophyllum, *'at my feild house by Bakestonbarth';* Saxifraga
stellaris, *Hardknott and Wrynose [another Raian record];* Hydrocotyle vulgaris,
Commonholme Bridge; Polygonum convolvulus, *Great Strickland Field*

Poſt Opus abſolutum & typis impreſſum literas accepi à Botanico non incelebri D.Tho. Lawſon *in* Weſtmorlandia *degente, quibus Catalogum inſeruit Plantarum à ſe obſervatarum in Septentrionalibus* Angliæ *ſponte naſcentium, quarum nonnullæ novæ & nondum editæ, aliæ à nobis in Catalogo Anglicanarum præteritæ & indictæ.*

Primi generis ſunt

1. CErasus ſylveſtris fructu minimo cordiformi, **The leaſt wild Heart Cherry-tree,** Ruſticis Ceſtrienſibus, **The Merry-tree,** cujus in Phytologia Britannica mentio. Hanc circa *Buriam* & *Mancunium Lancaſtriæ* oppida, & alicubi etiam in *Weſtmorlandia* inveniri ſcribit D. *Lawſon*; circa *Stockportum* & alibi in *Ceſtria* D.*Stonehouſe*, qui hanc Meraſum ſylveſtrem Ungarorum *Cluſ.* à nomine **Merry-tree** conjectaretur, ni color fructus dilutè ruber, qui Meraſo Ungarico niger eſt, obſtaret. Verùm errat D. *Stonehouſe*; Cluſius enim Meraſo ſylveſtri fructum nigrum non attribuit ſed rubrum; Meraſo autem ſimpliciter dicto nigrum; unde color fructus non impedit quò minùs Meraſus ſylveſtris Ungarorum *Cluſii* eſſe poſſit.
2. Cochlearia marina folio anguloſo parvo, in *Walney* vulgò *Waney Lancaſtriæ* inſula. Huic nulla quæ extat mihi ſaltem viſa neque icon, neque deſcriptio reſpondet.
3. Geranium hæmatodes flore eleganter variegato: in inſula *Walney* prædicta copioſiſſimè provenit. Hanc ſpeciem pro varietate Geranii hæmatodis vulgaris in Hiſtoria pag. 1061. habuimus, at nunc, ex obſervatione plantæ in horto cultæ melius edocti, diverſam agnoſcimus; non enim floris duntaxat variegatione quam etiam cultis retinet, ſed & parvitate ſua & humilitate, aliiſque accidentibus ab eo differt.
4. Lilium convallium anguſtifolium; ad pontem *Waterfall* in *Weſtmorlandia*.
5. Hieracium macrocaulon hirſutum folio rotundiore, prope *Shap* vicum in *Weſtmorlandia*.
6. Gramen ſparteum capite bifido vel gemino D. *Merret.* In *Weſtmorlandia* copioſè.

Secundi generis ſunt

1. Gramen ſparteum montanum ſpica foliacea graminea majus, à nobis in ſummis altiſſimorum *Cambriæ* montium verticibus copioſè naſcens obſervatum, quamvis in Catalogo per oblivionem omiſſum.
2. Lunaria minor ramoſa.
3. Lunaria minor foliis diſſectis, utraque *Stricklandiæ majori* in *Weſtmorlandia*.
4. Pyrola Alſines flore Braſiliana, prope *Gisburgum* oppidum in *Clevelandia*.
5. Sambucus foliis laciniatis prope *Mancunium Lancaſtriæ* in ſepibus.
6. Scabioſa pratenſis minor flore carneo *Park.* in *Weſtmorlandia*.
7. Sorbus ſylveſtris Anglica **Engliſh wild Serbice, Cheſs-Apple, Sea-Oulers.** Aſſerit *Parkinſonus* eam in *Witherſlake Park* ſponte naſci. Verùm arbor eo loci hoc nomine vulgo dicta **Aria** eſt Theophraſti.
8. Viola folio Trachelii D. *Merret*.
9. Viola paluſtris rotundifolia D. *Plot* Hiſt. nat. *Oxon.*
10. Geranium columbinum maximum fol. diſſectis *ejuſdem*, quorum deſcriptiones in Hiſtoria noſtra exhibuimus; ut &
11. Adianti foliis bifidis vel trifidis.
12. Helleborine minor alba *Park. Weſtmorland.*

His adde Varietates quarundam Plantarum inſignes, v. g.

1. Carduus monſtroſus Imperati.
2. Cotula non fœtida flore pleno *Weſtmorl.*
3. Gentianella flore lacteo *ibid.*
4. Geranium batrachioides flore eleganter variegato, *In old Deer-Park by Thornthwait Weſtmorland.*

List of northern plants sent to Ray (Historia Plantarum, *vol ii, 1688, preface*). *Headed: 'When this book was complted and in press I received letters from Dr Thomas Lawson, a celebrated botanist who lives in West Morland, in which was included a catalogue of plants observed by him growing wild in Northern England, of which some are new and not yet published, others have already been listed in the* Catalogus Angliae

If it happened at all like that, however, then surely Thomas invited his new friend home at some stage before he passed out of the country and on to fresh botanical pastures. From Kendal, it would have been new ground to Newton and, with a little deviation, there were places of botanical pilgrimage to see. John Ray had made the village of Orton known to all contemporary botanists. Lawson signalised it with a white-flowered variety of Ragged Robin, *Lychnis flos-cuculi* for which his other location was Pen-y-ghent, whilst Newton exercised himself with Fir Clubmoss, *Lycopodium selago* and the Dioecious Sedge, *Carex dioica* which was to prove a novelty to Ray when Newton showed it to him. One more place in this area with a name made known by a previous botanist remained – Crosby Ravensworth, where the Small Bistort, *Polygonum viviparum*, noted by Lawson in both his old notebook and the letter to Ray, had been known since the time of the herbalist Gerard.[35] Then Thomas was home. In our fanciful reconstruction, it is not too much to imagine that he entertained Newton there and cemented the basis of that acquaintance that was to lead Newton to call him 'our singular friend, Mr. Lawson' in his *Enchiridion Universale Plantarum* published about 1689.[36]

Acquaintance with other botanists led Thomas into new hunting grounds but it also encouraged in him a more discriminating eye and a better nose for likely spots when he returned to those botanising grounds that he had known before 1677. The nearest location where he could observe an upland vegetation was Shap and here 'on the rocks by the rivulet between Shap and Anna Well,' he made the discovery of a hieracium that, for a while bore his name. Another location for it was Buckbarrow Well in Longsleddale and, writing to Ray, he advises him to 'expect fair samples and my description.' These were duly sent and an account of *Hieracium lawsonii* may be found in Appendix 1. The same locality yielded Marsh Arrow-grass, *Triglochin palustris*, Bog Myrtle, *Myrica gale*, Horse-shoe Vetch, *Hippocrepis comosa* and Mountain St. John's Wort, *Hypericum montanum* which Thomas also knew from Cunswick Scar near Kendal. Between Shap and Threaplands grew Perennial Flax, *Linum anglicum* seen also at Crosby Ravensworth and by Hardindale Nab Musk Thistle, *Carduus nutans*. These were all plants with which Thomas was already acquainted and Shap produced nothing that Thomas had not seen before except the hieracium and white-flowered forms of two veronicas: Brooklime, *V. beccabunga* and Water Speedwell, *V. anagallis-aquatica*. As he passed on to Kendal over the old drove road, however, he took trouble to distinguish the three clubmosses, *Selaginella selaginoides*, *Lycopodium alpinum* (both by Buckbarrow Well) and *Lycopodium inundatum* (at the foot of Longsleddale). Buckbarrow Well, at the head of Longsleddale, was one of Thomas' new botanising spots. In addition to the newly discriminated clubmosses, he found Starry Saxifrage, *Saxifraga stellaris* 'copoise' and two plants that he already knew: Mountain Sorrel, *Oxyria digyna*, previously just listed under Westmorland and Alpine Lady's Mantle, *Alchemilla alpina*, for which his other location is 'on the rocks between Thornthwait and Mardale.' The old drove road was a favourite way of getting to Kendal. It was no shorter than the route over Shap, but at its highest point it rose to just under 1700 feet – an important consideration for a man interested in becoming thoroughly acquainted with moorland vegetation. Eastwards of the pass 'between Bannisdale Head and Water Sledale' Thomas already knew of the existence of the truly mountain Cloudberry, *Rubus chamaemorus*. When he sent the record to Ray he added Cross Fell as a location, perhaps its best known station in our area.

Dropping down through Longsleddale to Kendal, he found Red-rattle, *Pedicularis palustris* with a white flower at the lower end of the valley and, at Kendal itself, a plant last seen on the eastern side of the country, the Water Violet, *Hottonia palustris* growing in the River Kent. There was also a species of Usnea, unknown previously to Lawson that may have been *U. barbata*, and up on Cunswick Scar Dropwort, *Filipendula vulgaris* and Squinancy Wort, *Asperula cynanchica*, the latter a friend from Oxford, from Cambridge and even from 'Beltharrow in Witherslack' before he ever set out on his southern travels.

On again from Kendal and down the old route into Furness with the same mixture of familiar plants seen in new locations and completely new finds. The Greater Bladderwort, *Utricularia vulgaris* he already knew, now he saw it 'in the ditches by the causeway over the Moss to Fell-end near Witherslack.' So too, the White Bean, *Sorbus aria* now merits a brief note to Ray: 'Witherslack, Consick Scar, Silverdale, Arnside, places in Lancs and Westm. where they call it Chess apple and Sea-oulers.' Bog Rosemary, *Andromeda polifolia*, was not known to him in 1677; it grew in 'Brigsteer Moss, not far from Kendal, Westmorland; in Middleton Moss by Lancaster.'

Furness, only partially explored in 1677, was to produce several finds, many of them new but there were to be old acquaintances there as well. Two sites in particular claimed his attention: Humphrey Head, where the plants that he already knew were Ploughman's Spikenard, *Inula conyza*, Smallage, *Apium graveolens* and Common Meadow Rue, *Thalictrum flavum*. Nearby at Allithwaite there was Water Betony, *Scrophularia aquatica* and on the Isle of Walney he recognised Sea Bindweed, *Calystegia soldanella* and Sea Rocket, *Cakile maritima* which he sent to Ray with the old location at Roosebeck added in. His new finds on Humphrey Head were Common Centaury,

Centaurium erythraea, with a white flower and Hart's-tongue, *Phyllitis scolopendrium*. He was not, apparently, there at the right time of year to see Spiked Speedwell, *Veronica spicata* in flower which he had seen in the Avon Gorge, its other British station. A little later, it was discovered at Humphrey Head by John Fitz-Roberts, a Kendal man who contributed half a dozen plants to the third edition of Ray's *Synopsis*.[37]

At Walney, Thomas found the Lesser Meadow Rue, *Thalictrum minus* and Danish Scurvy-grass, *Cochlearia danica*, a plant which had caused Ray some puzzlement as to whether it was specifically distinct from *C. officinalis*. He had solved the problem by observing it under cultivation 'for although when transferred to gardens and propagating itself by seed it becomes larger in size, yet it never approximates in any degree to the dimensions of the other species.'[38] Thomas, however, sounds not entirely convinced: 'I saw nothing to distinguish it from the rest but its little cornered leaves,' he writes, promising to send 'fair samples and seeds' soon after Pentecost. This, we remember, was the Pentecost when he hoped to travel to the Isle of Man. Whitsun was a time when the schools were traditionally on holiday and Thomas was clearly intending an expedition then. We have too little information about Thomas' collecting after 1688 to know whether this ever took place but nothing that we have gives any pointer to it and I think we must conclude that he never went. With regard to another Walney plant, however, Thomas was to be proved right and Ray wrong: Ray had not believed that the var. *lancastrense* of the Bloody Cranesbill *Geranium sanguineum* would persist, but experience of the plant in cultivation proved him wrong. Lawson says 'thousands hereof I found in the Isle of Waney, and have sent roots to Edinburgh, York, London, Oxford, where they keep their distinction' – a tantalising hint of correspondents about whom we know nothing.

Outside the confines of the Lake Counties, Thomas' records tend to be widely and randomly separated. Perhaps we may assign Wood Speedwell, *Veronica montana* with the location 'at Lartington, in Yorkshire near Barnard Castle' (with the alternative 'in Buckham belonging to sir John Lowther, Westm[orland]') to one serious botanising trip that took him into the North-east. He had travelled the Barnard Castle road in 1677, but this time he was going further North, possibly he stayed with his kind old relative who had helped him with Hebrew so long ago, for there are several records from around Newcastle: Wild Mignonette, *Reseda lutea* 'by Clifford's Fort at Tinmouth Castle in Northumberland' last seen on the Gogmagogs, Star Thistle, *Centaurea calcitrapa* 'betwixt the Glasshouses and Dent's Hole, nigh Newcastle-upon-Tyne' for which Thomas' only previous records were second-hand from Merret and Ray. In the same place, he improved upon another record by finding Grass Vetchling, *Lathyrus nissolia* and another, also previously listed with the laconic memo 'Ray', Field Eryngo, *Eryngium campestre* at a site not far away 'on the shore called Fryer Goose near Newcastle-upon-Tyne' In the same place, grew Milk Vetch, *Astragalus glycyphyllos:* for that Thomas had his own location in Cambridge, though he also had it down under Durham on Ray's authority. The only novelty to him from this area was Sea Pearlwort, *Sagina maritima* 'on Whinneyfield Bank by Cullercoats by Tynemouth' but it is a less interesting find than the plants that he had searched out along the banks of the Tyne which show him taking an interest in the plants that sprang up amidst the ballast discharged by ships loading in the river.

Whilst he was in the North-east, he took time to go up Teesdale – Ray had found Shrubby Cinquefoil, *Potentilla fruticosa* there in 1671 and Thomas went up river to watch the Tees pour over an edge of rock and crash 70 feet to the river bed at High Force, like any other sightseer. Thereabouts, the Shrubby Cinquefoil grew in abundance. It cannot, however, have been on this occasion that he saw Lesser Twayblade, *Listera cordata* 'by the picts' wall' for he has this entry in his 1677 notebook – a solitary recording that does not fit into any of our supposed excursions of the late 1670s. Now, in the letter, Thomas repeats the location and adds 'Rogor park' presumably Roker Park at Sunderland.

If it was his learned relation who drew him North to Newcastle, it was probably old Quaker friends who drew him South into Cleveland and North Yorkshire. Botanical acquaintances seen at this time were Bristly Ox-tongue, *Picris echioides* recorded 'betwixt Stockton and Norton in the bishopric of Durham' plentifully, Spurge Laurel, *Daphne laureola* 'by Thornton in the bishopric of Durham', Purple Milk Vetch, *Astragalus danicus* 'close by Huntcliff Rock in Cleveland' and Alexanders, *Smyrnium olusatrum* 'within the walls of Scarborough Castle.'

By way of novelty on this southern leg of his trip, Thomas found a horsetail to which I have not been able to assign a binomial in Hell Kettles, near Darlington, another natural curiosity made famous by the sixteenth century antiquary, John Leland, who repeated a local legend that these deep dubs were bottomless and connected with the Tees by an underground passage. Thomas calls his Horsetail 'Equisetum sive hippuris lac. fol. mansu aren,' Gesner's name, and he gives 'Conzick Tarn ditches, Westmoreland' as another location. At Blackwall, not far away, he saw Bur Chervil, *Anthriscus caucalis* growing on mud walls – a favoured habitat for it for Thomas has seen it also on mud walls in and about Cambridge and again at Burlington in Yorkshire.

On to Guisborough then, where lived a Mrs. Ward 'very knowing in plants.' She may have told him where to find 'Pyrola Brasiliana' (?*Pyrola rotundifolia*). It was probably at her instigation that Thomas collected a few roots and planted them in his garden for, in informing Ray, he says 'it grew in my garden several years; whether [Parkinson's] major or minor I was not satisfied.'

Mrs. Ward's chief claim to fame was, however, her discovery of a plant which she called 'Sea-Beard', which appeared in successive editions of Ray's *Synopsis*. A specimen in the Dillenian herbaria under the appropriate polynomial is the Hydroid zoophyte, *Antennularia antennina*. In his edition of Ray's correspondence, Derham mistakenly entered this under Lawson's 'Asplenium' – i.e. *Ceterach officinarum*. It was, however, something entirely distinct which Mrs. Ward showed Lawson 'and after to Mr. Newton, who called it Bar[ba] Neptuni.'

A few Yorkshire and Lancashire plants complete the round-up of records outside the Lake Counties: Yellow Star-of-Bethlehem, *Gagea lutea* 'in the bushes at Bander Bridge-end, by Cotherstone, near Rombald church, Yorks[hire]'; Thrift, *Armeria maritima* 'in Bleaberry Gill under Hinkell Haugh at the head of Stockdale fields in Craven' – interesting to Thomas found far from the sea shore. Several seventeenth-century botanists were intrigued to find Thrift inland: Thomas Johnson had remarked upon it in the Welsh mountains[39] and William Nicolson was to observe it in the northern Pennines '30 miles from the sea.'[40] Another Yorkshire plant, *Ranunculus sceleratus* 'by Robin Hood's Well, nigh Wentbridge' was also found 'by Middleton near Lancaster.' Middleton, with its moss, interested Thomas. Besides *Andromeda polifolia*, he saw a species of Callitriche in flower which was probably *C. platycarpa*, Sea Spleenwort, *Asplenium marinum* 'under a shadowy sea rock by Middleton' and, at nearby Sunderland, he records Stinking Groundsel, *Senecio viscosus*. Between Bare and Pulton, now built-up areas of Morecambe, he records Brookweed, *Samolus valerandi* (also given from Marsh Grange) and on the road home from Lancashire he saw the Ivy Duckweed *Lemna trisulca* greening the ditches between Wharton and Carnforth.

On a few plants, Thomas has a brief note. Concerning Cotton-grass, *Eriophorum vaginatum*, so common on his native moors, he remarks 'its bluish spikes appear soon after Christmas. After it turns white sheep are greedy after it; so it is called Moss-crops about Clibburn, Water Sledale, and in all places here.' It is not in this letter, however, that he corrects Parkinson, so we must assume that there was further correspondence between Lawson and Ray. Of Common Oxlip, *Primula veris x vulgaris*, another plant not assigned to a location, Thomas says 'This, in the north, is commonly called Lady Candlestick' and of Sour Cherry, *Prunus cerasus*, found 'nigh Stockport in Cheshire, at Bery or Bury in Lancashire, at Rosgill in Westmoreland' he says 'in all these places it is called Merry-tree. I could observe no difference from other cherry trees save in its small cordiformous fruit.' These local names were of interest to Ray: he had published a *Collection of English Words* in 1673 – 'the first serious attempt to gather and preserve the folk-speech and to distinguish the local dialects of England.'[41] The Merry Tree and Lady Candlestick (or Lad Candlestick) joined Dead Tongue *Oenanthe crocata* 'about Kendal and Hiltondale . . . Scelsmoor', a plant used in Cumberland as a poultice for the galled backs of horses.[42]

And so Thomas ends his letter with an envoi that suggests confidence in his own opinion and supposes that Ray is interested in hearing it:

> As for Orchis palmata pal. mac., Park., and his Orchis pal. pal. dracontias, in my judgment you have truly referred them. I have consulted Park. and Ger. Emac., and see no reason to distinguish them. Pray consult Park. and Lobel. Lobel I have not. Park., I suppose, distinguishes them upon his authority. I purpose to mind them in this following season.

So ends the letter – in Derham's transcription as abruptly as it began, without good wishes or customary compliments. If Thomas did possess a Parkinson and a Gerard emac., they would, together with the up-to-date *Catalogus Angliae* have constituted a pretty comprehensive guide to the British flora.

The letter arrived barely a month before the publication of Ray's supplement to the second edition of the *Catalogus Angliae* his *Fasciculus Stirpium Britannicarum post editum Plantarum Angliae Catalogum observatarum*: a 32-page booklet which is witness to the enthusiasm that Ray had kindled up and down the country.[43] Brought out under the authorship of 'John Ray and his friends' it consists mainly of the records of those friends – Thomas Lawson might be proud to be counted amongst a company that included Dale and Doody, Plukenet, Sutherland, Sloane and Lhwyd. When this letter arrived, Ray managed to incorporate 19 of Thomas' records into the *Fasciculus* main list. He then selected a further 19 to compile two supplementary lists: one giving northern locations for plants previously listed in the *Catalogus Angliae* and the other of Lawson observations of abnormal or white-flowered forms. In the tables below, these lists are denoted fasc.b and fasc.c respectively, whilst those records that were integrated into the body of the *Fasciculus* are denoted fasc.a, following the similar notation used for the plants that originally first appeared in the *Historia*.[44] In order to complete the history of the 1687/88 letter(s), the tables also show, in column three, the use to which Ray put the letter(s) when he came to publish his *Synopsis Methodica Stirpium*

Britannicarum two years later. A few further plants are acknowledged to Thomas Lawson having arrived at Ray by other routes, and a brief note on each of these will be found in the last column. Three were transmitted through the agency of the Yorkshire botanist, Richard Richardson with whom Lawson enjoyed an expedition in 1690 and for three more: Dittander, *Lepidium heterophyllum*; Marsh Marigold, *Caltha palustris* and Tufted hair-grass, *Deschampsia cespitosa*, we have no known source. Perhaps they too followed an indirect route from Lawson to Richardson to Ray or perhaps there was yet another communication from Lawson to Ray that is now lost.

Explanation of the Table[45]

Intended to show Ray's use of Lawson's records after he had received them in:

(a) Hypothetical first letter, autumn 1687 or very early 1688.

(b) Letter of April 9th, 1688.

(c) Later communication either direct to Ray or through some intermediate stages (e.g. shown to Richardson).

The marginalia are excluded. (See Chapter XIV.)

H.P.a = 'Primus generis' = [plantae] quarum nonnulle novae & nondum edite.

H.P.b = 'Secundi generis' = [plantae] aliae a nobis in Catalogo Anglicarum praeterite & indictae.

fasc.a = The alphabetic list of plants, pages 1-22 that comprises the bulk of John Ray's *Fasciculus*.

fasc.b = The list in *fasc.* headed 'Loca quarundam rariorum Plantarum (praeter indicta in *Catalogo Angliae*) in quibus a D. Lawson inventae sunt.'

fasc.c = The list in *fasc.* headed 'Insignes quadedam & rariores nonnullarum speciarum varietatis a D. Tho Lawson observatae & communicatae.'

Achillea ptarmica	fasc.c		183 (*SYN* 1724 only)
Alchemilla alpina	fasc.a	158.2	TL showed Richardson
prob. *Allium oleraceum*		370.6	
Allium scorodoprasum		370.6	
Andromeda polifolia	fasc.b	472	

Armeria maritima			203	
'Barba Neptuni; muscus marinus equisetiformis non ramosus'		fasc.a	35.10	
Botrychium lunaria	H.P.b	fasc.a	128	
Caltha palustris			272	Ray's source not known
Cardamine pratensis		fasc.c	299.2	
Carlina vulgaris	H.P.c			
Centaurium erythraea		fasc.c	286 An	
Cephalanthera damasonium	H.P.b	fasc.a	283.3	
Cochlearia danica	H.P.a	fasc.a	303 An 5	
Convallaria majalis	H.P.a	fasc.a	264.2	
Deschampsia cespitosa			403.5	Ray's source not known
Dianthus deltoides			335.1	
Echinophora spinosa		fasc.a	220	
'Equisetum sive hippuris lac. fol, mansu arenosis'		fasc.b		
Eriphorum vaginatum			463.2	
prob. *Eruca sativa*			304.3	
Eryngium campestre		fasc.b		
Festuca ovina	H.P.b			
Gagea lutea			372.3	Record via Richardson
Gentiana pneumonanthe	H.P.c			
Geranium dissectum	H.P.b	fasc.a		
Geranium pratense or G. sylvaticum*	H.P.c	fasc.c	360.17	
Geranium sanguineum var. lancastrense*	H.P.a	fasc.a	360.1	
Geum rivale		fasc.a	353.13	
'Gramen sparteum capite bifido vel gemino'	H.P.a	fasc.a	430.11	
Helianthemum chamaecistus		fasc.c	341.1	
'Hieracium macrocaulon hirsutum fol. longiore'			169.9	
'Hieracium macrocaulon hirsutum fol. rotundiore'	H.P.a	fasc.a	169.8	
Hippophaë rhamnoides		fasc.b	445	
Hymenophyllum wilsonii	H.P.b	fasc.a	123.2	
Hypericum montanum			343.5	
Hypericum pulchrum			342.2	
Impatiens noli-tangere			316	
Lathraea squamaria			★288	Record via Richardson
Lathyrus nissolia			325 An	

Species	H.P.	fasc.	No.	Notes
Lathyrus sylvestris			319.1	
Lepidium heterophyllum			305 An 5	Ray's source not known
Linum anglicum			362.3	
Listera cordata		fasc.b	385.2	TL not acknowledged in Synopsis
Lobelia dortmanna		fasc.b	★287	
Mertensia maritima		fasc.b	228 An 4	
Oxyria digyna		fasc.a	143	
Phyllitis scolopendrium		fasc.c	116	TL not acknowledged in Synopsis
Polygonum viviparum		fasc.b	147.2	
Potentilla erecta		fasc.c	257	TL not acknowledged in Synopsis
Potentilla fruticosa			256.4	
Prunus cerasus	H.P.a	fasc.a	463.3	
Pyrola rotundifolia	H.P.b.	fasc.a	286.2	
Rhynchosinapis monensis			297	
Rubus chamaemorus		fasc.b	260.1	TL not acknowledged in Synopsis
Sagina maritima		fasc.a	345.4	
Sambucus nigra	H.P.b		461.3	
Saponaria officinalis		fasc.c	339.6	
Saxifraga hypnoides			354.3	
Scabiosa columbaria	H.P.b			
Smyrnium olusatrum			208	TL not acknowledged in Synopsis
Sorbas aria agg.	H.P.b			
Thalictrum minus		fasc.b	203.2	TL not acknowledged in Synopsis
Tripleurospermum maritimum	H.P.c	fasc.c		186 (*SYN* 1724 only)
Utricularia minor			★286.2	
Utricularia vulgaris			★286.1	
Vaccinium myrtillus		457.2		
Vaccinium uliginosum		457.1		
Vaccinium vitis-idaea			457.3	
Veronica beccabunga		280.8		
Veronica scutellata		280.9		
Vicia sylvatica			322.4	Record via Richardson
Viola hirta	H.P.b			
Viola palustris	H.P.b	fasc.a		
Wahlenbergia hederacea		277		

CHAPTER XI

David Restrained

THOMAS' INCREASED BOTANICAL ACTIVITY during the 1680s saw him through a period when life was far from easy for him. During the decade, domestic unhappiness was to cloud his life when his only son Jonah was to die suddenly and tragically and his eldest daughter, Ruth, of whom he was extremely fond, threatened to become alienated from the whole Quaker movement by marriage to an Anglican clergyman.

Jonah died in 1684, struck down with small-pox. Although he came through the worst of the illness, he appears, from the account his father gives, to have contracted pneumonia and, in a few days, he was dead. In the form of an admonishment to the young to live well, Thomas wrote his memorial to his only son, *A Serious Remembrancer*.

> Children and Young People, promise not to your selves many days; you know not how near your Glass is run out, when you shall be commended to Earthen Sheets, to your long home.[1]

Then follows a homily to children; a series of injunctions to follow good and eschew evil. Young children must be careful to do right in the sight of the Lord, to walk in God's light and turn away from darkness, to wrestle always against evil and 'in the Faith put on the Lord Jesus.'[2] It is the only document that we have of Lawson's that shows him speaking directly to children and if it seems rather heavily pious in a worldly age, it deals with things fundamental to a child's belief and code of honour: when he speaks of his own son he tells his readers that he was a clever and gentle boy but he also lists among his virtues the fact that he never told tales 'against any Scholar, or Servant I kept.' He also, incidentally, says that Jonah was never foul-mouthed – as much a schoolboy's vice then as now.[3]

The style in which the work is written is as simple as Lawson can ever be and he chooses for his illustration simple texts – dictates from the bible rather than doctrines from obscure learned texts. Even the format – 6″ x 3½″ – is small and suitable for little hands. When Thomas chooses, he can construct a parable to appeal to the imagination of his young readers:

> In Eastern Countries, they wear long and loose Garments, which several tucked and girded up, lest they should hinder them; as, Souldiers, Jewish Priests, Travellers, Runners, Wrestlers, Table-Servers, to serve more readily.

> Now the Apostle brings them to the Inward, to the Spiritual Girding up, saying, Gird up the loyns of your Minds, 1 Pet. 1.13. And 'tis of as absolute necessity now, as then, to wait in the Light of Life; gird up the loyns of your Mind, set your Affections on Heavenly things, otherwise you cannot be good Souldiers of Jesus Christ, to fight the Fight of Faith, neither can you be of the Royal Priesthood, nor perform the Heavenly Journey, nor run the Race of the Righteous, nor wrestle so as to obtain the Blessing, nor sit at Christ's Table, partake of his Blessings, manifold Spiritual Graces; so keep out of the Earth, growing up in Heavenly mindedness.[4]

To be a soldier, to run, to wrestle, to serve: these are things a child can feel are worth doing. But Thomas speaks to adults as well as children. He is not just another adult telling children to be good for he speaks to parents too, telling them they must be 'circumspect and tender over your Children.' No real results are to be had by harshness: 'Train up a Child (saith Solomon) in the way he should go: And when he is Old he will not depart from it. Prov. 22.6.'[5]

This concludes the admonitions. The painful part, the autobiographical reason for the work, fills the last seven pages of the booklet: 'This was my Exercise of late; I had a Son, one only Son, whose name was Jonah. . .'

The account that Thomas gives of his son's final hours is strongly devotional – the small boy dying with his eyes firmly fixed on the Eternal Kingdom:

> Then I said, Jonah, we will talk of another Kingdom: Our continuance here is very little; think of that City, whose Builder and Maker is God. This World is but at the best a Bitter-Sweet, but Heaven is nothing but Joy: Have God in thy Thoughts.[6]

But if Lawson set out to depict a saintly example, he also writes of a human tragedy – Jonah clinging to his father 'not willing to want me' and the anguished father – 'being afflicted for him, and filled with Love to him, I said, Jonah, thou knowest I was never harsh, but always tender to thee; he said, It is so.'[7]

His father and his eldest sister, Ruth, were with Jonah when he died. 'His Sister Ruth, weeping beside him, he said to her, Weep not, I hope we shall meet in a better place.'[8]

It is a pious account, no doubt, but no doubt too, it afforded some relief to Thomas to put on paper this memorial to his son. Jonah would not have lived in vain if his short life and early death could serve as an example to all. In an effort to come to grips with the fragility of creation, Thomas piles image upon image, with reckless hand:

> Read your Mortality in the Creation; the fair Damask Rose soon withers, the fairest Blossom is soon blasted, the most fragrant Aromatical Flower quickly fades, the Dewy Morning hastes away, the Sun (the glorious Lamp of the Firmament) soon sets, the Shadow is gone in a Moment; Jonah's Gourd presently withered; the Meadows, graced with Smaragdine Greeness, are quickly naked; the melodious Bird, now here, is presently gone, the Pearled Dew of the Spring soon ascends, an Hour is but a short time, or continuance, the bubble of a Brook is soon dispersed, the Course of a Shuttle is swift, a Writing on the Sand is soon obliterated, a Thought soon passeth away, a Dream is soon gone, the glyding of a Chrystal Stream soon passeth by, an Arrow from the Bow of the Mighty is quickly gone, the time betwixt Flood and Ebb is as no time, the Spiders Web is soon rent, Lightning from the Sky is soon vanished, a Post is quick in his Course, the Snow quickly dissolves whem [sic] summer comes: Such is the Life of Man, of short continuance here upon Earth, soon gone hence, and seen no more: Our Life (saith Petrarch) is a Race unto Death.[9]

It is a desperate stacking of fanciful images from a man for whom fancy was proscribed. The naturalist turns to the conventions of the poets, the teacher who had banished the lyrics of poets from his school curriculum turned to Petrarch, the most lyrical of Italian sonneteers for words to fit his sense of loss. The purpose of remembrance was, of course, that strength might be drawn from it:

> And I wish I may never forget his finishing of his Course; neither do I remember it, but I am bettered by the remembrance thereof.[10]

Such was no less than the duty of a good Christian. To what lengths this might go may be seen in the title-page of another tribute to a child's death-bed piety:

> The Living Words of a Dying Child. Being a True Relation of some part of the Words that came forth, and were spoken by Joseph Briggins on his Death-bed (1675)

> We whose names are subscribed, are Witnesses for the Lord in this matter, besides several others then present:

William Briggins)	his Father and Mother living in
Hesther Briggins)	Bartholomew-Close in London
John Goodson (surgeon)	Elizabeth Harford (the maid)
Margaret Adams (nurse)	Mary and Elizabeth Moux, Lodgers in the House

Besides such harrowing recitals, Thomas' piece, with its emphasis on gentleness and good behaviour from those remaining in this world and its few pages on the death of his own son is a tale told simply and movingly. At the end, the father, so proud of his son, seeks to rescue crumbs of comfort from oblivion by publishing a few of his schoolby verses. One, upon Man's Mortality, is its own sad elegy for the young life so abruptly cut short:

Death puts an end to all that do remain,
Or which this mortal wretched World contain.
Croesus his Riches nothing can prevail
Against the Darts of Death, when they assail;
'Tis to be moved by no means at all,
Nor any spares, but brings to all a fall[11]

– and so forth for another 16 lines of careful, though scarcely winged verse: very much the imitatory 'prentice work of a promising fledgling, carried off before he could attain maturity.

Jonah's death was but one of the trials that Thomas had to face in the 1680s: domestic troubles clouded his life at this period and he had little heart for exertions in the Quaker cause despite the fact that Fox was urging him to publish something more on its behalf. Towards the end of 1687 or early 1688, the Quaker Thomas Robertson came to see him, pressing him with a message from Fox. Robertson writes to Fox:

I was with Thomas Lawson lately and I asked him what he had done in order to the Booke and the Instructions ye g[a]vest him and he said that he had done something and did Intend to Come up to ye but as yet I have not heard whether he is Come or not.[12]

Thomas did not come, though he writes apologetically to Fox on 20th April, 1689 excusing himself by saying that he feels that, as things stand, there would be little point in travelling to London. There had been some excitement in Cumbria following the landing of William of Orange and Westmorland is in an unsettled state. Lawson, as a Quaker, might well fear to leave his home unprotected at a time when the taint of sedition attached all too readily to anyone whose life diverged from the norm. Besides, there was his school to think about:

I gladly received thy Lines, and I speak unfeignedly I should be very glad to answer the contents thereof, in comeing up to London, if way were made, and my comeing might be of any service. I follow my ancient employ of schooling, and makeing conscience thereof, fear to minister offence by over long absence. Many souldiers draw into these parts, and though they are pretty civill, yet many become much straitned, and more thorough want of provision for horse than men, the last year not yeilding its usual increase.[13]

Nevertheless, he would like to come to London but, if he did so, he would want to move permanently. If there were some way of doing so, he feels that he would be in a better position to complete all the writing that he has in draft:

I am sometymes thinking if Way were made answerable to my minde, it were better I were in, or near London, in order to complete somethings I have travel'd about. I have by me Manuscripts of many subjects, relating to the primitive order, and how it came to be lost, and then what fopperies and fooleries externals borrowed from and extracted out of the idolatry of paganism, as also from Judaism, entred and how the same or great Resemblances thereof is continued in Churches pretending to Reformation.

It is the cry of a scholar isolated in remote Westmorland – cut off from sources of reference and from the exchange of ideas with other workers in the field. But there is more to it still – his personal life has been upset and he had found it difficult to concentrate on his scholarly work:

That about the Wittnesses mention'd to Tho. Robartson, I have done nothing therein, except by way of Meditation, for indeed these 2 last years I have not writ any thing of these things, being driven out of my course my the enormous, irregular dealings of some.

These enormous and irregular dealings are partially explained in a letter that John Blaykling wrote to Fox on 29th January, 1688:

I saw thy letter to Tho. Robertson and touching T: Lawson whom in that thou mentions he is not a good Man. He hath been the weakening of Friends hands in every ex[ercise] these 2 yeares and never any helpe to them that any account cann be given by [. . .] Meeting he belongs to. A great ocasioner of evell to be spoken of the truth . . . a wrong society he hath amongst Men of the World, in sitting and Tipleing with . . . eldest Daughter was concerned with a young Priest as to Mariag and although [he] . . . seemed in words to oppose it: yet he took the Man Into his house and . . . ing that concerne, to teach him and not long after they maryed with a Priest and Thomas Lawson tooke him home to his house next day and hath kept him ever since above halfe a yeare: and yet will not acknowledge any Weakness in what he hath done.[14]

The events so described had come about when one of Lawson's pupils, Christopher Yates who was curate of nearby Thrimby, fell in love with Ruth and came to Thomas to ask for her hand in marriage. It is not difficult to picture what consternation this would have caused: rather as though an elder in the Free Kirk of Scotland had been asked to bestow his daughter on a Roman Catholic. Friends were not allowed to marry non-Quakers, let alone a clergyman of the Church of England. It was quite unthinkable and, lest Yates should think he was being turned away because his means were slender, Lawson informed him that, had he been the greatest Prebend in Carlisle cathedral he would have received the same answer. The following morning, he had the uncomfortable duty of speaking to his daughter whom he found very much in love with her suitor and, despite her father's 'many arguments mixed with much sharpness', not at all disposed to give him up.

For a while, Lawson continued to play the stern father, endeavouring to prevent the couple meeting and, in the end, forcing a parting upon them by sending his daughter away to Swarthmoor where Margaret Fell and others of the household tried to persuade her against uniting herself with Yates. But Ruth was undaunted and though the Swarthmoor household tried to alienate her affections and her father plied her with letters of paternal admonishment – 'if any question the truth hereof, the Letters I believe are yet extant'[15] says Lawson – she returned home in the same mind as she had departed. Her father was at his wits end. 'What should I have done?' he asks his critics in the letter that he wrote to vindicate himself over the affair. 'I am not a Man-Eater by pretence to chop [? for clap] her into a ship of Turk or pagan, and let her sink or swim as one of you said.'[16]

By now the matter had become common knowledge although most of the Quakers in and around Great Strickland and Shap seemed inclined to view the matter leniently. In contradiction to what John Blaykling said, I cannot find that Thomas was anywhere censured for his behaviour – or at least formally. He was, however, in difficulties with his family: his wife sided with Ruth against her father and there was a dramatic moment when Thomas threatened to leave his wife and to disinherit his daughter. This brought the Shap Friends to intercede, suggesting, perhaps, that he was over-reacting and that, provided he was 'clear' (that favourite Quaker word) of any complicity in the affair, then he had nothing to reproach himself with. Ruth had, at this point, given her word not to marry without her father's consent.

And so the year 1686 drew on towards a close in this position of stalemate.

'I when casually I met with Christopher Yeats,' says Lawson, 'I refused not to talk a little with him about other things, but if ever he mention'd the afforesaid concern I [b]ad him hold his peace, for my last words should answer my first, and not a man that spake with a tongue should start me one jot from my resolution, it being a matter of divine accompt.'

In this uneasy way, life went on until Christmas, when Thomas had three or four young men come to learn Hebrew with him and Yates 'unwilling to come behind in that accomplishment,' prevailed upon Thomas' sense of fairness by saying that if he gave him his word not to attempt to see Ruth but to go directly to the chamber above, then it was only common courtesy to admit him to the circle of scholars – to do less was to allow his personal feelings to stand in the way of justice. And Lawson, always susceptible where the advancement of learning was concerned, weakened – 'but I am sure he had no encouragement by it' – he says, disingenuously for, although Yates apparently kept to his promise not to try to see Ruth, their continued proximity can have done nothing towards cooling off the affair.

At this critical juncture, Thomas was away from home in the spring of 1687 for some time and in Whit week the inevitable happened. Christopher and Ruth were secretly married. Thomas' fury, according to his own account of it, knew no bounds – in a hyperbolic comparison, he likens himself to David, determined to destroy Nabal and to wipe out his household. But as David was prevented from the shedding of blood by Abigail, so Lawson was stayed from violence by the scriptures working within and possibly – though he does not say so – by an Abigail of his own house. If he chose the text for its appositeness, there may have been some such scene as that of I Sam. 25.24 in which Abigail falls at David's feet, saying:

> Upon me, my lord, upon me let this iniquity be: and let thine handmaid, I pray thee, speak in thine audience, and hear the words of thine handmaid

If there was such a scene, then it is likely to have been the wife's plea, rather than the daughter's. Frances, according to her husband:

> knowing how earnestly I had opposed that business stood in fear of my comeing home, so had got 3 or 4 men to a Neighbours house, hopeing they might pacify Me; or influence me to moderation.

His critics had misrepresented this by saying that Thomas had gone drinking with men of the world amongst whom was the priest who had married the pair. According to his version, Thomas' only traffic with the priest had been an angry debate about the justness of performing clandestine marriages.[17]

How much of this storm and fury we are to believe, we cannot know.

FASCICULUS
STIRPIUM
BRITANNICARUM,

Poft editum Plantarum Angliæ
Catalogum Obfervatarum

A *JOANNE RAIO* & ab Amicis :
Cum Synonymis & Locis natalibus.

Imprimatur,

CARBERY *Præf. Reg. Soc.*
Maii 16. **1688.**

LONDINI:

Apud *Henricum Faithorne* Regiæ Socie-
tatis Typographum, ad infigne Rofæ
in Cœmeterio D. *Pauli.* 1688.

Tombstone of Thomas Lawson, his wife and son in the Quaker Burial Ground at Nezeby Head [transcript page 188]

We only have the oblique remarks of John Blaykling's 1688 letter and Thomas' own paper of vindication to go upon. Blaykling, having fired his shots, is not too willing to be quoted. He urges Fox: 'if thou write to him againe I pray hurt not me in any Mistake.' Lawson, it seems, had friends as well as critics:

> I pray thee answere him not too much in publicke concerns of Truth untill he become more comfortable, the honest friends he lives amongst it will wound them more then I desyre.[18]

But if these afterthoughts on Blaykling's part tend to diminish his righteous wrath into tale-bearing the hard fact remains that Thomas Lawson's daughter did marry an Anglican clergyman and that his own account of it, written a year later, has a slightly melodramatic feel to it with its figures of the angry father, the disloyal daughter, the sly young man, the trembling wife, the restraining neighbours and the tricky priest. On the faded sheets of Thomas' letter of vindication they are propelled across the paper to play their parts. This effect is enhanced by the fact that only four sheets of manuscript remain – it is a paper without beginning and without end and in some places illegible like a letter concoted by a detective novelist to supply clues to the murder in a book. The beguiling young man who came to read Hebrew and stayed to carry off his mentor's daughter are as romantic as this latter-day David is scriptural, restrained from bloodshed only by holy self-discipline. Only the obstinate Ruth stays sharp and real, arguing at first with her father and then being packed off to Furness to stand up to the full weight of Margaret Fell's personality. Thus seen, she has a stronger reality than the weak and wandering daughter that Thomas took back into his house 'that she might be preserved from further straying' together with her husband.

The fact of the matter seems to have been that Lawson liked his young son-in-law. His request for Ruth's hand had followed a bare three years after the death of Thomas' only son. In those three years, perhaps, the company of his pupil had come to be precious to him – too precious to be thrown away in the gesture of rejection and anger that his fellow Quakers were demanding of him. He had not long lost his son – was he to lose his eldest daughter as well by disowning her and that son-in-law who had gained such a place in his affections? That he was fond of Christopher cannot be doubted – apart from leaving him in his will 'one parcell of ground called Backstanbar in the township of great Strickland with the feild house thereon,'[19] a bequest that might, perhaps, have been made with Ruth's interests in mind, he also left him his copy of Camden's *Britannia*, his Hebrew lexicon and all his manuscripts – personal legacies that speak eloquently of the esteem in which Thomas must have held young Yates. If these manuscripts were the unpublished works of Lawson that were discussed by London Friends a few years later,[20] then the gift speaks of a trust between the two men that transcended religious differences. To the scholar who had come to read Hebrew with him, Lawson left his scholarly possessions.

Sadly, Yates did not live long to enjoy his father-in-law's legacy. In the bitter April following her father's death, Ruth was to bury the man she had fought so hard to marry.[21] On the day following his burial, the snow fell thick and heavy to cover the new dug grave.[22] After only five years of married life, Ruth was left a widow with two small children. To the Quaker mind, brought up upon providences and the outward manifestations of God's will, it must have seemed like a judgment.

If children were any measure of the marriage's success, the four years were not without compensation: the children born during that time reflect, in their names, the closeness of Ruth to her family. If Yates was responsible for the fact that his children were baptised into the Anglican church, Ruth saw to it that they bore the names of the Quaker side of the family. The eldest, a girl baptised 15th June, 1688,[23] was named Frances after her grandmother. The next child, a boy, received his grandfather's name: Thomas. He was a premature baby, his baptism being recorded only eight months after the first child and three days later, 4th February 1689, he was buried.[24] The last child of the marriage, baptised on 14th March 1690,[25] was given the name of a Great-aunt: Jane, Frances Lawson's youngest sister who, we may remember, had lived with the Lawsons at the beginning of their married life.

The sum of worldly goods that Christopher Yates left to his wife upon his death amounted to £34.11.00, according to the inventory that was taken by some of the Trustees of Thrimby chapel/school.[26] A horse and two cows accounted for £9 of this, household goods and implements for £12.11.00 and his books were valued at £3.00. The remaining £10 was in clothes and money. Besides this, Ruth had the 'best cow . . . but one' of her father's legacy and, presumably the land called Backstanbar on which to pasture this cow and the two of Yates', together with his horse if she kept it. At 32 she had, in addition, a few household goods but no home of her own. It is not surprising to find her, two years after Yates' death, remarrying. What is a surprise is the choice of her second husband. On 7th June, 1694, she married John Ayrey of Shap – a dyed-in-the-wool Quaker if ever there was one. In the Strickland Monthly Meeting minute book,[27] John Ayrey's name appears frequently as one of the do-ers of the Meeting: a man called upon to speak to other members about laxness of all sorts, about domestic troubles between husband and wife, about the moral behaviour of their children and about the many other things in which Quakers watched over each other to prevent a falling away from the truth. And John himself was not immune from the friendly interest of the Meeting. On 2nd October, 1699 the minutes of the Meeting record:

> Wheareas a Case depending between Jo. Bowstead and John Arey has beene heard and examined this day is we find that John Bowstead has missed his way of proceeding against John Arey which upon a deliberate discourse with him he Is willing to owne and It is the scence of this meeting that Jo Arey should pas by All further dicourse [sic] and debate concerning the matter and so love and unity be brought up Againe As becomes All people of our Society professing the truth.

The formal phrases of the Clerk to the Meeting cannot disguise the fact that some high words had passed between Bowstead and Ayrey and there was a serious disagreement to be settled before the pious hope could come to pass that 'love and unity be brought up Againe.' Poor Ruth could not have had a very peaceful second marriage for, in 1703, her contentious husband was involved in another dispute with a man called Joshua Collinson. The Meeting tried, as Quaker Meetings were bound to do, to bring the two men to arbitration. But on 1st September, 1703 the despairing Clerk entered in the minute book that:

> The difference betwixt John Arey and Joshua Collinson is yet depending because John Arey now Refuses to Refer it to Any.

The dispute dragged on for the rest of that year and on into 1704. By now the matter had become serious. Quakers usually made every effort to settle their own affairs internally at Monthly Meetings, regarding recourse to the law as a falling away from Quaker ideals by trafficking with the World's people. Ayrey and Collinson, however, had resorted to the law and had, apparently, obtained satisfaction for, on 5th April 1704, the Clerk recorded that 'the difference between John Arey and Joshua Collinson is determined.' The Meeting, though, wanted its own satisfaction: an apology from both parties for using the law rather than the Meeting as an instrument to settle their differences. On 3rd May, 1704, they got it:

> As touching undue stops made by John Arey In a suite at Law without consent of this meeting he doth this day write a paper of Condemnation Against his unlawfull proceeding therein Contrary to order of truth. Also Joshua Collinson in Like manner doth Condemn his unlegal proceedings In a suite at law without the Consent of this meeting.

John Ayrey was rather good at apologising after the event. On 5th December, 1705, the Clerk records:

John Arey hath this day given a paper Acknowledging his Remisness
in Aquainting Friends that he had occasion to comense suite Against
Wm Granger which this meeting Aproves of.

The confession of Ayrey is then recorded and the minutes resume:

Also the visitors of friends families are desired to deal with John Arey
In order to see If he will be willing to sett the man Att Liberty that Is
prisoner Att his suite.

A charming man, Ayrey, but undoubtedly a pillar of the Quaker
community: he gave the ground on which the Shap Meeting House was
built[28] and his goods were repeatedly distrained during the 1680s and 1690s
by the 'servants or Tyth gatherers for Sir John Lowther.' Repeated entries
in the Book of Sufferings of Friends within Westmorland Quarterly
Meeting show corn, bigg [barley], oats and pease being taken from John
Ayrey of Shap[29] who was, at least, no half-hearted Quaker. And that his wife
should not come behind her husband in zeal, Ruth's tithe testimony is
recorded in Westmorland Women's Quarterly Meeting Book:

Dear friends this is my first publick testimony which I have born
against paying of tythes though for a time I have been convinced of
the unlawfullness thereof Blessed be the Lord God who through the
manifestation of his pur spirit and truth hath preserved me from the
evell thereof so that I Can Give in my testimony among my brethren
and sisters against them being fully satisfied that they are the wages
of unrightusness and maintinance of such as seek the[i]r gain from
their Quarter who feed with the full and Cloths with the Wooll not
sparing the flock which is pronounced against.

But Blessed be his name for ever he Is Come who will teach his
people himself and Gives freely and that without mony and without
price and thus my soull doth sencebely wittness magnified be his
name for ever who I trust will presarve me to the end to bear a
testemony for his name against that anticristian yoak of tythe
paying.

Ruth Ayrey
testemony

It is a longer and rather more exalted testimony than the average as befitted
a woman married to such a prominent Friend as Ayrey and conscious of a
lapse in her past. Her sister Deborah's, a little above, is a more prosaic
testimony:

Dear friends this Is my testimony Concerning the paying of tythes I
pay none and being made sencibell by the Inspiarition of the
Almighty who is able to Preserve me from the evel of such things as

the Lord hath made his way and truth known unto me I disiar to be
kept Clear from yelding to the paying of tythes or such things which
I see to be evell disiaring that I may be kept In the sence and feeling
of that which Gives me to see the right of such things.

Deborah Fallowfield[30]

The only document that I can find in Ruth's hand is a letter sent by her
to the Monthly Meeting in Lancaster to acquaint them that the bearer, John
Backhouse has gained her approval for his proposal to marry her daughter
Margaret. Below Ruth's old-fashioned hand, so like her father's, is
Margaret's clear, modern-looking script, giving her own approval of her
suitor:

Dear Friends

    I being Satisfied with what my Fr*ie*nd John Backhouse has to lay
before you respecting our Intended Marriage requests your
acceptance of his said proposal.

Which is all from your Fr*ie*nd
Marg^t Airey[31]

The witnesses to this testimonial are John Ayrey and Frances Yates, the
eldest daughter of Ruth's first marriage. Margaret married John Backhouse
in 1720 and her descendants remained good Quakers. Her mother's lapse in
marrying an Anglican curate was a mere temporary falling away from the
Society of Friends and by then a piece of almost forgotten history. The
curious thing about the earlier marriage, though, was that there appears
never to have been any formal censure passed upon it. What should have
happened was that the Monthly Meeting should have delegated a couple of
its members to go and remonstrate with Ruth in an attempt to dissuade her
from taking up with one of another persuasion. If that had failed, then the
Meeting would normally have instituted disownment proceedings and Ruth
would have been officially expelled from the Society 'till through godly
sorrow and unfeigned repentance she may obtaine mercy of the Lord and
soe come into unity with his people' as an eighteenth-century disownment
paper has it.[32] Apart from John Blaykling, however, the Quaker community
seems to have ignored Ruth's apostasy and no-one came to remonstrate with
Thomas who had taken the young couple under his roof. To the Quaker way
of thought, his offence would have been as great as hers. The children of
Friends were to be brought up in the truth and if they departed from it, the
fault lay heavily at the parents' door. But the Strickland Monthly Meeting
appear to have wished to spare Thomas embarrassment. There were
probably several reasons for this. Thomas' writings and his teaching had
won him an honoured place among Friends and the letter to Fox indicates

that he had re-opened his school after a lengthy break – 'I follow my ancient employ of schooling,'[33] he says. The community was probably unwilling to harass a man who was playing so useful a part amongst them.

Some, no doubt, were a little in awe of him: he was a man who had walked and talked with Nayler and Fox and Margaret Fell. Now he was winning a reputation in learned circles as the friend of John Ray and at the highest level as an acquaintance of William Penn who had the ear of the king himself. Such things might not impress the sturdy John Blaykling who was himself a man of the heroic age of Quakerism, but it could be that more timid and parochial souls of the Strickland Monthly Meeting were impressed and it is likely that Thomas Lawson himself did nothing to remind them that veneration was not in the Quaker way of doing things. It is about this time that he begins to be styled 'Gent.' in the Court Rolls. The next eminent friend that he was to make was in the very heart of the episcopal hierarchy of the established church itself – the Bishop's right hand man, William Nicholson, Archdeacon of Carlisle and Rector of Great Salkeld just five miles away. Botany was to acquaint Lawson with strange bedfellows.

CHAPTER XII

Northern Moss-cropper

IN THE LAST YEARS OF THOMAS' LIFE his reputation may have suffered a little amongst Quakers. In a sense it was the price of becoming an established figure. His London acquaintances were men in a world that was taking a more temperate view of religious differences: their avowed desire was that a common interest in science should bind them with a power that transcended religious differences.[1] When toleration came in 1689 it served to confirm a mood within the country. Whilst John Blaykling fumed, Thomas drew to him companions whose friendship was cemented in the love of plant hunting. The Joseph Sharps and Dan Abrahams of his early years had been joined by others: today he would have been President of the local Field Naturalists' Club, for we find William Sherard writing to Richard Richardson on 17th May, 1690 'I suppose you will see Thomas Lawson (who will furnish you with patterns of most of the Northern Plants) and his company a simpling.'[2]

Thomas, then, was recognised as a real 'moss-cropper'[3] and, by implication his herbarium had come to be regarded as a collection of reference material for the northern flora. Richardson did not become one of the company that season, but the summer did bring another distinguished addition to the plant-hunting brotherhood. William Nicolson, Cumbrian born, had been appointed in 1682 to the Archdeaconry of Carlisle, an office that he held in conjunction with the Rectory of Great Salkeld just nine miles to the North of Lawson's home. In temperament, the two men could not have been more different. Nicolson was a Church of England man through and through, a cleric who was comfortable with the orderly progression of the church's seasons and festivals; a natural administrator, efficient as the Bishop's executive in the governance of the temporal affairs of the diocese; a man, moreover, who had made the church his career and would eventually rise to high office in it as Bishop of Carlisle, Bishop of Derry and finally, just before his death, Archbishop of Cashel.[4] In private and public life he had a great regard for order. The Glorious Revolution of 1688 had come and gone and found him still in office when many others, having sworn fealty to the Stuarts, found themselves unable to take the new oaths to Dutch William. Nicolson saw nothing but the threat of national disorder in such loyalty: there were two parties to a sworn compact and James II had defaulted on his part. Any scruples that he might have had when it came to taking the new oaths were overcome and put behind him. He was not the man to fall upon the principles of swearing an oath and let it stand between him and political reality.

We cannot be certain when Lawson and Nicolson first became known to each other and what we do know comes from Nicolson and not from Lawson. For much of his life Nicolson kept a diary and, in 1690, he records meeting and botanising with Thomas. Prior to that, however, Nicolson had not kept a diary for five years and in still earlier diaries there is no mention of Thomas. It might be reasonable to think that Archdeacon Nicolson was a little shy of Friend Thomas until after the Act of Toleration in 1689 but, in any case, it is unlikely that Nicolson's real interest in botany started much before 1690 when a sudden spate of expeditions are entered in his diary with accompanying plant lists. During the winter of that year, he apparently became dissatisfied with this method of keeping field notes in a diary that contained other things besides and he started a botanical notebook, ceasing thenceforth to enter botanical expeditions in the diary. The bare record of July 3rd, 1690, then, is probably the first occasion of meeting of the two men: 'Mr Hume & I wth Mr Lawson at Trowgill & Clibburn moss.'[5]

Trough Gill is a couple of miles North-east of Great Strickland while Cliburn Moss lies another mile or so to the North-west. Mr. Hume had been botanising before with Nicolson: he was a colleague, Robert Hume the Vicar of Lazonby, and he had enjoyed botanising with Nicolson a month previously when, on 6th June, they had explored the area about Great Salkeld, Langwathby and Edenhall. On that occasion, they had been looking mainly at the plants and weeds of meadows and cultivated ground. Today, they were going to look at a bog: Bog Asphodel, *Narthecium ossifragum* heads the list that Nicolson wrote up later that day in his diary[6] and there are other lovers of moorland and peaty places: the Slender St. John's Wort, *Hypericum pulchrum*, Common Speedwell, *Veronica officinalis*, Bog Pimpernel, *Anagallis tenella*, the Lesser Clubmoss, *Selaginella selaginoides*. In the wetter places, the botanists were lucky enough to find the Nodding Bur-Marigold, *Bidens cernua*, together with a fern which may have been the Crested Buckler-fern, *Dryopteris cristata* and an unidentified rush, reed or sedge for which Thomas' name was 'Gramen Leptopursacaulon' as well as three that we can identify: Marsh

Arrow-grass, *Triglochin palustris*, Bur-reed, *Sparganium erectum* and the White Beak-sedge, *Rhynchospora alba*. The one remaining plant in the list is the little All-seed, *Radiola linoides* which, in the days when peat was widely cut for fuel,[7] favoured the bare places where the moor had been skinned preparatory to cutting. Some of these plants were already known to Thomas: *Narthecium ossifragum* had been recorded by him in his 1677 notebook from various stations around Westmorland and *Triglochin palustris*, *Selaginella selaginoides*, *Anagallis tenella* and *Hypericum pulchrum* all went into the 1688 letter to Ray, the last with Trough Gill given as the location. But the others may have been new finds for Thomas – they are not recorded anywhere amongst his known manuscripts.

He was probably delighted to be out plant hunting with such an interesting companion as William Nicolson: one, moreover, who was to prove himself a very capable botanist. Nicolson gives us no details of the outing: his diary is very much one of appointments kept and business transacted – rarely is there any elaborated commentary about his daily doings and the entry for this day is no exception: if it was his first encounter with the most proficient botanist in Cumbria, he does not say so. Nodding acquaintances they must surely have been – in their different ways they were both conspicuous figures in the area and they lived too close not to know one another by sight but until Nicolson became interested in plants there would have been no reason for them to have met and much, in their religious viewpoints, to keep them apart. Even now, despite the sharing of botanical interests, there may have been some constraint. It is true that there was a remarkable variety of political and religious opinion amongst men of science of the day: Thomas Sprat, the historian of the first years of the Royal Society, wrote that it had been formed so that men might have the satisfaction of breathing a freer air[8] and that this ideal of an agnostic science had been maintained in succeeding years, but Cumbria was not London and part of Archdeacon Nicolson's job as the Bishop of Carlisle's executive had been the suppression of Nonconformity within the diocese. A just man, a fair man and no zealot he was, nevertheless, not notably a lover of those who rejected the established worship. The outing with Lawson appears, however, to have been a success for Thomas invited the Archdeacon to come and look at his garden four days later. The diary records it: 'Julii 7o. I went wth Dr. Sutch and Mr. Robinson to Mr. Lawson's.'[9] Dr. Sutch was a Kendal man – earlier in the year he had enjoyed a botanising excursion down the Kent with Nicolson who had been over in Kendal to preach. The following day, the two men had had a pleasant round trip, going down the river from Kendal and coming back through Sedgwick and Natland. On that occasion, they had been joined by another Kendal man, John Robinson, also known as Fitz-Roberts, a noted botanist in his own right.

He, however, was not the Robinson who came to Lawson's garden that day. 'Mr Robinson' in Nicolson's diary always refers to Thomas Robinson of Ousby: his parish, some five miles away from Great Salkeld, was tucked in below the Pennine hills. It was something of an eastern outpost of Cumbria: the Pennines rise very sharply from the Eden valley and Ousby's ancient church is dominated by the great bulk of Cross Fell, the highest point on the whole Pennine chain. Thomas Robinson was rector there, a strange man and a dreamer of sorts whose friendship was always something of an embarrassment to Nicolson. He was to become keenly interested in mining and in the formation of the earth and later wrote a book putting forward a theory of the earth's structure that might have enjoyed some success a hundred years earlier but which, in the late seventeenth century seemed merely eccentric. As such, it might have been disregarded had not Robinson, in putting forward his own theories, rashly attacked those of the eminent and irascible John Woodward. The result was a severe mauling for Robinson and considerable embarrassment for Nicholson who was supposed to have endorsed his views.[10]

On the day of the visit to Lawson's garden, however, all this was in the future. Botany claimed the day and if we could wish that Nicholson had given a more descriptive and personal account of his visit, we must remain indebted to him for the notes that he does give relating to the plants that grew there.

On arrival, the party probably went indoors first where Thomas no doubt had a few of the curiosities that naturalists of the time collected so avidly. Indoors, too, would be his herbarium: he showed the visitors a sea-weed: 'Alga latifolia porosa maxima' before the party set off to view the garden. Clearly it was a good-sized plot – big enough, at any rate, to have several trees which Nicolson noted down in the diary. Thomas was proud of a beech-tree – beeches were not so common in Cumbria in his day – and he had, too, a white poplar which had been little known in England a hundred years before: the herbalist Gerard had said that there were 'in some places heere and there a tree.'[11] Other trees that took Nicolson's attention were a dwarf medlar and the wild cherry, *Prunus cerasus*, which Thomas regarded as distinctively northern. Amongst shrubs, there was Butcher's Broom and Jasmine, Honeysuckle, the showy hypericum, *H. androsaemum*, the Bladder-nut, *Staphylea pinnata* and Cress-Rocket, *Vella pseudocytisus* which reminded contemporaries of Broom with its yellow flowers and shrubby habit. These at least, were what caught Nicolson's eye: his list is obviously made out for his own purposes and he looked chiefly at trees and shrubs – perhaps with an eye to cuttings at Great Salkeld. Only three other plants receive his notice: two of them give us another slight indication that

Thomas could have been consulted for his medicinal knowledge of herbs. It seems that he grew Birthwort, *Aristolochia clematitis* which had a reputation for encouraging conception[12] and assisting ready delivery of the child and, by contrast, Barrenwort, *Epimedium alpinum* reputed to be efficacious in preventing conception. Certainly if Thomas, the most learned man in his village, was consulted for his herbal expertise one might suppose that conception or its prevention would be amongst the most frequent needs in a small country village. The remaining plant on Nicolson's list is entirely a botanist's curiosity: 'Geranium Haematodes flore eleganter variegato' – the var. *lancastrense* of *Geranium sanguineum* which Lawson originally found on Walney and, as we have seen, he was careful to check that it ran true to type both through his own experience of it under cultivation and by sending it to others to plant and grow.

The visit of the Archdeacon and his friends to Thomas' garden was another success: Nicolson was interested and keen to profit from his new acquaintance's knowledge. They made an appointment to botanise together three days later at Mayburgh near Penrith – possibly the choice of place was Nicolson's for it was a site of archaeological interest and the Archdeacon was well qualified to repay some of his host's kindness by discourse upon antiquities. When at Oxford, his interest in Anglo-Saxon studies had made him something of a pioneer and he had held a fellowship at Queen's for three years. Indeed, at one time it seemed as though scholarship might claim him altogether and it was only financial considerations that had induced him northwards to the Rectory of Great Salkeld. His desire to acquire skill in botany was, in some ways, a compensation for the life that he had left behind: it was hard to pursue scholarly studies without the necessary facilities. Botany required only an observant eye and a methodical habit of thought.

There was much of interest at Mayburgh, a large horseshoe of ground with standing stones within it. The name of King Arthur was connected with the remains and Nicolson was among many who speculated about their origin. Today, though, botany was to be the main object of the expedition and the diary records eight plants which Nicolson felt to have been of particular interest. The first, Keeled Garlic, *Allium carinatum* is noticed as occuring at Mayburgh itself but others are suggestive of a walk down the wooded banks of the Eamont. Several of them are plants that favour lime: Hairy St. John's Wort, *Hypericum hirsutum*, Shining Cranesbill, *Geranium lucidum* and Lily-of-the-Valley, *Convallaria majalis*. A white-flowered Gentian was probably *Gentiana pneumonanthe* and, close to the river grew Purple Loosestrife, *Lythrum salicaria*, Gipsy-wort, *Lycopus europaeus* and the Knotted Pearlwort, *Sagina nodosa*. It was obviously a very satisfactory outing – Lily-of-the-Valley, Gipsywort and the Pearlwort were all known to Lawson from other Cumbrian locations, but the others are not recorded anywhere by him and the two men parted in a mutual amity that ensured another meeting towards the end of the month. This was to be another garden outing: Nicolson was very interested in his own garden at this time and on 28th July he and Dr. Robert Law, later the Nicolson family physician, joined Lawson to visit gardens at Strickland and at Lowther where Sir John Lowther had recently opened up the views and enlarged the demesne by demolishing much of the old village of Lowther.[13] Thomas Robinson was among those who admired the hall and its surrounds:

> It is not only fenced from violent Winds by all kinds of Forest-Trees of Nature's own Production, but adorned and beautified by such Foreign Trees and Winter Greens as are raised by human Art.
>
> It hath by Nature such a gradual Ascent to the House, as makes the Avenue to it most noble and magnificent.
>
> Its Situation is upon a Lime-stone Rock, which does not only secure the Foundation, but so fertilizes the Earth and Soil, as to make it proper for Gardens, Orchards, Terras-Walks, and other most delightful Conveniences.[14]

This was nearly 20 years later. When Nicolson visited Lowther with Lawson, it was not the exotics that he chose to record. From here and from Strickland, it is mainly uncommon natives that he was interested in – many are southerners, their culture in gardens providing Nicolson with a welcome opportunity to become a more comprehensive botanist. His list for this excursion was as follows: Common Maple, *Acer campestre*; Alder Buckthorn, *Frangula alnus*; White Beam, *Sorbus aria* agg.; Musk Thistle, *Carduus nutans*; Sour Cherry, *Prunus cerasus*; Dogwood, *Thelycrania sanguinea*; Milk Vetch, *Astragalus glycyphyllos*; White Helleborine, *Cephalanthera damasonium*; Narrow-leaved Everlasting Pea, *Lathyrus sylvestris*; Yellow Loosestrife, *Lysimachia vulgaris*; a mint; Gold of Pleasure, *Camelina sativa*; Marsh Gentian, *Gentiana pneumonanthe*; Dark Mullein, *Verbascum nigrum* and Traveller's Joy, *Clematis vitalba*.

In August, Nicolson went botanising without Lawson – a miserably cold expedition up Cross Fell that does not sound as though it was much enjoyed by anyone. In September, however, the two men were together again for an outing that closed the season. Shap was old ground to Thomas: Horseshoe Vetch, *Hippocrepis comosa* and the Mossy Saxifrage, *Saxifraga hypnoides* had been recorded there in the 1677 notebook. Knotted Pearlwort, *Sagina nodosa* had been a Mayburgh find, Dogwood, *Thelycrania sanguinea* had been seen on the garden outing and Yellow Mountain-Saxifrage, *Saxifraga aizoides* had been sent to Bobart. The remaining plants were also all probably known to Thomas for, although they do not occur in his known records, he was to supply Nicolson with Cumbrian locations elsewhere for Hairy St. John's Wort, *Hypericum hirsutum*; Dutch Rush, *Equisetum hyemale* and the dock to which he gives the name 'Lapathum Bononiense.'[15] The Carline Thistle, *Carlina vulgaris*, however, appears to be new unless we count the monstrous form of it that he saw near his home, and he saw his own special hieracium – 'Hieracium leptocaulon.'

This ended the season in the field. Its main result was to fire Nicolson with an enthusiasm for botany so that he started his own field notebook along somewhat similar lines to Lawson's. The expeditions to gardens had also been to good effect. Nicolson determined upon planting up the Rectory garden at Great Salkeld and in his diary on September 25th, he records a visit by Thomas Lawson and the two gardeners of Lowther and Hutton.[16] With his characteristic organising ability, Nicolson had summoned the necessary expertise to his aid and for a list of what was planted that day we only have to turn to the back pages of his botanical notebook where five pages are devoted to plants 'Sett in my own Garden Sep. 1690. By Mr Lawson etc.'[17]

From this list, it would seem that much was being established from the beginning. There is, for instance, a long list of trees and shrubs amounting to a fifth of the total number. Several of these are things that Nicolson had seen and admired in visits to Lowther and Hutton. It is very likely that Sir George Fletcher, with whom Nicolson was well acquainted, had instructed the Hutton gardeners to help Nicolson with seedlings and young trees. Certainly we know that in November Nicolson received 'Apricock, Kentish Cherry, Black Hart, Plums, Vines'[18] from Hutton and we might suppose that the Lilac (purple and white), Horse Chestnut, Spindle-tree and the hardy *Coronilla emerus* with its yellow pea flower all came over with the Hutton gardener after Nicolson had seen and admired them earlier in the year. Other plants may have been contributed by Lawson: we find that Bladder Nut is being planted and White Poplar and Cress-Rocket, all of which he had in his own garden.

'On the Border above the green plot' – presumably a distant bed beyond a lawn – they planted Dogwood, Wayfaring Tree and a Lime and 'under the West Wall' they planted evergreens – a Pine tree, Juniper and the Cypress which, as Parkinson grandly says 'hath beene of great account with all Princes, both beyond, and on this side of the Sea.'[19] More utilitarian were a Filbert to give Nicolson nuts in the autumn, a Black Cherry and, against the warm wall of the house where Jasmine might be expected to flourish, they planted a Fig Tree.

When they came to the flowers, we see only a little of the influence of transatlantic imports: Virginia Creeper, Virginian asters and Candytuft. The others are old garden favourites: Wallflowers, Honesty, Martagon Lilies, Paeonies, Campion, Cornflower, Leopard's Bane, Wall Germander, popular in its day as a strewing herb for floors and a composite that Nicolson has down as 'Pilosella maxima.' A couple of varieties of exotic geraniums went in too – Perlagoniums, of course, had not yet appeared on the scene from South Africa – and there was a rose 'Rosea lutea simplex' of which Parkinson said unkindly 'this single yellow Rose is planted rather for variety then any other good use.'[20] Nicolson was obviously not a rose fancier; he planted no other varieties and perhaps this one was put in because 'it groweth to a good height' for it was put in 'the great border below the plott' with *Sisymbrium strictissimum* to grow beneath it.

Besides these exotics, Nicolson and Lawson planted numbers of wild flowers, chosen sometimes for their prettiness, sometimes because they were rarities. Tutsan was shrubby and robust and gave a good show, Yellow Loosestrife would blaze in the sunshine, whilst Rosebay Willow-herb was not so successful in Nicolson's day as to have achieved the despised status of a weed – indeed had been recommended by Parkinson for 'an out corner of our Gardens, to fill up the number of delightfull flowers.'[21] Not so Ground Elder – a surprising choice for even in Gerard's day it was a noxious weed being 'so fruitfull in his increase, that where it hath once taken roote, it will hardly be gotten out again, spoiling and getting every yeere more ground, to the annoying of better herbes.'[22] It was, however, good for gout.

In a small border by the door, where it could admire its strange beauty as he passed in and out, Nicolson planted the Lady's Slipper Orchid, a companion there for Rose-root and the ever popular Lily-of-the-Valley. For show, in the same bed, were Sweet Williams and White Lilies 'the ordinary White Lilly scarce needeth any description, it is so well knowne and so frequent in every Garden'[23] says Parkinson. In the spring, Anemones would bloom in that bed and, at the back end Autumn Crocuses, to give Nicolsons some colour next to their door all the year.

Other wild rarities that Nicolson was to nurture in his garden were Shrubby Cinquefoil, Starry Saxifrage, Solomon's Seal, Nettle-leaved Bellflower, Orpine, Water Germander, Jacob's Ladder, the 'lancastrense' variety of Bloody Cranesbill and Woody Nightshade which he was careful to plant in that distant border above the green plot. A few more natives were distributed in various beds: Meadow Rue, Alpine Lady's Mantle, Marsh Mallows, a Mint, Pellitory-of-the-Wall, Dropwort, Gipsy-wort and a plant which he calls 'Dentariae affinis.'

No seventeenth-century gardener would neglect herbs. Nicolson planted them in various places in the garden and their names are implicit with ancient lore: Asarabacca, Alcacangi, Comfrey, Cardiaca (Motherwort), Verbena to cure the King's Evil and three sorts of Balm to cheer the heart. Herbs with more prosaic names were grown to flavour food: Borage, Tarragon and Dittander which, in the days before pepper and Horse Radish were much used, served to provide a hot taste in food. These were distributed in various beds though most were in the '2d bed' where Nicolson also planted Lady's Laces and an ornamental reed. He and his helpers were not out that day to establish a complete herb or vegetable garden – no doubt the Nicolsons already had both, for they had been in the rectory for eight years. Still, there was room to try some Celery – used more like a herb in those days – and Rhubarb, always useful in early summer when vegetables are scarce.

It was a good day's work and it rounded off a very profitable summer. In the winter of the year, with time on his hands, Nicolson seems to have sat down to construct his own botanical notebook. This was compiled like Lawson's as a search list, but it was not divided into Counties. The basis of it was Ray's *Catalogus Angliae*, Nicolson listing the plants in alphabetical order as Ray had done with a view to inserting his own locations against them as he made discoveries around his own parish of Great Salkeld and elsewhere in Cumbria. This removed the records of collecting from his diary and from then on, it records no more expeditions with Thomas Lawson or anyone else. Lawson now had only a year to live, but he continued to be fit and active and he may well have botanised with Nicolson again during the summer of 1691. Some of the plants that Nicolson attributes to him in his newly-started notebook may possibly date from this period. A measure of the keenness of the two men is that their relationship appears to have been unaffected by a dispute that was even then brewing between the Dean and Chapter and young Isaac Thompson of Farmanby who was to marry Thomas' daughter Hannah. Farmanby is just two and a half miles from Great Salkeld and the property at Farmanby and Hillmire Head was left to Isaac when his father died prematurely in 1689. Probably Isaac was already a Quaker: his parents had dissented from the established religion and, on 12th June, 1666 they had been excommunicated for 'not resorting to their parish church either to service or sermon at any time during ye last year'[24] and, although it was said that Isaac joined the Society of Friends merely to gain the hand of Hannah Lawson and threw off its restraints afterwards, his children, for the most part, followed Quakerism.

Whether or not Isaac was, strictly speaking, a good Quaker, the reputation of his Nonconformity added leverage to the church's attempt to dispossess him of his property: they set about trying to wrest Farmanby from him with a most unrelenting persistence. In 1689, young Isaac was presented before the Court Baron of Little Salkeld for 'taking and engrossing the common belonging to the Lords of the Manor.' For this, he was to be fined 6s 8d and, as he refused to acknowledge the legality of the proceedings, his fines rose by 1693 to the sum of 39s 6d. His contention was, with regard to the disputed land that 'he and his ancestors have constantly held and enjoyed [it] . . . for some hundreds of years.' The evidence suggests that the Dean and Chapter really did not have any title to the land, but this did not prevent them from granting a lease of it to William Nicolson's brother John, who was then Chapter Clerk. On 22nd November, 1690, William noted in his diary that he had been granted the lease of Farmanby intake though he also notes that the matter was not yet quite legally settled. Indeed, brother John was having difficulty in ejecting the troublesome Isaac who fought on bitterly, doggedly and to the ruination of his fortune. In 1691, he was still contesting the matter and he filed a bill in Chancery, accusing 'the said Dean and Chapter John Nicholson and other persons aforsd' of 'confederating and combining together how to disseize and defeat your orator.' John Nicolson, for his part, threatened to bring the case against Isaac to trial in 1691 and 1692, but it was all bluster and, having put Isaac to expense, never proceeded with the cause. Eventually, the Dean and Chapter were to lose, but so too, in all real senses, was Isaac. The protracted fight had left him deep in debt and he was obliged, in the early years of the eighteenth century, to start selling the property that he had fought so hard to keep.

At what stage of this unhappy business Isaac married Hannah, we do not know. There was a daughter born on 29th March, 1692[25] (possibly called Dinah) so that it would seem that the couple were married before Lawson's death at the end of 1691. It seems likely, however, that the couple knew each other for several years prior to that date: it has been claimed, for instance, that Isaac was a pupil of Thomas. If Thomas' death spared him the knowledge of the final bankruptcy of his son-in-law and the consequent homelessness of his daughter, it was, nevertheless, evident in 1690 which way the wind was blowing. When John Nicolson claimed the Farmanby intakes, the rapacious intent of the church was made plain. Such vicissitudes were, however, no more than the stern background to Quaker life. It did not prevent Lawson and William Nicolson sharing a love of botany and discussing plans for future exploration. In the late March of 1691, Thomas is found writing to the Yorkshire botanist Richard Richardson about a plan that he and Nicolson had to obtain specimens of plants from Scotland.[26] The barriers of creed had been put aside for a mutual love and all was set fair for a profitable partnership between the two men. But in eight months Lawson was dead: the letter to Richardson is the last reference that we have to his botanical activity.

In that last year of his life, Thomas was full of plans for the future. New friends and new interests had broadened his outlook and he had become a little weary of the restricted life in Great Strickland: saddened by Jonah's death, disturbed by Ruth's marriage – perhaps a little tired by the new generation of Friends – he was as restless as he had been in the old days when the spirit had driven him all around England. As before, he looked to his teaching to anchor him in a new place. We remember how, in *Dagon's Fall* and *A Mite into the Treasury*, Thomas had argued that children should learn their Latin from classical authors who treated the natural world of 'Natures of Trees, Birds, Beasts . . . as also rules of Gardening . . . ordering of Bees, Propagation of Plants . . .'. The scheme that had been mooted in the 1670s to set up a school to teach such things had fallen through, but Thomas still had a dream of teaching boys in such a way and, on 18th February, 1691, he put out a feeler in the direction of John Rodes of Barlborough Hall near Chesterfield, introducing himself as a scholar and a man versed in botany:

> My Friend, – Though unknown by face, yet hearing severall months ago, that thou was tinctur'd with inclination after the knowledge of plants, the products of the earth, I am induc'd to write these lines unto thee. Severall years I have been concern'd in schooling, yet, as troubles attended me for Nonconformity, I made it my business to search most countries and corners of this land, with severall of promonteries, islands, and peninsulas thereof, in order to observe the variety of plants there described or nondescripts, as also, Monuments, Antiquities, Memorable things, whereby I came to be acquainted with most of the Lovers of Botany and of other rarities of the Royal Socity and others, in this Kingdom and other places.[27]

Thomas then recapitulates the scheme to set up a 'Garden Schoolhouse' and outlines its benefits to give John Rodes an idea of the kind of instructional programme that Thomas would like to pursue. He then offers himself as tutor:

> Now, if thou have an inclination after these things, and dost conclude the knowledge of them usefull, I could willingly abandon my employ of schooling here, and being with thee, lay out myselfe for thy improvement in Latin, Greek, and hebrew; and for the knowledge of plants, and without any great charge, could bring in 2 or 3 of the most parte or of all the trees and shrubs and plants in England into a plot of ground for that purpose prepared, and many outlandish plants also.
>
> And if thou would incline to the propagating of wood, we might prepare a nourcery, where seeds being sown, and young plants set to

grow till fit to be removed into other grounds – a work in no ways dishonourable, but very usefull and profitable.

Gardening, says Thomas, is a gentleman's occupation and, in its useful aspects, a suitable subject of study for a gentleman Quaker like John Rodes. One could wish one knew more about Thomas' own practice in gardening: we receive tantalising glimpses of him tracking Bobart and Morgan round the gardens of Oxford and Westminster; we watch him welcoming Nicolson to his own garden and co-ordinating the planting up of the Rectory garden at Great Salkeld; we open the pages of Newton's *Enchiridion Universale Plantarum* and find him receiving a cutting of a cultivated *Sorbus* from Mr. Pitts.[28] Now he writes to young John Rodes with a project very dear to his heart – the establishment of a demonstration garden as an adjunct to his cherished dream of a good and godly education. Such a scheme would, besides funds, require a pupil who wanted a very special sort of education. The parents of Great Strickland no doubt demanded a more conventional schooling for their children but, with a private pupil, anything was possible. With dignity, Thomas informs his prospective pupil that his motive in writing is idealistic, not financial:

> I have not much more to write, but unfeignedly to acquaint thee that want of employ or beneficial place is not the primum mobile, as I may say, or cause of my writing, for I have better ends, which, if I were with thee, I could satisfy thee herein.

And so, with a further paragraph giving a resumé of his scholarly interests and ambitions further to impress his pupil, Thomas ends the letter:

> No more, but unfeign'd love to thee and to thy Mother to whom I desire thee to shew this, and I desire a few lines shortly from thee, Thy truly Lo. ffrd,
>
>   Tho Lawson.

If Thomas had hoped that John Rodes' mother might incline her son to favour him, he was due to be disappointed. John did not rise to the attractive lure and his mother does not sound as though she had much intention of influencing her son. He was away in Bristol when the letter arrived and, writing to him there on 20th March, a whole month later, Martha Rodes lets him know about Thomas' offer and promises to forward the letter:

> Thos. Lawson sent A letter to thee to profer his servis to teach thee Lattine and Greek, and instruct thee in the product of Plants. It is A long letter. I think of sending it wn I send thy shirts, and then thou may write him an answer.[29]

It is difficult to see why the letter had to wait for the shirts, even if it was

'A long letter', but anyway it did and perhaps the shirts were never sent or the letter never forwarded with them or perhaps John Rodes had no time for educational theorists. At any rate, he declined to bite and Thomas' life in the North went on in the same old way. As always, he was looking forward to a break in his teaching duties in the Whitsun holiday and making plans for it. On 20th March, 1691 he wrote to the Yorkshire botanist Richard Richardson to propose a joint expedition at that time. As the letter gives a good indication of Thomas' plans and activities just eight months before he died, it is worth quoting in full:

> My Ffreind,
>
>   I know not what can be more acceptable to me than correspondence in this manner, till providence give us a meeting: if thy resolutions continue to see our countrey at the tyme called Pentecost, I shall, (God willing), be ready to meet thee upon a prefixt day, at Settle, or there abouts; and in our drawing this way, I can shew thee many topicall plants. If my neighbour, Arey, come into your parts about a month hence, I purpose to send thee a box of plants for thy garden: at present I send thee or two or three sorts of seeds, which I judge will be acceptable. The Archdeacon of Cumberland and I are treating with a young man, knowing in plants, to fetch us from Edenburgh and there about Scotch plants, a catalogue whereof I draw out of Sibbald's *Prodr.* and Sutherland's *Catalogue*, whose assistance he will not want: the man is desirous of the journey, if we can but raise him small assistance to beare his charges, not having much of his own. – Mr. Ray is about a *Synopsis Methodica Insectorum*: my small share of assistance is requested. I wish we could contribute any thing to that undertaking. I wish thou had any author that treats of them, with cuts, and could spare it me a little; indeed, I have none, neither have I much made it my study. I have little more to write but cordiall respects, and that,
>
>   I am, thy really Lo. ffrd.
>   Thomas Lawson.[30]

This is an interesting letter. Neighbour Arey was probably John Ayrey, who was to be Ruth Lawson's second husband, and the Archdeacon of Cumberland was William Nicolson: this tends to lend weight to the supposition that Nicolson and Lawson continued to botanise together in the last summer of Thomas' life. Lawson, as we have seen, was always keen to encourage others to help him collect: from Joseph Sharp and Dan Abraham he had gone on to gather his band of moss-croppers; now we see him entering into negotiations to subsidise a collector to go into Scotland. It was not the first time that he had employed someone on such an errand.

Eighteen months after Lawson's death, Nicolson was to remember how he sent a man across to Walney Island to gather for him:[31] the project to finance someone into Scotland was simply an extension of this. Interest in botany in Scotland rested largely with the Edinburgh men Andrew Balfour, Robert Sibbald and James Sutherland through whose joint efforts the Edinburgh botanical garden was founded in 1670 and a noble tradition of botany in Edinburgh was begun.[32] Thomas has been studying the work of these men in Sibbald's '*Prodr.*' the *Prodromus sive Scotia Illustrata*, published in 1684 which enumerated nearly 500 plants (though some were not Scottish natives) and Sutherland's '*Catalogue*', the *Hortus medicus edinburgensis*, 'a catalogue of the plants in the physical garden at Edinburgh; containing their . . . Latin and English names,' published in 1683.

Some correspondence regarding the young man who was to collect had obviously passed between Cumbria and Edinburgh if, as Thomas says, the assistance of Sibbald and Sutherland was to be at his disposal. A link with Scotland would have been very profitable, widening and deepening an understanding of what is distinctively northern in our flora. In later life, Nicolson was to exchange plant specimens with Sutherland[33] and he himself visited Edinburgh in 1699 and 1701.[34] But by that time his interests had turned to history and antiquity and some of the early enthusiasm for botany that Lawson had helped to generate was gone. Eight months after the writing of this letter, the death of Lawson dissolved the botanical partnership and, apparently nothing more came of the project to send the young man into Scotland.

Before that date, however, something did come of the suggestion that Richardson should join Lawson in a botanising trip 'at the tyme called Pentecost.' Richardson was himself an excellent botanist and, over 30 years younger than Lawson, he was to be one of the second generation of late seventeenth-century botanists who carried the work through to the eighteenth century. Dying in 1741, he links us with the age of Linnaeus who became Professor of Medicine and Botany at Uppsala University in that year. The chief focus of Richardson's work was the cryptogams and, when the third edition of Ray's *Synopsis* was prepared in 1724, he is coupled with Sherard as having contributed most largely to it.[35] Three of his contributions – two of which appeared also in the earlier edition of 1696 – refer back to the Whitsun holiday of 1691 when he had taken up Thomas' invitation to go botanising with him. The first time that he had distinguished Wood Vetch, *Vicia sylvatica*, had been with Thomas amongst tangled vegetation above the Devil's Bridge at Kirkby Lonsdale[36] and in the fields about Kendal they had dug up bulbs of the Field Garlic, *Allium oleraceum* which Richardson had borne home and planted in his garden – rather to his regret for they had proved ineradicable.[37] The third plant is something of a mystery. It appears only in the 1724 Dillenian edition of the *Synopsis* and should, from the polynomials there given, be *Stipa pennata*.[38] As Martindale points out, the pedigree of the record is doubtful and the grass not a member of our flora. If the record was not, by some error, concocted by Dillenius, then it is almost certain that Richardson and Lawson saw something else. A long note by Martindale may be found on pages 156-60 of the *Westmorland Note-Book*: rather more succinctly J. E. Dandy, providing where necessary modern names for those that Linnaeus had given to the plants in the *Synopsis*, writes against this plant – 'quid?'[39] The two botanists seem to have covered quite a bit of ground in each other's company for we find Lawson showing Richardson the narrow-leaved variety of *Convallaria majalis* at Levens in the South of the county.

The expedition with Richardson shows Thomas, even now, gaining in botanical acquaintance and the letter goes on to show how, through his enlarged circle of contacts, he was being stimulated and encouraged to make fresh observations in Natural History. Correspondence with Ray had brought a request that he should help in making a collection of insects from which Ray hoped to write a guide. The study of insects had hardly begun in his day – Thomas was not the only person who had not made it much his study. John Ray himself was only beginning to collect seriously and to study insects and, in 1690, was casting around for helpers and correspondents.[40] And Thomas was very ready to help: 'I wish we could contribute anything to that undertaking', he says, and writes off to Richardson for 'any author' that treats of the subject. This, as much as anything, reveals that Thomas is about to launch out upon unknown waters: he is all at sea regarding the literature of the subject and, had he known it, there was really only one author 'with cuts' that had made any real attempt to chart the insect kingdom and his work was nearly a century old. This was Thomas Muffet whose *Theater of Insects or Lesser Living Creatures* had been compiled before 1604 and published in 1654.

In the event, Thomas was not to be granted the time to contribute to the Synopsis of Insects, nor Ray the time to bring it to perfection. Derham, Buddle, Petiver and other naturalists sent Ray insects and, in the late 1690s, Ray's wife and daughters were all impressed to collect for the dying naturalist.[41] Towards the end of the decade, he began to write up but, before the task was properly complete, he was dead and the book that was published in 1710 was 'a medley, an unedited collection of material, such as any author undertaking a piece of research amasses before the final drafting of his work.'[42]

It was only to be expected that the study of insects should lag a good way behind botany. Botany had a good foundation in the herbal tradition and, initially, strong medical incentives to drive it forward. Insects never had the immediate popularity of plants. The science that, at this time, was gaining the fastest in popularity was the study of the earth. Enthusiasm for the study of stones and fossils was widespread and infectious in the last two decades of the century. So it is that we find Thomas sending off a parcel of fossils to Ray in 1689 which Ray speaks of in a letter to Edward Lhwyd:

> Mr. Lawson of great Strickland in Westmorland not long since sent me a parcell of Trochites or Entrochi found in ye channel of a rivulet near him or rather in ye bank thereof, being washed out of ye clay wn ye water overflows; they are of a clay colour on ye outside, & ye severall internodia (wch are short) are in some edged as sharp as a screw, in others flat: they are all taper, and some of ye bigness of my little finger, possibly they may not be unknown to you.[43]

These are probably the fossils that Ray at this time or later sent to Lhwyd for at least two of Lawson's finds appeared in the book about British geology that Lhwyd published in 1699, his *Lithophylacii Britannici*. Nos. 1136 and 1137 are attributed to Lawson and nos. 1146-1157 are recorded as having been found in Morland. All are classed as 'entrochi' a name used for the fossils of crinoidal limestone. The Morland fossils, though most probably Lawson's, could have been contributions from William Nicolson who, if Ray did not do so, may himself have forwarded nos. 1136 and 1137. Nicolson is credited elsewhere in the book and his nephew, John Archer, was also a keen hunter.[44] Young John was only 19 at the time of Lawson's death and still at Oxford, but he was already showing signs of a developing interest in Natural History. The names of all three men stand together in Lhwyd's book as the Cumbrian contribution to the first field guide to the geology of the British Isles.

Thus, right until the end of his life, Thomas Lawson was enlarging his contacts and his reputation. When he had impressed upon John Rodes that he was acquainted with most of the 'Lovers of Botany and of other rarities of the Royal Society,' it was no less than the literal truth. The botanist Sherard, writing to Richard Richardson from Ireland on 6th June, 1691 says:

> Pray my respects to Mr. Lawson (whom I once saw something of above two years ago, since at Chelsea with Mr. Watts;) and let him know, if I can be serviceable to him here, I shall be very ready.[45]

This looks as though Thomas made another trip to London in the late 1680s: 'above two years ago' would hardly refer to 1677 when Sherard was, in any case, only 18 and an undergraduate at St. John's College, Oxford. Moreover, if Sherard met Thomas 'with Mr. Watts' at Chelsea, then it would, at the very least, have been after 1680 for it was not until that year that Watts was appointed 'to undertake the Ordering management and Care of the Companys [the Apothecaries Company] Bottanick Garden at Chelsey.'[46] During the 1680s, Sherard spent most of his time abroad, but he visited England in the winter of 1689/90 – perhaps Thomas met him then. Once again, we have an elusive view of him in a garden. Winter was scarcely the best time to view, but the Chelsea garden was not to be missed. On Thomas' visit to London in 1677, it was barely established. In March of 1676, the building of a wall around the garden had been commenced but Chelsea was rather a remote place, the work was inadequately supervised, the workmen discontented and the plants, many of which were transferred from the Westminster garden, were frequently stolen.[47] In 1677 there would have been little to attract Thomas out to Chelsea, but by the late 1680s, things were much improved and if he was in London at that time it would be one place that he must see. Under John Watts' superintendence, the garden had become famous: his method of heating the conservatories was remarked upon by both Evelyn and Hans Sloane and, at that time of the year, would be the envy of Thomas Lawson – keen gardeners have green eyes as well as green fingers. The most famous plants in the garden were four Cedars of Lebanon planted in 1683. The timber from these trees still links us with Lawson's day for the wood of two of them, cut down in 1771 to gain space for more plants, was made into chairs (still in use) for the Master and Wardens of the Society of Apothecaries. The other two trees survived until 1878 and 1904, the last 'much painted and much photographed.'[48]

When Thomas visited the garden in the late 1680s, he probably met others of the London botanical virtuosi: Samuel Doody and James Petiver were to be on the committee of five that took over the running of the garden in the 1690s, and Hans Sloane, physician, collector, botanist and founder of the British Museum did much of his early botanising in the Chelsea Physic Garden[49] and took a great interest in it when he returned to England in May of 1689 after spending two years in Jamaica.

Thomas' botanical interests, however, always went hand-in-hand with his life as a Quaker. On this visit to London he would not omit to call upon Sarah Fell, Margaret's fourth daughter who had married William Meade, a prominent Friend and a man of property in Essex who kept a town house in Fenchurch Street. The couple had married in 1681 and Nathaniel, the only son of the marriage, had been born in 1684 when Sarah was 42. Letters of Sarah to her mother give details of the health and well-being of this late and, no doubt, very precious son.[50] If Thomas visited them in Fenchurch Street in 1689, Nathaniel would have been five and already started on his schooling. It was natural then, that in the March of 1691, when it looked as though nothing was going to come of the offer to teached John Rodes, that Thomas should have put out another feeler in the direction of the Meade family who might be expected to want their only son brought up as a good Quaker. This time, his offer met with acceptance and, although there seems to have been some slight difficulty in the way at first, by August of that year Meade is writing to Thomas from his country estate at Goose-eyes (Goosehays, near Barking, Essex):

> I have had thy kinde offer in my [tho]ughts; and now have an oppertunity to imbrace it. [I de]sire to know what summe of money yearly thou wilt [ex]pect, and also how soone thou cann settle thy affaires [and] come to mee; For I am now without one to Instruct [my] sonn and his Cousin Richard Lower; – Thou art to live at [my] Country House, with us, and have all things necessa[rie] for thee, vizt meate drinke, washing & Lodginge; – and [I would] have thee propse, what sume of money yearly thou dost Expect that thou mayst bee at a certainety as well as my selfe; – I would that my sonn, might not change his schoolmaster any more untill hee bee perfected in his [Latine, deleted] Learning; For I hope thou may stay with mee many yeares. The younge ladds cann made a peice of Latine, and pearce it and construe it, in some measure, – and are apt ladds to learne, such as I hope thou will take great delight in – I am now very cleare from this younge man, who was my sonns Tutor and hee is gone from us, and I was more Inclinable to part with him, haveinge thy kinde Letter by mee; – Thus with mine and my wives dear Love to thee, desireinge thy [s]peedy Answer I remaine
>
> > Thy Assured Loveing Friende
> > William Meade[51]

Such a position would have suited Lawson admirably. It was within 12 miles of London where he was increasing his scientific contacts and on the Goosehays estate he would doubtless have been allowed to develop the sort of 'Garden schoolhouse' or demonstration garden that he had long desired. But before the arrangements to take on the tutorship of Nathaniel Meade and Richard Lower had been finalised, Thomas was dead. Less than three months after Meade had written to him, he was to be buried in the family grave at Newby Head where his son had been laid to rest seven years previously. It was to be a sudden end to what, in the last 10 years of life had promised to be an autumn flowering. Recognition of his work had drawn him close to the new generation of botanists who, like himself, had been inspired by the work of John Ray to become keen plant hunters. It was left to William Nicolson to carry on Thomas Lawson's enthusiasm for cataloguing the plants on the northern counties.

In the autumn of 1691, Thomas' health began to fail him. That October, he drew up his will 'being sick and weak in body but in perfect remembrance (praised be god)'.[52] When the end came, it appears to have come suddenly at a time when his daughter Deborah was about to marry John Fallowfield. On the day after his burial, the simple Quaker ceremony went ahead as planned[53] and the Lawsons and Fallowfields, linked so often in the records of persecution, were formally joined by marriage. Three years later, Deborah's first children, twins Thomas and John,[54] were named for grandfather and father.

Thomas was buried at the Quaker Burial Ground at Newby Head where, contrary to usual Quaker practice, a tombstone was later placed over his remains. Some confusion exists over the Burial Ground and this stone. The Burial Ground was leased by John Morland (1620-83)[55] and his wife Elizabeth, both of Millflat, Morland Parish, to four local Quakers by an instrument, dated 10th April, 1669.[56] The lease was for a term of 99 years on consideration of a down payment of 40 shillings and an annual white rent of six pence if lawfully demanded – i.e. virtually a peppercorn. The instrument refers to 'all that Yard called by the name of Burieing Place' which suggests that the ground was already in use before the formal lease was drawn up.

Maria Webb[57] and Joseph Smith[58] both state that the Burial Ground was given to Friends by a former pupil of Lawson. Clearly this is incorrect, for John Morland would have been 39 years old when Lawson opened his school and in any event the tenure was leasehold. Again, Maria Webb is incorrect when she says that the same gentleman asked permission from Strickland Monthly Meeting to erect a tomb over the remains of the Lawson family. John and Elizabeth Morland were both buried in the Burial Ground before Lawson, his wife and their son Jonah died.

It is possible that the commemorative tombstone was placed by a former pupil although not the 'donor' [lessors] of the land. Towards the end of the nineteenth century, the tombstone was moved by Charles Thompson from its original horizontal position and inset into the perimeter wall in a vertical position to preserve the inscription.[59] Different versions of the Latin inscription on this stone exist[60] and some letters are now difficult to make out. In English:

> In the tomb below lies the body of Thomas Lawson, schoolmaster of Great Strickland and expert botanist, who died 12th November, 1691, aged 61.

Here also lies the body of his wife, Frances Lawson who died 3rd February, 1693, aged 55.

Buried with them also is Jonah Lawson, the only son of Thomas and Frances Lawson who departed this life 23rd February, 1683, aged 14.

Frances Lawson, so shadowy in Thomas' life, did not long outlive her husband and remains a shadow to the end. As for the worldly goods that Thomas left, they are detailed in the will that, as we have seen, he drew up in October when his health began to fail him. The legacy to Christopher Yates has already been described. The 'parcel of ground called Backstanbar' is of interest as being the one piece of Thomas Lawson's property which can be traced through to the present day. The name became corrupted first to Backsanbargh[61] and then to Baxen Bath[62] and the land now comprises two fields and part of a third a little under a half mile South-west of Great Strickland on the edge of a slope that drops down to the River Leith. To Ruth, Thomas left 'the best cow I have but one' and to his grandchildren, Frances and Jane, £5.

The specific legacies to his two younger daughters consisted of monies due from fellow Quakers on a mortgage and on various bonds, which amounted to £37-14s for Deborah and £38 for Hannah. There is also provision of 10 shillings for the 'poor of the private meeting' of Great Strickland. The remainder of his goods, moveable and immoveable, he left to his wife Frances and to Deborah and Hannah, the three being made joint executors. These legacies show Thomas as a man of substance, able to lend money. On 19th January, 1692, the will was proved at Penrith. In nine years, three deaths and three marriages had dispersed the family who had once lived in the Quaker schoolmaster's house at Great Strickland.

Quaker Burial Ground at Newby Head

SUB HOC TUMULO JA	In the tomb below lies
CET CORPUS THOMAE	the body of Thomas
LAWSON DE MAGNAE STRICK	Lawson of Great Strick-
LANDIA LUDIMAGISTER	land, Schoolmaster
ET BOTANICUS NON IMPE	and expert botanist
RITUS QUI OBIIT 12 DIE NO	who died 12th
VEMBR; ANNO DOMINI	November
1691 ANNO AETATIS	1691 aged
SUAE 61	61

[below this and now illegible through weathering:]

Here also lies the body of his wife, Frances Lawson who died 3rd February, 1693 aged 55.

CHAPTER XIII

Serviceable Pieces

THOMAS LAWSON'S DEATH CAME AT A TIME when the Quaker movement was deeply concerned about education. The 1689 Toleration Act gave them, they considered, the right to establish their own schools[1] but they faced enormous difficulties in finding adequate schoolmasters. Friends' children should be taught by Friends. There was no disagreement about that, and edicts went forth from London Yearly Meeting to that effect.[2] In many areas, however, Monthly Meetings found it difficult to implement central policy, especially in the years around the turn of the century when finances were at a low ebb. Strickland Monthly Meeting minute book reveals the difficulties of keeping a school there open. In August, 1701, there is mention of a collection 'for to defray the charge of the Schoolemaster'[3] and by December it has become necessary to apply to the Quarterly Meeting for financial assistance. The reply was only cautiously helpful: 'The report from the Quarterly Meeting concerning the schoole masters waige is that, if it was found to be an overcharge they would be assistant.' Strickland duly resolved to make sterner efforts on its own account: 'it is likewise agreed upon by this Meeting that a double collection be had for dischargeing the schoolmasters wage upon the first day come two weeks.'[4]

At this point, the school at Great Strickland and its master were living from hand to mouth. A minute of 4th March, 1702 records: 'it is . . . agreed upon that the schoolemaster continue for another quarter and for the future it is left to further consideration.'

Not surprisingly, perhaps, the schoolmaster left. Two years later, Quarterly Meeting is pressing Strickland Monthly Meeting to recruit a new man as a matter of policy. The Monthly Meeting minuted evasively: 'as touching the Advice from our last Quarterly meeting for getting a Schoolmaster to teach friends children It Is Left to the Consideration of our next monthly meeting.'[5]

It may seem strange that Great Strickland had such difficulty in maintaining a school in the more favourable times of the early eighteenth century when Lawson had managed to go on teaching – albeit intermittently – all through the very difficult years of Charles II's reign. This, though, is to misunderstand the differences between Thomas' school and the Quaker schools that were started up and down the land after the passing of the Toleration Act. These schools were the direct result of centrally-directed Quaker policy intended to provide a Quaker education under a full-time schoolmaster. The problems of paying the master arose from the comparative poverty of many of the members of the Society of Friends. The repeated collections that Monthly Meetings had to resort to in order to pay the schoolmaster are manifestations of this problem that the Quakers of the time never satisfactorily resolved: were the schools to be businesses or were they, in the interests of providing the right sort of education, to be subsidised institutions?[6] In the early days of the movement, such considerations never troubled Thomas. His pupils were almost certainly fee-paying, were not necessarily Quakers and he took them when he could get them to supplement a subsistence drawn from his land in Great Strickland. His teaching was an individual matter and, though he gave much thought to its direction within the Quaker ideal, he was not under 'advice' from Yearly Meeting. Quakers in the reigns of Charles II and James II were too busy just trying to survive and Thomas' stuggles were against the authorities who threatened to close him down. The view of him as the first of a great line of Quaker schoolmasters is true but it should not mislead one into thinking that his teaching had the stable, settled, distinctively Quaker character that such a view suggests or that he himself had any insight into the historical future: he fought for a right that became firmly established only after his death.

Perhaps if Thomas' son, Jonah, had lived the school would have continued. The need – as we have seen[7] – was certainly there. Jonah would have been a few days short of his 21st birthday at his father's death and of an age to have taken over. As it was, it was grandson Jonah, son of Hannah and Isaac Thompson who carried on the teaching tradition down in Dorset at Nether Compton. Of Thomas' other achievements – his books and his botany – the botany out-lived the books but the books outlived Thomas. Towards the end of the seventeenth century, there was a conscious effort made to review the works of the first generation of Friends. On 30th November, 1696, Second Day Morning Meeting met and determined that 'The Writings of Antient Friends' should be looked through by a committee of 18 members with the assistance of a further 18 Country Friends. The Meeting enumerates the Antient Friends whose work it is proposed to review. The list of 28 writers, headed by George Fox, comprises most of the great names of the early years – Howgill, Burrough,

Dewsbury, Penington, Nayler, Whitehead, Farnsworth – they are all there and Thomas is amongst them.[8]

The object of the editorial committee was to extract from the works of these early Friends suitable passages 'as they find propper to clear Friends from the Callumnies that are cast upon them with respect to the severall Doctrines hereafter mentioned.' These doctrines included Repentence, Perfection and Infallibility, Baptism and the Supper, Resurrection and all the issues that were raised by the doctrine of the inner light – 'how Christ is in Heaven and in the Hearts of his people.'

On 3rd December, the Meeting went into more details as to how, precisely, they wanted the editorial committee to set to work. The plan was to define a consensus of early Quaker belief by grouping together key passages which dealt with those important aspects of Quaker doctrine that they had enumerated. One is left with a gloomy feeling that out of this it is inevitable that what will emerge is a party line but that, after all, was what the Second Day Morning Meeting was about. The instructions state that extracts should be made of 'the most Materiall passages' relating to each of the doctrinal topics on which the Meeting aimed at consensus. Members of the editorial board are then assigned to specific authors: Thomas Lawson along with the well educated Stephen Crisp who died a year after Lawson, John Burnyeat who died a year before and the martyr James Parnell who died in Colchester jail in 1656, were all assigned to Richard Smith.

After his death, then, Thomas was given his place with the Quaker heroes of the first age of the movement. Fox had died in 1691, many others who had suffered imprisonment in the early days of fierce persecution were either dead or prematurely aged. By the end of the century even the dynamic William Penn was ageing and Margaret Fell, though apparently indestructible, was 86. It was time to consider reprinting some of the works of the founders before the memory of them passed away. On 10th June, 1700, the Second Day Morning Meeting recommended consideration of 'Thomas Lawson's Book about Baptizm.' Benjamin Bealing, who was an indefatigable collector of documents, was asked to bring a copy to the next meeting. When he did, he also raised the question of '6 other of [Thomas Lawson's] Books in Manuscript.' One of the six manuscripts was some loose sheets of *Baptismalogia* with marginal notes. These Thomas Ellwood, who had examined them in 1698, had thought 'might be usefully inserted to a New Edition: but not without great circumspection and care.' Obviously, these will be of interest to the Meeting and they make a start on the consideration of the whole work by reading to the eighth page on 17th June, 1700. In order to speed things up, the rest of the book is assigned to a committee of seven who are to meet again the following afternoon. In the

event, only three turned up: George Whitehead, John Tomkins and John
Thompson. Perhaps the others had not had time to do their homework. On
24th June, however, the members buckled down to it and, in committee,
read from page 8 to page 43. On 15th July, they were less successful,
managing only eight more pages and it took three more meetings to get to
the end of the printed matter.[9] That still left them with the marginal notes to
consider. On 12th August, the consideration of these was delegated to John
Tomkins and Richard Claridge 'to see they are brought in Right and
properly and then deliver it to the press and to Examin and Correct the
proofs.' For some reason, however the work was now laid aside – perhaps
the job of checking Lawson's references was too much for Tomkins and
Claridge. It is not until 1702 that we hear of *Baptismalogia* again. In the
spring of that year, Derbyshire Friends put forward a suggestion for the
reprinting of two of Lawson's works. Sir John Rodes of Barlborough Hall,
to whom Thomas had once applied for a job, was a great mover in getting a
good library built up in Derbyshire and it may have been at his instigation
that John Gratton and the Derby Friends requested the reprinting of *A Mite
into the Treasury* and *A Treatise Relating to the Call, Work and Wages of the
Ministers of Christ* on 11th May, 1702. This initiated debate as to whether
the time was ripe for a reprinting of all Thomas' works and interest in
Baptismalogia revived. This held things up a little. On 16th October, we
find John Tomkins writing to John Rodes:

> Give Dear Love to our Dear Friend J. Gratton. Tell him we shall
> take care of the Lawson manuscript, and it had been reprinted ere
> now or near it but that the M. Meet: [Morning Meeting, *not* Monthly
> Meeting] is under consideration about printing his whole works
> which yet they have not concluded.[10]

By autumn the idea of a collected Lawson was being implemented and in
the New Year of 1703, *A Mite into the Treasury* and *A Treatise Relating to the
Call, Work and Wages of the Ministers of Christ* were ready to be handed over
to Tacey Sowle for publishing in one volume: 'the volum to be figured
No 2'. This, as John Tomkins describes in another letter to John Rodes
dated 28th January, 1703, was volume 2 of the collected works:

> I understand by J. G. that your County much desieres two of Tho:
> Lawsons bookes should be printed in one vol and wil take of an
> hundred of, viz. Mite in the Treasury and of the Call, wages, etc of
> the ministry of Christ and of Anti Christ which our 2d dayes meeting
> have consented to, and they are in Press, to be Intituled the 2d vol –
> the first being to be printed afterwards, viz. of the Baptism and Supper
> and Dagon's fall before the Ark. There is also considerable quantity

of sheets in manuscript [these were the ones that Ellwood had looked at], which, if proper, may be printed for the 3d voll which will conclude the whole of his works.[11]

Tacey Sowle, however, appears to have been dilatory in getting the works off the press. The Friends were to have trouble with her in latter years and it is probably Lawson's works that are the subject of a letter from Henry Goulding in London to John Rodes, dated 3rd April, 1703:

> I did not forget thy orders to T. Sole; but how she forgot her owne interest, shall know better when I speake with her.[12]

The letter, apparently, remained unsealed until he had spoken to her, for a postscript reads:

> Tate Sole tells me the bookes thou wrote for is not yet printed, and thats the reasons, but I perceive they lost the memorandum and I cannot yet finde thy letter in which thou gives orders.

In the end Tacey Sowle was brought to understand her own interest and *A Mite into the Treasury* and *A Treatise Relating* duly appeared under the collective title *Two Treatises of Thomas Lawson deceased*.[13]

In the meantime, *Baptismalogia* was being got ready for the press. Its companion piece was to be *Dagon's Fall* and the two were to be volume 1 of the whole works. The checking of the references in *Baptismalogia*, however, delayed its publication. The job had been delegated to Samuel Crisp in December, 1702 but he did no better than Tomkins and Claridge had done and, five months later, at a meeting on 15th May, 1703 'Christopher Miedell to endeavour with Theodor Ecclestons assistance to have some of the most Remarkable Quotations in Thomas Lawsons Baptizmalogia Examined and put speedily to the press it having been long delayed.' This time, the Meeting was successful and the second edition of Baptismalogia was published in 1703, though there is very little evidence of any revision or amendment. With it was printed *Dagon's Fall*, the two works appearing under the title *Two Treatises More, by Thomas Lawson deceased*, a title that reflects the order of printing rather than the fact that it was actually volume 1 of the works.

These four works, published as volumes 1 and 2, comprised, in the view of the Second Day Morning Meeting, all Thomas' theological oeuvres that had been previously published. They ignored the pamphleteering of his early days and his memorial to Jonah. They were, however, as we have seen from Tomkin's second letter to Rodes, interested in assembling any manuscript material that might be used to produce a volume 3. To this end they were prepared to consider the six unpublished works that had been brought to the Meeting on 17th June, 1700. Benjamin Bealing's memo is still with the manuscripts:

That it be proposed to the 2d dayes meet*ing*'s: consideration
whether they think this may not be a proper time to order the
Reading over Thomas Lawsons books and manuscripts (that have
laine at the Chamber about 3 years) in order to be printed, they have
been viewed or the most part of them by Thomas Ellwood and some
Remarks made by him in a letter to John Loft which is with the
Bundle.[14]

This letter, fortunately, is still with the Bundle although of six works on
which Ellwood passed remarks, only three are now extant. The manuscripts
are almost certainly those to which Thomas referred when he wrote to Fox
on 20th April, 1689[15] and the three that survive certainly conform to the
description that he gave in that letter. Their titles, as listed by Ellwood are:

Adam Anatomized or a Glasse wherein the Rise and orriginall of
many Inventions vain Traditions and unsavory Customs may be
seen.

Babylons Fall being a Testimony Relateing to the state of the
Christian Church its purity soundnes seriousnes, weightines
heavenly-mindednes, spirituall worship and of its cruell sufferings
under the seven headed and ten horned Red Dragon, ethnick
Roman Emperours till Constantine the Great about the year 316 etc.

The Foolish virgin and the wise being A Testimony Relateing to the
Faith of the empty Formalist, that swaggers in the Court without
that bleses himself in the knowledge of Christ after the Flesh etc.

On these, Ellwood had given his opinion. In the case of 'Adam anatomiz'd'
he considered that the title is too ambitious for the matter: Ellwood
belonged to a generation that valued precision and he was out of sympathy
with such a hyperbolic title which promised to deliver a whole philosophy of
Man. The early sectaries had never balked at grandiose and fantastic titles
but Ellwood belonged to a more sober generation and even at his most
sympathetic he appears to damn with faint praise: 'His wise and foolish
virgins I take to be a serviceable Peice. I wish he had extended it further and
handled more Particulars in it.' 'Babylon's Fall' defeated Ellwood
altogether: 'His Babylon's Fall I have not lookt much into.' In so far as he
has, it seems to have prejudiced him against the work – if it had lived up to
its title it 'must needs be of good use.' However, Ellwood goes on, 'I
perceive it treats of the Mystical Number in Daniel and the Apocalyps
(about which most, that have hitherto travelled that way, have stumbled if
not fall'n) I think it requires the exactest care and most punctual
examination.' Mystic numerology was out of vogue in Ellwood's time: the

excitement of calculating the number of the Beast and the exact date of the end of the world belonged to the days of Protectorate and Restoration – Charles II had survived all the prophecies and life, after all, must be lived a little while longer. The end of the century was to see a reaction in favour of rationalism and a decline of interest in such esoteric subjects as mystic numerology.

Of the three manuscripts that are lost, one was the marginal notes on sheets of *Baptismalogia*. Ellwood provides us with titles for the other two, together with his succinct comments. A work that Lawson called:

> A Serious Apologie. For the energeticall panacea: or universall Light Grace and mercy of the Living God proved by a Cloud of witnesses now living to the Lord in the body etc.

was thought by Ellwood to be 'a very usefull Peice' and another, entitled:

> Of Christs Cross within and Antichrists Crosses Cruciffixes and Roodes without

seems to have received the same treatment as 'Babylon's Fall'. Ellwood has dipped into it and though it contained 'variety of good and useful reading' but he feels that it may need a very great deal of editorial work: 'the Authorities therein quoted had need be reviewed and ascertained' – a care that, he gloomily feels, will need to be extended to all of Lawson's works.

Ellwood's criticisms carried weight – they seem to have been enough to deter the Second Day Morning Meeting. It was Ellwood who had prepared the text of Fox's *Journal* for the 1694 edition which was to be reprinted many times without substantial alteration in England until 1902 and in America until 1892.[16] His strictures reach the heart of the matter – the fact was that in the early eighteenth century when the Second Day Morning Meeting was reconsidering Ellwood's verdict, the taste of the times was in agreement with what he had said. One is left with the distinct impression that, however much the Quakers of that age may have wished to perpetuate the works of the founders, they discovered, in practice, that they had grown out of sympathy with the ways in which those founders expressed themselves. Where it was easy to reprint Lawson's works from published copy, they dutifully did so, leaving little changed or up-dated. Where they were faced with a mass of closely worked notes and the possibility of inaccurate quotations and references, they balked the task. Isolated in Westmorland, Lawson had found it very difficult to check and cross-check and his works suffer from some confusion on that account. The Second Day Morning Meeting considered his unpublished manuscripts on 28th September, 1702 and on 6th April, 1703 and then quietly forgot about them. In the process, two manuscripts and the annotated sheets of

Baptismalogia disappeared. More seriously, a diary was lost and, with it, much of what we might have known about Lawson's early days. Ellwood, predictably, was not impressed with it:

> The Diary I have read throughout, and observe, it is much made up of visions, with their Interpretations, which seem to me not very clear, and such (at least some of them) as may rather amaze than benefit a Reader. Those visions set aside, the rest of the Diary is very short and scanty, for so long a life of so great a Man. It reaches no farther than the year 1666, or thereabouts so that a great part of his Life is wanting, and that in which there could not but many considerable Observables be likely to occur; which if they cann be recovered, so as to make it comprehend the whole Course of his Life I question whether it wil be any advantage to take notice of it. However, I conclude it cannot answer the Title; A Diary. I observe also, there is something unusual in the Style, which seems a little affected; such Expressions as these viz 'I let a deep meditation have an entrance into the Chamber of my heart, p 1. and 2.' and in other places, 'The Feilds of the heart; The Caves of the heart; The Eye of Eternity; The finger of Heaven, etc' Which sort of Periphrases sound, methinks, a little uncouth.

But Ellwood was out of sympathy with the mystical fervour of the early members of the movement and it may be that amongst passages reporting ecstatic experiences there are clues to Lawson's life and his movements in those crucial years following his convincement. And if Ellwood was disappointed in seeking greatness amongst Thomas' literary remains, his name continued to hold its place amongst the honoured founders. As late as 1793, we find the Second Day Morning Meeting still considering republication of one of Lawson's works. In the summer and autumn of that year the members are to be found working their way through 'Thomas Lawson's Treatise on the Divine and Human Calls to Ministers.' On 27th January, 1794, however, they minute:

> On solidly and deliberately considering the expediency of republishing Thomas Lawson's Treatise it is the Judgment of this Meeting that it is most expedient to omit it at present.

So Thomas' theological works were allowed to slide into oblivion like so much that was written in the last part of the seventeenth century when the presses clattered with controversy and the storm that had been raised in Civil War and Commonwealth blew through the reign of Charles II and fell still under the pedestrian eye of Dutch William. Urbanity became the fashion of the eighteenth century and, whatever one may say about Thomas' works, they were never urbane. But their message was irrelevant to the new times and though his name was revered, his works were largely unread. Only botany, less vulnerable to the breath of fashion, was to keep his name in remembrance into the nineteenth century and down to our own time.

William Nicolson, when Bishop of Carlisle (1703-1718)

CHAPTER XIV

Autumn Flowering

THE BOTANICAL DISCOVERIES OF THOMAS LAWSON may still be turned up in modern floras. They will always have a historic value because, many times, his was the first record of a plant in Cumbria. He who makes a botanical discovery, ensures that a small nugget of himself is preserved to posterity and, even for the Society of Friends, it was to be his interest in botany that marked him out as someone special amongst the early Quakers.

The first inheritor of his records was his old botanising companion, William Nicolson. We have seen how, in 1690, Nicolson opened a botanical notebook of his own and have suggested that it was Lawson who encouraged him in this. In some respects it is a modified version of Lawson's own ambitious 1677 notebook. It is, in essence, a regional flora: Nicolson's own title-page indicates the intended scope of the work:

> A Catalogue of British Plants . . . with locations given for the various plants in the counties of Cumberland and Westmorland, as well as the other regions of the old kingdom of Northumbria.

The old kingdom of Northumbria – in Saxon times that part of Britain which extended at various periods from the line of the Humber to the Firth of Forth – was a special interest of Nicolson's: as a Saxon scholar and an antiquary he had had an ambition, which was never realised, to write a history of the northern counties: had he executed the work, the botanical sections would have been largely drawn from this notebook.

Like Lawson, Nicolson used Ray's *Catalogus Angliae* as a basis for the work, but he limited his interest to the northern counties and made no County by County divisions as Thomas had done. Because he was not interested in arranging his Catalogue under County headings, he did not select records in the way that Thomas had done but he wrote down all the plants of the *Catalogus* to form a check list of about 1,450 species flowering and non-flowering. When he found a specimen in Cumbria or the other northern counties, he inserted its location against the plant. Like Lawson, he also accepted the finds of his predecessors. John Ray, as we have seen, made three tours into the North and the results of these tours were transferred by Nicolson from the *Catalogus Angliae* into his own Catalogue.

It is, however, his indebtedness to Lawson that chiefly interests us here. In his Catalogue, he adopts the abbreviation 'T.L.' to indicate those records that he owes to Thomas Lawson. There are exactly one hundred of these and although many of them are already known to us from the manuscript records of Lawson that are extant, there are no fewer than 23 plants which have no existence prior to Nicolson's ascription of them to Thomas.

These plants represent something of a mystery. Sometimes Nicolson gives no more than the ascription 'T.L.' – no location nor indication exactly as to what the letters T.L. represent. Did T.L. show them to Nicolson? Tell him of them? Or was the record taken from a Lawson manuscript or herbarium now lost to us? The last seems the most likely and there is, in fact, evidence that a Lawson botanical manuscript once existed which has not come down to us. When, in 1744, John Wilson, the Kendal botanist, compiled his *Synopsis of British Plants in Mr. Ray's Method*, he speaks in the Preface of incorporating several records 'such as I met with in an authentick manuscript of the late Mr. Lawson.' This cannot refer to any manuscript known to us, as only 10 out of a total of 21 plants are to be found in known material with the same locations as those cited by Wilson: 'Equisetum seu Hippuris coralloides' (Wilson p. 10), *Ceratophyllum demersum* (11), *Xanthium strumarium* (16), *Picris echioides* (36) 'Hieracium macrocaulon hirsutum folio rotundiore (38), *Crithmum maritimum* (71), *Mertensia maritima* (80), *Ranunculus lingua* (105), *Lathyrus nissolia* (205) and *Polygonum raii* (21).

Locations which differ from those of known Lawson records are given for seven plants. At his favourite old ground between Shap and Anna Well, Thomas has found Brittle Bladder-fern, *Cysopteris fragilis* (6) and by Buckbarrow Well the plant which he had previously found by the Blayklings home in Sedbergh, *Chrysosplenium oppositifolium*, mis-called *Sibthorpia europaea* (236). Another favourite spot, Marsh Grange, is cited in connection with Water Dropwort, *Oenanthe fistulosa* and 'in the ditches between Wharton and Carnforth' (67). There was also a Cumberland location for *Asplenium marinum* 'on the rocks between Parton saltpans and Whitehaven' (3). Journeys into and across the Pennines had led to the finding of Moonwort, *Botrychium lunaria* 'on Penniston green, by Dumma crag, on Stainmoor, plentifully' (8) and Common Hemp-nettle, *Galeopsis tetrahit* agg. 'on Cross Fell, and other places of Westmoreland and Cumberland' (95). In Yorkshire, Thomas had apparently found the Small Bistort, *Polygonum viviparum* growing 'by the lead-mill upon the river Tees, nigh Cotherstone plentifully; also in several places by Tees, between the said mill and Rombald church' (22).

These records used by Wilson show Thomas still extending his knowledge of the distribution of previously recorded species. In addition, are four species that are not listed anywhere in known Lawson material: (4) *Thelypteris palustris:* 'by Mickleforce in Teesdale, in the county of Durham, and in a ditch between Appleby and Brough.' (10) *Equisetum hyemale:* 'by the rivulet side between Anna Well and Shap.' (168) *Lathraea squamaria:* 'on the shelves of the scar below Waterfal bridge; near Dalston Westmorland.' (254) *Nuphar lutea:* 'in the moss river by Hawkshead.'

The use of these few records by Wilson, demonstrates beyond doubt the existence of a lost Lawson manuscript. In the letter Lawson wrote to John Rodes (see p. 179) he had spoken of an intention to put out a herbal, adding 'I am also pretty forward with a piece I call Floscuculi Britanniae'. It seems more than likely that this was the manuscript which Wilson saw and to which Nicolson had access when he compiled his notebook. As with Wilson, one might divide the plants into groups – those quoted by Nicolson with Lawsonian locations familiar to us from existing material and those where the location or the plant itself is not to be found in Lawson's writings. There is little profit, however, in speculating that Nicolson may have had access to this or that item of Lawson material. In the end, it is inherently more likely that Nicolson took all the records that he ascribes to 'T.L.' from this one source rather than using a variety of Lawsonian sources. The only exceptions to this assumption are those plants which Nicolson quite definitely says he took from Lawson's published records in Ray. His notation for these is 'T.L. fasc' 'T.L. et J. R.'etc. 15 plants are so designated though it must be said that in several cases Ray does not acknowledge Lawson nor do the stations given look like Lawson's.

Of the remaining 84 ascriptions to T.L., 46 of the plants occur in the 1688 letter from Lawson to Ray, some with Lawson's location only, others with new or added locations, all of which could be attributed to Nicolson. 15 plants occur in the notebook. To 9 of these, for which Lawson has only a southern location, Nicolson gives Cumbrian locations.

The balance of Nicolson's T.L. ascriptions, 23 plants, must exist outside all known Lawson material. The plants are as follows:

> 'Allium amphicarpon' Th. Lawson
> *Aphanes arvensis* T.L. S. [i.e. Salkeld]
> *Betonica officinalis* T.L.
> *Campanula latifolia* T.L. At Great Strickland. S.
> *Cardamine amara* T.L. in watery places in Selside. Baggra-lane near Ulndale.

Epipactis palustris T.L. In a wet meadow under Betham-bank; or Barrow-bank near Brigsteer. S.

Euonymus europaeus T.L. Natland. Skelton Wood. S.

'Filix montana florida perelegans' T.L. Skiddaw. Shap-Abbey.

'Fungus ophioglossoides niger' T.L.

Galeopsis speciosa T.L. [deleted] Orton and Burton.

Gentiana pneumonanthe (prob) T.L. About Great Strickland.

'Gramen sylvaticum tertium Tabernamontani' T.L. S.

Hypericum hirsutum T.L. At Great Strickland.

Lathraea squamaria T.L. [deleted] Great Strickland; under the Rocks below Water-fall-Bridge. [This is the only record also cited by Wilson.]

Lycopodium selago T.L. S.

Meum athamanticum T.L. [deleted] In a corn-close near Kendal Castle. About Shap. Nostras Baudmoney.

Ophioglossum vulgatum T.L. Helsfell-Woods S.

Paris quadrifolia T.L.

Pinguicula vulgaris T.L. Great Strickland S.

Salix fragilis T.L. [deleted] Salkeld, Edenhal etc. S.

Sedum villosum T.L. on Gatesgarth Fell. Hartside and Ingleborough.

Thlaspi arvense T.L. on Lancemoor. S.

Tragopogon pratensis T.L. At Great Strickland S.

This is in many ways a strange list. None of the locations are firmly and indisputably Lawson's, not even Great Strickland – Nicolson was only five miles away from the village. There is, moreover, that sprinkling of 'T.L.' with no location. It would be unlike the methodical Archdeacon, with access to a manuscript in which locations were given, to fail to transcribe these into his own notebook. It is true that we know that Lawson in his 1677 notebook sometimes jotted down a plant under a county heading without giving its station, but so many of Nicolson's ascriptions to 'T.L.' look as though they may have stood alone before Nicolson added a location of his own. We do know that Nicolson was in a position to borrow Lawson's *Catalogus Angliae*: he was to borrow it from his daughter Hannah at a later date (see p. 202). What if, like many another botanist, Thomas was given to putting ticks (and perhaps the occasional location) against plants seen in this, his reference book? What if, too, Nicolson actually borrowed Thomas' copy of the *Catalogus Angliae* in 1690 when he wished to compile a search list? Where a plant was ticked, he might well, then, put 'T.L.' against it in his own book (it is, perhaps, noteworthy that where there are locations they invariably follow the 'T.L.').

This is, however, only the most satisfying of several possible explanations. There is no denying the existence of the authentic manuscript since Wilson says that he actually saw it and the internal evidence of Lawson's 1688 letter to Ray demonstrates the existence of records that cannot be traced in the 1677 notebook. On pages 141ff we have discussed plants that appear for the first time in 1688. It is only reasonable to suppose that Lawson kept this new data in a new notebook. If this was the authentic manuscript and if Wilson and Nicolson were both using it, it is remarkable that they have in common only one record taken from Lawson.

The augmenting of his own notebook was not to be the only use to which Nicolson was to put the records of his predecessor. In the 1690s, he was invited to contribute to the Gibson edition of William Camden's *Britannia*, that splendidly produced county history of Britain. The main part of his contribution was antiquarian, assembling new material for the sections on Durham and Northumberland. But for Cumberland and Westmorland, he compiled short plant lists. To do so, he turned again to Lawson's records in 1694, relying upon his old friendship to borrow the *Catalogus Angliae* from Lawson's daughter, Hannah, to whom it had passed after Thomas' death. From the marginal notes that Thomas has made in the *Catalogus Angliae*, Nicolson obtained the list reproduced on pages 103-105 in Nicolson, *Flora*.

To what extent Nicolson edited Lawson's original notes, we cannot tell: there is certainly some evidence of editorial additions and it may be that there was some omission as well. Of Alpine Penny-cress, *Thlaspi alpestre*, Nicolson writes 'this Mr. Ray in his Synopsis has enter'd among his English plants: but takes no notice of his haveing it from Mr. Lawson' and of Wall Whitlow Grass, *Draba muralis* 'this Plant is in the former Catalogue [i.e. Nicolson's own plant list] I only repeat it here for Mr. Lawson's Description.'

These marginalia must include Thomas' last work in botany: although some records date back to the letter of 1688, more than half the plants are not recorded elsewhere than in the marginalia. Only the following are common to both letter and marginalia: *Lychnis flos-cuculi* (white), *Samolus valerandi*, *Saponaria officinalis* (double), *Potentilla erecta* (double), *Geranium sanguineum* var *Lancastrense*, *G. pratense/sylvaticum* (variegated flower), *Pedicularis sylvatica* and *P. palustris* (both white) and *Achillea ptarmica* (double). Double or white-flowered forms continued to divert Thomas: there was a double *Tripleurospermum maritimum* at Great Strickland, a white Daffodil, *Narcissus pseudo-narcissus* at Ulverston and another at Great Strickland gave him pleasure, a Doves-foot Cranesbill, *Geranium molle* grew under a wall by Mayburgh and his only record of Rest-harrow, *Ononis spinosa* in the Lake Counties was a white form 'by Bigger in the Isle of Walney'. Perhaps there was always something of the gardener in Thomas that made the abnormal as interesting to him as the typical. A double-flowered *Rosa canina* near Malham earns a marginal note: he adds Middleton in Lancashire as a place to see double-flowered Lady Smock *Cardamine pratensis* – in the 1688 letter he had mentioned seeing them at Great Strickland – and it was only with regret that he dismissed *Cephalaria alpina* to its rightful place as a garden escape. Two abnormalities near home were recorded: a three-leaved Twayblade, *Listera ovata* 'in the low Hagg over against the Mill at great Strickland' and a monstrous Water Avens, *Geum rivale* which had been sent in the letter but is here described in more detail.

Two good records come from Craven: Wall Whitlow Grass, *Draba muralis* 'on the sides of the mountains' and Alpine Penny-cress, *Thlaspi alpestre* 'on the pastures above the ebbing and flowing well near Gigleswick. In the mountainous pastures between Settle and Malham varijs in locis.' There are detailed descriptions of these and of a third plant 'Thlaspi minus Clusii' which was regarded by contemporaries as being identical with Ray's 'Thlaspi perfoliatum minus', modern *Thlaspi perfoliatum*, which also grew in the pastures above the ebbing and flowing well at Giggleswick. Ray grouped this plant with Bobart's record between Witney and Burford in Oxfordshire but it belonged properly with *Thlaspi alpestre* though Lawson, with two plants before him which he believed to be distinct, strove strenuously to discrimate between them on the grounds of colour, shape and profusion of leaves, describing too the pods, roots and general size and appearance.

Other Yorkshire finds were Jacob's Ladder, *Polemonium caeruleum* from Malham Cove and Dame's Violet *Hesperis matronalis* 'in the beck that parts Yorkshire and Lancashire, in the way from Westby in Craven to Pendle-Hill.'

None of the other records new in the marginalia – other than one from Carlisle – come from very far afield. Thomas found the Meadow Orchid, *Dactylorchis incarnata* near Common-holme Bridge and the mill at Great Strickland, another orchid, *Anacamptis pyramidalis* from Lancemoor (though also with a location on the Tees), and *Equisetum arvense* from Thrimby and Great Salkeld. Two plants are attributed to people, rather than places, *Galeopsis tetrahit* agg. being attributed to Merret (with only Merret's Nottingham station) and *Serratula tinctoria* to Lawson's old friend in Longsleddale, Reginald Harrison. Lastly, there were a few records that raised doubt and difficulty in Lawson's mind: Broad-leaved Ragwort, *Senecio fluviatilis*, *Geranium macrorrhizum* which he feels is probably a garden escape and *Tragopogon porrifolius* which was only grudgingly accepted by Ray although the record was later supported by John Fitz-Roberts and by

Nicolson who saw it near Rose Castle. It appeared and continued to appear amongst the plants which Nicolson selected for submission to Gibson's Camden. If we exclude *Polemonium caeruleum*, these consist of the last 10 plants named above.

It must be said that Nicolson, who now considered himself a good botanist in his own right, felt that he was at liberty to alter his predecessor's records at will or to add to them when he felt it necessary. The list that appeared in Camden was entitled 'An Additional account of some more rare Plants observ'd to grow in Westmoreland and Cumberland, by Mr. Nicolson, Arch-deacon of Carlisle.' Mr. Archdeacon Nicolson may well have observed these plants himself. But they were drawn to his attention by Mr. Lawson and they are essentially Lawson's records although Nicolson did add several of his own locations to the list and showed discrimination in selecting the most significant amongst the Lawsonian marginalia, ignoring Thomas' penchant for white-flowered forms and eliminating garden escapes. Nicolson's use of the notes is analysed in Nicolson, *Flora* xxxix-xlvi.

More of Lawson's records appeared in Camden through Ray. Ray attributes to Lawson one plant in Wiltshire, three in Yorkshire, two in Lancashire, seven in Westmorland and one in Cumberland. The locations given for a further five plants in the Westmorland list and three in the Lancashire list are almost certainly Lawson's although not acknowledged to him.

The list in Camden was not to be the end of the marginalia. Some 13 years later they were to prove their usefulness to Nicolson again. During those years, some of the first enthusiasm for plants which Lawson had helped to generate in his heart had been channelled into other interests, although he continued to botanise and his observations gave him a deeper and broader perspective on the marginalia. In 1708, he was approached by Thomas Robinson of Ousby with a request for a plant list. The egregious Robinson – whom we have met once before in the course of this story – was in process of writing *An Essay towards a Natural History of Westmorland and Cumberland* and he wished to include in it some note of the flora. Nicolson turned to Lawson again and the result of Robinson's appeal appeared in his book under the title:

> A list of several rare Plants (not observed by Mr. Ray) found in the Mountainous Parts of the Counties of Westmorland and Cumberland, by the late Eminent Botanist Mr. Thomas Lawson; and by him noted on the Margin of the said Mr. Ray's Catalogue of English Plants, now in the Possession of (his Daughter) Mrs. Thompson of Farmanby.

It is from this alone that we know that Thomas' copy of the *Catalogus* had passed to Hannah and S. L. Petty assumes that Robinson borrowed it direct from Hannah. Nicolson's diary, however, tells us that Robinson – who was, in any case, no botanist – had asked Nicolson to prepare a list of rare plants for him and the following day such a list was compiled. It is safe to assume that the list referred to is the one that Robinson published. It was a much longer list – albeit still not the whole of the marginalia – than the one which had been submitted for the Camden and there was more Nicolsonian addition. Much of what is new is the sort of material that Lawson might have added had he lived to do so. Where, for instance, Thomas saw the Spiny Rest-Harrow, *Ononis spinosa* 'by Bigger in the Isle of Walney', Nicolson gives a more general location 'on sandy Hillocks near the Sea-shore.' Even before Lawson's death, discussion between the two men had led to a broader appraisal of the occurence and distribution of certain plants. Where in his marginalia Lawson had noted the finding of a specimen of Twayblade, *Listera ovata* 'in the Low-Hag over against the Mill at Great Strickland,' he later reported to Nicolson that he had found other examples elsewhere and Nicolson, when he compiled the list for Robinson, took cognisance of the fact that 'he afterwards met with it in sundry other places of the Neighbourhood, as likewise elsewhere in the County of Westmorland.'

Such additions by Nicolson make the list published in the *Natural History of Westmorland and Cumberland* valuable in giving a last view of Thomas' botanical activities at the very end of his life. By the extended nature of his additions, Nicolson gives us a lively picture of Thomas, happy in diligent search and consideration of plants to the very end of his life. If we read between the lines, we can draw out a pleasing picture of co-operation between the two men. The Horsetail, *Equisetum arvense*, for instance, was 'first shew'd to Mr. Lawson at Great Salkeld' – surely by Nicolson. The early appearance of the fruiting stem led both men to suppose that they had seen something different from *Equisetum arvense* which had been known from the time of Gerard and Lawson was puzzled to know why it had been previously overlooked, since it grew 'in so great plenty' at Great Salkeld 'and every where on the Banks of the River Eden.' Nicolson, expanding the marginalia for Robinson's benefit, remembered what he had said at the time:

> 'tis an early, and quickly fading Vernal Plant, which might probably be the occasion of its not being hitherto taken notice of by those Curious Gentlemen, who commonly began their Circuits too late in the Year for such a Discovery.

Martindale, commenting upon this plant, notes that it was not amongst those records that were sent to Ray in 1688 supposing that 'before that date' Lawson had discovered that he had seen no more than the Common Horsetail. It seems more likely that it was not actually discovered until *after* that date, especially since Nicolson, who took such a part in its discovery, knew of no second thoughts on Lawson's part and sent the record to Robinson as a novelty.

Again, it is William Nicolson who expands for us the brief note about *Cephalaria alpina* 'sponte an ab ejectamentis horti incertum' into a picture of Lawson's natural optimism disappointed, as he is forced to conclude that it is not a British native:

> This Plant is well known to be a Native of the Italian and Helvetick Alps; and Mr. Lawson reasonably enough concluded from thence, that it might also have a spontaneous growth in this Country, when he found it near the Lord Lonsdale's Seat at Lowther; but he was afterwards rather inclined to believe (as he confesses) that the place where he gathered it, had probably been heretofore a Garden.

There is always something slightly deprecating in Nicolson's tone when he writes of his friend's discoveries. He was a more methodical man and, building upon Thomas' foundation, he produced a longer list of the flora of Cumbria. But he was never quite the enthusiast that Thomas was and he never travelled with quite the same hopeful expectation that Thomas retained to the end of his life of seeing something new every time he took a botanical ramble. Thomas was always looking out for unusual forms, enthusiastic to claim them as new species. In the list that Nicolson sent to Robinson, there are nine double or white-flowered forms. These Lawson was prepared to check upon, year after year, to try to establish their persistence over a period and to make sure that they were not the result of some freak of soil or condition. Of the white *Geranium molle*, we hear that it was 'observ'd several Years together in good fruitful Ground, under a Wall near the Round-Table at Eamont-Bridge.' And of Pyramidal Orchid, *Anacamptis pyramidalis*, later experience enabled Nicolson to write:

> This was look'd upon as a choice Rarety, when he first met with it, (about the Fairy Holes) on Lancemoor near Newby in Westmorland: But 'twas afterwards found abundantly in the Meadows upon both the Banks of Eden, throughout several Parishes.

The hint of patronage in Nicolson's tone is common to all who have made advances upon earlier workers and, on the whole, Nicolson has made a good and faithful job of preserving Thomas' last records. We should, perhaps, be thankful that the busyness of his own later life led him to turn so readily to Thomas' marginalia when he was asked to contribute to Camden and to Robinson's book. It also says much for Lawson's reputation. Certainly Nicolson's use of the marginalia not only preserved them for us but ensured for them a relatively long life. Both the Camden list and the list in Robinson's *Natural History* were subsequently used by Dillenius in the preparation of the third edition of John Ray's *Synopsis* in 1724: the Camden list being attributed to Nicolson, the Robinson list to Lawson. In the *Britannia* itself, the Camden list had a still longer life, being reproduced in editions in 1753 and 1772. In the Gough Camden of 1789, the list was severely pruned when the Linnaean binomials that William Hudson had adapted to the British flora in his *Flora Anglica* were used for the first time. Hudson was a Kendal man, born at the White Lion in 1734 and the publication, in 1762, of the *Flora Anglica* was the principal means by which the Linnaean system was introduced to British botanists.

In many ways, Nicolson and Lawson complemented each other. Nicolson was a born editor and we must be grateful for the numbers of Thomas' records that have been preserved through his efforts. Thomas was less well-organised, apt to be distracted by botanical oddities, probably more of an experimenter in garden-craft. When he died, Nicolson lost the one real botanist who was close enough to him to stimulate him: Lawson, knowing Nicolson too late, never received the encouragement that might have led him to put his botanical records in order and publish them as he had been encouraged to order and publish his theological works.

At times, we may feel disappointed that Lawson went no further than the mere record of what he had seen. We have only his field notebook by which to judge him and that, of its nature, is not a work of speculation: we look in vain for some indication that he studied habitat types or puzzled over the relationships of plants to each other and to their total environment. What we should not forget is that he lived at a time when the meticulous collection of data was important as never before. The schoolmen and philosophers had pondered and speculated about the nature of the world but the way that they went about it had tended to retard rather than advance the cause of science. At the time that Lawson lived, the best service to botany was being performed by those who patiently and methodically collected data. What was becoming urgent, was the need for some sort of system as an organisational framework for looking at that data. John Ray made some hesitant attempts at this but, in the end, it was left to Linnaeus to produce his artificial but workable system. Before taxonomists and ecologists can look at the world with any sort of intelligence, a large body of data must be available to them. It was Lawson's century which gave them that data.

Nevertheless, we may regret that we have only Thomas Lawson's field notebook by which to judge his stature. In extended work intended for publication, he might have given us more. Such work was never undertaken: his speculation was limited to private conversation and the man closest to him in the last years of his life was William Nicolson whose own bent was practical rather than speculative. If the two men had had more time together, the reaction between two very different minds might have produced more than it did. As it was, Nicolson built on Lawson's records but death robbed him of that speculative interest which only the living presence of a like mind can bring.

With Nicolson, the last direct link with Lawson is snapped. John Wilson, though he speaks of 'the late Mr. Lawson' with the courtesy applied to the revered and recently dead, published his work more than 50 years after Lawson's death. When interest revived in the nineteenth-century, the production of a number of county floras set men to hunting up the first records. In the first published flora of Cumbria, *A Flora of the English Lake District* (1885), J. G. Baker credits Lawson with 25 first records. Shortly afterwards, J. M. Martindale made a special study of the earliest Westmorland records. This 'Early Westmorland Plant Records' (which includes records from Furness) was published in *The Westmorland Natural History Record* (London and Kendal, 1888-89) and it credits Lawson with some 150 first records and Albert Wilson, in *The Flora of Westmorland* (1938) credits Lawson with 100 first records.

These floras bridge the long gap of years between the end of the seventeenth century and the end of the nineteenth. The years between never knew quite the same sort of interest in field botany at a local level. The compilation of local records has always been an essentially popular interest. The natural history societies of the Victorian age were the true successors of Ray's band of moss-croppers and simplers. Lawson's name has a natural place amongst the many other contributors to Baker and Wilson. If Nicolson and Lawson had joined forces earlier, we might have had a Cumbrian flora nearly 200 years before Baker's. John Wilson's *Synopsis*, though it included some local stations for plants 'that are not very common' never had records as its primary aim. With Lawson's death, we hear no more of plans to send young men into Scotland, no more of the despatch of specimens, hopefully submitted as new species to the patient and courteous Ray. Nicolson turned to fossil-hunting and Lawson rested quiet below the stone which praised him as a schoolmaster of Great Strickland and BOTANICUS NON IMPERITUS.

Postscript

DURING THE YEARS THAT SEPARATE US from the death of Thomas Lawson, he has become a somewhat different figure from the man that he actually was. I hope that I have restored a little of his actuality. In part, this change was effected by his contemporaries in the changing mood of eighteenth century Quakerism, in part it was effected by sketches of his life drawn up in the nineteenth century. For S. L. Petty, Thomas was the 'Father of Lakeland Botany' – a sobriquet with which it is impossible to quarrel but which confers upon Thomas a sort of elder statesmanship that tends to obscure the fact that he was also a rebel, a polemicist, a dreamer. More modern mentions of Thomas have followed the lead of Bennet and Petty and made of Thomas a sort of early day Gilbert White: a clergyman-schoolmaster botanising peacefully in a remote country village in Westmorland. Hence we have Thomas described as vicar – or at the very least, curate – of Rampside. He appears in biographical notices as the 'Rev. Thomas Lawson' and he is said to have resigned a 'very lucrative clerical living'[1] when he joined the Quakers – 'the first person of his station and eminence who embraced their principles.

What was this 'station and eminence?' Bennet and Petty make him son of Sir Thomas and Lady Ruth (or Lucy) Lawson, with brothers Gilbert and Guildford and connections with the great northern family of Lawsons. A third brother, John Lawson of Lancaster, himself a noted Quaker, was added by Maria Webb on no better grounds than the common surname. Another Lawson, Hugh Lawson, recorded in the register of Christ's College as born near Giggleswick is the likeliest candidate to have been a brother, but his birth is not recorded in Clapham Parish Register.

The true facts of his birth and parentage so far as I have been able to ascertain them, have already been given. They will be found tabulated in the family tree on page xiv. Not recorded in the tree, are the doubtful Hugh and a possible younger sister Katherine who would have been five years Thomas' junior. Her birth is recorded in the Clapham Parish Register, but probably she is of different parents.

With Thomas' own descendants, the record is much clearer. He married on 24th May, 1659, Frances Wilkinson of Great Strickland. The *DNB* and Petty, failing to follow seventeenth century observance in dating, give us the date as 24th March, 1658. The family tree has been taken down to Lawson Thompson of Hitchin in order to show how Thomas Lawson's botanical notebook was handed down the family to remain with them until Lawson Thompson gave it to Mr. R. L. Hine of Hitchin from whom it was presented to the Linnean Society of London.

On Thomas' abilities as a botanist and a scholar there is general, if pious, agreement. His contemporaries thought well of him – Ray speaking of him as a 'diligent, industrious and skilful botanist.'[2] This is the compliment of the age from the age's greatest botanist and was justly merited. But Croese's opinion that Thomas was the most noted herbalist in England[3] cannot stand up against the supreme figure of John Ray and the statement that he gave a series of lectures on botany in London appears to be a piece of pure fancy that does not even have a basis in Croese to whom it is attributed. In similar fashion, the statement that Thomas practised medical skills at Great Strickland would appear to have a basis in some sort of notion that all seventeenth century botanists were necessarily herbalists in the narrow sense.

On the subject of his schoolmastering, his contemporaries are the best guides. To them, Thomas was known as a schoolmaster rather than a scholar – as a scholar he was caught in the web of Quaker polemics and though his name was remembered his works were largely forgotten.

For us, he will always be a botanist first, a schoolmaster second and a religious controversialist last. It is an order of priorities with which his own age would not have quarrelled.

Notes

Convinced at Rampside

1 John Fell, 'The Guides over the Kent and Levens Sands, Morecambe Bay' *CWAAS*, o.s., vii (1884) p. 10.
2 J. C. Dickinson, *The Land of Cartmel* (Kendal, 1980) p.45.
3 Ibid, p. 46.
4 Ross, *Margaret Fell*, pp. 10-11.
5 Ibid, p. 4.
6 Fox, *Journal*, p. 115.
7 Ibid.
8 H. Barbour and A. O. Roberts, *Early Quaker Writings 1650-1700* (Michigan, 1973) p. 61.
9 Fox, *Journal*, p. 115.
10 Barbour and Roberts, pp. 61-62.
11 Fox, *Journal*, p. 115.
12 Ibid, pp. 115-16.
13 Raven, *Ray*, p. 57.
14 Fox, *Journal*, p. 131. Thomas also described himself as such. See p. 20. It was common usage for the parson in the North Country at that date.
15 Lambeth Palace Library MSS, COMM XIIa, Copies of Surveys, 1647-1657. 'Survey of Church Lands Anno 1649' vol ii, p. 76. The Commission met at Lancaster, 17th June, 1650.
16 S. L. Petty, 'Thomas Lawson, the Father of Lakeland Botany' *The North Lonsdale Magazine and Furness Miscellany* (Ulverston) vol i, no. 12, pp. 234-35.
17 Jane Houston, *Catalogue of Ecclesiastical Records of the Commonwealth 1643-1660 Lambeth Palace Library* (1968). COMM XIIc.
18 Lambeth Palace Library MSS, COMM XIIc/4.
19 See p. 209.
20 Lambeth Palace Library MSS, COMM XIIa, pp. 73-74. Preachers were very often supported, at least in part, by voluntary contributions. The Seeker, Thomas Taylor, later a Quaker, ministered in Swaledale as well as in his own community at Preston Patrick. Seekers at Richmond were grateful to him and hoped to contribute at least £20 per year towards his maintenance. (Braithwaite, i, p. 81).
21 See p. 209.
22 ed. J. Charlesworth, *The Parish Register of Clapham part 1, 1595-1683* (Yorkshire Parish Register Society, vol 67, 1921).
23 Ibid.
24 Rufus M. Jones, *Mysticism and Democracy in the English Commonwealth* (Harvard, 1932) p. 79.

25 Ibid. For an account of the Seekers and their relationship to the Quakers, see pp. 58-104.
26 A. F. Leach, *Early Yorkshire Schools* (Yorkshire Archaeological Society, vol. xxxiii, 1903) vol. ii, p. lxxviii.
27 Ibid, pp. lxxiv-lxxvii.
28 ed. H. B. Atkinson, *The Giggleswick School Register 1499-1921* (2nd ed. Newcastle, 1922) pp. 65-66.
29 'That is to say, my will and minde is that the rentes, proffits, and commodities arisinge yearely of all the foresaid howses, landes woodes and premisses shall be for eight schollershipps and two Fellowshipps in their Colledge, And my will is that everie Schollershipp be worth five poundes yearely and everie Fellowshipp twentie markes yearly if the rentes proffits and commodities of the said premisses will arise to so much.' Giggleswick School MSS. Extract from will of Richard Carr, dated 20th April, 1616. Printed in Leach, *Early Yorkshire Schools*, pp. 271-77.
30 Hugh Kearney, *Scholars and Gentlemen* (1970) pp. 112-13.
31 Ibid, p. 120.
32 Ibid, p. 123.
33 Raven, *Ray*, p. 233.
34 Ibid, p. 46.
35 The first reference to Lawson's interest in botany is 5th July, 1674. See p. 67 for further discussion of possible meeting between Lawson and Ray.
36 Letter of 11th February, 1685. See p. 138.
37 ed. A. H. Ewen and C. T. Prime, *Ray's Flora of Cambridgeshire* (Hitchin, 1975) p. 22.
38 *Clapham Register.*
39 Leach, *Early Yorkshire Schools*, pp. lxxviii-lxxix.
40 E. M. Leonard, *The Early History of English Poor Relief* (Cambridge, 1900) p. 164.
41 F. H. MSS, Swarth., i, 246. ?about 1653.
42 F. H. MSS, A. R. Barclay, xlii.

Chapter II   (pages 11-20)
Slandered at Clapham

1 Ross, *Margaret Fell*, p. 10.
2 Elfrida Vipont, *George Fox and the Valiant Sixty* (1975) p. 43.
3 Gerard Croese, *General History of the Quakers* (1696) p. 49.
4 Elfrida Vipont, *George Fox and the Valiant Sixty* (1975) p. 45.
5 Ross, *Margaret Fell*, p. 14.
6 The account that follows is from the Lancaster Quarterly Meeting Minutebook, published in extract in H. Barbour and A. O. Roberts, *Early Quaker Writings, 1650-1700* (Michigan, 1973) pp. 61-63.
7 F. H. MSS, Box C²/13, pp. 24-25.
8 Fox, *Journal*, p. 129.
9 Ibid, p. 131.
10 ''The Valiant Sixty' was a name coined by the late John Handley of Brigflatts near Sedbergh, for the first Quaker missionaries' (Elfrida Vipont, *George Fox and the Valiant Sixty* (1975) p. xiii.) She goes on to point out that, although the

name does not appear in Fox's *Journal*, 'valiant' was a favourite word with him and the name has stuck as true as though he himself had coined it.

11 Fox, *Journal*, p. 174.
12 Ernest E. Taylor, *The Valiant Sixty* (1951) pp. 40-41.
13 Elfrida Vipont, *George Fox and the Valiant Sixty* (1975) pp. 128-129.
14 F. H. MSS, Swarth., i, 246. A paper given forth by Tho. Lawson. The account which follows of Lawson's reception by the vicar and congregation of this town is taken from Lawson's own report in this paper.
15 In J. Venn and J. A. Venn, *Alumni Cantabrigiensis* (Cambridge 1922-27), Benjamin Place is described as son of Christopher Place, Vicar of Clapham, Yorkshire 1649-1679.
16 Matthew xiii, 55.
17 Braithwaite, i, p. 52.
18 Ibid, p. 72.
19 Fox, *Journal*, p. 116.
20 G. Lyon Turner, *Original Records of Early Nonconformity under Persecution and Indulgence* (1911) vol. i, p. 175.
21 G.B.S., vol. ii, Yorkshire, p. 13.
22 ed. James Raine, *Depositions from the Castle of York relating to Offences committed in the Northern Counties in the Seventeenth Century* (Surtees Society, 1861).
23 Stephen Allot, *Friends in York* (Sessions of York, 1978) p. 3.
24 It seems to me most likely that the affair at Clapham took place very shortly after Lawson's convincement and that his incarceration at York followed upon it. This would date the affair to some time late in 1652 or very early in 1653, since we know that he must have been in York Castle before February, 1653 (see n. 25 below). The dating of Lawson's paper of vindication rests upon the endorsement 'about 1653' by Fox many years after. It seems probable, therefore, that Thomas employed some of his time in the Castle in composing this paper. However, these early events in Lawson's life are difficult to date and it is equally possible, if less plausible, that Clapham was subsequent to York.
25 'A Description of the true and false Temple'. These two, together with 'The Idols Temple, where the Beast is Worshipped' (unsigned) and 'A copy of a letter to some friends concerning George Foxes tryal' by James Nayler, written from Kellet 27th October, 1652 were put together by Samuel Buttivant, himself briefly an inmate at York, to make up *A Brief Discovery*. A letter of Aldam's dated 19th February, 1653 and written from the Castle gives some particulars concerning publication. He asks for 200 or 300 copies for distribution amongst the prisoners (Barbour and Roberts, p. 474).
26 G.B.S., vol. ii, Yorkshire, p. 8.
27 Ibid.
28 Ibid, p. 15.

Chapter III (*pages 21-37*)
Missionary in Sussex
1 Page 23.
2 This would conveniently explain why Thomas did not set out on his missionary journey in 1654 when so many other of the Valiant Sixty did. If he was in prison from 1653 until early 1655, however, it is extraordinary that such a

long imprisonment goes unrecorded in the Great Book of Sufferings or Besse.

[3] See Bennet, p. 347.

[4] Henry Winder, *A Critical and Chronological History of the Rise, Progress, Declension and Revival of Knowledge, Chiefly Religious* (2nd ed., 1756) p. 3.

[5] Henry Winder, *The Spirit of Quakerism, And the Danger of their Divine Revelation laid open* (1696) p. 39.

[6] Winder, *A Critical and Chronological History*, p. 3.

[7] Winder, *The Spirit of Quakerism*, pp. 1-17.

[8] George Whitehead, *A Collection of sundry Books, Epistles and Papers written by James Nayler* (1716) p. vi.

[9] Page 14.

[10] Mabel Richmond Brailsford, *A Quaker from Cromwell's Army: James Nayler* (1927) p. 78.

[11] Ibid, p. 81.

[12] 'Financial Statements sent to Swarthmore, 1654 and 1655,' *J.F.H.S.*, vi (1909) pp. 49-52.

[13] F. H. MSS, Caton, vol. iii, p. 268.

[14] Page 235.

[15] F.H. MSS, Caton, vol. iii, p. 172.

[16] ed. Norman Penney, *The First Publishers of Truth* (1907) p. 234.

[17] Ibid.

[18] Ibid.

[19] The first spelling is that of the Quarterly Meeting at Thakeham; the corrected spelling, Wilkinson, appeared in Besse i, p. 708.

[20] *First Publishers*, p. 235.

[21] Ibid.

[22] Ibid.

[23] Ibid, p. 231.

[24] Ibid.

[25] Page 29.

[26] F.H. MSS, Swarth., iii, 131: Letter of Richard Roper to Margaret Fell, 1656.

[27] On the subject of Ranters, see Rufus M. Jones, *Mysticism and Democracy in the English Commonwealth* (Harvard, 1932) pp. 132-33; G.S.F. Ellens, 'The Ranters Ranting: Reflections on a Ranter Counter Culture' *Church History* xl (1971) pp. 91-107; and Christopher Hill, *The World Turned Upside Down* (Penguin 1975) pp. 184-258.

[28] F.H. MSS, Swarth., i, 242.

[29] G.F. Nuttall, Early Quaker Letters from the Swarthmore Manuscripts to 1660 (F.H. unpublished typescript, 1952) Letter 168.

[30] Although Nuttall's dating of the letter depends partly on the incorrect inference he has drawn regarding Byne, the circumstantial evidence points to the letter having been written in the summer of 1655.

[31] F.H. MSS, Swarth., Vol. VII 23B.

[32] Christopher Hill, *The World Turned Upside Down* (Penguin 1975) p. 197.

[33] B. Nightingale, *The Ejected of 1662 in Cumberland and Westmorland* (Manchester University, 1911) vol. ii, p. 1181.

[34] F.H. MSS, Swarth., i, 244. The dating of this letter presents problems. Thomas has given us the day and month but no year date. From the reference to 26th July as a 'fifth-day', it must have been a year in which 26th July fell on a Thursday. 1655 and 1660 are both possibilities. Nuttall dates it as 1655 for the above reason and 'from recent coming to Morland as Vicar of Pearse Burton'

(Early Quaker Letters from the Swarthmore Manuscripts to 1660, F.H. unpublished typescript, 1952, Letter 166) but Burton remained at Morland until 1668 and a dispute over tithe could have arisen at any time during his incumbency. The chief objection to 1655 is that we must suppose that Thomas Lawson, who set off to convince Sussex in May of that year, was back in the North after a comparatively brief period. This, however, is not improbable – Fox, on occasion, would travel through six counties in as many months and other itinerant Quakers were similarly mobile. Thomas, as I see it, could well have spent a few weeks back in the North in the middle of his mission to Sussex. The deciding factor in favour of Nuttall's dating would seem to me to be the fact that Thomas writes from Penrith, hears of the debate on an apparently casual visit to Strickland – 'beeing at Strickland, and heareing of it', and proposes to remain in Penrith until the affair is over. It is not the way a man would write who was married and had a home in Great Strickland as Thomas had by 1660.

35 Francis Higginson, Vicar of Kirkby Stephen, 1648-1673 (B. Nightingale, *The Ejected of 1662 in Cumberland and Westmorland* (Manchester University, 1911) vol. ii, p. 1089).
Percy Burton, Vicar of Morland 1654-1668 (Ibid, p. 1181).
Christopher Jackson, Rector of Crosby Garret in the time of Cromwell, ejected in 1662 (N. & B., vol. i, p. 531).
Ambrose Rowland, Vicar of St. Lawrence, Appleby, 1656-1661 (Ibid, vol. i, p. 325).
36 *A Brief Relation of the Irreligion of the Northern Quakers* (1653) and *A Brief Reply to some part of a very scurrilous and lying Pamphlet called Sauls errand to Damascus* (1653).
37 Alan Wharham, 'Tithes in Country Life', *History Today*, xxii, no. 6, June 1972, pp. 426-433. The long list of titheable produce will be found on pages 398-439 of Richard Burn's *Ecclesiastical Law* (1763).
38 C.R.O.(K) MSS, WDFC/F/1 Strickland Monthly Meeting Minute Book No. 1 1675-1714. The testimony is undated. It is located between minutes dated 26th November, 1679 and 25th December, 1679.
39 Joseph Smith, *Bibliotheca Anti-Quakeriana* (1873). Some account of Caffyn's life is to be found in Florence Gregg, *Matthew Caffin, a Pioneer of Truth* (1890).
40 *First Publishers*, p. 235.
41 Besse, i, p. 708.
42 Ibid.
43 *First Publishers*, pp. 236-7.
44 Ibid, p. 237.
45 Besse, i, p. 708.
46 Magnus Byne, *The Scornfull Quakers Answered and Their railing Reply refuted* (1656).
47 Ibid, A2v.
48 Matthew Caffyn, *The Deceived, and deceiving Quakers Discovered* (1656) p. 54.
49 Christopher Hill, *The World Turned Upside Down* (Penguin, 1975) p. 239 also raises the question whether Laycock was a Ranter. His Chapter 10 'Ranters and Quakers' is illuminating on contemporary views of the two groups.
50 Francis Bugg, *The Pilgrim's Progress from Quakerism to Christianity* (1698) p. 137.
51 Thomas Lawson and John Slee, *An Untaught Teacher Witnessed against* (1655) p. 39. Details and date from title-page.
52 Ibid, p. 39 [for p. 4].

53 Ibid, p. 3.
54 Ibid, p. 7.
55 Ibid, p. 11.
56 Ibid, p. 12.
57 Ibid.
58 Ibid, p. 18.
59 Ibid, p. 16. Quotation from Job 19, 26.
60 Ibid, p. 20.
61 Fox, *Journal*, p. 96.
62 F.H. MSS, The Great Book of Sufferings, vol. ii, Sussex, p. 7.
63 Matthew Caffyn, *The Deceived, and deceiving Quakers Discovered* (1656) p. 2.
64 Ibid, p. 35.
65 Ibid, p. 5.
66 Ibid, p. 19.
67 Ibid, pp. 41 and 43.
68 Ibid, p. 55.
69 Ibid, p. 56.
70 Ibid, p. 54.
71 James Nayler, *The Light of Christ, and the Word of Life Cleared from the Deceipts of the Deceiver* (1656) p. 2.

Chapter IV   *(pages 38-49)*
An Abode in the Earth

1 Ross, *Margaret Fell*, pp. 105-106.
2 Luella M. Wright, *The Literary Life of the Early Friends 1650-1725* (New York, 1966) p. 98.
3 Quoted by Magnus Byne in *The Scornfull Quakers answered* (1656) p. 63.
4 F.H. MSS, Swarth., Vol. VII 23B.
5 Thomas Lawson, *The Lip of Truth Opened, against a Dawber with untempered Morter* (1656) p. 3.
6 Letter of Parker and Audland to Fox, Lancaster, 7th March, 1656 (F.H. MSS, Swarth., i, 1. Quoted in Braithwaite i, p. 448.
7 Mabel Richmond Brailsford, *A Quaker from Cromwell's Army: James Nayler* (1927) pp. 102-117.
8 Ibid, pp. 141-42.
9 Nuttall dates it as ?December, 1655 (Early Quaker Letters from the Swarthmore Manuscripts to 1660: F.H. unpublished typescript, 1952, Letter no. 214) on the grounds that Thomas demanded money that month from the Kendal, or General, Fund. Presumably Nuttall considered that this was to repay the loan mentioned in the letter. But Lawson specifically says that he was reluctant to apply to the Kendal Fund and did not do so. Ross, *Margaret Fell*, p. 66, dates the letter 1657 but gives no reason. The tone and contents of the letter suggest a date later than 1655.
10 F.H. MSS, Swarth., i, 241. Lawson's phrase is 'a man some thing related to mee in the outward.' He is using the theological distinction between outward, on the outside of the body or person as opposed to the inner nature or character (O.E.D.). So Burrough excuses his inability to go home after his parents' death by saying 'it is only pertaining to outwards.' (Braithwaite, i, p. 91.)

[11] e.g. Ross, *Margaret Fell*, p. 13.
[12] A. F. Leach, *Early Yorkshire Schools* (Yorkshire Archaeological Society, vol. xxxiii, 1903, vol. ii) p. lxxv.
[13] Page 66.
[14] Page 24.
[15] 'Leave this with Thos. Turner, shopkeeper, upon the bridge at Newcastle, to be sent by the first carrier to Geo. Taylor in Kendal, Ironmonger, with care and trust' – endorsement on a letter of Howgill and Robertson from Leith to Fox. (Braithwaite, i, p. 231n from F.H. MSS, Portfolio 2, no. 77.)
[16] Wright, *Literary Life*, p. 8, from information in John Whiting, *A Catalogue of Friends Books* (1708).
[17] Fox, *Journal*, p. 7.
[18] Short gap in manuscript. Presumably Lawson intended to insert a name.
[19] . This letter is endorsed by Fox: 'Thomas Loson to Margret read over.'
[20] Brailsford, *James Nayler*, pp. 169-170.
[21] F.H. MSS, Swarth., i, 243. Bordley Hall, the home of Elizabeth Proctor, lies 3 miles East of Malham over the hill in the next valley.
[22] H. Barbour and A. O. Roberts, *Early Quaker Writings 1650-1700* (Michigan 1973) p. 550.
[23] Howard H. Brinton, *Children of Light* (New York, 1938) p. 160.
[24] F.H.MSS, Digest Copies of Registers.
[25] In 1668, *Eine Antwort auf ein Buch* was published abroad.
[26] Thomas Lawson, *An Appeal to the Parliament* (1660). Four-page pamphlet.
[27] Ibid, p. 3.
[28] Isabel Grubb, *Quakerism and Industry before 1800* (1930) pp. 133-35.
[29] 14 Charles II. c. 4. 1662. An Act for the Uniformity of Publique Prayers and Administration of Sacraments and other Rites and Ceremonies and for Establishing the Form of making, ordaining and consecrating Bishops, Priests and Deacons in the Church of England.
17 Charles II. c. 2. 1665. An Act for Restraining Non-Conformists from inhabiting in Corporations.
Braithwaite ii, Chapter I, gives a good account of the Restoration Settlement as it affected Quakers.
[30] Henry R. Plomer, *A Dictionary of the Booksellers and Printers who were at work in England, Scotland and Ireland from 1641 to 1667* (1907).
[31] Ibid.

Chapter V   (pages 50-65)
Schoolmaster at Great Strickland

[1] The progress towards a limited toleration may be followed in Charles Mullet, 'Toleration and Persecution in England 1660-89,' *Church History*, xviii (1949) pp. 18-43.
[2] Braithwaite ii, p. 9.
[3] Ibid, pp. 29-30. (A full account of the Westmorland incident is given in Francis Nicholson, 'The Kaber Rigg Plot, 1663' *CWAAS*, n.s., xi (1911) pp. 212-32.)
[4] Ibid, p. 31.
[5] Ibid, p. 32-37.
[6] Ibid, p. 7.
[7] Christopher Hill, *The World Turned Upside Down* (Penguin, 1975) p. 241.

8 C.R.O.(C) MSS, D/LONS/L Manors of Great Strickland and Melkinthorpe, Court Roll, 1661.

9 C.R.O.(C) MSS, D/LONS/L Manor of Great Strickland 1/13, Court Roll, 1665.

10 Ibid, Court Roll, 1666.

11 Ibid, Court Roll, 1667.

12 Ibid, Court Roll, 1668.

13 When Thomas died, Frances Lawson's name went down on his will as having sworn in order to obtain probate.

14 C.R.O.(C) MSS, D/LONS/L Manor of Great Strickland 1/13, Court Roll, 1670.

15 Ibid, Court Roll, 1665.

16 Ibid, Court Roll, 1667.

17 Ibid.

18 C.R.O.(C) MSS, D/LONS/L Manors of Great Strickland and Melkinthorpe Court Roll, 1686.

19 Ibid, Court Rolls 1689, 1690 and 1691.

20 F.H. MSS, A. R. Barclay, no. 42.

21 Lawsons of Brough; Lawsons of Cramlington; and Lawsons of Longhirst. Martlets do not feature in the arms of the Cumbrian Lawsons, Lawsons of Isel and Brayton.

22 C.R.O.(C) MSS, DRC 5/2 Correction Court Act Book, 26:1:1663/4 – 13:3: 1667/8 f. 198v.

23 Ibid, f. 210.

24 C.R.O.(C) MSS, DRC 5/3 Correction Court Act Book, 13:3:1667/8 – 7:10:1670 f. 24v.

25 W. E. Tate, *The Parish Chest, a Study of the Records of Parochial Administration of England* (Cambridge, 1946) p. 92.

26 J. A. Williams, *Catholic Recusancy in Wiltshire 1660-1791* (Catholic Record Society, 1968) p. 72.

27 G. F. Nuttall, Early Quaker Letters from the Swarthmore Manuscripts to 1660, F.H. unpublished typescript, 1652, p. 66.

28 See p. 162.

29 *Registers of Morland.*

30 C.R.O.(C) MSS, D/LONS/L Manors of Great Strickland and Melkinthorpe, Court Rolls 1632, 1639 and 1647.

31 *Registers of Morland.*

32 Two Wilkinsons appear in the court rolls of this time: Peter and Margaret. The usual practice of the court would lead us to conclude that Margaret must be either a widow or an unmarried woman holding a tenancy in her own right. Had she been Peter Wilkinson's wife, her name would not have appeared at all in the court roll even if she was the holder of the tenancy. In such a case, the husband's name would have appeared, representing his wife at the court and the clerk would have noted on the roll that the man was appearing 'in jure uxoris'.

33 When Thomas died, his name is deleted in the court roll and the names of Ruth Yates and Jane Yates, his daughter and granddaughter, are inserted as inheritors of the tenancies. (C.R.O. MSS, D/LONS/L Manors of Great Strickland and Melkinthorpe, Court Roll 1692.)

34 F.H. MSS, A. R. Barclay, no. 169.

35 Hubbard, p. 85.

36 Besse, ii, p. 3.

37 Ibid, p. 11.

38 *Eine Antwort*, p. 6.

[39] Besse, ii, p. 22.

[40] Hubbard, p. 89, quoting from the 1708 report of the Somerset Quarterly Meeting to the London Yearly Meeting: 'Many people who are of different persuasions send their children to Table at a friends school [Sidcot].'

[41] Ralph Randles, 'Faithful Friends and well Qualified' in Michael Mullett, *Early Lancaster Friends* (University of Lancaster, 1978) p. 39.

[42] John Nichols, *Literary Anecdotes of the Eighteenth Century, comprizing Biographical Memoirs of William Bowyer, Printer, F.S.A. and many of his learned friends 1812-1815*, vol. i (1812) p. 233.

[43] *A Serious Remembrancer*, p. 30.

[44] Appendices F and G of J. H. D. Bate, The Schools of Westmorland in Tudor and Stuart Times, unpublished M.Ed. thesis, Manchester University, 1968 (Copy C.R.O.(K)).

[45] Hubbard, p. 89.

[46] Ibid, p. 199.

[47] Ibid, pp. 88-89.

[48] C.R.O.(C) MSS, D/LONS/L TH 21. Indenture made 2nd February, 1685.

[49] N. & B., i, p. 441.

[50] F.H. MSS, G.B.S. i, p. 376.

[51] Fox, *Journal*, p. 452.

[52] F.H. MSS, G.B.S. i, p. 376.

[53] Ibid, ii Westmorland p. 11.

[54] Ibid, p. 15.

[55] An Acte for the due Execution of the Statutes against Jesuits, seminarie Preists, Recusants etc.

[56] See n. 29, Ch. IV.

[57] Besse i, p. 202.

[58] C.R.O.(C) MSS, DRC 5/2 Correction Court Act Book, 26:1:1663/4 – 13:3:1667/8 f. 45v.

[59] Ibid, f. 37.

[60] Ibid, f. 75.

[61] Ibid, ff. 95-95v.

[62] F. D. Logan, *Excommunication and the Secular Arm in Medieval England* (Pontifical Institute of Medieval Studies, Toronto, 1968).

[63] J. A. Williams, *Catholic Recusancy in Wiltshire 1660-1791* (Catholic Record Society, 1968) pp. 71-72.

[64] ed. G. Lyon Turner, *Original Records of Early Nonconformity under Persecution and Indulgence* (1911) vol. iii, p. 63. Document 4. Concerning schoolmasters & Instructors of Youth ('Sheldon's Enquiries').

[65] Ibid, vol. i, pp. 173-76.

[66] C.R.O.(K) MSS, WQ/I/2 Indictment Book 1661-1685 (Appleby).

[67] C.R.O.(C) MSS, DRC 1/4 General Register of the Bishop 8:12:1660 – 24:2:1668, p. 517.

[68] Ibid, p. 518.

[69] C.R.O.(C) MSS, DRC 5/4 Correction Court Act Book 23:9:1670 – 6:10:1681 f. 37.

[70] Ibid, f. 55v. Quoted in *J.F.H.S.*, vi (1909) p. 169.

[71] C.R.O.(K) MSS, WDCF/F2/51D Book of Sufferings of Friends within Westmorland Quarterly Meeting.

[72] C.R.O.(K) MSS, WQ/I/2 Indictment book 1661-1685 (Appleby).

Chapter VI

Swarthmoor Interlude

(pages 66-78)

[1] ed. Norman Penney, *The Household Account Book of Sarah Fell of Swarthmoor Hall* (Cambridge, 1920) p. 95.

[2] Ross, *Margaret Fell*, p. 324: 'Table of Four Generations.'

[3] Page 42.

[4] Raven, *Ray*, p. 233.

[5] ed. Edwin Lankester, *Memorials of John Ray* (Ray Society, 1846) pp. 131-63.

[6] Ray, *Corr.* pp. 25-28.

[7] M. Bennet, 'Thomas Lawson, the Westmorland Botanist', *The Westmorland Note Book* (London and Kendal 1888-89) vol. i, p. 347.

[8] ed. R. T. Gunther, *Further Correspondence of John Ray* (Ray Society, 1928) p. 22.

[9] S. L. Petty, 'Thomas Lawson, The Father of Lakeland Botany,' *The North Lonsdale Magazine and Furness Miscellany* (Ulverston) vol. i, no. 12, p. 236. Only the briefest and most cryptic of clues is to be found to Lawson's supposed practice of medicine. It occurs in *George Fox's 'Book of Miracles'* which was edited by Henry J. Cadbury and published, Cambridge 1948: on p. 130 'And there was a woman . . . Lawson . . . sick . . . she would recover.' We cannot even be certain that this was Thomas.

[10] *Household Account Book of Sarah Fell*, p. 113.

[11] Edward Cocker, *The Young Clerks Tutor* (6th ed., 1670) A3-A3v.

[12] Ibid, A4v.

[13] Ross, *Margaret Fell*, pp. 266-68.

[14] *Radio Times*, 31st October, 1982.

[15] Raven, *Ray*, p. 61.

[16] John Dury, *The Reformed School* (1651) p. 57.

[17] Ibid, p. 58.

[18] Richard Richardson (c. 1623-1689) was a schoolmaster in Wheeler Street, Spitalfields in 1679. In 1681, he was appointed to the salaried clerkship of various Friends' committees and meetings, an appointment which he held until his death at Stratford-le-Bow in 1689.

[19] *J.F.H.S.*, vol. vii (1910), p. 74.

[20] Hubbard p. 223.

[21] ed G. L. Lampson, *A Quaker Post-Bag* (1910) p. 21.

[22] Raven, *Ray*, p. 9.

[23] Page 112ff.

[24] For compilation of the notebook, see Appendix 2. So far as Lawson's local records are concerned, I have imposed a pattern of supposed outings, expeditions and journeys that can only be conjectural since his movements outwith his tour of 1677 are not detailed.

[25] Size and weight of Gerard's *Herball*, Johnson, 1633 edition.

[26] Page 147.

[27] Page 163.

[28] In naming the plant, Lawson was confused by adopting Ray's polynomial which is that for *Malva alcea*, but the plant which he saw would have been *Malva moschata*. See Martindale, plant 226.

[29] John Ogilby, *Britannia* (1675) Map 38 London to Carlisle road. The modern O.S. grid reference is NY 549037.

[30] Martindale plant 241.

[31] Ibid, plant 71 and p. 183.

[32] Ibid, plant 243 [*Atriplex Babingtonii*].

[33] E. J. Salisbury, '*Echinophora spinosa* L. – A member of our flora,' *Watsonia*, vol. viii, pt. 4, July 1971, p. 397.

[34] The Kendal botanist, John Wilson, who quotes Lawson's Dunnerholme record, remarks upon Samphire's use as a pickle 'being a very agreeable one', *A Synopsis of British Plants, in Mr. Ray's Method* (Newcastle, 1744).

[35] J. M. Mawson, 'Deadly Nightshade', *Barrow Naturalists' Field Club . . . Annual Report and Proceedings*, vol. iv (1883), pp. 9-10.

Chapter VII   *(pages 79-97)*
On Tour – walking to London

[1] Ross, *Margaret Fell*, 255-57.

[2] *Baptismalogia* (1678), A2.

[3] Ibid, pp. 2-7.

[4] Ibid, pp. 8-27.

[5] Ibid, pp. 28-42.

[6] Ibid, pp. 43-51.

[7] John Aubrey (1626-1697), Natural History of Wiltshire, unpublished by its author, was published edited by J. Britton in 1847; William Nicolson (1655-1727) for a long time collected material for a history of the counties that had comprised the old kingdom of Northumbria, some of which was used in the 1695 edition of Camden's *Britannia*.

[8] On the second page of the notebook, Thomas has written down John Ray's address: 'Mr. Ray at Middleton in Hemlingford hundred in Warwickshire.' In the winter of 1675/76, Ray moved from Middleton (although he remained in the area until late summer of 1677 when he moved to Essex). Charles Raven uses this to imply that the notebook was compiled no later than 1676 ('Thomas Lawson's Note-book' *Proceedings of the Linnean Society of London*, 1947, p. 3). I think, however, that it is more likely that Lawson wrote the address down in 1677 because he thought it possible that he might visit Ray and simply did not know that he had moved. Other names and addresses were jotted down for this purpose (see Appendix 2).

[9] NB pp. 326-27.

[10] Raven, 'Thomas Lawson's Note-book' p. 11.

[11] Ray, *Corr*, pp. 209-10.

[12] Ross, *Margaret Fell*, pp. 224, 227.

[13] NB p. 326.

[14] Sir Walter Scott, *The Heart of Midlothian* (1893) p. 389.

[15] NB p. 326.

[16] William Camden, *Britannia* (1722) col. 593.

[17] ed. Joseph Hunter, *The Diary of Ralph Thoresby* (1830) vol. i, pp. 89-90, 20th July, 1681.

[18] Ibid, p. 90.

[19] NB p. 50.

[20] John Gerard, *Catalogus Arborum, Fruticum ac plantarum tam indigenarum, quam exoticarum in horto Johannis Gerardi* (1599) p. 16.

[21] Besse, i, p. 219.
[22] Ibid.
[23] Alan Wharham, 'Tithes in Country Life' *History Today* xxii, no. 6, June 1972, pp. 426-33.
[24] R. T. Gunther, *Early British Botanists and their Gardens* (Oxford, 1922) pp. 75-77.
[25] Besse, i, p. 53.
[26] Ray visited St. Vincent's Rock on 19th June, 1662 and published plants found there in the *Catalogus Angliae* (1670). Raven, *Ray*, p. 127.
[27] J. W. White, *The Flora of Bristol* (Bristol, 1912) p. 334.
[28] Ibid, p. 335.
[29] M. Dermott Harding, *Bristol and America* (Bristol, 1929) preface.
[30] NB p. 127.
[31] William Camden, *Britannia* (1637) p. 236 and (1722) col. 93.
[32] NB p. 156.
[33] *SYN* p. 304.
[34] For a description of the Oxford Garden see ed Humphrey Baskerville, *Thomas Baskerville's Account of Oxford c. 1670-1700* in *Collectanea* (Oxford Historical Society, 1905) 4th ser, vol. xlvii, p. 187ff.
[35] Ibid.
[36] Ibid, p. 191.
[37] Ibid.
[38] NB p. 329.
[39] Baskerville gives a description of the garden (pp. 187-88) and catalogues were published in 1648 and 1658 (Henrey 279, 281).
[40] NB 2.
[41] See p. 137.
[42] NB, unpaginated leaf facing p. 3. Ducke Lane joined Little Britain Street in London (John Stow, *Survey of London*, Everyman, 1956, pp. 331, 335).
[43] Henrey, pp. 119-20.

Chapter VIII *(pages 98-117)*
On Tour – return journey

[1] R. H. Jeffers, 'Edward Morgan and the Westminster Physic Garden,' *Proceedings of the Linnean Society of London* (1953) p. 106.
[2] The above facts about the Westminster Garden have been taken from Jeffers' article. A subsequent article 'A Further Note on Edward Morgan and the Westminster Physic Garden' (1957) pp. 96-101 gives an interesting account of the history of the Cluster Pine in Britain. Lawson's was the first record of its being grown in this country.
[3] p. 622-3
[4] NB p. 2.
[5] Rufus M. Jones, *The Quakers in the American Colonies* (1911) pp. 70-75.
[6] S. H. Vines and G. C. Druce, *An Account of the Morisonian Herbarium in the Possession of the University of Oxford* (Oxford, 1914).
[7] Diary of John Evelyn, 3rd January, 1666.
[8] D. H. Kent, *The Historical Flora of Middlesex* (Ray Society, 1975) pp. 77, 548.
[9] G. C. Druce and S. H. Vines, *The Dillenian Herbaria* (Oxford, 1907).

[10] Kent, *Middlesex Flora*, pp. 187-88.

[11] Ibid, p. 3.

[12] ed. J. S. L. Gilmour, *Thomas Johnson, Botanical Journeys in Kent and Hampstead* (Pittsburgh, Pennsylvania 1972) p. 15.

[13] Ibid, p. 16.

[14] G. Grigson, *The Englishman's Flora* (Paladin, 1975) p. 311.

[15] NB p. 2.

[16] F.H. MSS, Minutes of 2nd day Morning Meeting of Ministering Friends, fol. 18: At a Meeting 6th August, 1677.

[17] Luella M. Wright, *The Literary Life of the Early Friends 1650-1725* (New York, 1966) pp. 97-99.

[18] Nathaniel Kite, *Antiquarian Researches among the Early Printers and Publishers of Friends' Books* (Manchester, 1844) p. 17.

[19] ed. A. H. Ewen and C. T. Prime, *Ray's Flora of Cambridgeshire* (Hitchin, 1975) p. 22.

[20] Ibid.

[21] *SYN* p. 341.

[22] Ewen and Prime, *Ray's Flora of Cambridgeshire*, p. 129.

[23] NB p. 327.

[24] Besse, ii, p. 165.

[25] Ibid, p. 95.

[26] Ibid, p. 164.

[27] Fox, *Journal*, p. 491.

Chapter IX   *(pages 118-133)*
Educational Theorist

[1] G.B.S., vol. iv, p. 442. Also Besse, ii, p. 24.

[2] Ibid, p. 438.

[3] Ibid, p. 441.

[4] A. W. Pollard, 'Some Notes on the History of Copyright in England, 1662-1774' *The Library*, 4th ser., iii, 102-103.

[5] e.g. NB p. 258ff = *Dagon's Fall* p. 46ff: NB p. 103ff = *A Treatise Relating* p. 225ff.

[6] Christopher Hill, *AntiChrist in Seventeenth-Century England* (Oxford, 1971) p. 141.

[7] The works of Arthur Raistrick give much information on the scientific and industrial achievements of Quakers in the northern counties and elsewhere.

[8] ed. Stephen Medcalf, *Joseph Glanvill, The Vanity of Dogmatizing: the Three 'Versions'* (Sussex, 1970) 'The Vanity of Dogmatizing' pp. 5-6.

[9] Ibid, p. 7.

[10] Ibid, 'Scepsis Scientifica', pp. 5-6.

[11] *Dagon's Fall*, p. 3.

[12] ed. Douglas Bush, *Milton, Poetical Works* (Oxford, 1966) p. 433.

[13] *Dagon's Fall*, Ch. IV 'A rehearsal of Testimonies, born by several men eminent in the Church, since the Apostles days, against Heathen learning, or the teaching of it, in Christian Schools, as also of others.'

[14] Ibid, p. 9.

[15] William Turner, *A New Herball* (1551).

[16] *Dagon's Fall*, p. 85.
[17] Hugh Kearney, *Scholars and Gentlemen* (1970) pp. 141-56.
[18] See Dorothy Stimson, *Scientists and Amateurs, a History of the Royal Society* (New York, 1948).
[19] *Dagon's Fall* pp. 86-87.
[20] Ibid, p. 88.
[21] See below.
[22] F.H. MSS, A. R. Barclay no. 42.
[23] Quoted by D. G. Brinton Thompson, 'John Thompson of Nether Compton, Dorset, and Philadelphia, Quaker Schoolmaster and Merchant,' *Pennsylvania Genealogical Magazine*, vol. xxiii, pt. 3 (1964) p. 143.
[24] Rufus M. Jones, *The Quakers in the American Colonies* (1911) p. 419.
[25] Ibid, p. 420.
[26] Ibid.
[27] Quoted by Brinton Thompson, *Pennsylvania Geneaological Magazine*, vol. xxiii, pt. 3, p. 143.
[28] Ibid.
[29] Ibid pp. 147-48.
[30] *A Mite into the Treasury*, p. 3.
[31] Ibid, p. 10.
[32] Ibid, p. 19.
[33] Kearney, *Scholars and Gentlemen*, p. 162.
[34] *A Mite into the Treasury*, p. 24.
[35] Ibid, p. 36.
[36] Ibid, p. 41.
[37] Ibid, pp. 45-46.
[38] Ibid, p. 46.
[39] *A Treatise Relating*, p. 19.
[40] Ibid, p. 21.
[41] Ibid, pp. 21-23.
[42] Ibid, p. 102.
[43] Ibid, p. 47.
[44] Printer and bookseller in London, George Yard, Lombard Street 1674-98. Henry R. Plomer, *A Dictionary of the Printers and Booksellers who were at work in England, Scotland and Ireland from 1668 to 1725* (Oxford, 1922).
[45] *Dagon's Fall*, p. 1.
[46] Ibid, p. 2.
[47] Ibid, p. 42.
[48] Pliny, *The Natural History*, ed. Philemon Holland (1635) Book 9, Chap IV, pp. 235-36.
[49] NB pp. 173-74.
[50] Charles E. Raven, 'Thomas Lawson's Note-book' *'Proceedings of the Linnean Society of London* (October, 1947) p. 6.

Chapter X   *(pages 134-155)*
Contact with Ray

[1] David M. Butler, *Quaker Meeting Houses of the Lake Counties* (Friends Historical Society, 1978) p. 81.
[2] T. R. Newbold, 'Newby Head, Westmorland', *The Friend*, vol. xxxiii (1893) pp. 537-38.

[3] Butler, *Quaker Meeting Houses*, p. 81.

[4] *Epistles from the Yearly Meeting of Friends, vol. i, 1681-1769* (1858) p. 4.

[5] C.R.O.(K) MSS WDFC/F2/103, The Booke of Minutes of General Meeting of Northern Counties 1658-1700, p. 118.

[6] F.H. MSS, Gibson, iii, 11.

[7] C.R.O.(C) MSS, DRC 5/5, 15th December, 1682.

[8] Besse, ii, p. 35.

[9] Robert Morison, *Plantarum Historiae Universalis Oxoniensis* (Pars secunda, Oxford, 1680) 193.5, 555.7 and 583.10.

[10] Ray, *SYN*, 436.2: I understood by Mr. Lawson, that this is the same Plant which Parkinson p. 1188. calls Gramen junceum montanum subcoerulea spica Cambrobritannicum. The same Observation I find in Phytol. Britan. So that Parkinson errs in putting it for a distinct Species, and I inadvertently following him in my History of Plants, p. 1306. cp Morison, *Historia* (Pars tertia, 1699) 224.6.

[11] See Appendix 1.

[12] S. H. Vines and G. C. Druce, *An Account of the Morisonian Herbarium in the Possession of the University of Oxford* (Oxford, 1914).

[13] Ibid.

[14] Morison, *Historia* (Pars tertia, 1699) 450.12, 575.17.

[15] ed. R. T. Gunther, *Further Correspondence of John Ray* (Ray Society, 1928) p. 187.

[16] Morison, *Historia* (Pars tertia, 1699) pp. 473.34, 431.9, 477.4.

[17] Vines and Druce, *Morisonian Herbarium*.

[18] ed. Gunther, *Further Correspondence*, p. 286.

[19] Ibid, p. 288.

[20] Ray, *Corr*, p. 139.

[21] ed. Gunther, *Further Correspondence*, p. 195.

[22] Ray, *Corr*, pp. 197-210.

[23] Ibid, p. viii.

[24] ed. Gunther, *Further Correspondence*, p. viii.

[25] Raven, *Ray*, p. 233.

[26] John Ray, *Historia Plantarum*, vol. ii (1693) Preface.

[27] ed. Gunther, *Further Correspondence*, p. 155.

[28] Ibid.

[29] *SYN*, p. 129.

[30] Nicolson *Flora*, p. xlii.

[31] Ibid.

[32] Ray, *Historia Plantarum*, vol. i, p. 141.

[33] Ray, *Corr*, p. 139.

[34] Thomas West, *A Guide to the Lakes* (10th ed., Kendal, 1812) p. 97.

[35] John Gerard, *The Herball or Generall Historie of Plantes* (1597) p. 323.

[36] James Newton, *Enchiridion Universale Plantarum* (?1689) sect. I, pt. 2, cap. 11.2.

[37] Nicolson, *Flora*, p. 92.

[38] Raven, *Ray*, p. 125.

[39] John Raven and Max Walters, *Mountain Flowers* (1956) p. 8.

[40] Nicolson, *Flora*, p. 22.

[41] Raven, *Ray*, p. 169.

[42] Geoffrey Grigson, *The Englishman's Flora* (Paladin, 1975) pp. 234-35.

[43] Raven, *Ray*, pp. 244-46.

44 See above p. 140.
45 The numbers in this table refer to the 1724 edition of Ray's *Synopsis* edited by J. J.
   Dillenius as this became the definitive edition, being used by British botanists
   well into the eighteenth century. It was also the edition used by later botanists
   when they wished to quote Ray's names in synonymy with Linnaean
   binomials.

Chapter XI   *(pages 156-168)*
                        David Restrained

1 Thomas Lawson, *A Serious Remembrancer to Live Well* (1684) p. 3.
2 Ibid, p. 11.
3 Ibid, p. 26.
4 Ibid, pp. 15-16.
5 Ibid, p. 19, p. 23.
6 Ibid, p. 27.
7 Ibid.
8 Ibid, p. 28.
9 Ibid, pp. 4-6.
10 Ibid, p. 29.
11 Ibid, pp. 30-31.
12 F.H. MSS, A. R. Barclay no. 150.
13 Ibid, no. 42.
14 Ibid, no. 139.
15 These letters are now lost.
16 F.H. MSS, Vol 101/50.
17 A Clandestine marriage was defined as one which did not meet the requirements
   of canon law with regard to publication of banns, consent of parents or
   guardians, clearness from prior attachment or consanguinity and place and
   time of celebration. In theory, the parties to such marriages were punishable
   under canon law, though it was not generally possible to render the marriage
   void. Thomas Lawson, as he would be bitterly aware, was not likely to appeal
   to a church court. The principal canons enacted in England after the
   Reformation were those at the beginning of James I's reign in 1604. See Giles
   Jacob, *A New Law-Dictionary* (1729) and R. S. Mylne, *The Canon Law*
   (1912).
18 F. H. MSS, A. R. Barclay no. 139.
19 Page 188.
20 Page 193ff.
21 *Registers of Morland part I: 1538-1742* (Kendal, 1957).
22 T.H. MSS, William Nicolson's Diaries.
23 *Registers of Morland.*
24 Ibid.
25 Ibid.
26 C.R.O.(C) MSS, P.1692, An Inventory of all the goods and chattels of
   Mr. Christopher Yates of Great Strickland.
27 C.R.O.(K) MSS, WDFC/F/2/1 Strickland Monthly Meeting Minute Book
   No. 1, 1675-1714.
28 Ibid, 5th May 1703.

[29] C.R.O.(K) MSS, WDFC/F1/51D Book of Sufferings of Friends within Westmorland Quarterly Meeting. e.g., f. 21, 24v, 26, 27, 29, 32v, 35, 59, 61v, 66v,

[30] C.R.O.(K) MSS, WDFC/F1/37 Westmorland (Women's) Quarterly Meeting Testimonies and Minute Book, 1677-1719.

[31] Friends Meeting House, Lancaster, MSS, xiii(a) 67: Ruth and Margaret Airey's (Shap) acceptance of John Backhouse's proposal to Margaret 1720.

[32] An example of such a disownment paper may be seen on F.H. MSS, Gibson iii, 43.

[33] F.H. MSS, A. R. Barclay no. 42.

Chapter XII   (pages 169-188)
Northern Moss-cropper

[1] See note 8 below.

[2] John Nichols, *Illustrations of the Literary History of the Eighteenth Century* (1817-1858) vol. i, p. 341.

[3] The name was a whimsical one. William Vernon refers to the botanist Adam Buddle as 'the top of all the moss-croppers.' (ed. Dawson Turner, *Extracts from the Literary and Scientific correspondence of Richard Richardson*, Yarmouth, 1835, p. 73.)

[4] The standard biography of William Nicolson is F. G. James, *North Country Bishop, a biography of William Nicolson* (Yale, London and Oxford, 1956). A brief account of his life, concentrating upon his botanical interests may be found in Nicolson, *Flora*, xix ff.

[5] T.H. MSS, Nicolson's Diaries.

[6] The material that follows of William Nicolson's joint expeditions with Thomas Lawson may be found in Nicolson, *Flora*, pp. xxx-xxxviii.

[7] Ibid, p. 60.

[8] Thomas Sprat, *The History of the Royal-Society, 1667*, facs. ed. Jackson I. Cope and H. W. Jones (St. Louis and London, 1959) p. 53.

[9] T.H. MSS, Nicolson's Diaries.

[10] Nicolson, *Flora*, p. xxiv.

[11] John Gerard, *The Herball or Generall Historie of Plantes* (1597) p. 1302.

[12] Geoffrey Grigson, *The Englishman's Flora* (Paladin, 1975) p. 243.

[13] N & B, vol. i, p. 440.

[14] Thomas Robinson, *An Essay towards a Natural History of Westmorland and Cumberland* (1709) p. 51.

[15] 'Lapathum Bononiense' is the polynomial for *Rumex pulcher*, but see p. 142.

[16] T.H. MSS, Nicolson's Diaries.

[17] Nicolson, *Flora*, pp. 111-113.

[18] T.H. MSS, Nicolson's Diaries.

[19] John Parkinson, *Paradisi in Sole Paradisus Terrestris 1629* (1904) p. 602.

[20] Ibid, p. 417.

[21] Ibid, p. 270.

[22] Grigson, *Englishman's Flora*, p. 233.

[23] Parkinson, *Paradisi*, p. 39.

[24] R. Denton Thompson, 'Farmanby and the Thompson family' *CWAAS* n.s., 1v, pp. 179-190, p. 184. The details of Isaac's battle with the Dean and Chapter of Carlisle are taken from this article.

[25] Ibid, p. 188.

[26] See page ?.

[27] ed. G. L. Lampson, *A Quaker Post-Bag* (1910) pp. 20-21.

[28] James Newton, *Enchiridion Universale Plantarum*, (?1689) Sect. I, pt. 2, cap. ii.2.

[29] Lampson, Post-Bag, pp. 19-20.

[30] Turner, *Richardson Correspondence*, pp. 5-7.

[31] ed. John Nichols, *Letters on various subjects to and from William Nicolson D.D.* (1809) p. 36.

[32] H.R. Fletcher and W. H. Brown, *The Royal Botanic Garden Edinburgh 1670-1970* (Edinburgh, 1970) pp. 1-19.

[33] Nicolson, *Flora*, pp. 108, 114-116.

[34] James, *North Country Bishop*, p. 87.

[35] *SYN*, Preface.

[36] Ibid, p. 322.

[37] Ibid, p. 370.

[38] Ibid, p. 393.

[39] Ibid, p. 47.

[40] Raven, *Ray*, p. 392.

[41] Ibid, pp. 394-95.

[42] Ibid, p. 404.

[43] ed. R. T. Gunther, *Further Correspondence of John Ray* (Ray Society, 1928) p. 203. 3rd November.

[44] Letters from Lhwyd to both Nicolson and Archer were published in the *Lithophylacii Britannici Ichnographia*, 1760. See R. T. Gunther, *Early Science in Oxford*, vol. xiv, *Life and Letters of Edward Lhwyd* (Oxford, 1945) pp. 359-369.

[45] Turner, *Richardson Correspondence*, pp. 11-12.

[46] *A History of the Worshipful Society of Apothecaries of London*, notes of Cecil Wall, ed. H. Charles Cameron, revised E. Ashworth Underwood (Oxford University for Wellcome Historical Medical Museum, 1963) p. 165.

[47] Ibid, p. 164.

[48] Ibid, p. 165.

[49] Blanche Henrey, *British Botanical and Horticultural Literature before 1800* (Oxford, 1975) p. 146.

[50] Ross, *Margaret Fell*, pp. 335, 351, 353.

[51] F.H. MSS, Gibson, v, 155.

[52] C.R.O.(C) MSS, P. 1691/2 Will of Thomas Lawson.

[53] F.H. MSS, Digest Registers give the date of Thomas Lawson's burial as 11th November, 1691 and Deborah's marriage as 12th, although his tombstone (see below) has Thomas' burial as also on 12th.

[54] Ibid.

[55] R. S. Boumphrey, C. Roy Hudleston and J. Hughes, *An Armorial for Westmorland and Lonsdale* (Lake District Museum Trust and CWAAS, 1975).

[56] I am indebted to Mrs. Betty Shilston, secretary of the Strickland Monthly Meeting Property Trust for access to a copy of this lease.

[57] Maria Webb *The Fells of Swarthmoor Hall and their Friends* (1865) p. 377.

[58] Joseph Smith, *A Descriptive Catalogue of Friends' Books* (1867) p. 89.

[59] T. R. Newbold, 'Newby Head, Westmorland,' *The Friend*, vol. xxxiii (1893), p. 537.

[60] Webb's *Fells*, pp. 377-78; Smith, *Catalogue*, p. 89; Newbold, p. 537; R. S. Ferguson, *Early Cumberland and Westmorland Friends* (1871) p. 67; M. Bennet, 'Thomas Lawson, the Westmorland Botanist' *The Westmorland Note Book* (London and Kendal 1888-89) p. 348.

[61] C.R.O.(C) MSS, D/LONS/L. G.S.7.

[62] C.R.O.(K) MSS, Tithe Map of Great Strickland, 1838.

Chapter XIII
Serviceable Pieces

(pages 189-197)

[1] Ralph Randles 'Faithful Friends and well qualified', ed. Michael Mullett, *Early Lancaster Friends* (University of Lancaster, 1978) p. 33.

[2] Ibid. Quoted from *Epistles from the Yearly Meeting of Friends*, vol. i, p. 48.

[3] C.R.O.(K) MSS WDFC/F2/1 Strickland Monthly Meeting Minute Book no. 1, 1675-1714.

[4] Ibid, 4th February, 1702.

[5] Ibid, 2nd February, 1704.

[6] Randles, 'Faithful Friends', pp. 38-39.

[7] Page 60.

[8] F.H. MSS, Minutes of 2nd day Morning Meeting of Ministering Friends.

[9] 29th July, 5th August and 12th August.

[10] G. L. Lampson, *A Quaker Post-Bag* (1910) p. 184.

[11] Ibid, p. 192.

[12] Ibid, p. 95.

[13] Printed and sold by T. Sowle, in White-Hart-Court in Gracious-street, 1703. Bibliographical details regarding the printing of these works will be found in Joseph Smith, *A Descriptive Catalogue of Friends' Books* (1867) pp. 91-92. Another edition of *A Treatise Relating*, not listed by Smith, was published in 1706.

[14] F.H. MSS, Box C²/13.
Contains: Letter, dated 1st September, 1698. Thomas Ellwood from Hunger Hill to John Loft.
A List of the Bookes and Manuscripts of Thomas Lawson.
Three works of Lawson in MS: Adam Anatomized, Babylons Fall, The Foolish Virgin (full titles in text).
Note by Benjamin Bealing of minute of 17th June, 1700.

[15] Page 159.

[16] Fox, *Journal*, pp. vii, ix-x.

Chapter XIV
Autumn Flowering

(pages 198-208)

[1] John Wilson, *A Synopsis of British Plants in Mr. Ray's Method* (Newcastle-upon-Tyne, 1744) p. a4.

[2] A Thomas Lawson, described as 'schoole Mr. att Rombald kirke' appears in the *Calendar of State Papers* (see Norman Penney and R. A. Roberts, *Extracts from State Papers relating to Friends 1654 to 1672* (1913) p. 259. He appears to have been a government spy reporting upon the Quakers and on 23rd

September, 1666, he signed a paper promising to make discovery of any 'plot or designe against the Kings Majestys person, or his Government.' At this time Thomas Lawson of Great Strickland was appearing regularly in the court rolls (1665, 1666, 1667) and must be cleared of any suspicion that he could have been the same man.

[3] Thomas Robinson, *An Essay towards a Natural History of Westmorland and Cumberland* (1709) p. 89.

[4] William Camden, *Britannia* (1695) p.846.

[5] S. L. Petty, 'Thomas Lawson, the Father of Lakeland Botany', *The North Lonsdale Magazine and Furness Miscellany* (Ulverston) vol. i, no. 12, p. 236.

[6] Martindale no. 210.

Postscript   *(pages 209-210)*

[1] Maria Webb, *The Fells of Swarthmoor Hall and their Friends* (1865) p. 63.

[2] John Ray, *Synopsis Methodica Stirpium Britannicarum* (1690) Preface. Plukenet, *Almagestum Botanicum* (1696) p. 8, praises Lawson in similar vein.

[3] Webb's *Fells*, p. 63. Gerard Croese, *The General History of the Quakers* refers to Lawson on p. 49.

Eine Antwort 7.

Auf ein Buch/ in Lateinischer Sprache außgegeben; genant

Der Unstahe der Quäcker/

Abgemahlet nach ihren Auffkommen/ Fortgang/ und greulichen Leeren.

Außgegeben durch
M. Johan. Joachim Zentgraff.

Gutgeheissen von
Dn. Johan Conradus Danhauer &c.

beyde von der hohen Schule zu Straßburg/

THOMAS LAWSON.

Wer den Gottlosen Recht spricht/ und den Gerechten verdamt/ die sind beyde dem HErrn ein Greuel.

Aus der Englischen Sprach verteutscht/ aus Liebe zu der Wahrheit von Johannes Clauß, von Straßburg.

Gedruckt im Jahr 1668.

Hieracium Lawsonii

IN THE LETTER THAT LAWSON WROTE TO RAY on 9th April, 1688, he included the following:

> Hieracium Macrocaulon hirsutum fol. rotundiore. This I found by Buckbarrow Well, in Longsledale, and on the rocks by the rivulet between Shap and Anna Well, Westmoreland; expect fair samples and my description.

By the time that Lawson came to send his fair samples, he had realised that he was dealing with two different plants, since Ray, presumably following Lawson's notes in a covering letter, divides the locations that were originally assigned to the one plant between two different *hieracia*. They appeared in the 1724 ed. of his *Synopsis* as follows:

169.8 Hieracium macrocaulon hirsutum folio rotundiore D. Lawson. An Hieracium fruticosum folio subrotundo C.B. Pin. 129. Pr. 67. Round-leaved rough Hawk-weed with a tall stalk. Found by Mr. Newton in Edinburgh Park in Scotland; by Mr. Lawson near Buckbarrow Well in Langsledale, Westmorland. (In loco declivi Gordil dicto prope Malham Cravoniae vicum; Dr. Richards. Hieracii murorum folio pilosissimo C.B. varietatem facit D. Vaillant Comm. Ac. R. Sc. A. 1721. p. 185 quo etiam refert sequentem speciem.)

169.9 Hierac. [leptocaulon] hirsutum folio longiore D. Lawson. On the Rocks by the Rivulet between Shap and Anna Well, Westmorland . . .

• • •

169.8 'Hieracium macrocaulon'

It is not now possible to know what this plant was. Identifications made in the past are as follows:

1. *H. pallidum.* Accepted by Baker, *A Flora of the English Lake District* (1885) pp. 125-6, adding 'It was from this that the name

Lawsoni took its origin' (this is incorrect, however. See 'H. leptocaulon' below). Baker probably relied upon James Backhouse's identification of a specimen in the Sherard herbarium in *A monograph of the British Hieracia* (York, 1856) p. 36. Lees, *The Flora of West Yorkshire* (1888) pp. 307 and 791 doubted Backhouse's identification.

2. *H. murorum* L.   J. E. Smith, *The English Flora* (1824-28) vol. iii, p. 359 equates 'Hieracium macrocaulon' with *H. murorum* L. as did C. C. Babington in the binomials that he supplied for Lankester's edition of Lawson's letter.

Neither *H. pallidum* nor *H. murorum* L. are specific names which have any status in the modern taxonomy of *hieracia*.

169.9 'Hieracium leptocaulon'

1. *H. anglicum.*   A specimen of 'Hieracium leptocaulon' was sent by Lawson to Morison and is identified by Vines and Druce as *H. anglicum* Fr. in *An Account of the Morisonian herbarium in the possession of the University of Oxford* (Oxford, 1914) p. 80. We may therefore accept it as *H. anglicum* Fr. in the *H. cerinthoides* group.

2. *H. lawsonii* Vill. *H. lawsoni* Sm.   Lawson's name thus passed away from the *hieracium* with which he had been associated. But by one of those strange accidents that are of frequent occurence in the labyrinths of botanical nomenclature, his name was diverted to another species. *Hieracium lawsonii*, the name established by M. Villars in the *Histoire des Plantes de Dauphine* (1786) vol. i, p. 273, whose range is the Pyrenees, the mountains of S. France and the S.W. Alps, was believed by J. E. Smith to be a British plant and, in the *English Flora* vol. iii, p. 362, he equated it with Lawson's 'Hieracium leptocaulon'. A figure of the plant, by Sowerby, used to illustrate Smith's *English Botany* (1809) vol. xxix, p. 2083, brings us back, however to *H. anglicum* in the *H. cerinthoides* group. Backhouse assigned the figure to *H. cerinthoides* and Lees, in the *Flora of West Yorkshire*, p. 306, assigns *H. lawsoni* Sm. to *H. anglicum.*

The winding paths of botanical nomenclature are as full of specialised reference as Lawson's own writing. When we have won through to the breezy uplands to find *H. ang licum* Fr. at our feet, we deserve the pleasure of remembering the man in this typical hawkweed of the hill country of northern Britain. That his name should actually be transferred to another *hieracium* growing in hills far removed from his Westmorland fells, is just one of the quirks of taxonomy. That it should be a *hieracium* at all, is somehow symbolic of a man who, in the many aspects of his interesting life, still remains something of a puzzle.

The Botanical Notebook

History

Lawson, in his will dated 19th January 1691, bequeathed to his son-in-law, Christopher Yates, his copies of Camden's *Britannia* and Buxtorfius' Hebrew Lexicon, together with all his manuscripts. The botanical notebook was either not considered to be amongst these last, or was given by Ruth Yates to her sister Hannah, married to Isaac Thompson at some later date, for it would appear to be through the children of Hannah and their descendants that the notebook was handed down. Hannah certainly had her father's copy of Ray's *Catalogus Angliae* which was used by William Nicolson in preparing a list of plants for the 1695 edition of the *Britannia*: Bennet suggests that she inherited her father's love of botany and perhaps he is right.

From Hannah, the notebook passed down the Thompson family to its last Thompson owner, Mr. Lawson Thompson, who died unmarried at Hitchin in 1919 (see Family tree p. xiv).

Lawson Thompson gave the notebook to R. L. Hine of Hitchin, who presented it to the Linnean Society of London in October, 1947, in whose library it is now lodged. A microfilm of the notebook has been taken and is in the library of Durham University.

Description

The notebook measures 6" x 3½", contains 165 leaves, is paginated and is bound in contemporary leather.

pp. 1-2 Miscellaneous jottings, including names and addresses.

3-178 Search List: the English counties in alphabetical order, followed by Wales and the Isle of Man. Plants listed alphabetically under each county.

179-194 Tour Notes. Begins 'In my journey -77' followed by list of plants found in Cambridgeshire.

195-223 Blank.

224 Note from Trapp (q.v. below).

225-228 Notes on tithe, used in the compilation of *A Treatise Relating*.

229-245 Tour Notes: plants seen in the Westminster garden.

246 Blank

247-298 Notes and extracts from religious commentaries, mainly from the works of Rudolph Hospinian (1547-1626) protestant divine and John Trapp (1601-1669) author of *A Commentary or Exposition upon the four Evangelists and the Acts of the Apostles* (1647). Much of this material used in the compilation of *Dagon's Fall*. (In the middle, p. 271 is a list of fishes and p. 272 is blank.)

299-325 Tour Notes: including plants seen in the Oxford garden.

326-327 Itinerary (see p. xiii).

327-329 Miscellaneous jottings.

Definition of Lawson records

In the Search List, Lawson includes records from other botanists, signed with abbreviations (Ger emac., Mer., Ray's Cat. pl. etc). Plants that have been claimed as Lawson's own finds were defined following the rules below:

1. All unsigned entires have been accepted.

2. In the Search List, any plant which has a cross against it has been accepted as having been observed by Lawson. In some counties, Lawson has used ticks, but these seem to have been employed in connection with the compilation of the notebook and do not denote that he saw the plant: e.g. in Wales, the first 11 plants listed have been ticked, but there is no evidence that Lawson was ever in Wales, nor is it likely that the first 11 plants only of an alphabetical list should have been ticked as sightings.

3. In the case of additions to the Search List, these, if signed, have been checked against the appropriate authority. Only if the location given by Lawson differs from that of his authority, or if the authoritiy gives no location, have these plants been accepted.

4. Special treatment has been given to the northern counties of Cumberland, Durham, Northumberland, Westmorland and Lancashire. In the case of these counties, the whole Search List has been treated as in paragraph 3 above.

5. All plants listed in the Tour Notes have been accepted as Lawson finds.

Writings of Thomas Lawson

Published works

'Of the false Ministry' in *A Brief Discovery of a threefold estate of Antichrist* by T. Aldam, B. Nicholson, J. Harwood and T. Lawson (1653).

An Untaught Teacher Witnessed against [with John Slee] (1655).

The Lip of Truth Opened, against a Dawber with untempered Morter (1656).

An Appeal to the Parliament, concerning the Poor That there may not be a Beggar in England (1660).

Eine Antwort auf ein Buch (1668).

Baptismalogia, or a Treatise concerning Baptisms: whereto is added a Discourse concerning the Supper, Bread and Wine, Called also Communion (1677/8).

Dagon's Fall before the Ark (1679).

A Mite into the Treasury (1680).

A Treatise Relating to the Call, Work and Wages of the Ministers of Christ; As also to the Call, Work and Wages of the Ministers of Antichrist (1680).

A Serious Remembrancer To Live Well (1684).

Unpublished manuscripts

Linnean Society of London: Botanical notebook. Microfilm, Durham University Library.

F.H. Box C²/13. 'Adam Anatomized', 'The Foolish virgin and the wise', 'Babylon's Fall being a Testimony Relateing to the State of the Christian Church'.

F.H. Swarth. i. 246. 'A paper given forth by Tho. Lawson' [relating to the visit to Clapham. Undated, probably c. 1653].

F.H. MS vol. 101/50. A paper relating to Ruth's marriage [undated]. Included in part in Webb's *Fells*, pp. 373-376.

Published letters

To:

John Ray, 9th April, 1688. *The Correspondence of John Ray*, ed. E. Lankester (Ray Society, 1848) pp. 197-210. First published by W. Derham, *Philosophical Letters* (1718). Lawson's MS now missing.

[Sir] John Rodes at Balber [Barlborough] Hall [near Chesterfield] 18th January, 1691. G. L. Lampson, *A Quaker Post-Bag* (1910) pp. 20-22.

Richard Richardson, 20th March, 1691. *Extracts from the Literary and Scientific Correspondence of Richard Richardson*, ed. Dawson Turner (Yarmouth, 1835) pp. 5-7.

Unpublished letters (all F.H.)

Swarth. i. 241. To Margaret Fell (undated). Included, not very accurately and with some omissions in Webb's *Fells*, pp. 64-65.

Swarth. i. 242. To Margaret Fell (undated).

Swarth. i. 243. To Margaret Fell, from Bordley Hall, month i, day 11, 1657 [11th March, 1658].

Swarth. i. 244. To Margaret Fell from Pearyth [Penrith], 17 5mo [17th July, ?1660].

Swarth. i. 245. To Margaret Fell, 1653. Included, not very accurately and with some omissions in Webb's *Fells*, pp. 63-64.

Vol. VII 23B. To John Webster (undated).

A. R. Barclay xlii. To George Fox, from Great Strickland, 20 Mo 2 1689 [20th April, 1689].

Manuscript Sources

Christ's College, Cambridge.
    Admission Register.
Cumbria Record Office, Carlisle.

DRC 1	General Register of the Bishop.
DRC 5	Correction Court Act Books.
D/LONS/L	Court Rolls.
P. 1691/2	Will of Thomas Lawson.
P. 1692	An Inventory of all the goods and chattels of Mr. Christopher Yates of Great Strickland.

Cumbria Record Office, Kendal.

WQ/1/2	Indictment Book 1661-1685 (Appleby).
WDFC/F2/1	Strickland Monthly Meeting minute book (no. 1) 1675-1714.
WDFC/F1/13	Kendal Monthly Meeting minute book 1699-1723.
WDFC/F1/32	Westmorland (Men's) Quarterly Meeting minute . . . book 1691-1743.
WDFC/F1/37	Westmorland (Women's) Quarterly Meeting minute . . . book 1677-1719.
WDFC/F1/51D	Book of Sufferings of Friends within Westmorland Quarterly Meeting.
WDFC/F1/103	The Booke of Minutes of General Meeting of Northern Counties 1658-1700.
	J. H. D. Bates, The Schools of Westmorland in Tudor and Stuart Times, unpublished M.Ed thesis, Manchester University, 1968.
	Tithe Map of Great Strickland, 1838.

Friends Meeting House, Lancaster.

xiii(a) 67	Ruth and Margaret Airey's (Shap) acceptance of John Backhouse's proposal to Margaret, 1720.

Friends House, Euston Road, London.
    Digest copies of Registers of Births, Marriages and Burials.
    The Great Book of Sufferings.
    Minutes of 2nd day Morning Meeting of Ministering Friends.
    Letters from the following collections:
        Swarthmore
        A. R. Barclay
        Caton
        Gibson
    Unpublished typescript, G. F. Nuttall, Early Quaker letters from Swarthmore manuscripts to 1600 (1952).
    D. G. Hubbard, Early Quaker Education, unpublished M.A. thesis, London University, 1939.

DQB	Dictionary of Quaker Bibliography.

Lambeth Palace Library.

COMM XIIa	Copies of Surveys, 1647-1657.
COMM XIIc/4	Registers of the union and division of parishes, 1655-1659.

Tullie House Library, Carlisle.
    William Nicolson's Diaries.

Printed Sources

Stephen Allot, *Friends in York* (Sessions of York, 1978).
ed. H. B. Atkinson, *The Giggleswick School Register 1499-1921* (Northumberland Press, Newcastle-upon-Tyne, 2nd ed. 1922).
J. G. Baker, *A Flora of the English Lake District* (1885).
H. Barbour and A. O. Roberts, *Early Quaker Writings 1650-1700* (Michigan, 1973).
Thomas Baskerville, '*Thomas Baskerville's Account of Oxford c. 1670-1700*', ed. H. Baskerville in *Collectanea*, 4th series, vol. xlvii (Oxford Historical Society, 1905).
M. Bennet, 'Thomas Lawson, the Westmorland Botanist', *The Westmorland Note Book* (London and Kendal, 1888-89).
Joseph Besse, *A Collection of the Sufferings of the People called Quakers*, 2 vols (1753).
C. M. L. Bouch, *Prelates and People of the Lake Counties* (Kendal, 1948).
R. S. Boumphrey, C. Roy Hudleston and J. Hughes, *An Armorial for Westmorland and Lonsdale* (Lake District Museum Trust and CWAAS, 1975).
M. R. Brailsford, *A Quaker from Cromwell's Army: James Nayler* (1927).
W. C. Braithwaite, *The Beginnings of Quakerism*, 2nd ed. revised by H. C. Cadbury (Cambridge, 1955, Sessions of York, 1961).
—— *The Second Period of Quakerism*, 2nd ed. prepared by H. C. Cadbury (Cambridge, 1961, Sessions of York, 1979).
Howard H. Brinton, *Children of Light* (New York, 1938).
F. Bugg, *The Pilgrim's Progress from Quakerism to Christianity* (1698).
Richard Burn, *Ecclesiastical Law* (1763).
David M. Butler, *Quaker Meeting Houses of the Lake Counties* (Friends Historical Society, 1978).
Magnus Byne, *The Scornful Quakers Answered, and Their railing Reply refuted* (1656).
Matthew Caffyn, *The Deceived and deceiving Quakers Discovered* (1656).
W. Camden, *Britannia or a Chorographical Description of Great Britain and Ireland* ed. Edmund Gibson (1695).
—— 2nd Gibson ed. (1722).
A. R. Clapham, T. G. Tutin and E. F. Warburg, *Flora of the British Isles* (2nd ed. Cambridge, 1962).
Clapham Register: ed. J. Charlesworth, *The Parish Register of Clapham, part 1 1595-1683* (Yorkshire Parish Register Society, vol. 67, 1921).
Edward Cocker, *The Young Clerks Tutor* (6th ed. 1670).
G. Croese, *The General History of the Quakers* (1696).
Cumberland and Westmorland Antiquarian and Archaeological Society, *Transactions* (Kendal, 1874-   ).
J. C. Dickinson, *The Land of Cartmel* (Kendal, 1980).
Dictionary of National Biography.
G. C. Druce and S. H. Vines, *The Dillenian Herbarium* (Oxford, 1907).
John Dury, *The Reformed School* (1651).
G. S. F. Ellens, 'The Ranters Ranting: Reflections on a Ranter Counter Culture' *Church History*, vol. xl (1971).
Epistles from the Yearly Meeting of Friends, vol. i, 1681-1769 (1858).
John Evelyn, *Diary and Correspondence of John Evelyn*, ed. W. Bray (1898).
A. Everitt, *Change in the Provinces: the Seventeenth Century* (Leicester University, 1969).

John Fell, 'The Guides over the Kent and Leven Sands, Morecambe Bay', *CWAAS*, o.s., vol. vii (1884), pp. 1-26.
Sarah Fell, *The Household Account Book of Sarah Fell of Swarthmoor Hall*, ed. Norman Penney (Cambridge, 1920).
R. S. Ferguson, *Early Cumberland and Westmorland Friends*, (1871).
H. R. Fletcher and W. H. Brown, *The Royal Botanic Garden Edinburgh, 1670-1970* (Edinburgh, 1970).
George Fox, *The Journal of George Fox*, ed. John L. Nickalls (revised ed., 1975).
—— *George Fox's 'Book of Miracles'* ed. Henry J. Cadbury (Cambridge, 1948).
Friends Historical Society, *The Journal of the Friends Historical Society* (1903-   ).
John Gerard, *The Herball or Generall Historie of Plantes* (1597).
—— (2nd ed. 1633) ed. Thomas Johnson.
—— *Catalogus Arborum, Fruticum ac plantarum tam indigenarum, quam exoticarum in horto Johannis Gerardi* (1599).
Richard Gilpin, *Daemonologia Sacra*, ed. A. B. Grosart (1867).
G. Grigson, *The Englishman's Flora* (1958, Paladin 1975).
Isabel Grubb, *Quakerism and Industry before 1800* (1930).
R. T. Gunther, *Early British Botanists and their Gardens* (Oxford, 1922).
F. J. Hanbury and E. S. Marshall, *Flora of Kent* (1899).
Blanche Henrey, *British Botanical and Horticultural Literature before 1800*, 3 vols (Oxford, 1975).
Christopher Hill, *AntiChrist in Seventeenth-Century England* (Oxford, 1971).
—— *The World Turned Upside Down* (1972, Penguin 1975).
Jane Houston, *Catalogue of Ecclesiastical Records of the Commonwealth 1643-1660 Lambeth Palace Library* (1968).
F. G. James, *North Country Bishop, a biography of William Nicolson* (Yale, London and Oxford, 1956).
N. G. B. James, *The Growth of Stuart London* (1935).
R. H. Jeffers, 'Edward Morgan and the Westminster Physic Garden', *Proceedings of the Linnean Society of London* (1953) pp. 102-133.
—— 'A Further Note on Edward Morgan and the Westminster Physic Garden', *Proceedings of the Linnean Society of London* (1957) pp. 96-101.
Thomas Johnson, *Thomas Johnson, Botanical Journeys in Kent and Hampstead*, ed. J. S. L. Gilmour (Pittsburgh, Pennsylvania, 1972).
R. M. Jones, *The Quakers in the American Colonies* (1911).
—— *Mysticism and Democracy in the English Commonwealth* (Harvard, 1932).
H. Kearney, *Scholars and Gentlemen* (1970).
D. H. Kent, *The Historical Flora of Middlesex* (Ray Society, 1975).
Nathaniel Kite, *Antiquarian Researches among the Early Printers and Publishers of Friends' Books* (Manchester, 1844).
ed. G. L. Lampson, *A Quaker Post-Bag* (1910).
A. F. Leach, *Early Yorkshire Schools* (Yorkshire Archaeological Society, vol. xxxiii, 1903).
Edward Lhwyd, *Lithophylacii Britannici Ichnographia* (1699, 2nd ed., 1760).
—— *Life and Letters of Edward Lhwyd*, ed. R. T. Gunther (Early Science in Oxford, vol. xiv, Oxford, 1945).
F. D. Logan, *Excommunication and the Secular Arm in Medieval England* (Pontifical Institute of Medieval Studies, Toronto, 1968).
J. A. Martindale, 'Early Westmorland Plant Records', *The Westmorland Natural History Record, a quarterly magazine*, vol. i (London and Kendal, 1888-89).

J. M. Mawson, 'Deadly Nightshade', *Barrow Naturalists Field Club Annual Report and Proceedings*, vol. iv (1883).

Christopher Merret, *Pinax Rerum Naturalium Britannicarum* (1667).

Robert Morison, *Plantarum Historiae Universalis Oxoniensis* Pars secunda, (Oxford 1680) and Pars tertia (Oxford 1699).

Morland Register, *Registers of Morland Part I 1538-1742* (Kendal, 1957).

Charles Mullet, 'Toleration and Persecution in England 1660-89', *Church History*, vol. xviii (1949), pp. 18-43.

M. Mullett, in *Early Lancaster Friends* (University of Lancaster, 1978).

James Nayler, *The Light of Christ, and the Word of Life Cleared from the Deceipts of the Deceiver* (1656).

T. R. Newbold, 'Newby Head, Westmorland', *The Friend*, vol. xxxiii (1893).

James Newton, *Enchiridion Universale Plantarum; or An Universal and Compleat History of Plants with their Icons in a Manual* (?1689).

J. Nichols, *Literary Anecdotes of the Eighteenth Century, comprizing Biographical Memoirs of William Bowyer, Printer F.S.A. and many of his learned friends* (1812-1815).

—— *Illustrations of the Literary History of the Eighteenth Century* (1817-1858).

F. Nicholson, 'The Kaber Rigg Plot, 1663', *CWAAS* n.s. xi (1911).

J. Nicolson and R. Burn, *'The History and Antiquities of the Counties of Westmorland and Cumberland* (1777).

William Nicolson, *Letters on various subjects to and from William Nicolson D.D.* ed. John Nichols (1809).

—— *A Seventeenth Century Flora of Cumbria. William Nicolson's Catalogue of Plants 1690*, ed. E. Jean Whittaker (Surtees Society, 1981).

B. Nightingale, *The Ejected of 1662 in Cumberland and Westmorland* (Manchester University, 1911).

John Ogilby, *Britannia* (1675).

John Parkinson, *Paradisi in Sole Paradisus Terrestris, 1629* (1904).

—— *Theatrum Botanicum* (1640).

ed. Norman Penney, *The First Publishers of Truth* (1907).

S. L. Petty, 'Thomas Lawson, The Father of Lakeland Botany', *The North Lonsdale Magazine and Furness Miscellany*, (Ulverston) vol. i, no. 12.

Henry R. Plomer, *A Dictionary of the Booksellers and Printers who were at work in England, Scotland and Ireland from 1641 to 1667* (1907) and *1668 to 1725* (Oxford, 1922).

A. W. Pollard, 'Some Notes on the History of Copyright in England 1662-1774', *The Library*, 4th series, iii, pp. 97-114.

R. Pulteney, *Historical and Biographical Sketches of the Progress of Botany in England* (1790).

ed. James Raine, *Depositions from the Castle at York relating to Offences committed in the Northern Counties in the Seventeenth Century* (Surtees Society, 1861).

Charles E. Raven, *John Ray Naturalist, his Life and Works*, (Cambridge, 1942).

—— 'Thomas Lawson's Note-book', *Proceedings of the Linnean Society of London*, October, 1947 pp. 3-12.

John Raven and Max Walters, *Mountain Flowers* (1956).

John Ray, *Ray's Flora of Cambridgeshire, 1660*, ed. A. H. Ewen and C. T. Prime (Hitchin, 1975).

—— *Catalogus Plantarum Angliae* (1670, 2nd ed. 1677).

—— *Fasciculus Stirpium Britannicarum* (1688).

—— *Historia Plantarum*, 3 vols (1686-1704).

—— *Synopsis Methodica Stirpium Britannicarum* (1690, 2nd ed. 1696).

—— (3rd ed. 1724) ed. J. J. Dillenius, facs ed, William T. Stearn (Ray Society, 1973).

—— *Memorials of John Ray*, ed. E. Lankester (Ray Society, 1846).

—— *The Correspondence of John Ray*, ed. E. Lankester (Ray Society, 1848).

—— *Further Correspondence of John Ray*, ed. R. T. Gunther (Ray Society, 1928).

Richard Richardson, *Extracts from the Literary and Scientific correspondence of Richard Richardson M.D., F.R.S.*, ed. Dawson Turner (Yarmouth, 1835).

Thomas Robinson, *An Essay towards a Natural History of Westmorland and Cumberland*, (1709).

Isabel Ross, *Margaret Fell, Mother of Quakerism* (1949, Sessions of York, 1984).

E. J. Salisbury, 'Echinophora spinosa L. – a member of our flora', *Watsonia*, vol. vii, pt. 4, July 1971.

J. E. Smith, *The English Flora* (2nd ed. 1828-30).

Joseph Smith, *A Descriptive Catalogue of Friends' Books* (1867).

—— *Bibliotheca Anti-Quakeriana* (1873).

Thomas Sprat, *The History of the Royal-Society 1667*, facs ed. J. I. Cope and H. W. Jones (St. Louis and London, 1959).

E. H. Swete, *Flora Bristoliensis* (1854).

W. E. Tate, *The Parish Chest, a Study of the Records of Parochial Administration of England* (Cambridge, 1946).

Ernest E. Taylor, *The Valiant Sixty* (1951).

D. G. Brinton Thompson, 'John Thompson of Nether Compton, Dorset, and Philadelphia, Quaker Schoolmaster and Merchant', *Pennsylvania Genealogical Magazine*, vol. xxiii, pt. 3 (1964) pp. 141-160.

R. Denton Thompson 'Farmanby and the Thompson family', *CWAAS* n.s., lv, pp. 179-190.

Ralph Thoresby, *The Diary of Ralph Thoresby* ed. Joseph Hunter (1830).

—— *Letters of Eminent Men addressed to Ralph Thoresby*, ed. Joseph Hunter (1832).

G. Lyon Turner, *Original Records of Early Nonconformity under Persecution and Indulgence* (1911).

J. Venn and J. A. Venn, *Alumni Cantabrigiensis* (Cambridge, 1922-27).

S. H. Vines and G. C. Druce, *An Account of the Morisonian Herbarium in the Possession of the University of Oxford* (Oxford, 1914).

Elfrida Vipont, *George Fox and the Valiant Sixty* (1975).

Cecil Wall, *A History of the Worshipful Society of Apothecaries of London*, notes by Cecil Wall, ed. H. Charles Cameron, revised E. Ashworth Underwood (O.U.P. for Wellcome Historical Medical Museum, 1963).

Maria Webb, *The Fells of Swarthmoor Hall and their Friends* (1865).

C. Welch, *History of the Monument* (1921).

A. Wharham, 'Tithes in Country Life', *History Today*, vol. xxii, June 1972, pp. 426-433.

J. W. White, *The Flora of Bristol* (Bristol, 1912).

George Whitehead, *A Collection of sundry Books, Epistles and Papers written by James Nayler*, (1716).

J. A. Williams, *Catholic Recusancy in Wiltshire 1660-1791* (Catholic Record Society, 1968).

A. Wilson, *The Flora of Westmorland* (Arbroath, 1938).

John Wilson, *A Synopsis of British Plants in Mr. Ray's Method* (Newcastle-upon-Tyne, 1744).

Henry Winder, *A Critical and Chronological History of the Rise, Progress, Declension and Revival of Knowledge, Chiefly Religious* (2nd ed., 1756).

—— *The Spirit of Quakerism, And the Danger of their Divine Revelation laid open* (1696).

Luella M. Wright, *The Literary Life of the Early Friends 1650-1725* (New York, 1966).

Plant Index – Latin

It has been possible to assign modern botanical names to most of Lawson's polynomials. A few present difficulties and the polynomials stand alone in the index. Where Lawson has given alternative polynomials in a single record, the first polynomial only has been listed. Where he has used alternative polynomials in separate records, each is given. Where a polynomial is expanded at a separate recording, the expansion is given in brackets. In a very few cases, the record is not to be found amongst Lawson's extant writings, but has come through an intermediate source (e.g. Ray's *Synopsis*). In such cases, the polynomial is that of the intermediate source.

The sources for Lawson's records are as follows:

NB Thomas Lawson's notebook c. 1677
RM Records attributed to Lawson in Robert Morison's *Historia Plantarum* 1680 and 1699
HP Records, for which there is no other source, attributed to Lawson by Ray in the preface to *Historia Plantarum*, vol ii, 1688
L Lawson's letter to John Ray, dated 9th April, 1688
M Marginal notes made in Ray's *Catalogus Angliae*. Recorded by William Nicolson, 1690. Published Nicolson, *Flora* pp 103-5
WN Records found in joint expeditions with Nicolson in 1690 or attributed to Lawson by Nicolson in *Flora*
SYN Records, for which there is no other source, attributed to Lawson by Ray in *Synopsis* 1690 and subsequent editions. Page refs to 1724 ed
AM Records said by John Wilson to have been seen in an authentic manuscript of the late Mr Lawson and published in his *Synopsis* 1744
CFW Plants found in Cumberland, Furness and Westmorland

Records of plants found in other counties may be turned up in the General Index under the appropriate county heading.

Modern Botanical Name		Thomas Lawson's Complete Plant List
	ACER CAMPESTRE, 174	Acer minus (WN xxxvi)
	Aceras anthropophorum, 105-6	Orchis anthrophophora (NB 5)
	Achillea millefolium, 107	Millefolium fl rubro aut purpureo (NB 186)
W	*ptarmica*, 145, 153, 202	Ptarmica flore pleno (L; M)
	Acinos arvensis, 102	Clinopodium minus (NB 186)
	Actaea spicata, 132, 141, 145	Christophoriana (NB 174; L)
W		Adiantum aureum fol bifidis etc, 75 (NB 149)
	Aegopodium podagraria, 109	Herba Gerardi (NB 99)
	Aethusa cynapium, 107	Cicutaria fatua (NB 190)
W	*Alchemilla alpina*, 83, 84, 148, 153	Alchemilla alpina quinquefolia (NB 154, 194; L)
		Alga latifolia porosa maxima (WN xxxv)
		Allium amphicarpon, 200 (WN 8)
W	*Allium carinatum*, 173	Allium montanum purpureum proliferum (WN xxxvi)
W	*oleraceum*, 153, 182	Allium sylvestre bicorne flore exherbaceo albicante (*SYN* 370)
W	*scorodoprasum* 153	Lawson's polynomials (L) are confused but specimens sent to Ray were referred *SYN* 370, 6 to *A. scorodoprasum*
	vineale, 94, 116	Allium sylvestre (NB 180, 323)
	Alopecuros geniculatus, 108	Gramen aquaticum geniculatum (spicatum cum parva cauda muris) (NB 188, 190)
	Althaea officinalis, 116	Althea (NB 91)
W	*Anacamptis pyramidalis*, 203, 206	Orchis cynosorchis militaris purpurea odorata (M)
	Anagallis arvensis,	Anagallis fl albo aut carneo (NB 83, 186)
	ssp *arvensis*, 102	
	ssp *foemina*, 97	Anagallis flore coeruleo (NB 114)
W	*tenella*, 84, 90, 97, 117, 143, 170, 171	Nummularia minor (fl purpurascente) (NB 154, 306, 319, 324; L; WN xxxv)
W	*Andromeda polifolia*, 148, 151, 153	Rosmarinum syl minus nostras (L, WN 78)
	Anemone pulsatilla, 113	Pulsatilla purpurea (NB 179)
W	*Antennaria dioica*, 74, 76, 144	Gnaphalium montanum album (NB 149; L)
		Anthora, 84, (NB 153)
	Anthriscus caucalis, 114, 150	Myrrhis sylvestris seminibus asperis (NB 181; L)
F	*Anthyllis vulneraria*, 86	Anthyllis leguminosa (NB 88)
	Antirrhinum orontium, 93, 102	Antirrhinum minus (NB 186, 322)
	Aphanes arvensis, 200	Percepier anglorum (WN 68)

F   *Apium graveolens*, 78, 94, 148
W   *inundatum*, 78, 143
    Arctium lappa, 108
    Arenaria serpyllifolia, 93, 100
    Aristolochia clematitis, 173
F   *Armeria maritima*, 2, 78, 132, 151, 154

    Arnoseris minima, 107
    Artemisia maritima, 94
W   *Asperula cynanchica*, 97, 114, 148

W   *Asplenium adiantum-nigrum*, 93, 142
C   *marinum*, 151, 199

F   *Aster tripolium*, 77, 94, 116, 141
    Astragalus danicus, 113, 150
        glycyphyllos, 90, 97, 114, 133, 150, 174
F   *Atriplex glabriuscula*, 77
        hastata, 109
        patula, 109
        pedunculatus, 109

F   *Atropa bella-donna*, 77
    Avena fatua, 103
W   *BALDELLIA RANUNCULOIDES*, 103, 143

W   *Barbarea vulgaris*, 73
W   *Bartsia alpina*, 138

    Beta vulgaris, 94
    Betonica officinalis, 200
W   *Bidens cernua*, 170
    Blackstonia, perfoliata, 90, 91, 141
    Blechnum spicant, 97, 110
W   *Botrychium lunaria*, 143, 154, 199
    Brassica rapa, 102
    Bryonia dioica, 78, 141
    Bupleurum rotundifolium, 95
    Butomus umbellatus, 91, 96, 141

F   *CAKILE MARITIMA*, 77, 148
    Callitriche platycarpa, 151
    Calluna vulgaris, 107, 110
    Caltha palustris, 153, 154
    Calystegia sepium, 91
F   *soldanella*, 75, 103, 148
    Camelina sativa, 174
W   *Campanula glomerata*, 143
        latifolia, 200
        rapunculus, 103, 105, 106

        rotundifolia, 114

W   *Cardamine amara*, 200
W   *pratensis*, 143, 154, 203
W   *Carduus nutans*, 105, 133, 147, 174

    Carex dioica, 97, 147
        divisa, 103
        otrubae, 108
        pendula, 103

Apium palustre seu off (NB 85, 323; L)
Sium minimum (NB 88; L)
Bardana (rosea) (NB 90, 190)
Alsine (minor multicaulis) (NB 182, 185), A. petraea (NB 323)
Aristolochia rotunda (WN xxxv)
Caryophyllus marinus minimus (NB 85; L), C. montanus (NB 174)
Hieracium minimum clusii (NB 190)
Absinthium marinum album (NB 323)
Rubia cynanchica (flosculis albis tetrapetalis) (NB 301, 306; WN 78)
Dryopteris nigra dodonei (NB 320; L; WN 30)
Filix marina anglica (L; AM 3)
Aster atticus, 110 (NB 93)
Tripolium (NB 88, 91, 322; L)
Glaux dioscoridis (NB 179; L)
Glaux vulgaris (ad lob) (NB 55, 301, 305; L)

Atriplex maritima nostras (NB 85)
Atriplex syl altera, A deltoides (NB 191)
Atriplex sylvestris angustifolia (NB 191)
Not a Lawson find
Atriplex halimi folio, 109 (NB 191)
Atriplex syl latifolia seu pes anserinus, 94, 109 (NB 191, 323)
Solanum lethale (NB 88)
Aegilops (NB 185)
Plantago aquatica minor (NB 187; L)
Barba neptuni muscus marinus equisetiformis non ramosus, 151, 154 (L)
Barbarea nasturtium hybernum (NB 147)
Euphrasia erecta foliis brevibus et obtusis veronicae Westmorlandica (RM pt 3 431)
Beta alba vulgaris (NB 323)
Betonica vulgaris flore albo (WN 17)
Eupatorium folio integro (WN xxxv)
Centaurium luteum perfoliatum (NB 320; L)
Asplenium exiguum hirsutum (NB 93); Lonchitis etc (NB 305)
Lunaria ramosa (L), L. minor (WN 56; AM 8)
Napus sylvestris (NB 185)
Bryonia alba (NB 55; L)
Perfoliata (NB 324)
Gladiolus palustris cordi (NB 322; L)

Eruca marina (NB 86; L)
Stellaria aquatica (L)
Erica vulgaris fl purpureo et albo (NB 188, 193)
Populago (*SYN* 272)
Convolvulus major fl albo (NB 319)
Soldanella (marina) (NB 88, 187; L)
Myagrum (WN xxxvi)
Trachelium minus fl albo (L)
Trachelium majus belgarum seu giganteum (WN 88)
Rapunculus campanulata (NB 192), R. esculentus vulgaris (NB 186)
Campanula minor rotundifolia (NB 179)
Campanula lactescens, 73 (NB 148)
Campanula persicifolia alba (NB 154)
Nasturtium aquaticum amarum (WN 63)
Cardamine fl pleno (L; M)
Carduus nutans (NB 55; L), C. capite nutante (NB 192), C. moschatus (WN xxxvi)
Gramen cyperoides spica echinata simplici (NB 115)
Gramen cyperoides ex monte ballon spica divulsa (NB 186)
Gramen cyperoides palustre majus spica compacta (NB 188)
Gramen cyperoides spica pendula longiore (NB 187)

Gramen (cyperoides) pulicare (NB 115, 194)
Carduus monstrosus imperati (L; WN 21), Carlina sylv (WN xxxvii)
Betulus (NB 94)
Not a Lawson find
Carduus stellatus (NB 55, 94; L)
Cyanus coeruleus (NB 319)
Jacea nigra vulgaris laciniata (NB 184)
Centaurium min fl albo (L)
Helleborine minor alba (L; WN xxxvi, 46)

Scabiosa montana maxima (M)
Auricula muris pulchro flore (NB 179)
Alsine hirsuta altera viscosa (NB 183)
Hydroceratophyllon folio aspera, quatuor cornibus armato (AM 11). See also *Ranunculus circinatus* p. 96
Asplenium (NB 147, 322; L)
Antirrhinum arvense minus (NB 184)
Chamaemelum nudum odoratum (NB 306)
Chamaenerion (latifolium), C. (angustifolium) (NB 105, 189)
Equisetum foetidum (sub aquis repens) (NB 115, 306)
Atriplex syl folio sinuato candicante (NB 191)
Atriplex syl latifolia (altera) pes anserinus sive ramosior (NB 191, 323)
Atriplex syl latifolia seu pes anserinus (NB 191, 323)
Atriplex olida (NB 185, 191)
See *Sibthorpia europaea*
Cichoreum sylvestre (NB 319)
Carduus acaulis (NB 192)
Carduus ceanothos sive viarum et vinearum repens (NB 94)
Carduus capite tomentoso (NB 179), C. tomentosus corona fratrum dictus (NB 314)
Cirsium britannicum clusii repens (NB 147)
Carduus palustris fl albo (NB 186, 193)
Viorna (NB 319; WN xxxvii)
Clinopodium majus (NB 186), Acinos (NB 323)
Cochlearia longiore et sinuato folio (NB 95)
Cochlearia marina fol anguloso parvo (L)
Not a Lawson find
Orchis batrachoides (NB 116)
Colchicum (NB 180)
Lilium convallium (angustifolium) (NB 188, L, WN xxxvi, RM, pt 3 539, *SYN* 264)
Convolvulus minor fl albo (NB 319)

Coronopus ruelli (flos albis tetrapetalis) (NB 306, 320, 323)
Fumaria alba latifolia (NB 182; L), F. alba claviculata (NB 318)
Brassica marina monospermos (NB 85)
Crithmum marinum vulgare (NB 86; AM 71)
Cuscuta (NB 95, 188)
Calceolus Mariae (NB 318)
Dryopteris alba dodonei (L), Filix saxatilis caule tenui fragili (AM 6)

Orchis palmata palustris dracontias (M)
Plantago aquat minor stellata (NB 191; L)
Laureola (NB 192; L)
Elaphoboscum sive pastinaca sylvestris (NB 318)
Gramen miliaceum segetale majus (*SYN* 403)
Caryophyllus etc fl rubris pentapetalis (NB 181)
Caryophyllus virgineus (NB 149; L; WN 22)
Digitalis fl albo (L; WN 30)
Thlaspi veronicae folio (M)
Ros solis fol oblongo (NB 193; L)
Ros solis fol rotundo (NB 193; L)
Filix aquatica (WN xxxv)

Primula farinosa, 137
  veris x vulgaris, 151
Prunella vulgaris, 87
W Prunus cerasus, 88, 151, 155, 172, 174

W   padus, 73
F Pulicaria dysenterica, 76
  vulgaris, 102, 115

? Pyrola rotundifolia, 151, 155

QUERCUS ILEX, 99

W RADIOLA LINOIDES, 83, 105, 144 171

Ranunculus arvensis, 114
W   auricomus, 114
  bulbosus, 114
  circinatus, 96

  hederaceus, 102
F lingua, 146, 199
  sceleratus, 116, 151
Raphanus raphanistrum, 114

Reseda lutea, 113, 133, 149
W Rhamnus catharticus, 73, 143
CF Rhynchosinapis monensis, 146, 155
W Rhynchospora alba, 171
Rorippa amphibia, 102, 115
Rosa canina, 203
W Rubus chamaemorus, 83, 148, 155
Rumex conglomeratus, 103
  crispus, 105
F hydrolapathum, 86
W pulcher, 105, 142, 227

Ruscus aculeatus, 101, 110, 141
SAGINA MARITIMA, 150, 155

W   nodosa, 74, 143, 173, 174

W   procumbens, 75, 133
Sagittaria sagittifolia, 91, 97, 108

W Salicornia europaea, 76, 78, 103
  perennis, 103

Salix caprea, 101
  fragilis, 201
Salsola kali, 103
Sambucus nigra, 76, 94, 140, 155
F Samolus valerandi, 75, 114, 115, 116, 151, 202
Saponaria officinalis, 75, 141, 155, 202
Saxifraga aizoides, 138, 174
W hypnoides, 74, 144, 155, 174
W stellaris, 75, 84, 148

W Scabiosa columbaria, 144, 155
Schoenoplectus triquetrus, 108

Scirpus maritimus, 100
FW Scrophularia aquatica, 85, 87, 116, 148
W nodosa, 144

Primula veris minor rubra eboracensis (RM pt 2 555)
Primula pratensis inodora lutea (L)
Prunella fl albo (NB 193)
Cerasus sylvestris fructu minimo cordiformi (NB 41; L; WN xxxvi), C. sylvestris septentrionalis fructu parvo rubro serotino (WN xxxv), Populus alba altera (NB 318)
Cerasus avium nigra et racemosa (NB 147)
Conyza media (NB 85)
Conyza graviter olens (NB 186), C. minor tragi (NB 301)
Pyracantha, 85 (NB 154)
Pyrola brasiliana (L)

Ilex (NB 99)

Herniaria minor (NB 191, 194), H. minima (NB 193), Millegrana minima (NB 192; L; WN xxxv)
Ranunculus arvorum echinatum (NB 181)
Ranunculus nemorosus dulcis secundus tragi (L)
Ranunculus bulbosa radice (NB 179)
Not a Lawson find. Millefolium aquaticum cornutum (NB 116, 316. But see p. 96)
Ranunculus hederaceus rivulorum se extendens (NB 186)
Ranunculus flammeus major (L; AM 105)
Ranunculus apii foliis (NB 180), R. palustr. rotundifolius (L)
Rapistrum album articulatum (NB 180)
Regia hasta, 132 (NB 173)
Reseda vulgaris (NB 55; L), R. italica (NB 179)
Rhamnus catharticus (NB 150; L; WN 76)
Eruca monensis lacin. lutea (L)
Gramen junceum leucanthemum (WN xxxv)
Raphanus aquaticus (NB 181, 185)
Rosa sylvestris inodora (M)
Vaccinium nubis (NB 194), Chamaemorus (L; WN 24)
Lapathum acutum minimum (NB 187)
Lapathum foliis crispis (NB 306)
Lapathum maximum aquaticum (NB 317)
Lapathum pulchrum bononiense (NB 100, 306; L). L. bononiense sinuatum (WN xxxvii, 52) But see p. 142.
Ruscus (NB 103, 186; L; WN xxxv)
Saxifraga graminea pusilla foliis brevioribus crassioribus et succulentioribus (L)
Saxifraga palustris anglica (NB 151; L; WN xxxvi), Alsine palustris anglica (WN xxxvii)
Alsine tenuifolia muscosa (NB 55, 149)
Sagitta major (NB 65, 320) S. minor (NB 65, 320) Sagittaria minor (NB 190)
Kali geniculatum (majus) (NB 55, 87, 187)
Kali perenne multis ramis fruticans (NB 187), K. fruticosum lignosum perenne (NB 189)
Salix latifolia rotunda (NB 184)
Salix folio splendente (WN 79)
Kali spinosum cochleatum (NB 187)
Sambucus fol laciniatis (NB 86, 87, 324; HP; WN 80)
Anagallis aquatica (rotundifolia tertia lobelii) fl albo (NB 39, 91, 147; L), Alsine beccabungae folio (M)
Saponaria fl pleno (NB 88; L; M)
Sedum minus alpinum luteum (RM pt 3 482; WN xxxvii)
Sedum alpinum trifido folio (NB 151; L; WN xxxvi, 81)
Sanicula guttata (NB 152, 153, 317), Cotyledon hirsuta (L; WN 28)
Scabiosa minor prat fl carneo (L)
Juncus caule trianguli (NB 99), J. acutus maritimus (NB 189, 190)
Scilla, 132 (NB 174)
Gramen cyperoides palustre panicula sparsa (NB 182)
Betonica aquatica polius scrophularia aquaticus (NB 180, 317; L)
Scrophularia major (L)

Plant Index – English

Notes: 1. English names of garden plants have not, in general, been indexed but may be found by reference to 'Gardens' in the General Index. 2. Where references are given in bold, thus **123** the modern botanical name only appears on the page. The English equivalent may be discovered by turning up one of the other references.

General Index

ABRAHAM, Daniel, 76, 169, 181; *m* Rachel Fell (*q.v.*)
Act of,
1553 (1 Mariae c. 3) against Offenders of Preachers and other Ministers in the Churche, 16, 19
1581 (23 Eliz c. 1) 62,118 and 1586/7 (28 & 29 Eliz c. 6), 118
1604 (1 Jac I c. 4) 62 and 1606 (3 & 4 Jac I c. 4), 118
1661, Corporation Act, 51
1662, (14 Car II c. 4) Uniformity, 48, 62, 67, 70, 119
1662 (14 Car II c. 23) for preventing the frequent Abuses in printing etc. 119
1664 (16 Car II c. 4) & 1670 (22 Car II c. 2) Conventicle Acts, 48, 51
1665 (17 Car II c. 2) Five Mile Act, 51
1689 (1 W&M c. 18) Toleration, 169, 170, 189, 190
Adamson, William, 40
Aldam, Thomas, 19, 213
Aldingham, 2, 3, 76
Allegiance, Oath of, 52, 56, 170
Alpines, *see* Mountain plants
Appleby, 22, 29, 50, 56, 58, 62, 64, 65, 200
Archer, John, 184
Arundel, 31
Ashton, Sir Ralph, 87-88
Atkinson, Robert, 50
Audland, John, 23
Ayrey, John, 164-7, 181; *m* Ruth Lawson: (*q.v.*); *Dau,* Margaret, 167

BACKHOUSE, John, 167
Bainbridge, Bernard, 64
Balfour, Andrew, 182
Banks, Sir Joseph, 93
Baptists, 30, 34, 48, 80
Bax, Richard, 25
Baxter, Henry, 54
Baycliff, 12
Barrow, Robert, 119
Bellingham, James, 75
Benson, Gervase, 40, 45
Bealing, Benjamin, 191, 193
Berkshire, plants found in, 97, 105
Bethell, Mr, 7
Binstead, 31
Blaykling, Francis, 132; John, 132, 160-8 passim, 169
Bobart, Jacob the elder, 95, 96, 180; Jacob the younger, 95, 96, 136, 138, 143, 174, 203
Bordley Hall, 45, 217
Bownas, Samuel, 134, 136
Bowstead, John, 165
Bradley, Margaret, wife of Thomas, 22
Breda, declaration of, 50
Brereley, Roger, 5
Bristol, 23, 40, 49, 56, 92-4, 95, 102, 108-9, 180
Buckinghamshire, plants found in, 105

Buddle, Adam, 183
Bugg, Francis, 33
Burns, Edward, 90
Burnyeat, John, 191
Burrough, Edward, 23, 26, 56, 190
Burton, Percy, 29, 62, 214-5
Buxtorfius, Johannes, *Lexicon Hebraicum et Chaldaicum,* 43, 233
Byne, Magnus, 27-8, 32, 38-9, 40, 44, 87, 214

CAFFYN, Matthew, 30, 33-7, 80
Cambridge, 4-9 passim, 16, 42, 44, 52, 59, 60, 70, 71, 72, 107, 112-5, 126, 127, 136, 148, 150
Cambridgeshire, plants found in, 113-6
Camden, William, *Britannia,* 82, 84, 89, 95, 163, 202-7, passim
Camm, John, 23
Capel, 25
Carlisle, diocese of, 54, 62-5, 169, 171, 177-88. *See also* Established Church
Carr, Richard, 7
Charles II, 9, 48, 50, 51, 62, 64, 100, 106, 190, 195, 196
Charlton, Walter, 111
Cheshire, plants found in, 88, 152
Chichester, 31
Church of England, *see* Established Church
Civil War, 5, 6, 10, 18, 22, 28, 32, 60, 106, 130, 196
Clapham, 5, 7, 15ff, 21, 209
Clarendon Code, 51
Claridge, Richard, 192, 193
Clayton, 32
Cocker, Edward, *Young Clerks Tutor,* 69
Colchester, 62
Coles, William, 82-3, 108
Cosin, Bishop John, 61
?Couplin, Christopher, 64
Crawley, 33
Crisp, Samuel, 193; Stephen, 191
Collinson, Joshua, 165
Cromwell, Oliver, 4, 5, 8, 9, 20, 41, 48, 62, 115; Henry, 56
Cudworth, Ralph, 71-2
Cumberland, plants found in, 143-6, 148, 199, 200, 201, 203, 205-6
Curwen, family, 144

DALE, Samuel, 152
Dalton, 4, 5, 12
Dalston, John, 53
Dell, William, 8
Denkin, Nicholas, 54, 118
Derbyshire, plants found in, 89
Derham, William, Dr, 138-40, 151, 152, 183
Dew, John, Joiner, 116
Dewsbury, William, 191
Diggers, 8
Dillenius, J. J., 183, 207, 226; herbaria, 109, 151
Dixon, Will, 116
Docker, Thomas, 65
Dodsworth, Matthew, 132

254